Computer Security for the Home and Small Office

THOMAS C. GREENE

Apress™

Computer Security for the Home and Small Office
Copyright ©2004 by Thomas C. Greene

ISBN (pbk): 1-59059-316-2

Printed and bound in the United States of America 12345678910

Technical Reviewer: Robert Slade

Editorial Board: Steve Anglin, Dan Appleman, Gary Cornell, James Cox, Tony Davis, John Franklin, Chris Mills, Steven Rycroft, Dominic Shakeshaft, Julian Skinner, Jim Sumser, Karen Watterson, Gavin Wray, John Zukowski

Lead Editor: Jim Sumser

Assistant Publisher: Grace Wong

Project Manager: Beth Christmas

Copy Editor: Nancy Conner

Production Manager: Kari Brooks

Production Editor: Kelly Winquist

Proofreader: Liz Welch

Compositor: Kinetic Publishing Services, LLC

Indexer: Kevin Broccoli

Illustrator: Mike Reed

Artist: Kinetic Publishing Services, LLC

Cover Designer: Kurt Krames

Manufacturing Manager: Tom Debolski

Distributed to the book trade in the United States by Springer-Verlag New York, Inc., 175 Fifth Avenue, New York, NY, 10010 and outside the United States by Springer-Verlag GmbH & Co. KG, Tiergartenstr. 17, 69112 Heidelberg, Germany.

In the United States: phone 1-800-SPRINGER, email orders@springer-ny.com, or visit http://www.springer-ny.com. Outside the United States: fax +49 6221 345229, email orders@springer.de, or visit http://www.springer.de.

For information on translations, please contact Apress directly at 2560 Ninth Street, Suite 219, Berkeley, CA 94710. Phone 510-549-5930, fax 510-549-5939, email info@apress.com, or visit http://www.apress.com.

Contents at a Glance

About the Author .... *vii*

About the Technical Reviewer .... *ix*

About the Illustrator .... *x*

Acknowledgments .... *xi*

Preface .... *xiii*

Introduction .... *xvii*

Chapter 1   Introducing the Dark Side *1*
Chapter 2   Vectors *31*
Chapter 3   Social Engineering *73*
Chapter 4   From Newbie to Power User *95*
Chapter 5   Treasure Hunt *155*
Chapter 6   The Open-Source Escape Hatch *195*
Chapter 7   Trust Nothing, Fear Nothing *219*
Appendix A   Glossary *279*
Appendix B   Procedures, Processes, and Ports *297*
Appendix C   Online Resources *389*

Index *393*

Contents

About the Author .... *vii*

About the Technical Reviewer .... *ix*

About the Illustrator .... *x*

Acknowledgments .... *xi*

Preface .... *xiii*

Introduction .... *xvii*

The Magic of Firewalls .... *xvii*
"Hackproofing" .... *xxiv*
An Open-Source Solution .... *xxvi*
Why Mozilla? .... *xxix*

Chapter 1   Introducing the Dark Side *1*

The Hacker's Lair *4*
Child's Play *13*
Free Porn and Easy Credit *21*

Chapter 2   Vectors *31*

Common Vectors *33*
Other Vulnerabilities *39*
"Unsafe at Any Speed" *41*
Defense *45*
Becoming a User *58*

Chapter 3   Social Engineering *73*

Serving Hackers with a Smile *75*
Mad Cows *88*

Chapter 4 From Newbie to Power User *95*

Network and Internet Monitoring *99*
System Monitoring *112*
Encryption *119*

Chapter 5 Treasure Hunt *155*

Local Stealth *156*
The Wibbly Wobbly Web *178*
Online Stealth *181*

Chapter 6 The Open-Source Escape Hatch *195*

A Fresh Approach *196*
The Sins of William Perfidious *204*

Chapter 7 Trust Nothing, Fear Nothing *219*

"Depend on Us" *220*
Disinformation *227*
Unintended Consequences *256*
Database Hell *264*
Trust Nothing, Fear Nothing *275*

Appendix A Glossary *279*

Appendix B Procedures, Processes, and Ports *297*

Procedures *297*
Notes on NAT *348*
Notes on Packet Filters *349*
Windows Processes *351*
Ports *354*

Appendix C Online Resources *389*

Security News *389*
Resources *390*
E-mail Lists *392*

Index *393*

About the Author

Thomas Greene is Associate Editor of the information technology journal *The Register* (www.theregister.co.uk), the leading independent tech news daily, where he has been a senior editor and columnist for five years. Tom covers cybercrime, computer and network security, and legislation related to information technology.

The Register is much loved for its irreverent editorial style and its exasperating ability to break stories that greatly inconvenience industry heavyweights.

Prior to his job at *The Register,* Tom covered the pharmaceutical industry for FDC Reports, a division of Elsevier Science. Prior to that he lived in Seoul, South Korea, studying Asian history and working in language education. He holds a bachelor's degree from Williams College, though he's not proud of it.

About the Technical Reviewer

Robert Slade started researching malware and other aspects of security before his grandchildren were born. He has written an eponymously titled guide to computer viruses, *Software Forensics,* a glossary of information security jargon, a bunch of magazine and encyclopedia articles, and coauthored *Viruses Revealed.* Despite all of this, he is best known for gleefully (and regularly) pointing out the errors in literally thousands of books written by other people, since it is easier and more fun. More information than anyone would want to know about him is available at sun.soci.niu.edu/~rslade/rms.htm. It is next to impossible to get him to take bio writing seriously.

About the Illustrator

Mike Reed is an illustrator and close observer of Internet culture. He currently teaches at the College of Visual Arts in St. Paul, Minnesota. His taxonomy of Internet personalities can be seen at www.flamewarriors.com.

Acknowledgments

I CAN'T THANK Jim Sumser, Beth Christmas, Nancy Conner, and Kelly Winquist from Apress adequately. Shouts as well to Neil Salkind and the folks at Studio B.

I'm indebted to the delightfully brutal critic Rob Slade, who graciously offered to do the tech review.

Thanks awfully to the lads at *The Register* for giving me a place to live and work and learn for the past five years, however virtually.

And above all, thanks to Eeleng Ong, who managed to put up with me while I worked on this project.

Preface

THIS IS A HANDBOOK for ordinary people concerned about computer security and online privacy. It addresses everyday computer users and Netizens with little or no background in information technology, concerned parents, business users, and corporate telecommuters. It speaks as well to corporate security managers struggling to articulate the necessary principles and procedures to nontechnical staff in understandable language. It involves both theory and practice: readers will learn the most common techniques used by malicious hackers, spammers, identity thieves, online marketers, and Internet fraudsters, and receive detailed instruction to defend their systems against exploitation, protect their privacy, and avoid identity theft. Whether one uses a desktop or workstation connected to a professionally managed network on the job, a single computer connected to the Internet at home, or a small network serving both business and personal needs and accommodating several users including children and teenagers, the basic approaches remain the same. No special skills are needed: anyone can understand and adopt the essential habits of computer security, data hygiene, and online privacy. If you can use a computer or workstation, log on to the

Internet or a company network, use an instant-messaging or chat client like ICQ or AIM, a Web browser, a search engine, and an e-mail client, then you can learn to use them safely, even anonymously. This book will show you how.

Surveys tell us that the majority of computer users are concerned about security, but they also tell us that very few people have a realistic grasp of the risks. For example, a 2003 study by the U.S. National Cyber Security Alliance found that 86 percent of home users erroneously believed their computers to be safe from online threats, though only a mere 11 percent had a "safe broadband connection with a properly configured firewall, recently upgraded antivirus protection, and, if children were present in the household, parental controls." Nevertheless, 86 percent admitted to keeping sensitive information on their computers, while 79 percent said they use their computers for transactions over the Internet. Only *three percent* of those polled with children in their households made use of Internet filtering, while a whopping 91 percent had at least one spyware program active on their machines about which they knew nothing.

Apparently, the public suffers either from overconfidence or from a fatalistic attitude that resigns them to regard computer and Internet security as too complicated for the average person to manage. The bad news is that most PCs are quite poorly defended and easily exploited, but the good news is that hardening them is relatively easy.

The corporate world is in no better shape. Cybercrime and intellectual property theft are profitable underground industries supported in part by the innocent mistakes of millions of computer users in a wired workplace. Even a professionally managed business network can be undermined by users innocent of the risks inherent in their daily activities. When the 2002 and 2003 Computer Crime Surveys by the national Computer Emergency Response Team for Australia (AusCERT) and the Australian Federal Police asked corporate security managers which aspects of their jobs they found most problematic, in both years' surveys "changing users' attitudes and behavior regarding computer security practices" emerged as the single leading challenge.

Clearly, proscriptive declarations and policy edicts from the IT department have not been a success. Users have long been called the weak link in the security chain, and so they are. A $35,000 firewall can be rendered useless by the accidental installation of a single malicious program behind it. IT managers often respond with increasing restrictions, but when security protocols inconvenience workers in their daily activities, they're routinely ignored. Overdoing security will often backfire in that way. This book is based on a belief that users will voluntarily change their behavior once they come to appreciate the risks. It will help management to articulate security information to nontechnical staff in understandable language, and it can serve as a manual to educate today's wired employees and bring them into the collective project of corporate network security by promoting awareness among everyday users. It is not a manual for professionals; there are plenty of good security books available for administrators and managers. It's a book written specifically for users that, I hope, can also make the professional's job a bit easier by promoting security awareness.

There is an air of myth surrounding cybersecurity and the hacking underground, one vigorously encouraged by celebrity hackers seeking to distinguish themselves, and by security and antivirus vendors who profit by promoting the fiction that only professionals dare confront the inscrutable denizens who lurk in the seedier districts of cyberspace. Today, computer and network security are extremely valuable territorial possessions belonging to highly trained, and highly paid, specialists, just as French *haute cuisine* was in the 1960s, before an ordinary housewife named Julia Child demystified and simplified it for the home cook. The analogy is a good one: just as the supposed mysteries of French cookery come down to a theoretical framework and a set of techniques that anyone can master, so does defensive computing. It is not rocket science; it is in fact almost entirely a matter of common sense. True, there is a theoretical framework and there are techniques, but these, just like a recipe for *pâte feuilletée* or *coquilles Saint-Jacques*, can be understood and mastered by anyone willing to learn.

Whether you're a home user concerned about software bugs and viruses, commercial profilers, identity thieves, and malicious hackers on the Internet; a parent worried about your children's exposure to online perverts, pornography, and mindless hate speech; or a corporate security manager struggling to communicate the rationale of network security to your nontechnical but wired staff, you'll find this book a faithful companion, one that will debunk the myths of security and cybercrime and offer instead realistic warnings, clear background explanations, and patient, step-by-step tutorials with a minimum of technical jargon.

The book is meant to be read through, not flipped through, because security is a cumulative process with many interdependent layers. Some chapters are devoted to practical steps for hardening systems and assuring privacy and Internet anonymity; others are more concerned with background and theory. I've tried to present these elements in an interlaced order that makes the whole easier to grasp, rather than adhere to some rationalistic scheme such as a textbook might follow. The twin elements of theory and practice must both be considered before good decisions can be made. Similarly, security and privacy must be applied together: it's impossible to harden a system without good privacy protection and data hygiene, yet privacy can't possibly be assured on a soft system. I'm separating these elements into digestible bits and arranging them in a more "natural" sequence to make them easier to grasp, but they all work together and need to be applied in an integrated manner. You will encounter tutorials with detailed procedures throughout the book, starting with the Introduction, and these can be applied at any time to advantage. But it's better to read through and get a sense of the larger picture before carrying out the instructions, because something you learn in Chapter 6, say, might affect your approach to a tutorial back in Chapter 4. While I'm loath to discourage tinkering, an initial read-through will help you avoid backtracking and duplicating your efforts. Generally, the practical information—the "what to do" guidance—comes first, and the background information—the "what to know" guidance—comes later. The book is loosely structured that way, and most chapters are as well.

Because this book is written primarily for home and small business users, and desktop users in the corporate world, when we talk about Windows we'll focus on the user-friendly Windows XP for our practical examples, though these should be easy for users of Windows NT and Windows 2000 to adapt to their systems. Similarly, UNIX-related tips will be based on GNU/Linux, which is popular in home and small business environments, though UNIX and BSD users should not have difficulty adapting them to their systems. Because Windows represents the majority of installed systems among likely readers of this book, I will naturally be giving it more attention than Linux, but the basic principles of security and privacy are fairly universal, so Linux users can certainly benefit from material addressed to Windows users. And of course there will be Linux-specific material throughout the book, including a chapter detailing its numerous advantages for the security-conscious user, and in particular, the novice. One of the more controversial tenets of this book, though one that will be proved handily, is that Linux is better suited than Windows to the security novice. This might seem counterintuitive now, but it will gradually become evident that the procedures for securing Windows are more complicated, more numerous, and less effective than those for Linux. As recently as two years ago, Linux was difficult to install and use, but great strides have since been made in accommodating novices, especially by the big vendors such as SuSE and Mandrake. Users who want the best computer security with the least bother and expense will be better served by Linux. But Windows enthusiasts need not despair; Windows XP can indeed be configured for improved security. It's not at all difficult, but it is more involved than securing a Linux system.

It will sometimes be necessary to use technical terms in passing that will be explained in later chapters. Readers need not be concerned if a term or concept seems unfamiliar when it's first introduced; as you progress through the text, your knowledge will broaden and the context will deepen, as one chapter illuminates another. Readers will gradually become conversant in the peculiar lingo of systems vulnerabilities and the tools and techniques used to control them, though in Appendix A there is an alphabetical glossary of all technical terms, jargon, and acronyms used in the book. Expressions that might be unfamiliar are italicized when first mentioned as a reminder to consult the glossary, but patient readers can rest assured that all mysteries will be explained in due course.

Despite what you may have been led to believe, security is not a black art and the Internet is not some spooky realm of pure evil like the enchanted forest through which Hansel and Gretel wandered. Risks can be managed, systems hardened, and hackers and privacy invaders frustrated. There is no reason to be apprehensive, though there is reason to be both cautious and skeptical. Computer security is *not* rocket science: you can learn it, and you will.

Introduction

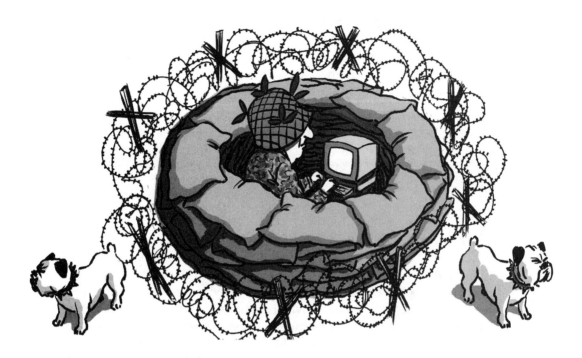

The Magic of Firewalls

THERE IS PERHAPS no piece of security equipment more shrouded in superstition than the firewall. It's a familiar item, though poorly understood, likely to be the first thing most people think of when computer security is mentioned. Almost everyone, regardless of skill level, talks about them, recommends them, and secretly worries that theirs might not be quite up to the task. Many home users have one whether they know it or not, either in the form of a small router for connecting several computers to a single modem, or in the form of a software program like BlackIce Defender or ZoneAlarm, which are called *packet filters* or *personal firewalls*.

Indeed, there is much that a firewall can do to improve security, but there is also a great deal that it can't. Many users, even many IT managers, erroneously imagine it to be a panacea of network and Internet security. A firewall does not create the equivalent of a digital bunker within which we're safe from attack. In truth, it addresses only a small, though important, set of vulnerabilities. Relying on a firewall for general security is very much like relying on a locked door at home when the windows are open. There are scores of routes by which a computer or a network can be attacked and compromised, both remotely and locally. Firewalls defend against only a fraction of them.

In its basic form, a firewall is a physical device. This type can be as simple as a NAT (network address translation) router for home users, such as the popular Linksys and Netgear cable/DSL broadband routers sold at retail for $100 or so, or as elaborate as an entire computer system loaded with various types of software for commercial users costing tens of thousands of dollars. Either way, a firewall is essentially a separate box that sits between your computer and a network, or your local network and another, larger one such as the Internet.

> **NOTE** *NAT routers are relevant to broadband users who connect to the Internet with an Ethernet card rather than a telephone modem. Dialup Internet users who connect with a standard phone modem can install a packet filter, or personal firewall, instead.*

This physical buffering is useful because when you make an Internet connection through a router-style firewall, the traffic you generate appears to originate from it and the traffic you receive appears to end at it. This makes it difficult for the many unsophisticated would-be hackers called *script kiddies* populating the Internet to locate your computer. When a computer's location can't be pinpointed, a number of attacks become awkward for the vast majority of mediocre, wannabe hackers to mount. Of course, to a sophisticated attacker with a thorough grasp of software programming and network protocols, a basic firewall is little more than a speed bump. For this reason, firewalls used in defense of corporate networks contain a great deal of added capability and may be custom designed, generally at great expense.

There are four basic types of firewalls, but only the first two are relevant to home users:

Packet filters: These are software programs running on a client machine such as a PC. On an Internet-connected PC, they block access to particular ports behind which insecure services may be running. They are commonly used on home systems, particularly by dialup users for whom a router would be superfluous. Most are inexpensive and quite effective.

Circuit proxies: These are physical boxes that create a gateway through which a computer connects to a network or the Internet. They forward data between the computers they're protecting and the network, and hide the IP addresses of each user's PC. Circuit proxies are physical buffer zones: they establish their own IP address on the Internet, then assign internal IP addresses that are not Internet-routable to each machine they're defending. A NAT router is an example of a circuit proxy for home systems using a broadband Internet connection.

Application-layer firewalls: Unlike a routing firewall such as a circuit proxy, these actually stop and filter network traffic, examine it for malicious content, then forward it to the host if the traffic or request is legitimate. They examine traffic for malicious code and malformed packets meant to attack specific applications on the host system. Generally, they are designed to protect only a single application that cannot be blocked, such as the Apache Web server, and are therefore used in combination with other, more general defenses. A good one will eliminate malicious traffic related to individual application vulnerabilities, but the chief drawback is a fair bit of computational overhead that can slow system performance.

Swiss Army knives: There are security appliances that claim to combine the benefits of routing and proxying, flood protection, application-layer filtering, intrusion detection, encryption, and more. Often they carry additional costs from required support services and impose a significant performance drain. Their added complexity is itself a security issue. And remember, a Swiss Army knife may be invaluable when nothing better is available, but it really doesn't do anything terribly well. Always beware of any security pitch promising a catch-all panacea. If it "slices, dices, chops, and grates," it probably won't handle any of those tasks with much grace.

Home users with dialup connections are quite well served by a good packet filter. For the Linux home user with a broadband connection and no Internet servers, a simple, hundred-dollar NAT router is perfectly adequate. Windows home users with a NAT router also need a packet filter capable of *egress filtering,* which we will learn about in the following section. For an office or small business network with no Internet servers but client PCs with both local network and Internet connections, there are routers or circuit proxies with added capability in the $200 to $500 range that will usually prove adequate, especially if a packet filter is installed as well. Of course, when you offer services over the Internet, firewalling gets more complicated. However, we won't be getting into server-side security because plenty of resources already exist. Our concern is securing the client system, whether a stand-alone PC or home network, or a thousand desktops in a business environment, because this is an element of computer security that has received too little attention. Remember, a single insecure client program can open a home PC to remote exploitation in spite of diligent defensive efforts, and even undermine thousands of dollars' worth of professional security services and equipment in the workplace.

Home and small business users should beware of overspending on firewall products. A bank or corporate network contains assets valuable enough to attract the cleverest of blackhat hackers. Attacks against such targets are expensive in terms of time and effort, but the goal is well worth it. By comparison, the home PC and small business network are insignificant targets for an elite blackhat, but are often sought by script kiddies looking for credit card data or seeking to commandeer a number of machines for launching DDoS (distributed denial-of-service) attacks and similar nuisances. A simple packet filter or router-style firewall is an important element in making attacks against a home or small business system too expensive for the mediocre intruders it tends to attract.

Any good, inexpensive firewall should be capable of *stateful packet inspection* (SPI), a routine in which packets destined for any port not in use will be dropped, but where ports the user activates will be opened automatically. Packets are the basic units of data exchanged over the Internet. E-mail memos, instant messages, even the Web pages that show up in our browsers, are a function of packets, or *datagrams*. When a large chunk of data is sent, it's broken into several packets for ease of transport and reassembled at the destination. A port is a logical structure, not a physical opening, but it can be imagined as a virtual opening through which data packets flow both out of and into networked computers. Ports are numbered sequentially, and there are standard ones enabling particular applications, *servers,* and *clients* to communicate with each other across a local network or the Internet.

Let's look at a familiar example. When you click on a hyperlink or type a URL into your browser's address field, your PC communicates with a remote Web server and asks to be sent the contents of a particular Web page via a protocol called HTTP (Hypertext Transfer Protocol). In order to make the request, your browser, acting as a client, opens a port on your computer and exchanges several small packets with the server in a routine called a *handshake* to establish a two-way connection, or *session*. The Web server, acting as a *host*, is listening on port 80 for just this sort of initial request and is programmed to answer it. After a brief handshake, a session is established and the data you've requested is sent to your computer in several packets to be reassembled as a Web page in your browser.

NOTE *The words* client *and* host *can be confusing. A client is a machine or an application, such as a browser, that requests a service, and a host is a system, such as a Web server, that offers a service. We think of the PC as primarily a client system reaching out for services offered by host systems, but it also makes services available, and in so doing sometimes functions as a host as well as a client.*

We'll learn the actual nuts and bolts of how one computer interacts with others in later chapters; for now, the important thing to note is that the Web server is available on a particular port and is designed to accommodate requests for any services it's offering that have been sent to it through that port. Home computers, especially Windows computers, have a great number of open ports because Windows is designed with a tremendous amount of networking capability that's installed and enabled by default. Much of this capability is superfluous to Internet users, and some of it is actually dangerous, being meant for use only on a local network, not the Web. These extra functions leave us exposed on the Internet. If someone happens to be scanning the Net for vulnerable machines and *pings* yours on the right port, your computer will answer. You likely have several *services* running on your PC, all listening for requests on their respective ports. If they're pinged, they'll respond. This is how malicious hackers and script kiddies find your machine on the Internet. Without a firewall or packet filter, your computer will respond to packets sent from anywhere on the Internet.

If you have a firewall capable of stateful packet inspection, it will automatically drop any packet destined for a particular port on your computer when that port is inactive. A simple firewall or filter will block incoming connections to particular ports, but stateful packet inspection allows your firewall to open a port automatically when you want to use it, and close it automatically when you're done. It records the *state* of a connection and recognizes connections you've deliberately made. This prevents your computer from responding to probes from machines with which you haven't established a connection, while allowing machines with which you've deliberately established a session to contact you.

For example, let's say that you have an active connection with a remote machine at the IP address 123.1.1.1. When stateful packet inspection is active, only packets originating from that IP address will be forwarded to your computer by the firewall. A packet sent from any other location on the Internet will be ignored, even though your computer is active and listening for data. On the server side, stateful packet inspection can defeat some denial-of-service attacks by recording the origin and state of packets sent to the host machine. If packets start arriving from a remote location, yet no connection or session is ever established, the firewall will "remember" this and automatically ignore additional contacts from that location, and therefore not waste system resources trying to accommodate bogus requests.

This is all good because it's common for malicious script kiddies to scan the Internet looking for unprotected computers, servers, and networks. They use automated port scanners capable of searching large swaths of the Internet, automatically sending packets to chosen IP addresses port by port. For example, such a tool might be configured to scan the IP range 123.1.1.1 to 123.1.1.100. The program will ping, or send a packet to, each port at each IP address in turn. It might begin by pinging 123.1.1.1 port 21 (FTP), then 123.1.1.1 port 22 (SSH), then 123.1.1.1 port 23 (Telnet), and continue in this manner until the entire list is exhausted.

Most script kiddies are mere opportunists searching for vulnerable machines, much like a thief trying doors in a hotel corridor. A locked room is usually all that's needed to discourage this type of attack. Most thieves will simply move on, looking for an unlocked, unoccupied room. In a very broad sense, stateful packet inspection is similar to locking your hotel room from the outside but not from the inside. You can open the door whenever you please, to whomever you please, but others can't. Your computer can have an open connection, or several of them using a number of different clients and services, yet your firewall will drop any packet that arrives from an address that does not correspond to one of the connections you've made. Suppose you have an active connection with a server at 123.1.1.1 and a packet arrives from a kiddie scanner at a completely different IP address, say 123.2.2.2. The packet will be dropped by the firewall because you do not have a connection established with that address. To the script kiddie using the scanner, there will be no reply and it will appear that there is no computer at your *IP address*.

So, what if your router doesn't support stateful packet inspection? Should you run out and buy a new one? Definitely not; in this case you can install a personal firewall or packet filter to create an additional line of defense. Windows users with simple, router-style firewalls can use products like Tiny Personal Firewall, BlackIce Defender, ZoneAlarm, or Sygate Personal Firewall, which are all easy to handle. Linux users can install IPchains for the 2.2.x kernel and IPtables for the 2.4.x kernel. These Linux packet filters are difficult for novices to configure manually, but there is a user-friendly frontend called Bastille that will configure packet filtering and also tighten other security elements, such as file permissions and the like.

A simple NAT router, used at home to connect several PCs to a single broadband Internet connection, serves quite well as a firewall. If you're using one, it's important to know whether it supports stateful packet inspection: some do and some don't. If it doesn't, you can deploy a packet filter to extend its capability. If you're using a dialup connection, you won't be using a NAT router, so you *definitely* need a packet filter or personal firewall capable of stateful packet inspection.

Firewalls and packet filters are important, but there is a great deal they can't do. While they may accept outside traffic only when you have an active connection, they can't determine whether you made the connection voluntarily or a malicious program running without your knowledge made it on your behalf. If someone sends you a malicious program via e-mail or instant messaging, or by enticing you to download it from a Web site, it may establish a connection to the Internet without your knowledge. To a firewall, these connections are no different from ones you make voluntarily. Thus a stranger can easily connect to your PC remotely, right through your personal firewall or your company's very expensive professional firewall. It happens every day.

Some packet filters will pop up an alert message, warning users whenever a program installed on their PC attempts to contact the Internet. This is called *egress filtering*, and it's one way of dealing with spyware and other malicious programs hidden on your machine. Egress filtering is a *very* useful feature that can alert you to the presence of *malware*, and it's important to know that Microsoft's Internet Connection Firewall, shipped with Windows XP, *does not* offer it. It performs *ingress filtering* only. If a malicious program hidden on your PC were to make a connection to the Internet, the standard Microsoft firewall would allow it to do so without warning you. Thus egress filtering, like stateful packet inspection, is an important feature that one should look for in any firewall product. And it's not expensive. You can buy a router capable of stateful packet inspection and a packet filter capable of egress filtering for about $100. All Windows users, regardless of how they connect to the Internet, need a packet filter capable of egress filtering. There is too much phone-home capability built into Windows itself, and into the applications it runs, for a user to depend on a router alone. It is essential that outbound connections be monitored.

Egress filtering is good, but it's hardly foolproof. If a malicious program is given a familiar name or is integrated into a familiar program, users may not realize that they need to block it when it attempts to connect to the Internet. For example, one particularly stealthy piece of spyware from SpecterSoft, called eBlaster, records a user's every keystroke, including their passwords, every Web site visited, and the contents every online chat and every e-mail sent and received. It then silently forwards all this data to the e-mail account of a remote spy. The eBlaster program is difficult to detect because it integrates itself with the familiar Windows shell, Explorer. When eBlaster runs for the first time, packet filters capable of egress filtering like ZoneAlarm will alert the victim with a popup, warning that Windows Explorer (explorer.exe) is attempting to connect to the Internet. But because Explorer is such a familiar program, and because it normally phones home to Microsoft when the Windows Search Assistant is activated, users may believe its activity to be innocent and permit it to connect when eBlaster invokes it. (For additional information about egress filtering, see Appendix B.)

Another thing that no firewall can do is shield your identity from the Web sites you visit. It cannot deter commercial profilers and spammers. It cannot protect your privacy or anonymity on line. It cannot defend you against spyware and viruses, except marginally if it performs egress filtering. It cannot *eliminate* insecure clients and services running on your computer; it merely blocks or conceals them. It cannot secure your machine against unauthorized action taken by local users. In short, *a firewall does not make your PC more difficult to hack.* It only blocks certain ports associated with insecure clients and services, if used properly, and makes your computer more difficult for remote attackers to locate on the Internet. That's all good, certainly, but it's only the tip of the iceberg.

"Hackproofing"

By the time you've finished reading this book, you will indeed be able to "hackproof" your computer, company workstation, home network, or small business network. By hackproofing I *do not* mean making your system an impenetrable bunker; nothing can do that. Instead, I mean using common sense and layers of protection to make compromising your system more trouble than it's worth. This involves three general principles that we will learn in detail:

Prevention: Reducing your target footprint through firewalling, keeping a low profile on the Internet, patching software and operating system vulnerabilities, and declining to open e-mail attachments and other risky files

Resistance: Setting sensible file and user permissions, disabling unused services and daemons, and installing reliable software—in other words, *hardening* the system

Tolerance: Securing the private data stored on your PC and your personal communications via e-mail and chat clients against interception on the Internet and against access by remote attackers and local snoops (e.g., nosy housemates), thereby limiting the damage that a system compromise or other security snafu can cause

Those are the three elements of effective computer security: prevention, resistance, and tolerance. Unfortunately, there is no magic bullet. Regardless of what the marketing departments of the security and antivirus vendors might lead you to believe, there are threats that no one can defend against; therefore it is *impossible* to make a computer or network truly hackproof. Internet service and software vendors like to give the impression that whatever they have to sell will make us safe, but this is mere marketing hype.

For example, the MSN-8 television ads from the spring of 2003 with the slogan "it's better with the butterfly" show an actor in a killer-bee costume dutifully shielding a mother and her small children from nasty bits of life on the street, implying that one need only switch one's ISP (Internet service provider) to MSN and all will be well. In fact, Microsoft Windows, MSN, Hotmail, and Microsoft Passport are all notoriously buggy. Hotmail's spam filters are among the weakest in commercial use. Exploits against Hotmail and Passport surface regularly, and exploitable Windows bugs are reported at a rate of roughly one a week. Indeed, during the time when the TV ad was running, Microsoft was forced to sue a number of bulk spammers precisely because its technical solutions have been a failure.

AOL is guilty of the same marketing hype, touting its automatic McAfee virus scanning feature as a veritable panacea of online security. "If you want your computer to be able to play with other computers without getting sick, get AOL for broadband with automatic virus protection," the advertising copywriters urge. Virus scanning is indeed a useful tool, but it's hardly adequate to prevent computers "getting sick."

Cisco Systems also joined the security-based advertising carnival with a TV ad showing a group of hipster "international hackers" tearing out their hair in frustration while trying to own the network of a Cisco customer. The scene then moves to a group of clueless Yuppies in suits on the other side of the equation, marveling at their presumably impenetrable Cisco server. "It's got self-protective features," one remarks with much awe and little comprehension. The others nod in deference to Cisco's magic technology, unwilling to speak lest they offend the mysterious pixies and sprites responsible for this feat of security sorcery.

None of these vendors actually claims that their gimmicks and slogans add up to invulnerability, however, and with good reason: Oracle CEO Larry Ellison made that mistake in November of 2001 and soon came to regret it. During his keynote speech at the Comdex technology conference in Las Vegas, Ellison stated flatly that Oracle is "unbreakable." Security researchers David and Mark Litchfield of Next-Generation Security Software (NGSS) then spent the better part of the next 18 months publishing exploit after exploit against Oracle in a seemingly endless and humiliating series. Ellison was soon forced to rewrite history, suggesting that he'd meant *unbreakable* in the sense of relatively difficult to break, not in the sense of impossible to break. So much for unbreakable products. No one will repeat Ellison's blunder in public again, but so long as computer and network security remain popular issues, vendors and their marketing copywriters will urge us toward the belief that their products offer a unique safety advantage. And they may indeed offer one—only what's needed is a comprehensive approach, not any particular gimmick.

Security is not a product you buy; it is not a gizmo you bolt on to your server rack; it is not a service you subscribe to. It is a process: one that begins with good information combined with common sense and skeptical thinking. And that doesn't mean just being skeptical of the claims of vendors; it means being skeptical of your own habits, your own equipment, your own software. The risks can never be eliminated, but they can be managed quite well. The more you know, not just about what you can do to defend yourself, but also about what you *can't* do, the better equipped you'll be to make wise choices whenever you're using a computer.

An Open-Source Solution

Microsoft Windows is far and away the most popular desktop operating system and far and away the least secure. There are many reasons why this is so. For one thing, Windows wasn't developed with Internet security in mind; the Net wouldn't become popular until near the end of the Windows 3.x development cycle, by which time the operating system was well established. The first retail edition for desktop users with Internet use in mind, Windows 95, was filled with 3.x *legacy code* and based on extremely naive assumptions about the security implications of the Internet, which had been engineered as a convenient way to *transfer* data, not *protect* it. The Internet was never designed to be secure, and Windows was designed primarily to be feature rich and convenient for users. Indeed, Windows is *too* feature rich. Because it's meant to be all things to all people, it contains far more networking capability than home users need. And because so many components are deeply integrated with the operating system kernel, there are many superfluous and insecure features that can't be disabled without affecting other, desirable ones.

There is a tremendous amount of legacy code in Windows and other Microsoft applications, written years ago when security was the least of the company's concerns, and this code is a constant obstacle to security, privacy, and data hygiene. Bad legacy code can be likened to bad genetic material and its consequences to hereditary disease. Thus we can say that new versions of Windows and MS applications are plagued by the digital equivalent of hereditary birth defects.

Windows is also quite obscure, with many hidden functions. It's often difficult for a user to observe system processes and understand their purpose. Windows frequently reaches out to the Internet without invitation and in ways that users don't anticipate, and it even quietly phones home to Microsoft on occasion. This lack of system transparency is a security challenge in itself.

Another problem with Windows comes not from Redmond but from the thousands of closed-source applications and utilities written for it, many of which have serious security holes. Indeed, some of them—especially "free" applications supported by advertising on your desktop—cross the line into malware. These programs can track users across the Internet and help advertisers develop marketing profiles of people as they go about their business on line.

Yet another problem is the very architecture of Windows: it is highly interlaced with many deeply integrated and *interdependent* components. The alternative to this engineering scheme would be a *modular* architecture such as one finds in

UNIX, BSD, and GNU/Linux. UNIX, as well as Linux and BSD, which share much in common with it, is designed so that a security vulnerability in one component will not typically extend into another. Vulnerable processes can be isolated, shut down if necessary, and patched without fuss. But because Windows is so interlaced and its many components so interdependent, shutting down a vulnerable process may cause system instability or even a crash. This complex architecture also makes the operating system tricky to patch when security vulnerabilities are discovered, leaving Windows users at a disadvantage.

For example, in July of 2003 Microsoft discovered that a service called RPC (remote procedure call) was vulnerable to a *buffer overflow* that could yield complete ownership of a Windows system to a remote attacker. Three weeks after the vulnerability was announced and a patch issued, the MSBlaster worm was launched, exploiting RPC through another service called DCOM, and automatically infecting hundreds of thousands of Windows systems. RPC allows a program running on one computer to execute code on another. This can be useful, particularly for networked machines sharing a hardware device like a printer over a LAN (local area network), say. However, there is no reason why any computer should run RPC if it is not supplying services to other machines on an internal network. Computers primarily meant to access the Internet should always have RPC disabled because many exploits against it have been discovered over the years. Unfortunately, RPC is deeply integrated into the Windows operating system and cannot be disabled safely: scores of other Windows components depend on RPC to function. On the other hand, users of UNIX, BSD, and Linux can disable RPC if they don't need it, because on those more modular systems RPC is an isolated service running on top of the operating system kernel. RPC is an integral part of Windows, but it's not part of UNIX; it's merely a function that can be switched on and off.

It's not uncommon for Windows users to find themselves stuck with insecure system components that can't be shut off because desirable, even crucial, processes depend on them. Therefore, this book will focus primarily on securing Microsoft Windows, but it will often do so by urging security-minded users to take advantage of the many open-source applications and utilities designed to run on it.

Let's look at another example. On 12 August 2002, I reported in my daily column for *The Register* a serious flaw in the way the Windows Internet Explorer and Linux Konqueror browsers handle SSL (Secure Sockets Layer) certification. SSL is the encrypted Web protocol used by e-commerce sites and banks to establish a "secure" browser session, indicated by a little padlock icon in the browser's status bar and a Web address beginning with HTTPS instead of HTTP.

A security researcher named Mike Benham had discovered a vulnerability in Internet Explorer's implementation of SSL certification and notified Microsoft before publicizing his discovery. The open-source Mozilla browser was not vulnerable, even when running on Windows; but while researching the story I did a bit of tinkering and discovered that the Konqueror browser for Linux was vulnerable.

Benham had already notified Microsoft, but my article was the first indication that Konqueror needed a fix too. Microsoft had been given a head start.

One day later, the Konqueror developers integrated a fix into the *CVS* (concurrent versions system) tree for the latest version. On 19 August, seven days after Benham's public announcement, all previous versions of Konqueror were fixed, despite the fact that the developers had a shorter warning period than the coders at Microsoft had gotten.

It was not until 5 September that Microsoft began issuing patches for the vulnerability, starting with Windows NT and XP. It had taken them three weeks to begin the job, and it would take them well over a month to complete it, in spite of the advance warning Benham had given them.

One might conclude that Microsoft was slowed by the sheer size of the bureaucracy associated with such an enormous company, but that would be a mistake. The Microsoft security response team is conscientious and usually pounces on published exploits as quickly as humanly possible. The delay resulted from the essential nature of Windows' architecture. The Internet Explorer browser may appear to be a stand-alone application, something, in a sense, running on top of Windows, but it's very much integrated with the operating system kernel. The broken cryptographic function that IE used for its implementation of SSL was buried deep in the bowels of Windows. Because several other Windows components and applications used the same crypto API (application programming interface), the patch developers had to be mindful of its many uses, and the patch itself had to be tested against scores of variables. While Internet Explorer was the thing that, in this case, exhibited the risky behavior, it's more accurate to say that Windows itself was broken and needed to be fixed—not an easy task when you're dealing with over 35 million lines of code.

On the other hand, Konqueror, like most open-source applications, really can be thought of as a stand-alone module running on top of the Linux kernel. In its case, the broken cryptographic function belonged solely to the Konqueror browser, not to Linux. Fixing it was a straightforward affair.

For another example, in June of 2002 a serious exploit against the popular, open-source Apache Web server, available for both Linux and Windows, was revealed by a security vendor called Internet Security Systems (ISS). The company posted their discovery to the BugTraq security mailing list without knowing the full extent of the flaw, and without giving Apache.org time to investigate and develop a patch or even propose a workaround. To sugar the pill, ISS had developed its own patch, which Apache later said didn't address all the issues.

Clearly, ISS was more concerned with taking credit for the discovery than mitigating the risks associated with it—behavior all too common within the "security community"—and this left the developers at Apache.org in a lurch. Nevertheless, they were able to issue fully patched versions within 24 hours. Why? Because the Apache Web server, unlike its Microsoft counterpart, IIS

(Internet Information Server), is a stand-alone application. *Only it* needed fixing, not the operating systems that run it. This provided a clear advantage to users running Apache on Windows; the lack of deep integration with the operating system kernel made patching the application far easier than it might otherwise have been.

There is another advantage to the modular approach of open-source applications. No matter how hard the security team at Microsoft works to ensure that a patch is safe to use, occasional problems necessarily arise whenever one is dealing with such a complicated, deeply interdependent system as Windows. Bad patches do come along from time to time, and for this reason professional system administrators (sysadmins) never install one on a mission-critical system without first installing it on a test system. In spite of the efforts made to ensure compatibility, Microsoft has at times been forced to recall patches. Thus it's not unusual for Windows admins to neglect patches entirely and seek their own workarounds to security vulnerabilities. Windows is a complicated beast, and Microsoft can't possibly test every patch against every possible system configuration.

Here again, because open-source applications are generally modular in design, a bad patch stands less chance of damaging the system than one designed for Windows. Generally, it will affect only the application to which it corresponds; if the patch is flawed, it's unlikely to cause a system failure. Of course, patches must *always* be tested before integration into mission-critical systems, but users of UNIX, BSD, and Linux, and users of open-source applications for Windows, have less to worry about than strict MS-only users. This is simply true by design.

With this in mind, let's take our first practical step toward improving online security by installing and configuring the free, open-source Mozilla Web browser and e-mail client on Windows.

Why Mozilla?

There are many reasons why Mozilla is a better choice for the security-conscious user than Internet Explorer and Outlook Express. We've already touched on one reason: it's not integrated with the Windows kernel, so security issues can be addressed quickly and with little danger of causing wider system difficulties. Also important is the simple fact that it's open source and therefore transparent: anyone is welcome to review the *source code* and see for himself exactly what it does and how it works. There are no secrets in Mozilla. On the other hand, Internet Explorer and Outlook Express (and Netscape and Opera) are closed-source products. Microsoft doesn't permit consumers to look under the hood, so to speak. All we know about these products is what's stated in the documentation, but Microsoft has for decades included undocumented functions in many of its products. Obviously, any software containing secret functions is an obstacle to good security.

Furthermore, the Mozilla browser offers users more control over potentially risky features like Java and JavaScript. It doesn't run ActiveX controls, a dangerous gimmick with which Microsoft is much enamored. It offers superior user privacy with better management of the URL history, page cache, cookies, plug-ins, and passwords.

Even better, the Mozilla e-mail client can be configured to display messages in plain text rather than HTML (Hypertext Markup Language), perhaps the single most productive step a user can take toward online security. Or, said another way, allowing HTML rendering and scripting in e-mail is one of the most common risky habits. It is not HTML *per se* that's at issue; it is, rather, the scripting support in HTML rendering engines (the programs that cause HTML to display as it was intended) that allows malicious code in e-mail memos to run, even when the recipient takes no action. Such scripts can cause major system compromises, allowing an attacker to take over a victim's machine. The deeper the integration of the Internet client into the operating system kernel, the more dangerous these scripts can become.

Microsoft's solution has been to issue patch after patch, fixing each type of scripting vulnerability individually as it becomes known. You can see the problem here: the flaw has to be known before it can be addressed, but of course the blackhat community likes to keep its discoveries and exploits secret for as long as possible. Yet Microsoft has for years refused to allow users to employ the simplest and most effective solution to scripting vulnerabilities whether they're known or unknown: to shut off HTML rendering and scripting support in their e-mail clients.

After all these years of difficulty, Outlook Express and Hotmail didn't receive HTML "off switches" for incoming mail until the summer of 2003, while Outlook is, at this writing, not scheduled to get its own until the next release (Outlook 2003). Why the company should have demanded for so many years that HTML formatting be displayed in e-mail, whether the user wishes to see it or not, is open to speculation. It could be that Microsoft feared that users would be disappointed in the look and feel of their e-mail if it should fail to throb with color advertisements, pornography, and clever animations. Or it could be that the company has a quiet financial interest in accommodating the direct-marketing industry, which wants its torrents of spam to be as eye-catching as possible.

Even the simplest HTML elements, like an image to be fetched off the Web and displayed in your e-mail, can give spammers the confirmation they need that your address is valid, even if you delete the message immediately after it arrives. A tracer image can be hidden in the HTML code and fetched automatically from a remote server in such a way that a unique identifier—possibly as simple as your e-mail address—will be logged along with your IP address for later harvesting as a known, valid contact. By the time the image appears, you have, in a very real sense, already replied to the message and the spammer has got your number, so to speak.

A typical tracer will look like this example from a spam message I received recently for lip augmentation products, urging me, illogically, to "kiss [my] thin, ordinary lips goodbye."

`<IMG src=http://home.optinaffiliate.info/a/header.tif?thomas.greene@theregister.co.uk>`

The IMG tag tells my mail client to fetch an image called header.tif from the `optinaffiliate` spam server and display it. It also plugs my e-mail address and probably my IP address into the server's log files when that happens, confirming that my e-mail address is valid and so keeping it in circulation among spammers. But because my e-mail client is configured with HTML rendering off, the raw HTML code was displayed to me as plain text instead of being executed, no tracer image was fetched, and the spammer received no response. However, if HTML had been switched on, I would *not* have seen the IMG tag as plain text; I would have seen the tracer image, or "Web bug," in its place. The image would have been fetched without my noticing that a spammer had just got confirmation of my address.

Turning off HTML prevents dangerous scripts from running. It also reduces spam because your e-mail address can't be verified unless you take deliberate actions, like replying to the message or following the link provided to remove yourself from the spammer's list. Often, the removal links are a scam designed to confirm your address in case you're smart enough to disable HTML, so you should *never* follow them.

For an added, and significant, bonus, an HTML-off setup for e-mail prevents pornographic images from being fetched and displayed in spam messages that small children might encounter—an important consideration on home machines.

Now that Microsoft has finally begun to address the security problems with HTML rendering and scripting support in their e-mail clients, the chief problems remaining are the numerous duplicate data traces that Internet Explorer and Outlook Express scatter about the system, the difficulty of removing them, and the integration of these applications into the low-level realm of the Windows kernel, where risky client behavior can lead to radical system difficulties.

Fortunately, Windows users can employ numerous workarounds, and, where necessary, sidestep such problems altogether. Accordingly, replacing a number of MS clients with safer and more transparent open-source substitutes is a crucial bit of housekeeping that this book will explain and encourage throughout. As Internet Explorer and Outlook Express can't be made secure enough no matter how hard one might try to overcome their shortcomings, we will simply bypass these problems by installing Mozilla in their place.

> **NOTE** *Mozilla Mail is a superior replacement for Outlook Express, but hardly an adequate one for MS Outlook. Readers looking for a safer alternative to Outlook should check out Ximian Evolution, a free, open-source Outlook clone that's fully compatible with MS Exchange. Unfortunately, it's available for Linux and Solaris only. Windows users who can't do without Outlook are stuck with it for now.*

Getting Mozilla

The first step is to point your browser to `mozilla.org` and find the latest stable release for your operating system. You will find it linked on the home page. If you're not a power user, don't download any of the *release candidates*, indicated by the initials *RC* in the file name. If you are a power user, then by all means feel free to experiment with the newest, bleeding-edge candidate. Otherwise, stick with the most recent stable build.

The file you will download first is the Mozilla installer; this will take only a few minutes on a fast connection. You can then run it as you would any Windows installation wizard. If you are new to Mozilla, when you reach the Setup Type dialog you should select the Complete option. In the next dialog, you will be asked if you want to use the Quick Launch feature. This helps Mozilla launch rapidly, the way Internet Explorer does, by preloading it at boot time. There is no harm in selecting this option. Next, you will be invited to save the installation files in case you should wish to reinstall the current version of Mozilla without downloading it again. Broadband users needn't bother, but 56K-ers might wish to choose Yes.

You will also be given an opportunity to configure your proxy settings if your ISP requires you to use one, though this can be dealt with later, using the browser's Preferences menu if you wish. Users not required to use a proxy may ignore this setting for now, though we'll be learning a great deal about proxies, and how to use them for online privacy, in later chapters.

Mozilla will be ready to use without a reboot, which is a good sign because this means it doesn't depend on the *Windows Registry*, a mysterious complex of data files that is read at boot time, where other browsers and Web-enabled applications may leave data traces indicating your online comings and goings. For example, URLs (uniform resource locators)—that is, Internet addresses—that you type into the address field of Internet Explorer are recorded in the Registry, along with numerous other bits of potentially sensitive personal data that ought to be under your control but are not, such as a list of the files you've searched for on your hard drive, files you've accessed recently, and several other items that we'll learn about in due course.

When Mozilla has finished installing itself and pops up on your desktop, you will be asked one more thing: whether you want it to become your default browser. I recommend that you make it so. You should *not* remove or disable Internet Explorer because you'll need it for Windows Update, although I would not recommend using it for any other purpose.

Now it's time to set up the mail and news client. You can launch it from the Mozilla browser by going to the menu bar and selecting Window ➤ Mail & Newsgroups. But let's make a desktop icon for it instead. From the Windows desktop Start menu, go to Programs ➤ Mozilla ➤ Mail. Right-click on the Mail icon and drag it to the desktop. When you activate it, a setup wizard will start, allowing you to enter your account information just as you would in setting up Outlook Express. Again, you will be asked if you want to make Mozilla your default mail client, and again I recommend that you do just that.

Secure Configuration

You've now got a Web browser and an e-mail client that you can configure for security considerably better than the disappointing levels established by Internet Explorer and Outlook Express. Only you do have to configure them. What follows is a walk-through of the various settings and available options with recommendations for improving online security, data hygiene, and user privacy.

Fortunately, Mozilla is a good deal simpler to configure than Internet Explorer, with all of its confusing "zones" and individual permissions, most of which are easily exploitable with malicious scripts anyway. Most, though not all, browser exploits affect IE exclusively, so merely replacing it with Mozilla will protect you from a host of online threats. But to make it even more secure, open Mozilla, go to the menu bar, and select Edit ➤ Preferences to bring up the Preferences menu. Items where the Mozilla defaults are generally good will not be covered.

Figure 1 shows the History option, where I prefer to use a value of zero days. This makes the browsing history available so long as Mozilla is open. When it's closed, the history will be deleted, except for the typed-URL history. Notice that there is a button enabling you to clear the URLs that you've typed into the address bar, or location bar.

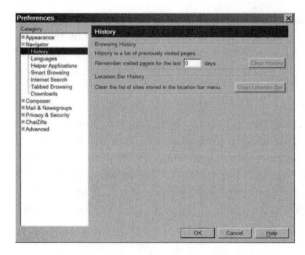

Figure 1. Controlling data traces with the History options dialog

Next is the Downloads menu (Figure 2), where I recommend choosing the progress dialog option over the download manager, which makes it too easy for other users to see what you've been up to. Mozilla will still record your downloads, but in Chapter 5 we will learn how to prevent the recording of *any* of our download history. The download history is the only item where Mozilla records your comings and goings without enabling you to control your data traces easily from the Preferences menu.

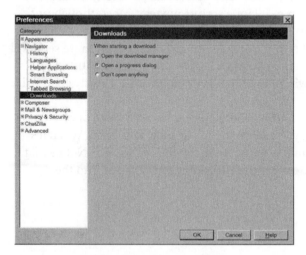

Figure 2. The Downloads setup dialog

The option for sending automatic replies that confirm your receipt of an e-mail memo appears in Figure 3. Obviously, it's best left off because spammers, marketers, and other Internet parasites can abuse this feature.

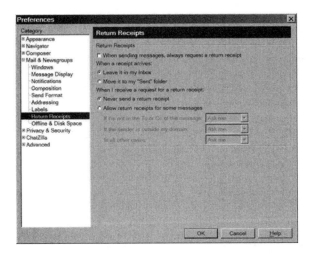

Figure 3. Blocking return receipts

Figure 4 shows a good, yet simple setup for handling cookies. Accepting cookies only from the originating server prevents third-party marketers from tracking you, though some Web sites, such as banking and e-commerce outfits, will sometimes use third-party cookies for authentication. In that case, you can accept cookies from those sites by using the Manage Stored Cookies feature. However, I prefer to leave third-party cookies blocked and simply toggle the setting occasionally, because the sites I visit that have legitimate uses for third-party cookies are few. It is also important to block *all* cookies in the Mozilla mail client using the second option, *Disable cookies in Mail & Newsgroups,* to help defeat spammers. Finally, limit the lifetime of cookies to your current browser session as indicated. This way, cookies will stay alive for as long as you have Mozilla open, then be deleted automatically when you close the browser. This prevents cookies from accumulating data about your comings and goings over time.

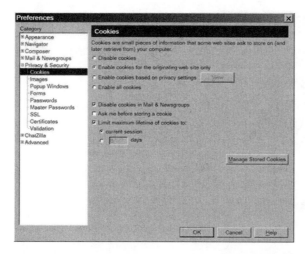

Figure 4. Blocking third-party cookies in the browser and e-mail client

Next we have the Images setup (Figure 5), and I strongly recommend limiting images to the originating server. This will cut down on third-party Web bugs and on third-party advertisements that only cause Web pages to load slower. You will miss a bit of content, but most of it will be junk anyway. It's very important to check *Do not load remote images in Mail & Newsgroup messages,* as indicated. This will help defeat spammers' tracer images and porn. Images attached to a memo will still display normally.

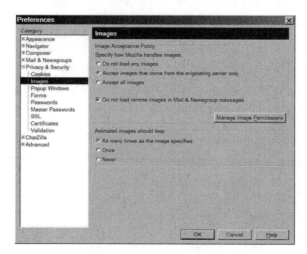

Figure 5. Blocking third-party images in the browser and e-mail client

The option for preventing popup windows from launching is shown in Figure 6. It's a good feature, but it doesn't work all the time. To defeat popups with certainty, you need to disable Java and JavaScript, but this will make Web surfing rather inconvenient because the majority of sites stubbornly insist on using both. On the plus side, disabling Java and JavaScript will positively eliminate popups and cause Web pages to load faster, which is an issue for 56K-ers. Choose your poison.

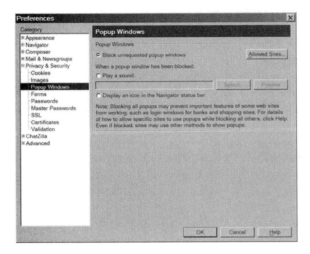

Figure 6. Blocking popup ads

Now we come to a tricky set of options. Mozilla can collect a good deal of user information related to Web shopping, including credit card data, so that it can be entered quickly and conveniently during an online purchase. If this is configured right, it can be made adequately secure. If it's done carelessly, remote attackers and local snoops can easily obtain this data from you. The Forms, Passwords, and Master Passwords options need to be set as shown in the four examples that follow. However, it is reasonable to let Mozilla save form data (Figure 7).

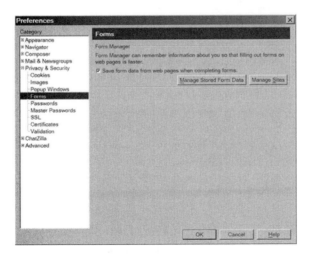

Figure 7. Saving form data, step one

When the options are set correctly, you will receive a password prompt whenever you attempt to access the data using the Manage Stored Form Data button (Figure 8).

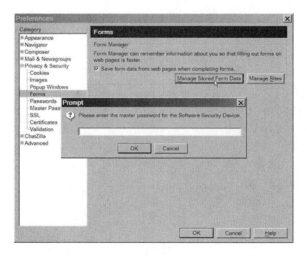

Figure 8. The password prompt

The Passwords menu should be set so that Mozilla will remember and enter Web site passwords for you, but only if the option *Use encryption when storing sensitive data* is also selected, as shown in Figure 9.

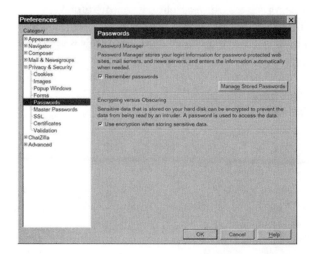

Figure 9. Saving passwords and encrypting them

Finally, it is necessary to set a good password using the Master Passwords menu, and also to require the password each time the information is accessed (Figure 10).

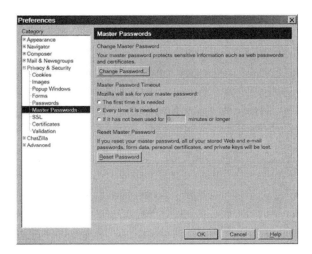

Figure 10. Proper settings for the Master Password

Once this is done, your Web site passwords and form data will not be accessible without the master password. To verify this, go to the Form Data and Passwords menus and select the Manage buttons. You should be prompted for the master password each time. It's important that the master password be very difficult to guess, but you mustn't forget it. You can write it down and keep it in a secure place until you're confident you've memorized it, then destroy the record.

The Advanced menu enables you to toggle Java on and off (Figure 11). Java is not much of a security hassle with Mozilla on Windows, and even less of one on Linux. There are annoyances, and there have been exploits, but the inconvenience of trying to surf the Web with it shut off is fairly daunting. If your computer is otherwise well configured for security, which it will be by the time you finish reading this book, Java should not be a problem.

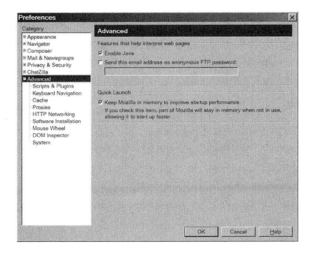

Figure 11. Enabling Java and letting Mozilla load at boot time

The toggle for JavaScript (Figure 12) is an item with a bit more potential for mischief, including exploit code, popups, cookie manipulation, and the like. On a Windows computer, even with Mozilla, I would be somewhat more inclined to disable JavaScript, though on a well-configured Linux machine I wouldn't worry about it, so long as the popups are under control. Incidentally, the Internet is swarming with all this blinking, throbbing rubbish because Web developers charge for it and therefore insist on using it. (Ever try to buy a car without under-coating and ScotchGuard or a major appliance without an extended warranty? Try getting a Web site built without Flash, JavaScript, etc....) Allowing JavaScript, but denying its most offensive "features," as pictured in Figure 12, is a reasonable compromise between security and convenience. Note in particular that both JavaScript and plugins are disabled for Mozilla Mail, which is quite important. Like remote images and cookies, these are things you do *not* want in your e-mail.

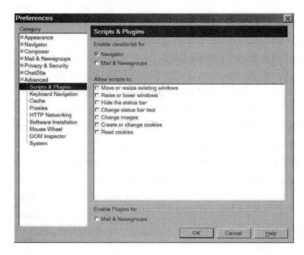

Figure 12. Enabling JavaScript in the browser but restricting its functions, and disabling it in e-mail

The browser cache stores local copies of all the Web pages you've visited. Obviously, this is a security issue on shared computers. You can control it by limiting the available disk space and clearing it periodically (though not securely) with the Clear Cache button. I would recommend a value of 0 MB for disk space if you have a fast Internet connection (Figure 13). Dialup users should limit its size to a few tens of MB and remember to clear it regularly.

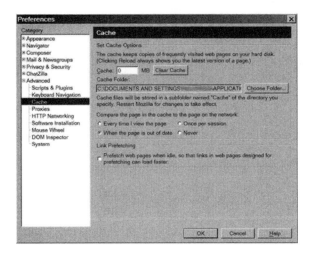

Figure 13. Controlling the page cache

Finally, to make Mozilla Mail display incoming memos in plain text, open the mail client, go to the menu bar, and choose View ➤ Message Body As ➤ Plain Text (Figure 14).

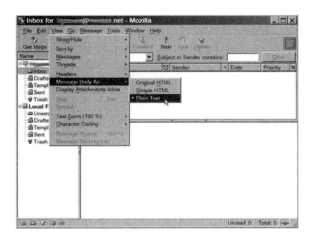

Figure 14. Choosing plain-text display in Mozilla Mail

And that's all there is to it. If you use Mozilla with these settings, your Windows computer will become appreciably more secure. There's a lot more to be done, but this is a solid, and relatively painless, beginning.

CHAPTER 1

Introducing the Dark Side

THE DARK SIDE OF THE WEB is represented by two general categories of unpleasantness: nuisances and plausible threats, with the former greatly outnumbering the latter. The threats are represented in turn by virus writers, script kiddies, spammers, carders (credit-card fraudsters), identity thieves, marketing profilers, social engineers (con artists), phreaks or phreakers (telephone system experts), overzealous law enforcement officials practicing the art of entrapment, and finally, a few exceptional, all-around hackers with superb programming skills and an intimate knowledge of network infrastructure. However, this last group is a small minority: any notion that the Net has been infiltrated by legions of elite blackhats is purely a product of Hollywood exaggeration and a gullible mainstream press hungry for technical wonders.

Such movies as *Johnny Mnemonic, Blade Runner,* and *The Matrix* attribute near-supernatural abilities to elite hackers, spawning a substantial genre we might call the "hacksploitation" film. The movie industry needs to infuse the hacking underground with airs of superior intelligence and evil wizardry for a simple reason: it has already inflated the technical prowess of the national security establishment to comic-book heights, as in the 1998 movie *Enemy of the State,* with Gene Hackman and Will Smith, and must therefore propose worthy adversaries who, like the underground hacker played by Hugh Jackman in the 2001 movie *Swordfish,* can crack military-grade encryption by "just sort of seeing the code in his mind"—a capacity no less impressive than faster-than-light space travel, and no more realistic.

If Hollywood and the cyberpunk novels of William Gibson were the only force driving hacker mythology, the average person would readily see it for the fiction that it is. Unfortunately, many hackers are eager to cultivate an image that sets them apart as superior. They've been quite successful at co-opting the mainstream press into further legitimizing the mystique, chiefly because the reporters who cover cybercrime have little technical background, drawing much of what they know about hacking from the underground personalities they interview and from the movies and cyberpunk sci-fi novels they've encountered. Lacking a nuts-and-bolts grounding in software design and network architecture, they simply don't *see* why it's impossible for a teenager to break into NORAD and initiate a nuclear holocaust using a laptop in his bedroom. It's one thing for such a scenario to appear in an enjoyable piece of Hollywood entertainment like the 1983 movie *WarGames;* it's quite another for a journalist to treat it as a plausible scenario, as John Markoff did in his legendary *New York Times* series on hacker celebrity Kevin Mitnick. It's a sad reflection on the state of big-media journalism, but it is nevertheless true that many reporters covering cybercrime and the hacking underground for major newspapers and television outlets illuminate their work with what they've seen in the movies and on TV shows like *The X-Files* because they simply don't *know* anything else.

Of course, hackers eagerly encourage these popular myths. "I watched myself morph, adapt, and change to my world," renowned überhacker Simple Nomad explained at the 2003 Defcon hacker exhibition in Las Vegas. "I literally watched myself circle the digital wagons. And in doing so, I watched the air-gap between nym and psyche—between the virtual world and the physical world—disappear. To understand the truth about something like a computer is not only to understand how the components fit together, how they interact, when they can be bent or broken, when you can exploit sublevels of trust between components to bypass a control—it is also about understanding that computer's placement within a network of others.

"We are plugged in," Nomad claimed, "and there ain't no going back. We *have* to hack ourselves. Not just the surface tension that is wrapped in a nym, but the core of your hacker self. Explore mental ring zero. Live to hack, and hack to live."

This sort of vague portentousness has an effect on journalists who lack the technical chops to see it for the empty gibberish that it is. But it can get a lot worse. Self-anointed techno-visionary Richard Thieme imagines hacking as a route to metaphysical insight. In an essay entitled *Hacker Generations*, Thieme purports to explain life, truth, and role of hacking in safeguarding both:

> [First Generation] hackers were alive with the spirit of Loki or Coyote or the Trickster, moving with stealth across boundaries, often spurning conventional ways of thinking and behaving. Hackers see deeply into the arbitrariness of structures, how form and content are assembled in subjective and often random ways and therefore how they can be defeated or subverted. They see atoms where others see a seeming solid, and they know that atoms are approximations of energies, abstractions, mathematical constructions. At the top level, they see the skull behind the grin, the unspoken or unacknowledged but shared assumptions of a fallible humanity.[1]

The essay reads like a parody of the late Joseph Campbell, and *still* it gets worse. Later we're told that Generation-Three hackers possess the unique vision required to liberate mankind from bondage imposed by a grand, universally shared illusion, a tired notion embroidered with material from the *I Ching*, Plato's *Republic*, and *Star Trek*, with a careless sprinkling of scientific words like *fractal* and *cyborg* and *planetary*:

> Third Generation hackers [must] be expert at every level of the fractal that connects all the levels of the network. It includes the most granular examination of how electrons are turned into bits and bytes, how percepts as well as concepts are framed and transported in network-centric warfare/peacefare, how all the layers link to one another, which distinctions between them matter and which don't. How the seemingly topmost application layer is not the end but the beginning of the real challenge, where the significance and symbolic meaning of the manufactured images and ideas that constitute the cyborg network create a trans-planetary hive mind. That's where the game is played today by the masters of the unseen, where those ideas and images become the means of moving the herd, percept turned into concept, people thinking they actually think when what has in fact already been thought for them has moved on all those layers into their unconscious constructions of reality.[2]

"Masters of the unseen" indeed. As film critic Roger Ebert pointed out in a smart review of *The Matrix Reloaded:* "The idea that the world is an illusion was old news when Plato said it."

---

1. See www.thiemeworks.com/write/archives/HackerGenerations.htm.
2. Ibid.

So what can we really say about hackers? First, they're hobbyists, much like the shade-tree mechanics who muscled up their cars in the 1950s and '60s and competed in the streets, but who had dignity enough not to speak of themselves as prophets merely because they could make their cars run faster and handle better than most people could. They "hacked" their cars and "transcended" design limits as well as the law—accomplishments which, coincidentally, also form the basis of computer-hacker narcissism. Hacking is nothing more than using or modifying computer hardware, software, networks, and their related systems in ways the designers didn't anticipate—which is interesting and fun, certainly, but hardly a basis for some new mystical cult.

Johnny Mnemonic and *The Matrix* may be good enough for the news media and broadsheets like the *New York Times*, but for those of us wishing to harden our systems against *real* threats, they simply won't do. The mythology has got to go. Forget about Loki and the Trickster, whoever they may be, and the "trans-planetary hive mind." Hackers are by no means special. They are quite ordinary people, affected by the same ambitions, foibles, and motives—both good and bad—affecting anyone else. They are not necessarily malicious. Some hackers, called *whitehats*, may never have broken a law in their lives, while some cybercriminals are so inept that calling them "hackers" would be a preposterous overstatement. They may be motivated by benign curiosity, by vanity, or by greed. But they are not superior; they are people you chat with on line, people you work with every day, and people you send upstairs with an affectionate pat on the bottom to do their homework. They are good and bad, young and old, bright and stupid. They are people just like you and me.

The Hacker's Lair

The lexicon of the dark side is filled with technical jargon, profanity, and geeky slang, often employing numerals as substitutes for the letters they resemble. The letter *O* looks like a zero; the capital letter *A* looks like a four, the capital letter *I* and the lowercase *L* both look like a one, and so on. Words are often misspelled in a sort of casual Esperanto. Thus, *script kiddie* can become *skr1p7 k1dd13* and *hacker h4x0r*. In this way, hackers and wannabes actively promote the aura of antisocial genius and elitism surrounding the computer underground. Script kiddies trade exploits, or *sploits*, in chatrooms. Successfully compromised systems are said to be owned *(0wn3d)*, or rooted *(r00t3d)*. Capable hackers are said to be elite, or *leet (l33t)*. *Eleet* can be, and often is, spelled numerically as *31337*, though this form is almost always reserved for mockery as in, "What a hopeless 31337 wannabe you are." Script kiddies often accuse each other of being "gay," which has nothing to do with sex and everything to do with hacking skills, or *skillz*, and the relative lack thereof. You're gay if you can talk the talk but can't walk the walk, a condition that applies to the overwhelming majority of script kiddies and their inept female counterparts, called "scene whores," who swarm the Internet like so many malicious tadpoles. Most dream of the day when they'll be total l33t h4x0rz with mad skillz, though most will progress toward adulthood, discover sex, find jobs, and lose interest in the "scene" without having contributed the merest scrap of useful knowledge or original insight to either the hacking underground or the security mainstream.

They have online aliases like *w1ck3d, 2kewl,* and *tekn0.* They are chiefly a nuisance, but in spite of their essential incompetence they can manage considerable mischief using packaged exploits and tools created by the minority of blackhat hackers who actually know what they're doing. Many of these utilities feature a GUI (graphical user interface) and can be controlled by clicking buttons on a mouse rather than entering commands with a keyboard. Point-and-click attack tools are plentiful, as are the lamers who rely on them.

Unless you're responsible for a company network representing a high-value target, script kiddies are the people you need to worry about, not the elite blackhats. Script-kiddie and scene-whore hacking may be child's play, but with so many software vulnerabilities in place and so many cracking tools available, child's play suffices to make serious trouble for online businesses and home systems, and even corporate networks. It's not that the hackers are so good; it's that the software is so bad. A would-be hacker doesn't have to be terribly bright to compromise a remote system—at least one outside the enterprise/banking/military arena where tens of thousands to millions of dollars are budgeted for security each year. But this is not such bad news. Thwarting your chief adversary, the script kiddie and the journeyman cracker, is really a matter of common sense, good habits, and skepticism. Your adversary has no deep background in computer science. It makes no sense to suppose that frustrating him should require *you* to have one.

Hewlett-Packard security manager Ira Winkler likes to say that he can "teach a monkey to hack." Statements like this have earned him frequent ridicule among the more capable members of the hacking underground. Indeed, it is a foolish slogan, because no one should doubt that there are people with less-than-noble intentions out there who know far more about the security flaws in software and hardware systems than the engineers who designed them. Yet there is an element of truth in Winkler's motto, though he would do better to say that he can teach a monkey to do what script kiddies do. I don't doubt that he could.

It may seem counterintuitive, but it's nevertheless true that the online adversary most of us will encounter is a semiskilled teenager armed with a cracking toolbox that he would have little hope of developing on his own. But it is a big and quite potent arsenal nonetheless: there are Trojan horse programs and password crackers, Web site exploiters and rootkits, vulnerability scanners and do-it-yourself virus assembly kits, all painfully easy to use and available for free download off the Web.

Let's take a brief inventory of the script kiddie's 31337 toolchest.

Trojans

As the name implies, these are seemingly harmless programs with concealed malicious payloads. Among the more common ones plaguing Windows users is *SubSeven*, a small yet powerful server that yields remote administration rights to an outsider. Indeed, it can offer an attacker *greater* control over a machine than the owner enjoys: it includes a keystroke logger and a screen grabber among several other features that the victim's machine may not possess. However, a Trojan is so named for way it's distributed, not for any particular payload that it delivers. For example, the SubSeven server is called a Trojan because it can be delivered concealed within another program, but the actual malicious payload is a *rootkit*, that is, a program that gives an attacker *root*, or administrative, privileges on a remote machine. Many people use the word *Trojan* to indicate any backdoor program like SubSeven, but this is not correct. A Trojan is simply a piece of evidently benign software that contains a hidden, malicious payload, just like the original wooden horse for which it's named.

Rootkits and RATs

The name *rootkit* derives from the administrator account on UNIX, BSD, and Linux systems, which is called root. The root user is the one who has total control of the system. A rootkit, then, is a software package that gives a remote attacker, or a nonprivileged local user, the same level of control. Although Windows has no root account, but has instead *administrator* and *system* accounts, a program allowing this sort of remote takeover is usually called a rootkit or a *RAT* (remote-access trapdoor). A RAT is similar to a rootkit, though simpler. These programs create a virtual back door through which other people can connect to your machine and control it. They will often open a particular port and listen for the attacker's instructions. Some of the more popular rootkits for Windows are SubSeven and Back Orifice, the latter of which, comically, listens on port 31337. Both of these programs can be delivered as Trojans, which has led many people to believe that Trojans and rootkits are the same. As we noted above, a Trojan does not necessarily deliver any particular payload, though many Windows rootkits are delivered in that way. Rootkits can also be installed automatically by worms, or manually by leveraging software vulnerabilities and system misconfigurations. UNIX and Linux rootkits are often installed manually, though Trojan delivery is increasingly common through infected patches, updates, and software packages.

Rootkits are also a significant danger to corporate networks, in spite of the steps taken and money spent to secure these networks with elaborate firewalls and security monitoring services. For example, employees who telecommute may connect to the company system from compromised laptops or home machines, inadvertently spreading an infection from their local machine to the remote network. Even when encrypted connections such as SSH (secure shell) or VPNs (virtual private networks) are used for remote access, an attacker can easily harvest company passwords with a keystroke logger planted on an employee's home PC or laptop. In that situation, even the strongest password is useless. *Many* professionally defended networks have been compromised in this way.

Dictionary Crackers

These programs automatically log on to a password-protected remote service using names and passwords from a list until a match is found. They work very quickly, in some cases making 200 attempts per second. They can be configured to try passwords only, using lists of single words, or login/password pairs from lists of combinations. Among the more popular ones are AccessDiver, GoldenEye, and Ares. Most are free and very easy to use. An attacker need not have a clue how password authentication works; all he needs is a cracker and a few wordlists, many of which are also available for free download. This sort of attack is called a *dictionary attack*. Many cracking programs are also capable of *brute force attacks*, an extremely time-consuming routine in which characters are tried exhaustively.

A related tool is the *passfile cracker*, which attempts to break encrypted password files stolen from remote systems. The best known passfile cracker is called John the Ripper (JtR), available free on the Net. It is a command-line (text-only) tool not quite so user-friendly as the many GUI dictionary crackers available, but it is not beyond the reach of many script kiddies.

HTTP Exploiters

Also called Web site exploiters or *directory exploiters*, these programs automatically search for unprotected (i.e., *world-readable*) directories on a server. Many commercial Web servers have been hastily run up and are poorly configured for security, and it is often possible for a remote attacker to find a directory containing user passwords, credit card data, or other useful files simply by following a URL to it. Let's say you have a Web site at yourdomain.net. And let's say you have a password file in a directory called passwords, in a file called paswd.txt. If you fail to configure your server properly, an attacker could easily use a browser to follow the URL yourdomain.net/passwords/paswd.txt and navigate directly to the file. An HTTP exploiter automates this procedure, trying scores or even hundreds of URLs to common directory locations within minutes.

In addition, there are CGI (common gateway interface) exploiters, which focus on vulnerabilities in CGIs, the "flat" HTML pages used for logging on to a Web service or entering user data. Web mail services such as Hotmail and most e-commerce shopping carts make liberal use of CGIs.

Vulnerability Scanners

These programs automatically query a remote system in search of known vulnerabilities, unprotected services, and susceptibility to scores of exploits. They are double-edged swords: although extremely valuable to administrators in assessing the security of their own systems, they can easily be turned against unsuspecting victims. While it might seem logical to design such programs to work only against a local target, this would create a problem in practice: professional admins often manage numerous systems that are geographically separate and must therefore do so via a remote connection. Thus, the ability to scan a remote host is necessary even for quite innocent purposes. Two popular vulnerability scanners are Nessus, which is free, and SAINT, which was free until fairly recently.

Port Scanners

Similar to vulnerability scanners, these programs query a remote machine to learn which ports are active or ready to accept a connection. Since many services use standard ports, an attacker using a port scanner can often guess which services are running on a remote system and decide which attacks are most likely to be fruitful. A well-configured firewall will close unnecessary ports, though there are some that can't be blocked without impeding a machine's basic functions. However, home desktop machines used primarily as client systems for accessing the Internet can be configured with virtually no running services, and ports need not be open unless the user is initiating a connection.

Again, we have a double-edged sword: port scanners are extremely useful to attackers, but running them against one's own machine is an excellent way of ensuring that there are no unnecessary services or daemons listening for network traffic. This is especially important for Windows users with home desktop systems, who may be surprised to discover that services they've never heard of have been installed along with their operating system. The most popular port scanner is Nmap; it's free and available for both Windows and UNIX-compatible systems.

Malware

This is a very general, catch-all term. Stated simply, malware is any software code or firmware code that

- Causes your computer to behave in ways you don't intend, or

- Prevents your computer from behaving in ways you do intend

There are hundreds of types of malware, from viruses to Trojans to adware, which we will examine below. Incidentally, by my definition, *Windows* is malware because Microsoft maintains more control over some of its functions than the end user. As we'll see in later chapters, Windows both causes a computer to behave in ways the user may not intend and prevents a computer from behaving in ways the user may intend.

Viruses

These familiar nuisances have been around for ages, and the Internet has only helped them propagate. A virus is any code that can be transferred from one computer to another without being observed directly, much the way one might infect another person with a cold simply by sneezing in their vicinity. There's almost no limit to the purposes for which viruses can be created. Some viruses are completely harmless, while others can cause severe damage to a system. It's possible for malicious hackers to use them to gain control of your computer, then use your machine, in turn, to attack others. There are even do-it-yourself virus creation kits available on the Web for malicious kiddies with no programming skills.

There are tens of thousands of viruses with virtually unlimited potential to create difficulties, though most are "lab strains" that haven't been released into the wild but are instead collected by antivirus (AV) vendors for research. Some viruses are viciously destructive, others are merely irritating, and still others do no harm at all. They can be delivered as Trojans concealed in other software; they can be spread by instant messaging clients, P2P (Peer-to-Peer) file-sharing utilities such as KaZaA, and infected e-mail; or they may be inadvertently downloaded from the Web. They can also be spread by sharing removable media such as floppy disks and CDs. A virus spreads through human interaction, though it is designed to escape observation.

Suppose you ask a friend for a copy of an MP3. He copies it from his computer onto a disk and brings it to work the next day. Only there's a virus on his home computer, so when he copies the file, the virus silently copies itself without his knowledge. Later, when you copy the MP3 file onto your own computer, the virus automatically and silently copies itself at the same time and, in this way, replicates itself with your assistance. Viruses depend on human action to replicate, though the process may be invisible to the victim.

Children and teenagers are a major source of malware and viruses on home systems because of their inclination to trade and share files, whereas workgroups are a major source on corporate networks, because members tend to trust each other and often exchange files without much concern. Telecommuters may infect a company network simply by connecting from an insecure computer. Large companies use expensive firewall products and filtering services to block infected files and spam at the border. For home users and small businesses with tighter budgets, there are two basic approaches to defense:

- Use Windows and purchase a virus-scanning tool or service such as those provided by F-Secure (www.f-secure.com), Sophos (www.sophos.com), and AVG (www.grisoft.com)

- Use Linux and forget about the vast majority of viruses

While Linux is not invulnerable, viruses affecting it are rare. Windows is far and away the chief target of virus writers, though this may change as the Linux desktop continues to grow in popularity. The best general defense against viruses is *never* to open any e-mail attachment or file downloaded from the Internet or received via instant messaging, and never to copy a file from removable media to your own machine, without first scanning it for the presence of malware.

Worms

A worm is an infection that can spread without any user interaction. It takes advantage of software vulnerabilities that may not be widely known and is therefore difficult to defend against. Worms may contain several components: they are often able to connect to and scan the Internet for vulnerable machines, automatically install themselves, and transform each infected host into another point of propagation, in turn scanning for additional hosts and infecting them as well. Malicious attackers can use worms in a targeted manner to deliver rootkits or other malware designed to commandeer a computer and use it to attack others, though most often they are released indiscriminately. If your computer is vulnerable to a worm, it can be infected, and it can infect others, without the slightest action on your part. Recent examples include the Code Red worm, which exploited a flaw in the Microsoft IIS server; the MSBlaster worm, which exploited a flaw in Windows; and the Slapper.A worm, which affected Linux machines.

Virus scanners, used periodically to check the local hard disk, can alert users to the presence of viruses and worms *after* the fact, but they cannot *prevent* infection unless all new files are scanned before being copied or installed. A worm is especially hard to detect because it's designed to exploit software vulnerabilities automatically and, well, worm its way into the system. It is not necessary for you to install anything for a worm to infect your machine, so it's difficult to prevent it with any sort of antivirus software. Large corporate networks employ specialized firewalls and security monitoring services to catch suspicious activity in real time, but those solutions are far too costly for small companies and home users. In those cases, the best defense is to remain informed of new vulnerabilities, to apply patches as soon as possible, and to scan the system regularly for the presence of malware. You'll detect it after the fact, but if you scan regularly, the interval of infection will be brief. As in the case of Trojans, when we talk about worms we're talking primarily about a delivery mechanism, not any particular payload.

Packet Sniffers

These are at once excellent security tools and potent weapons. They intercept each packet exchanged over a network connection and reveal every byte of data that's not encrypted, along with the origin and destination. Used as defensive tools, they can reveal spyware and Trojans overlooked by virus-scanning software and firewalls, and I recommend that everyone run a packet sniffer on their own connection from time to time as a precaution against hidden malware. Windows users in particular may be surprised to see that their computers will phone home and exchange data with servers at Microsoft at unexpected times. Packet sniffers are the best tools to detect this sort of behavior. Used as weapons, however, they can compromise security just as surely as they can protect it. They can harvest passwords sent in plain text, an all-too-common occurrence with e-mail services and ISP accounts. They can capture every unencrypted e-mail, instant message, and every bit of Web traffic between your browser and the Internet. Although it's not trivial to install a sniffer on a remote network, it's not brain surgery, either. The most popular free sniffer is called Ethereal, available for both Linux and Windows. TCPdump is an old command-line sniffer well known to UNIX admins.

Scripted Exploits

The word *exploit*, or *sploit*, is a generic term covering an enormous territory. When a security vulnerability is discovered in a piece of software or hardware, the mechanism for leveraging it is called an exploit. Usually, a security researcher who discovers a vulnerability releases exploit code along with it, to allow others to confirm that the problem involves a practical, real-world security risk. Generally, the people discovering vulnerabilities and their associated exploits are very knowledgeable and skilled in programming, so information of this sort is rarely of use to script kiddies.

However, competent blackhats are capable of repackaging exploits so that unsophisticated attackers can use them with ease. These are *scripted exploits*, and they can be quite destructive in the wrong hands. Often, the vulnerability involved is newly discovered, meaning that it may not have been patched or that the patch may not have been widely deployed. In many cases, the first warning users receive is a sudden, widespread infection such as those caused by the Code Red and SirCam worms in 2001 and the MSBlaster worm in 2003. Interestingly, the software vulnerability that Blaster exploited had been addressed with a patch from Microsoft about a month *before* the worm struck. The same was true of Code Red, which exploited a vulnerability for which a patch existed three weeks prior to its release. Many admins neglected to install the patches, however, so the worms spread quickly once they went live. Ironically, Microsoft's Hotmail servers became infected with Code Red, as did a number of the company's own internal network servers. Even at the home of "Trustworthy Computing," the application of crucial software patches can be slow.

A number of exploits are known only to a handful of people who keep their discoveries secret in order to use them without detection. This sort of exploit is virtually impossible to defend against, because no one outside a small, core group knows that it exists. The day of its public debut is called zero day, or 0-day, at which point its value as a secret weapon rapidly diminishes. It is impossible to estimate how many unknown exploits are in circulation at any given time. Although they're not part of the script-kiddie toolchest but are instead used primarily against high-value targets by advanced blackhats, it is crucial for everyone concerned with security to understand that there are vulnerabilities and threats against which no specific defense exists.

Adware and Spyware

It's safe to assume that nearly every Windows system not managed by professional admins, along with a significant portion of those that are, will be hosting some form of adware or spyware. There are thousands of purportedly free applications written for Windows that cost nothing to purchase but are supported by advertisements that appear on the desktop or in the application window. Gator, now known as Claria Corporation, and WhenU are two companies that use advertising revenue to develop and distribute software: the companies earn money, while the only cost to the consumer is the occasional banner or pop-up ad, though there are significant security and privacy issues inherent in this software distribution model. The advertisements you see are fetched off an *ad server,* which may not belong to the company you think you're doing business with. Allowing your computer to contact third-party servers about which you know nothing is a security risk.

Gator and WhenU are quite unabashed about what they do. Indeed, Gator openly calls itself "one of the world's largest behavioral marketing networks." Other Internet marketing companies and software developers are not so forthcoming. A good deal of Windows so-called freeware secretly tracks users for marketing purposes. If you've installed this type of software, then it's nearly certain that you've also installed spyware. You can assume that your Internet use is being monitored, that advertisements are being fed to you based on your surfing habits, and that this data has been accumulating in company databases along with personally identifying information.

Free applications that involve spyware include P2P file-sharing software, media players and jukeboxes, computer games, browser and desktop toolbars, screen savers, system "optimizers," instant messaging clients, Internet telephony or VoIP (Voice over Internet Protocol) dialers, and innumerable other clients and utilities.

It is often impossible to remove the spyware portion of the application without disabling the useful portion, though in some cases running the vendor's program uninstaller will eliminate the good parts but *not* disable the spyware functions. Such programs are generally designed with little or no concern for security: not only do they pose a privacy risk in the best case, they are generally riddled with bugs and notoriously easy for potential intruders to exploit. All such software should be strictly forbidden on corporate Windows-based workstations. It represents an unpredictable security risk that is very difficult to assess and manage, and some applications, such as P2P software, may open a company to legal liability for intellectual property and copyright infringement.

For home users, a simple Web search on the term *adware* will yield numerous Web sites offering advice on detecting and removing most spy programs. There is also a free utility called Ad-aware from Lavasoft that will detect and remove spyware programs. Once they've been removed, the best solution is to install comparable open-source applications in their place, because there are no secret functions in open-source products: if it's not in the source code, it's not in the application. Fortunately, many of the features and conveniences offered by popular freeware applications have been duplicated in open-source alternatives that run on Windows as well as UNIX, BSD, and Linux.

Child's Play

Now that we've got an overview of the tools available to the mischievous but unskilled majority of online reprobates, it's time to put them to use. The following exercise is based on actual cases in which a script kiddie's blunt implements proved adequate to compromise a professionally managed system. The purpose is not so much to turn readers into hacker newbies, but to illustrate the ease with which systems can be compromised and to explain why unsophisticated attacks continue to yield fruit. We've all heard the standard security prescriptions and proscriptions: back up often, update virus signatures, and never open e-mail attachments from unknown sources. But familiar bromides of this sort fall on deaf ears because, for one thing, they're completely inadequate and even nontechnical people can sense this, and for another, too few computer users understand exactly what can happen if they drop their guard. Many corporate IT managers issue good policies but avoid explaining the underlying technical details to rank-and-file employees because they don't believe that ordinary users will be able to grasp the finer points, and sometimes because they fear educating them in network sabotage and intellectual property theft. But experience has shown that uninformed users are themselves a major security vulnerability. Ignorance of the real consequences leads to innocent mistakes among users, which in turn leads to trouble both at home and on the job. When it comes to computer security, there is far more to gain from educating the majority of honest people than there is from denying information to the minority of miscreants.

"What's the worst that can happen?" an employee may ask himself with a shrug as he slides a disc given to him by a trusted friend into the CD-ROM drive of his workstation, quite against company policy. He knows it's against policy, but he also knows that his friend would never give him something dangerous. He trusts his friend, whom he has known for years, unlike the company's IT manager, whom he's never even met. The friend has proved his trustworthiness repeatedly over the years. The manager, on the other hand, communicates through memos that increasingly restrict everyone's computer and network privileges, typically with little in the way of explanation. Like many security managers, this one doesn't like to give employees too many ideas about how the network might be compromised. But rank-and-file staff sense that through his memos he's patronizing them, talking down to them as if they were children. His restrictions on company computer use and network access are strict enough to interfere with work, so they're flouted routinely. After all, everyone knows the difference between some risky executable file and a harmless MP3 music file.

In the employee's mind—and this is perfectly natural, even universal—the long-term relationship of trust with a friend takes precedence over the presumed expertise of a stranger, so he plays the CD on his workstation with hardly a second thought—and inadvertently installs a malicious virus on his company's professionally defended network behind a $60,000 firewall. He does this because no one has explained to him in truthful, adult language exactly what can happen when good security practices are ignored.

So let's just see what can happen.

Legal Beagle

Robbie is 15 years old. For years, he's had what might politely be called "anger-control problems." His girlfriend, who's seen more than enough evidence of them, has filed a lawsuit seeking a judgment for property damage she says he caused in a fit of pique. Her lawyer is named Samuel Wise. To better prepare a defense, Robbie wants to know exactly what the opposition knows about him. Unfortunately, Wise's law firm employs a professional security team and the hope of simply bypassing their firewall, finding the information, and escaping undetected is slim to none. Robbie is a script kiddie, not a sophisticated blackhat; all he's got are the point-and-click tools available on the Web. Obviously, it will be far easier to attack Wise's home system, if he's got one, and use it as a springboard, though first Robbie's got to find it.

So, how does he find Wise's home computer among the millions connected to the Internet? It's not difficult. The first step is to find Wise's home e-mail address. If Robbie can get Wise to send him an e-mail memo from his home machine, it will reveal the IP address of his computer.

First, Robbie does a bit of background research, visiting the law firm's Web site. He knows that sometimes a home phone number and home e-mail address will be listed on the staff pages for an emergency contact. In this case, unfortunately, there is no such information about his target, but there is a nice bio with plenty of details about Wise's past, including his work and educational history, his areas of specialization, and the like. This may prove useful, but Robbie still needs the lawyer's home e-mail address; he wants to receive a memo from that account in order to locate Wise's PC. He considers sending an e-mail to Wise's work address after hours. Wise might monitor his work account from home, and if Robbie gives him a good reason to reply right away, he may do so from home. Of course, Wise may not bother to download his work e-mail during off hours, so it's better if Robbie can find his home e-mail address and approach him there directly.

Thanks to the increasing power and convenience of Internet search engines, there's an excellent chance that Robbie will find a document somewhere on the Web showing Wise's home e-mail. Using Wise's name and several of the details provided by his company's employee profile, Robbie begins to search.

As it turns out, Wise has spoken at a number of professional conferences dealing with legal issues. Several of the conferences maintain Web sites, and at one of these Robbie finds Wise's home e-mail address listed on a page of speaker profiles. Now, he refines his search, using his target's name and e-mail address together. This will eliminate hits from other Samuel Wises.

By searching in this manner, Robbie soon discovers something interesting: Wise has made numerous posts to a cigar aficionado bulletin board. The board is configured to catalog the IP address and domain name of each person posting to it. He immediately notices that Wise's e-mail and domain relate to the same ISP. His e-mail, `samwise@mail.uswest.net`, harmonizes with the location logged by the forum: `poolND12345.uswest.net` (123.231.2.3). This tells Robbie that Wise is not using a *proxy server* to access the Internet, which in turn means that any e-mail he sends will reveal his true IP address in a portion of the memo called the header.

Robbie makes a note of the IP address logged by the bulletin board, but he knows that many ISPs use DHCP (Dynamic Host Configuration Protocol), a system that assigns an IP address to users dynamically whenever they connect. He checks to see if Wise has a permanent IP address by examining several of his older posts at the cigar forum. Sure enough, his computer's location changes from time to time. His ISP does in fact use DHCP to assign him a new IP address whenever he connects. Therefore, Robbie will have to work quickly to locate Wise's computer once he persuades the lawyer to send him an e-mail, because his PC may be at a different location a day or two later. This is good information; it helps him to organize his attack.

NOTE *Can you spot Wise's chief mistake here? How would you avoid having your e-mail, your computer's IP address, and your identity harvested from Internet forums and bulletin boards and later correlated? Check the analysis at the end of this section for answers.*

Robbie's next step will be to e-mail Wise at home and persuade him to reply. Robbie does *not* want to send any malware in that message; if Wise later discovers that his machine is infected, he may associate it with the mail. Robbie's safest bet will be to run a vulnerability scan against Wise's machine and look for a software flaw that he can exploit to gain leverage. Coming in through the back door, so to speak, is less risky.

Preparation is crucial. Robbie must have a number of tools ready to scan Wise's machine as soon as he locates it, and he must be prepared to look up any vulnerability he discovers, using a search engine to find an easy way of exploiting it.

A real hacker would own Wise's machine within 15 minutes of finding his home e-mail address, but Robbie, unfortunately, is a script kiddie. However, like most of his breed, he hangs out in several forums and in a few IRC channels devoted to hacking. One of his buddies is a bit more advanced and runs his computer on Linux. Robbie knows that he'll have to learn to use Linux or another flavor of UNIX in order to become better at what he does, but, like most script kiddies, he's essentially lazy and doesn't want to learn how to do things for himself. Linux is a superior platform from both a defensive and an offensive point of view, and while the major, packaged distributions like SuSE, Mandrake, and Red Hat are as easy to use as Windows, Linux is not a handy platform for the PC games that take up most of Robbie's time with his computer.

He connects on ICQ and quickly finds his Linux-savvy friend, who goes by the online alias av3ngr, appealing for help: "d00d, can i get u 2 do me a solid?" Robbie asks. He explains his predicament with the lawyer and asks av3ngr to scan the target computer with Nessus, a powerful vulnerability scanner that runs on UNIX-compatible computers. Robbie may not be much of a hacker, but he knows that there are no free scanners of comparable power for Windows users.

It's about 9:00 p.m. when av3ngr agrees to help, a good hour to catch the lawyer working in his home office. Robbie sends an e-mail memo to Wise, asking if his girlfriend would be willing to consider an out-of-court settlement. Wise replies right away that he can only address the matter with Robbie's lawyer and suggests having him get in touch. It's a short reply, but it's all Robbie needs: in the header of Wise's e-mail is the current IP address of his computer. Now Robbie and av3ngr must work quickly to attack it, before Wise disconnects.

The Nessus scan reveals a number of vulnerabilities, but av3ngr isn't familiar with most of them. He's really not much of a hacker himself, having no programming skills, but compared to Robbie he's elite. However, ports 137, 138, 139, and 445 on Wise's Windows machine are open to the Internet, and av3ngr knows what that means: SMB (server message block) file sharing is enabled on Wise's computer, and it's been badly misconfigured. No doubt he uses it to exchange document revisions with his workstation at the law firm to keep both machines' versions in harmony, but he's going about it wrong.

"omfg d00d--this gimp has shares open on his box," av3ngr tells Robbie. "u got legion? u can attack it easy."

Robbie does a search for a cracking tool called Legion, developed to attack Windows machines with open shares. He finds it, and immediately downloads and installs it on his PC.

"d00d u got a good wordlist?" av3ngr asks. "u got 2 copy it into the legion thing. then u just point it at the ip and it will log in 4 u off that list."

Robbie copies his best wordlist into the Legion directory and sets it to working against Wise's machine. While that's happening, he and av3ngr debate what to do next. After a bit of discussion, it's decided that the best approach would be to replace a file in Wise's shared folder with a rootkit. This way, the next time he accesses the file, the rootkit will become active. It will alert Robbie that Wise is on line and allow him full access to the computer, even if the IP address should change in the meantime.

"u don't need a proxy for this gimps box but u better proxy up big time if u try anything on that office net," av3ngr advises. "tha guys runnin it gonna be logging everything, u can bet."

Once Legion connects to Wise's shared folder with the simple dictionary password *private*, Robbie changes the folder view to show him the files most recently accessed, which he reckons are ones Wise is still working on and likely to be accessed again soon. He also changes the folder's view settings to hide known file extensions, since he will be changing that from .doc to .exe when he installs the rootkit. Wise will probably not notice the difference.

Robbie chooses the SubSeven rootkit because of its power and ease of use. It consists of two parts: a server that is installed on the victim's machine, and a controlling client that provides the attacker with an intuitive, GUI interface with the server.

Robbie configures the server to notify him via ICQ whenever Wise is on line. He also protects the server with a password so that only he can connect to it. He doesn't want someone else connecting to it and possibly taking action that would alert Wise.

He will rename the SubSeven server to match the name of a Word document that Wise appears to be working on. He will also insert the same icon into the server file that Word uses, with the help of a free icon editor downloaded from the Web. Finally, he copies it over the existing file on Wise's PC. The next time Wise accesses the file, he will install the rootkit. The file he's expecting won't launch properly, of course, but he'll likely assume that it's a typical computer glitch and simply download a good copy from his archive at the office.

Two days later, the remote server on Wise's machine alerts Robbie via ICQ that Wise is on line and ready to be exploited. Robbie connects, using SubSeven's easy-to-use GUI client, and begins monitoring the desktop with periodic screen grabs and logging Wise's keystrokes. Within a few minutes, Wise connects to his network at the office, and Robbie intercepts the password. He can now connect to the law firm's network with the same level of access that Wise enjoys.

A more ambitious script kiddie would try to parlay user-level access into ownership of the company network by trying a number of exploits, but Robbie is only interested in documents related to his upcoming court case. Once he finds them, he copies them to his own computer and never again attempts to trespass on the law firm's network, for fear of getting caught by an alert sysadmin. As for Wise, Robbie calculates that a man foolish enough to share files over the Internet and use a simple dictionary word for a password is unlikely to figure out that he's been hacked; still, Robbie connects to Wise's computer one last time and deletes the SubSeven server and its traces from several Windows configuration files, just to be safe.

Analysis

Robbie is not going to get caught. He and his mentor may be far from elite, but they've made a number of sensible decisions. By initially attacking Wise's misconfigured computer with Legion, they avoided detection by exploiting a system vulnerability instead of trying to trick the owner into taking action. An infected file sent via e-mail might have worked, but it could have established a trail back to Robbie. However, Legion left no traces; Windows does not log the IP addresses of those who connect remotely to exposed SMB shares. Had Wise ever become suspicious, he would have had no way of knowing who had connected to his shared folder.

Second, by using the feature-rich SubSeven rootkit, Robbie was able to log on to the law firm's network *through Wise's computer.* Not even a watchful admin would be suspicious of this activity, because Wise himself connects from home regularly. Furthermore, Robbie resisted the temptation to explore the network or attempt to increase his (or, more properly, Wise's) privileges on it, which would have appeared suspicious to any competent admin. He hit and ran, and later covered his tracks by clearing evidence of his attack on Wise's home machine. He didn't get greedy.

There are a number of points along the way where Wise could easily have frustrated Robbie, if only he'd been more aware of basic computer and Internet security. First off, he could have avoided publishing his home e-mail address on Internet bulletin boards and in conference programs by using a couple of non-identifying aliases through a free, Web-based e-mail service like Yahoo Mail or Hotmail. If the e-mail alias Wise used on the cigar forum were, for example, cigarfan@hotmail.com, and the personal e-mail address he used for the conference were, say, samadvocate@yahoo.com, it would be extremely difficult for a third party to associate the two aliases by using a search engine. While these e-mail services require registration and do request identifying information, there is no reason why the registration information must be truthful. If Wise were in the habit of using several different aliases on line, he would have made himself difficult to identify and track across the Internet. A neophyte attacker like Robbie would have had little hope of locating his personal e-mail address to contact him at home.

Next, Wise could have used an *anonymous proxy server* to connect to the Internet. This would have hidden his true IP address in his posts to the cigar forum and elsewhere on the Web, and, more importantly, would have hidden it from Robbie when Wise answered his e-mail query. Robbie would have found only Wise's proxy address in the e-mail header, not the location of his PC.

Finally, Wise could have educated himself about common system vulnerabilities. There is no excuse for exposing shared directories to the Internet: they are meant to be shared over a LAN (local area network) like a home or office network, not a WAN (wide area network) like the Internet. A properly configured personal firewall or packet filter would have prevented this intrusion by blocking the relevant ports. Simply learning about the services he made available on his computer and disabling unnecessary ones also would have prevented it. Robbie would have been forced to use a riskier strategy against Wise, setting himself up to be caught. Indeed, if Wise had been even marginally cautious, Robbie might well have declined to attack his machine. An elite blackhat would likely have tracked Wise and owned his machine and his company network with relative ease, but not these two script kiddies. There is no reason for anyone to be afraid of attackers like Robbie and av3ngr.

The Real World

In October of 2000, Microsoft conceded publicly that its internal network had suffered just such an intrusion by script kiddies. Valuable source code for Windows Me, Windows 2000, and MS Office was taken from the company's internal development network and possibly manipulated. That is, the attackers might have downloaded the code, implanted back doors in it, and then uploaded it once again in modified form. Fortunately, MS learned of the intrusion, so there is little likelihood that any malicious code would have found its way into the marketplace.

The intruders are believed to have used a Trojan rootkit called QAZ, a good choice because it automatically copies itself throughout shared folders on a LAN. Once an attacker gets a copy of it onto someone's internal machine, it automatically spreads to others and silently e-mails the attacker with the IP addresses of each infected computer.

QAZ masquerades as the familiar Windows utility Notepad. Once launched, QAZ searches for notepad.exe and copies itself in place of the standard Notepad file, simultaneously renaming the genuine file to note.com. When someone executes the malicious Notepad file, QAZ also launches note.com, or the original Notepad, so the application appears to behave normally. The only odd thing a user might notice is that when Notepad is open, both note.com and notepad.exe will be running, where note.com is the actual Notepad utility and notepad.exe is QAZ. However, this is not evident unless a user hits the keys Alt+Ctrl+Delete or launches the Task Manager (taskmgr.exe) to bring up a list of running processes.

Once installed, QAZ searches the entire LAN for additional copies of Notepad to infect, thereby combining the delivery mechanisms of a Trojan and a worm.

To get QAZ implanted on a LAN in the first place, an attacker must feed it to someone with access to the LAN who is willing to execute it. It's easy enough to distribute as an executable e-mail attachment, but not everyone will fall for it. Thus, there are two chief obstacles to getting the infection started, neither of which is terribly difficult to overcome.

First, there is *social engineering*—that is, persuading the victim to accept it. The wording of the e-mail message must make executing the attached program both desirable and sensible. Presenting it as a software patch or upgrade is a common tactic, though there are others. Archiving and compressing it with a program such as WinZip or PKZip and naming it PornCollection.zip or DirtyJokes.zip is another. If the e-mail message makes sense in the context of the attachment, and if it's sent to enough potential victims, the combined laws of probability and human nature ensure that some fool will activate the payload. And with QAZ, an attacker needs only *one* victim with access to the target LAN; QAZ will propagate on its own once the infection begins.

The second obstacle is antivirus software. Not a tough one, either, despite all the glowing claims of superior technological wizardry touted by AV vendors. When I covered the Microsoft intrusion for my column in *The Register,* I performed a simple test: I took an assortment of Trojan rootkits—Back Orifice, Deep Throat, SubSeven, NetBus, and Hack'a'Tack—and verified that my copy of Norton AntiVirus (NAV) would detect them, both as-is and compressed with WinZip. I then tried several other compression utilities to see how NAV would react. When I compressed them using a tool called NeoLite and ran Norton AntiVirus again, only the Deep Throat rootkit was detected, because its *compressed signature* is widely known. That is, Deep Throat is distributed already compressed by NeoLite, so the AV software is looking for it in that form. But that was not the case with the other malicious files: my AV software was not looking for versions compressed with NeoLite, a rather glaring oversight that I hope has since been addressed. A further advantage to NeoLite is that the archives it creates are self-extracting: no third-party software like WinZip need be loaded on the victim's machine for the compressed programs to be unpacked and executed.

Once the infection is active on the target LAN, an intruder can begin connecting to vulnerable machines as they notify him of their presence on the Internet. By exploring these machines, the attacker can begin searching for high-value targets. Such an ultimate target is unlikely to be connected to the Internet, but it may well accept connections from other machines that are. The attacker can only connect to machines facing the Internet, but he will likely find that some of these boxes are trusted by other, high-value ones that are quarantined from the Net. The system from which Microsoft's source code was stolen was probably not connected to the Internet, but it likely trusted several machines that were. The attackers found one of these intermediary machines and used it to attack the target, just as Robbie and av3ngr used Wise's home computer to attack his office network.

How the intruders targeted Microsoft is not known, but we can make an educated guess. Many companies have naming conventions for e-mail addresses: first-name-dot-last-name, as in `Thomas.Greene@theregister.co.uk`; first-name-last-initial, as in `JosefK@kompany.com`; or first-initial-last-name, as in `JPeterman@catalog.net`; and so on. The attackers might have created a little script to assign random names to e-mail addresses according to Microsoft's naming conventions and simply blanketed the field. Or they might have targeted a few employees at home, finding their PCs and exploiting them, as Robbie and av3ngr did in the preceding example. There are tens of thousands of postings on the Web by, and regarding, MS employees, some of which undoubtedly include a home e-mail address as an alternate point of contact.

It's also possible that the attackers delivered the malicious file by exploiting a vulnerability in Microsoft's network configuration. However, there is reason to prefer the e-mail Trojan theory.

Back when the story of Microsoft's humiliation was still a popular news item, *The Register* learned that company employees worldwide were temporarily denied remote network access, suggesting that the original infection began on the home PC of a software developer, probably delivered as a Trojan via e-mail. There were rumors to that effect as well, but Microsoft's statements about the affair were highly inconsistent and never satisfactory, so it's likely that we'll never know the whole story. It has been suggested that MS deliberately leaked news of the QAZ debacle while its source code was being pilfered by a trusted employee. That is, the two incidents were actually separate, but Microsoft lumped them together to confuse the press. It did so, the theory goes, because it found the idea of internal betrayal more embarrassing than an external attack.

The intruders were never caught—or if they were, MS has since dealt with them very quietly. But assuming that *The Register's* reading of the incident is reasonably accurate—that an employee's workstation or home PC was compromised and the QAZ Trojan spread from there to the internal network—then this is a good illustration of why there is far more to gain from educating the majority of honest employees about the realities of computer security than there is from denying such information to the minority who would misuse it.

Free Porn and Easy Credit

The typical script kiddie spends much of his time on line figuring out how to obtain digital pornography without paying for it: hence, the plethora of HTTP exploiters and dictionary password crackers available on the Web, and their incredible ease of use. A visit to any of hundreds of popular cracking-related Web sites will reveal an arsenal of automatic cracking tools and essays on the art, in which attacking porn sites looms large. There are also thousands of forums devoted to advising the clueless and trading tips.

There is, of course, plenty of free porn available through P2P services like KaZaA and numerous free Web sites and bulletin boards, but many young people find it strangely satisfying to scam the pay sites, perhaps on the theory that charging for porn on the Internet is a bit like charging for air. Porn sites are also fairly safe targets for newbies to practice on; lost revenues among smut mongers are a rather low priority among most prosecutors.

The lion's share of cracker forum activity centers on ways into porn sites and past third-party billing processors like iBill and CCbill. Newbies stick with dictionary crackers and secondhand wordlists downloaded off the Web, while the journeymen play around with exploits against CGIs and server software, looking for misconfigured administrator interfaces and passfiles they can steal or to which they can add their own passwords. Stealing and then cracking a Web site's passfile with John the Ripper (JtR) is an excellent way to assemble a collection of wordlists for dictionary attacks. Some of these files are enormous, and as people tend to use the same passwords on multiple sites, such lists can be effective in many situations. Passfiles foolishly kept in plain text are tremendously valuable. That's because cracking an encrypted, or *hashed*, file will yield only a small percentage of working passes.

Passfiles are not encrypted per se. Instead, they're hashed, which means that the original input is not meant to be reconstructed. We'll get into encryption and hashing and their distinctions in more detail later, but for now we can say that encrypted text must be reconstructed to be at all useful, whereas hashed text must not. Hashing is a way of making authentication a bit stronger, because no actual passwords are stored. Instead, a mathematical product of each password, called a *hash,* is collected. When the user logs in, the hash created by his password is compared against valid hashes contained in a list, called a *passfile*. If the password entered generates a valid hash, the user is granted access.

A hashed password is never decrypted. Instead, it passes through a mathematical formula called an algorithm. This is a one-way function. The algorithm creates a hash (a jumble, a mess, just like it sounds) that in theory can't be reconstructed. No two passwords should create the same hash, so cracking a hashed list involves considerable trial and error. Complex, unique passwords create hashes that are generally not crackable unless the algorithm or the cryptosystem are flawed. For this reason, cracking tools like JtR are successful against only a fraction of the hashes in a passfile, whereas a plain-text passfile is pure gold. Often, the best wordlists for dictionary attacks are taken from stolen passfiles that were foolishly stored in plain text.

The basic concepts will become clear if we perform an attack. Let's imagine that we've already created a large cracking wordlist from a plain-text passfile that we stole from a careless Web merchant. We can use this wordlist to attack other Web sites with a dictionary cracker, and we may get lucky because many people use the same password in several places.

But we can also use the plain-text passfile to help crack a hashed passfile stolen from another merchant who's a bit more careful. First, we load our plain-text wordlist into a dictionary attack tool like Ares, which will try to log in with each password in our list, and attack the second site from which we stole the hashed file. Ares will try each of our passwords in succession. Each time it successfully logs on to the Web site, it tells us two things: first, the password or combination that succeeded, and second, the number of attempts that came before. Let's say that bob22 is successful, and that it was our fifth attempted password. We then check our stolen copy of the hashed file, which contains no passwords, naturally, and find the fifth hash. Let's say it's hU38fHoz5C4i46. We now know that the hashing algorithm created hU38fHoz5C4i46 from bob22.

So we continue our dictionary attack, noting the particular hash that corresponds to each successful password. Eventually, we can compile a list of working passes for the Web site from which we stole the hashed passfile. We can also compile a list of hashes matched to their corresponding passwords. This is useful: if we should obtain another hashed file, we can start attacking it by searching for hashes whose corresponding passwords we already know.

Alternatively, and more commonly, we can simply hash a list of passwords using various algorithms and see if the resulting hashes match any of the hashes in our stolen file. If any do, we've found a working password. For example, let's say we hash the password bob22 using the MD5 algorithm and get hU38fHoz5C4i46. Now we search for hU38fHoz5C4i46 in our stolen passfile. If we find it, we know the password that created it had to be bob22, and we can use it to log in. This is the basic principle on which JtR works, although it's a bit more complicated in reality. Essentially, though, it automates this trial-and-error procedure.

Simple dictionary attacks work well regardless of whether the authentication mechanism uses hashing. A good cracker's wordlist will contain plenty of valid passes, especially if it's been built up over time from several stolen passfiles. But even if not, dictionary attacks work because people choose simple passwords. No one likes a complicated password that's hard to memorize and easy to forget. Unfortunately, this makes the cracker's job easy, even when he knows nothing more than how to run an automated tool.

Stealing a Web site's passfile is child's play if the directory containing it is accessible to the Internet. Obviously, if someone is serving Web pages, documents, and software to the public, they must locate these items in directories that people can simply point their browsers at. It may seem obvious to suggest that a passfile needs to be in a directory that's not accessible via the Internet, but experience shows that there are many thousands of badly misconfigured systems out there, especially among small- to medium-traffic porn and merchant sites, which, not surprisingly, are also the sites that most crackers prefer to attack.

There is a tool created by a programmer called Gaa Moa (the author of Ares) that automates the process of searching for passfiles and other goodies located in world-readable directories. It's called Gaa Moa Exploiter (GME), and it's a sort of brute-force directory locator. The user supplies a list of the directory paths to be searched, then simply aims the tool at a Web site. GME will attempt to connect to each directory in succession and locate useful files. It does this very quickly.

A simple attack like this won't succeed if the passfile or other important files are properly located in protected directories. There are more sophisticated directory attacks that we need to watch out for, but obvious ones like this account for a good deal of the malicious activity on the Internet. However, it should be noted that URL manipulation and directory path searches can be a very sophisticated business among hackers who know more than the standard approaches. GME can be an excellent tool, speeding up the work of advanced crackers. The attacks it makes possible are as sophisticated—or as unsophisticated—as the person using it.

Still, the typical script kiddie can be frustrated simply by requiring difficult passwords and by locating passfiles and other sensitive items in directories not accessible via the Web. Better crackers require better defenses, naturally, and we'll get to these in time. But once again we should emphasize that the majority of clueless newbies are painfully easy to stop with simple precautions like using tough passwords, hashing them properly, and protecting directories containing passfiles and other sensitive data.

Free Passwords

An amusing side-phenomenon related to porn-site cracking has to do with password request boards, IRC channels, and Web sites promising "custom hacks" and freshly cracked passes to unlimited smut. Virtually all of these are scam sites run by porno Webmasters to attract visitors to their pay sites. The passes given away are, naturally, either dead or fake, and using them only exposes one to a blizzard of hardcore pop-up ads and Flash animations. But the something-for-nothing pitch does reliably pull in the suckers. A Google search on the term *xxx passwords* will yield thousands of such Web sites. Caveat emptor!

Crackers pilfering porn are one thing, and not a terribly worrisome thing at that. Of somewhat greater concern are *carders*: people who steal online credit card databases and sell or trade the contents, or who attempt to buy products using stolen or counterfeit card numbers.

Many e-commerce sites do a very poor job of verifying the credit card numbers that online shoppers use. Quite a few merely verify that a proffered card number conforms to the Luhn algorithm, which every valid card number does. To verify a card with the Luhn number test, you start with the second-to-last (penultimate) digit and, moving left, double the value of every other digit. Then, starting with the second digit on the left, you add all the skipped digits. Double digits are added individually (e.g., 15 is treated as 1 + 5). If the sum of all the digits counted in this manner is divisible by ten, then the credit card number conforms to the Luhn algorithm and *might* be valid. Checking card numbers in this way only ensures that impossible numbers will be rejected; any valid Luhn number will be accepted, even if there is no account corresponding to it. This is a very poor verification system that begs to be abused, yet it's fairly common in online transactions. Verifying an account takes time, and Web merchants don't like to inconvenience shoppers. The faster a transaction can be completed, the more likely it is to be completed. To keep sales moving swiftly, a valid Luhn number is often all that's required.

Predictably, there are easy-to-use software tools available for download from the Internet that will generate random Luhn numbers. Carders can use such tools to gain instant access to Web services and product downloads. Any online account created in this way will be closed as soon as the merchant discovers that the card number is counterfeit, but by that time, the attacker will likely have made off with everything he wants, such as an expensive application or several gigs of porn.

Carders also like to find online credit card databases whenever they can. A surprising number of e-commerce sites and smaller Web merchants are in the habit of storing this data on their Web servers, and worse, in plain text. Such data ought to be stored on a secure back-end database server that does not connect directly to the Internet, and the data should be maintained in an encrypted file. Unfortunately, this is rarely the case with small to medium merchant sites, because it's an expensive solution. Many e-commerce sites tout their security measures, such as their use of SSL (Secure Socket Layer), a Web protocol that encrypts data exchanged between the buyer and the seller, but they then store the collected data very carelessly. Quite mediocre hackers can often locate unprotected and unencrypted database files filled with credit card numbers, and there are numerous IRC channels devoted to carding where such discoveries are traded openly.

More worrisome are skilled hackers who can exploit major commercial databases by leveraging software flaws. Even professionally defended sites with big security budgets can be compromised by patient, competent attackers. In June of 2003, a whitehat hacker named Jeremiah Jacks found common vulnerabilities allowing *SQL injection* in database servers belonging to PetCo and Guess, Inc., with which he gained access to 700,000 credit cards. Jacks reported the flaws rather than exploit them, but if a nonmalicious hacker can penetrate two major, and well-heeled, sites in two weeks, we have to wonder what the blackhats are up to.

Internet Fraud Prevention Advisory Council (IFPAC) cofounder Joe Barrett calls online losses to credit fraud the "dirty little secret" of the retail industry. Whereas the fraud rate in face-to-face credit card transactions is in the range of two- to three-tenths of one percent, the overall rate for online transactions is in the range of one to two percent, in spite of the credit associations' insistence that the rates are roughly equivalent. A rate below one percent is considered good for a commercial Web site, while the rate for porn sites is in the range of eight to twelve percent, Barrett says.

Still, card numbers are most often gathered in the traditional fashion, with a technique called *skimming*. A simple electronic scanner, small enough to fit in a pocket or a waitress' apron, which can read and write to the cards' magnetic strips, is readily available for purchase. The fraudster, presumably in a position to handle a card unobserved for a few seconds, swipes it through the scanner, which records all the necessary information. Later, the device can be used to write to the magnetic strips of blank, outdated, or canceled cards, giving them valid account numbers. The Internet may not be the preferred source of card numbers yet, but it makes shopping with bogus cards convenient and relatively safe, and it provides many opportunities for carders to trade their collections of numbers through chatrooms, bulletin boards, and forums.

Turbo Skimming

There are more than 350,000 ATMs (automatic teller machines) in the United States, the cheapest of which can be bought for a mere $3,000 and installed almost anywhere: a bar, a convenience store, a gas station. In a busy location, a malicious ATM can skim thousands of cards a week. In the summer of 2003, one Iljmija Frljuckic was indicted for skimming 21,000 cards and stealing $3.5 million in goods and services with the pilfered card numbers, simply by purchasing a number of these personal units and installing them in several Manhattan locations. ATMs operated by banks are generally well protected, but those owned by private individuals and small businesses are highly susceptible to fraud. So think twice before you swipe.

All of this is vehemently denied by the credit associations like Visa and MasterCard, by the issuing banks, and by Web merchants. They would have us believe that the online shopping experience is as private as the confessional. Guess, Inc., a company that gave up 200,000 plain-text credit card numbers to Jeremiah Jacks, had assured its customers that "all of [their] personal information including credit card information and sign-in password are stored in an unreadable, encrypted format at all times." That statement was, in fact, a bald-faced lie, one that prompted the Federal Trade Commission (FTC) to pressure the company to get its story straight under penalty of a $22,000 fine for *each instance* of future violation.

But we shouldn't single out the Guess debacle as unique. Problems of this sort surface almost daily, though the FTC rarely condescends to involve itself. The Commission has gone after other big targets, like pharmaceutical giant Eli Lilly for leaking sensitive patient information and software behemoth Microsoft for grossly overstating the security of its Passport and Wallet services, but the majority of privacy and credit card stuff-ups come and go well beneath the federal government's radar. However, in the five years I've spent researching security and privacy issues for *The Register,* I can count only three occasions when a hacked Web merchant or bank didn't employ the three Ds of public relations—deny, delay, and dissimulate— and, when confronted with evidence, slam down the phone. Security flaws are routinely treated as public relations problems, with the consumer's interest repre- senting the lowest priority.

It's virtually impossible for cardholders to take positive steps toward protect- ing their credit details from script-kiddie carders, because the online credit card sales process is largely hidden and well outside our control. We can protect sen- sitive data on our own computers from local and remote attacks easily enough, but we obviously can't protect Web merchants who have our credit details stored carelessly on their systems. Online shopping is one situation in which your secu- rity is poor whenever someone else's security is poor. The same is true in the real world. Every time a waiter, a clerk, a gas station attendant takes possession of a credit card and moves out of the owner's sight, skimming is a possibility. Meanwhile, credit card numbers used for online transactions routinely end up in very poorly protected databases, and even big-name Web merchants with hefty security budgets can be exploited by clever hackers—that is, when they haven't made foolish mistakes exploitable by script kiddies. And there's little you can do to protect yourself.

In a July 2003 study, IT-industry consulting outfit Gartner found that 5.5 percent of American adults surveyed, or an estimated 11 million nationally, had become vic- tims of credit card fraud, while 3.4 percent, or an estimated 7 million, had become victims of identity theft during the preceding 12 months alone. Furthermore, prose- cutions for identity theft are virtually unknown, happening at a rate of only one per 700 cases reported, Gartner says. While we must always take such survey results with a grain of salt, it's a safe bet that credit card fraud and identity theft are going on at a positively scandalous rate, yet little is being done to prevent it—or even to address it after the fact. The credit associations, issuing banks, and merchants are collectively mishandling, underreporting, and soft-pedaling the problem, the Gartner report concludes.

Gartner isn't alone in its pessimism. The U.S. Federal Trade Commission con- ducted its own survey about two months later and came up with similar estimates. According to the FTC, roughly 10 million Americans fell victim to ID theft in the preceding year, suffering a collective loss of nearly $5 billion. Banks and merchants fared even worse, suffering losses of $48 billion to ID thieves alone.

One would think that the banking and consumer credit industries would bring their immense financial resources to bear on this problem and find ways to reduce it, but one would be wrong. The industry is already adapting to the threat and learning to profit from it. Rather than educate consumers and introduce more secure methods of distributing cards and maintaining customer data, all of which would cost them money, issuing banks are beginning to sell what amounts to identity theft insurance to offset their losses. A typical package might include advisory services to aid in ID theft recovery and an Internet security package involving antivirus software and a personal firewall. The first is probably useful; recovering from identity theft is a time-consuming and often exasperating exercise. The second is a hoax. Carders and identity thieves only occasionally obtain the data they need from hacking a home computer, and then only in an opportunistic fashion. Such an approach would be absurdly inefficient. There is no systematic effort to hack home PCs for identities and credit card details, and there won't be.

Carders and ID thieves attack online merchant databases where the data they want is concentrated, or they use mass mailings of hoax e-mails in connection with a malicious Web site to harvest identity details. But skimming, telephone fraud, and snail-mail fraud remain their preferred techniques. While it's certainly a good idea to run a personal firewall and an antivirus utility, neither of these defenses can prevent common Internet-based attacks against your identity. It's true that your home PC might be hacked and that your identity could be stolen, but it's extremely unlikely that anyone will hack your machine *in order* to steal your identity. That's far too inefficient. When it comes to ID theft and credit card fraud, you should worry about your merchant's online security a lot more than your own.

The best defense is always to remain informed and to be proactive. Unfortunately, in the world of plastic payment there's little possibility of doing either. The consumer credit system does not welcome scrutiny or cardholder involvement. The best advice I can offer is to be *very* selective about the Web sites you choose to do business with, which means avoiding porn sites like the plague, and always to be as stingy as possible with your personal information. The more data collected about you in online databases, the greater the potential for identity theft. There is absolutely no reason why a Web merchant needs to know your Social Security number or date of birth in order to sell you a pair of shoes. Simply refuse to do business with merchants who demand more than your name, card number, phone number, e-mail address, and snail-mail address. Even that's useful for an identity thief to work with, but volunteering additional information is only asking for trouble.

It's also wise to use a credit card allowing you to shop on line with a *dynamic account*, a scheme in which a unique card number is generated for each transaction. The number is valid for one purchase only, and you can usually arrange a preset spending limit if you wish. It's not much protection against identity theft, but it will help to prevent fraudulent use of your card if a merchant's database is compromised. Keep in mind that there is a window of opportunity during which you can get a fraudulent charge dropped, so you should always review your statements promptly and carefully. If you fail to act on a questionable item in time, you may be stuck with the charge.

Scare tactics and dire predictions are antithetical to the philosophy of this book, which is confidently based on the proposition that anyone can learn computer and Internet security, and, once educated, take control of their patch of cyberspace and operate without anxiety. Our mantra is "Be *aware*, but never frightened." Unfortunately, online shopping is one area where too much goes on outside our control, too many incompetents are in positions of responsibility, and the tendency to conceal, deny, and even lie about vulnerabilities and compromises is commonplace. Therefore, using a credit card on line involves risk that we simply cannot assess or manage for ourselves. In this situation, withholding trust is not a sign of irrational fear or timidity. It is, rather, plain common sense.

CHAPTER 2

Vectors

NO DOUBT MOST OF US can sympathize with this *Register* reader:

Hi Mr. Greene, I have just read your article on the severe Windows security hole and I still cannot for the life of me fathom ports—there are so many! I have been on line now for two years and have had to reformat my hard drive so many times due to viruses, etc., that I'm getting bored with it—lol! I have the latest antivirus software and a firewall up and running, but still I get problems. Any help will be so greatly appreciated; I'm not IT informed in any way—as u can tell! I can work my way round a PC with the basics. Any help at all with the security of a PC (is there such a thing?) will be much appreciated.

Thanks,
–Rich in the UK

Rich's good-natured attitude may be concealing a trace of exasperation as he closes, wondering if securing a PC is even possible. It *is* possible, of course, and not even terribly difficult, but there's a good deal more to it than antivirus software and firewalls. He seems to have learned the conventional wisdom well enough, yet his computer is still getting infected with malware. Although we may use security products conscientiously, malicious programs still find their way onto our systems in large numbers. How does this happen? Blame it on software bugs, system vulnerabilities, malware, and the *vectors* that deliver them to us. Vector comes from the Latin *vehere, to carry*. Our computers are in constant contact with vectors, or carriers, of infection and exploitation. Generally speaking

> A *bug* is any programming error that causes unforeseen and undesirable conditions, including, but not limited to, vulnerabilities.
>
> A *vulnerability* is any security weakness that can be attacked deliberately, either with software or with a series of commands, to cause undesirable system behavior or impede desired behavior.
>
> An *exploit* is any command or any sequence of commands that can leverage a bug or a vulnerability (and when the command sequence is designed to be executed automatically, we call this a *scripted* exploit).
>
> *Malware* is any software program or any component such as a plugin or an ActiveX control that can exploit a bug or a vulnerability, or cause undesirable system behavior or impede desired behavior in and of itself.
>
> A *vector* is any mechanism or agent that spreads, or enables the spread of, malware and scripted exploits.

From a security point of view, the Internet is a vast, virtual ecosystem filled with predators and parasites as well as "prey" and "hosts," much as we find in any biological system. Just as living things are susceptible to attack from parasites and disease germs, software systems are vulnerable to malware and exploits, and some more so than others. And just as parasites, germs, and the vermin that carry them are everywhere in the real world, the Internet too is teeming with malware and exploit code and the vectors that deliver them—and that's why Rich's firewall and AV software have let him down. He is, in a sense, relying on a flu shot to protect against lice.

There's an important advantage in the real world that has no analogy in the realm of information technology: biodiversity. The entire IT ecosystem is divided into a few technological *monocultures,* analogous to the agribusiness and livestock industries, where a lack of genetic diversity can lead to blights and epidemics. The world of computing is very much the same, with Cisco Systems running much of the Internet and high-end network infrastructure; Microsoft, Oracle, and Sun running much of the enterprise application (e.g., database) and server realm; and

Microsoft acting as the McDonald's of personal computing, running nearly every-thing in the consumer desktop arena. In this environment, if you've got an exploit against Cisco, then you've got an exploit against most routers on the Internet; if you've got an exploit against Windows, you've got an exploit against virtually every client system and quite a few servers as well. Monocultures, whether biological or artificial, invite epidemics. Just as the operators of agricultural conglomerates and factory feedlots must aggressively control disease-carrying vermin to protect their genetically challenged inventory of plants and animals, so we must control the many vectors of contagion affecting our rather inbred computer systems and networks.

Common Vectors

The Internet may not be crawling with dangerous hackers as the news media like to pretend, but it is inundated with billions of bytes of incredibly lousy and often malicious code, while most PCs are loaded with gigabytes of wretched software that either offers no protection or is itself malicious. Hackers are *not* your primary security concern; bad software is. This may not be terribly sexy news, but it's true. Your computer is insecure because your software is insecure and because you've probably got several malware applications installed on it to boot.

Before we dig into the details, let's take a brief survey of the most common malware vectors and other common routes to exploitation.

E-mail

The Microsoft e-mail clients Outlook and Outlook Express have for years been the Internet's most prolific virus and worm vectors. They are joined by instant messaging (IM) clients and P2P file-sharing utilities for that dubious distinction. However, the Microsoft e-mail applications are particularly dangerous because they are deeply integrated into the Windows system, and also because, like most clients, they are *code-execution environments*. That is, the e-mail client itself is capable of executing code, such as HTML, ActiveX controls, and JavaScript, auto-matically in the body. Such code is said to be delivered *in line* when it appears in the body of a memo, as opposed to code contained in a file attached to it. Virtually all modern e-mail clients are capable of executing code, though the Mozilla mail client recommended in the Introduction allows users to disable all remote images, HTML, and in-line scripts and plugins. Others do as well, but I recommend Mozilla because it's not deeply integrated with the Windows operating system, its data traces are easy to control, and it's both free and open source.

In addition to executing code, e-mail also transports a great number of malicious file attachments. People are repeatedly warned never to open attach-ments without first scanning them for malware, but still they do so every day. Some mass-mailing viruses are capable of sending themselves automatically to each correspondent in a victim's e-mail address book. The next recipient recognizes the sender as a known contact and is therefore more likely to open the attachment and infect himself, propagating the virus to his own contacts, and so on. The Melissa, IloveYou, and Slammer e-mail worms used this technique and managed to clog up portions of the Internet for brief periods, though they contained no destructive payloads. However, many in-line scripts and e-mail attachments *do* contain malicious payloads, so it is very important to disable code execution (i.e., switch off HTML and all scripting and plugin support) and *never* to open any attachment, regardless of who sent it, without first scanning it for the presence of malware. E-mail attachments are probably the single largest vector of malware. Switching off HTML is also an important step because spam is often loaded with malicious scripting and remote images that can track recipients. Admittedly, it can be irritating to read HTML-formatted mail rendered in plain text. If your friends and regular correspondents have the habit of sending HTML e-mail, take a moment to explain the security risks of in-line scripting, and suggest that they consider sending mail in plain text.

Browsers

Most of us think of the browser as a simple window on the Internet. It is that, of course, but it has developed considerably since the early days of the humble Mosaic browser in the early 1990s, gradually swelling into what it is today: a major code-execution environment. We now have Java, JavaScript, Flash, ActiveX, PHP (Hypertext Preprocessor), XML (Extensible Markup Language), ASP (Active Server Pages), and other pulsating, decorative accessories to make our browsing experience memorable, and risky. After all, if a browser can execute code, it can execute malicious code.

It's easy for an attacker to force a victim's browser to run malicious code and scripts, and this is especially true of Internet Explorer. Sometimes an attack involves redirecting a browser session to a malicious Web site without the user's knowledge; sometimes it involves enticing a user to visit a malicious site with a link in an e-mail message; sometimes it involves spoofing or obscuring URLs and filenames; sometimes it involves sending malformed packets to the browser, and sometimes it involves tricks that cause code from untrusted sites to execute in the "trusted" Internet Explorer security zone. Cookies can be misused to compromise privacy and even to hijack browser sessions and gain access to private online accounts. Local files can be read by remote attackers; downloaded files can be forced to execute automatically; and *buffer overflows* can be caused, allowing arbitrary code to run on a victim's machine without any user interaction. There are literally hundreds of ways for an attacker to turn a victim's browser against him. Some have been patched; others have not.

Here again, Windows users are at a disadvantage. The Internet Explorer browser is designed primarily as a code-execution environment and is deeply embedded in Windows. This makes it particularly dangerous because there are a vast number of exploits against it and because attacks against the browser can more readily become attacks against the system. For one ironic example, in July of 2003 an online "security scan" offered by security services giant Symantec was found to be loading a dangerous, and exploitable, ActiveX control on Windows users' machines, which in turn allowed external code to run with the victim's level of privilege. An ActiveX control is an executable program that can operate at a very low level within the Windows operating system, often delivered as Web content.

Internet Explorer also makes it difficult for users to clear their computers of data traces from their browsing sessions. A great deal of data is stored in the Windows Registry; and the default directories where the URL history, page cache, and cookies are stored can be difficult to clear.

Internet Explorer also does not permit fine-grained control of images to be loaded and so offers little protection against *Web bugs*, a commercial tracking and profiling gimmick that uses tracer images embedded in Web pages by third-party marketers. The scheme is similar to the tracer images in HTML e-mail, by which a spam victim's e-mail account is verified. In this case, the bugs track a person's surfing habits by logging their IP address, and possibly cross-referencing this behavior with login information and data stored in cookies.

According to Coremetrics, a marketing outfit that supplies tracer images for use on Web sites, their LIVE (lifetime individual visitor experience) profile technology (i.e., Web bugs) will "deepen and enhance customer relationships by gaining a better understanding of *individual users' behavior* on your site and product preferences, giving you the insight you need to cross-sell financial products more effectively." As you can see from the Coremetrics sales boilerplate, surfers can be identified personally with the bugs, though no doubt the decorative "privacy policy" on many of the Web sites using them will claim that personally identifiable data is not gathered. Web bugs, like tracer images in e-mail, are difficult to spot. The images themselves can be one pixel in size, making them invisible. The only way to avoid this sort of abuse in Internet Explorer is to deny *all* images, which makes surfing a rather dull affair. However, Mozilla allows the blocking of third-party images and cookies, which in turn helps surfers to defeat marketers while allowing a fair bit of image content to enliven their surfing experience.

Scripts

This is a generic term for quite a few similar things. Essentially, a script is a series of *commands* to be executed without user interaction. They are not programs per se but, rather, commands that programs will respond to or instructions they will execute. The simplest ones are called *batch files* in Windows parlance and *shell scripts* in UNIX parlance. Most users have entered commands at a shell prompt or a command prompt. A batch file or shell script would simplify this by entering the commands in sequence automatically until the desired task is completed.

A *macro* is a scripted series of commands taking fairly complex action at the touch of a few keys. Many people use macros to automate repetitive tasks with word processors and spreadsheets. Not surprisingly, a command is translated into code that your computer can understand by a *command interpreter*. There are various interpreters, just as there are different scripting languages, such as JavaScript, VBScript, Perl, and so on.

Scripts are everywhere and come in many forms. They often appear in Web pages and e-mail memos, where they provide interactive features and dynamic content. What they all share is the ability perform tasks without user interaction. They are wonderful tools for automating repetitive chores and therefore of great value to sysadmins, Webmasters, and users alike. They are also of tremendous value to attackers. Scripts in Web pages and e-mail are frequently used as weapons because scripting languages are easy to learn: an attacker does not need any experience in programming to hack out a malicious script. A trick called *cross-site scripting* (XSS) allows an untrusted Web site to execute code in the security context of a trusted Web site without the user's knowledge. Therefore, scripting support in *any* type of Internet client, including instant messaging, and in programs that invoke Internet clients (such as a word processor might do when one activates a hyperlink in a document file) is inherently risky. Scripting support is a significant and ever-present vector of compromise, and it must be controlled by the user with prejudice against allowing it except where necessary.

Instant Messaging

Instant messaging, or IM, is one of the more enjoyable services available over the Internet, one that can bring people together from anywhere in the world in real time for the price of an ISP account. However, graphical IM clients like MSN Messenger, AIM, and ICQ, as well as the text-based IRC (Internet relay chat) clients, are major vectors of infection. One reason is that the clients offer scripting support. There are many useful and innocent capabilities associated with IM and IRC scripts, though it should be said that the vast majority of packaged ones available for download have at least some malicious function, such as mass messaging (spamming), channel and network flooding, grabbing user IP addresses and other data, hijacking accounts and screen names, and the like. Another problem is that IM attracts children and teenagers and makes exchanging files very convenient. Young people tend to trust their peers and so typically end up accepting a great number of malicious files that can compromise not only their own privacy, but the overall security of a home network. Finally, it is important to know that many of the graphical IM and IRC clients contain adware and may reveal more about a user than he is willing to share with the IM service provider.

Businesses are also using IM as an inexpensive way for telecommuters to touch base with workmates on site in real time, and even for virtual conferences. This is an extremely insecure method of communication. IM clients can reveal a user's true IP address; they can leave one open to *man-in-the-middle attacks* where one's chat session is intercepted by a third party; they can be hijacked by scripts; and users can easily be impersonated. IM is fine for casual communication, but it is *not* an appropriate substitute for teleconferencing via a secure VPN (virtual private network). Simply permitting IM clients on a company network is a moderate security risk; using them for sensitive communication is positively reckless.

The MSN Messenger IM client is tied to a user's Passport and Hotmail accounts and is deeply integrated with Windows as well. Browser action, such as logging into Hotmail, can invoke the IM client and vice versa. There is also a very dubious feature in Messenger called "shared browsing," which enables two people on different computers to synchronize their browsers. "Even if you're in Hollywood, CA, and your friend is in Hollywood, FL, you can both be on the same page—literally. You'll see each other's cursors on screen and you can chat in real time via MSN Messenger," an MS marketing copywriter gushes. This level of integration and "synergy" is an open invitation to system compromise and privacy violation from *many* fronts. Exploits against Passport, Hotmail, and MSN Messenger are common, and a weakness in one increasingly implies a weakness in the others, since Microsoft's trend is toward more, not less, application and Internet service integration. It is not a bad idea to replace MSN Messenger with a third-party clone like Trillian, which does not burrow so deep in the bowels of Windows and allows connections to numerous other IM networks. Even better from a security point of view is Gaim for Windows or Linux, which is both open source and adware-free, and, like Trillian, features cross-network compatibility. Gaim lacks the handsome user interface of many IM clients, but it is a fine choice for security reasons. However, *all* IM clients have been found susceptible to numerous exploits in the past and need to be patched regularly.

P2P Software

Much loved by young people for trading music files, illegally cracked editions of expensive software, and pornography, P2P applications like Morpheus, KaZaA, Grokster, and the like are major malware vectors even worse than IM clients. For one thing, most are infected with adware or spyware to help fund the developers. A great deal of user behavior is tracked across the Internet in this way, though the companies producing the applications soft-pedal this fact with the same dissimulating PR-speak that any flack from the music lobby would use. For example, KaZaA "contains no spyware," developer Sharman Networks claims. The company "does not condone the use of spyware nor support the distribution of spyware to others," we're told. However, the KaZaA application feeds advertisements to users through third-party ad servers. Sharman assures us that this is all benign, that no one is tracked. But since you cannot possibly verify this claim, you would be foolish to believe it. "No spyware" is pure marketing spin. The company can call it what they please, but to any security-conscious user, adware *is* spyware.

P2P applications also function as servers so that users can upload files to each other's machines, which means that their potential to spread malware is tremendous. Most of them are also capable of acting as *super nodes,* meaning that they can relay search requests from potentially millions of users. Enabling (or, rather, *not disabling*) the super-node function may cause users to violate their ISP's use policy by inadvertently exceeding bandwidth limits, and the server function can expose users to every manner of malware known. These dangerous functions are often *enabled by default,* so users should take care to ensure that their P2P application is not behaving more promiscuously than they wish.

Permitting strangers to load files on your machine is essentially foolhardy. So is taking files from machines to which anyone can perform uploads. All such files must be scanned with antivirus software before activation, and users who permit uploads should scan their share directory periodically. However, AV software is only effective against known malicious files; it is hardly foolproof, so some risk will always remain no matter how careful or conscientious one is. Files downloaded via P2P applications or stored in an open share directory should be treated as malicious until proven otherwise. Careful scrutiny of file extensions is not an adequate defense: even seemingly normal MP3 files have potential to cause buffer overflow conditions against media players and use them as springboards to further system exploitation. While it may seem antisocial to use P2P software only to find and download files for yourself, this is, if not quite safe, the least risky way to go about it.

Assuming that the embedded adware and real potential for attracting rootkits hasn't daunted you, there is yet another hazard. A powerful and quite ruthless lobbying organization for the music labels, the Recording Industry Association of America (RIAA), initiated a vendetta against file sharing in the summer of 2003. Armed with federal legislation called the Digital Millennium Copyright Act (DMCA) of 1998, written by the music and film lobbies and pushed through Congress on the wings of lavish campaign donations, the labels have begun identifying and suing file sharers with a streamlined subpoena process made possible by the DMCA. According to the Act, any copyright owner is permitted to file a simple subpoena obtained from a court clerk against anyone suspected of copyright violation, without a judge's approval. There is no standard of evidence or probable cause.

The RIAA has been serving these inexpensive, do-it-yourself court orders against ISPs and obtaining the identities of P2P users, who are then sued. Usually, the accuser will be a simple software robot automatically trawling P2P networks, identifying likely candidates for legal persecution by their online nicknames or screen names. The subpoenas, essentially fishing licenses enabling the RIAA to accuse first and gather evidence later, are then used to obtain the suspected infringer's true identity from their ISP. The RIAA is conducting an intimidation campaign in the form of a vendetta, lashing out at random members of a virtual "family" in order to chasten everyone else.

Meanwhile, telecommunication outfit Verizon objected to revealing its customers' names on the basis of these flimsy subpoenas and fought the RIAA in court. The U.S.

Court of Appeals for the District of Columbia ruled against the quick-and-dirty subpoena process, though no doubt a long, bitter legal battle over the music industry's tactics will ensue. The practice may be reprehensible, but it may yet be upheld by the U.S. Supreme Court, thanks to the eternal inflooding of entertainment industry money into the U.S. political system. While there are valid political reasons for defying the RIAA and its sister organization, the Motion Picture Association of America (MPAA), and the custom-designed legislation they purchased on Capitol Hill, from a security point of view, P2P sharing is moderately risky at best, and positively self-destructive if all the features are enabled.

Users of P2P applications would do well to run a packet sniffer on their Internet connections from time to time and observe directly what sort of data is being exchanged, and with whom (we will learn to do this in Chapter 4). One should be especially suspicious of *encrypted* data shuttling back and forth between their computers and some Internet marketing outfit. It's also wise to seek an open-source P2P application so that no secret functions can be hidden in the code. When choosing any open-source product, always look for the availability of source-code packages. Many P2P developers like to call their products "open," a marketing label with no more meaning than any other PR copywriter's phrase, such as "all natural." Unless the source-code files are available so that you can build the application yourself, it is *not* open source.

Other Vulnerabilities

Now let's look briefly at several other common weaknesses that computer users need to remain aware of.

Operating System Vulnerabilities

Every operating system has vulnerabilities that are constantly being discovered. Some of these may be very old, having propagated in *legacy code* through numerous versions of an operating system before their security implications ever become known. The only practical defense is to remain aware of newly discovered vulnerabilities and to patch systems promptly. There are several e-mail lists, such as the Focus-MS and Focus-Linux lists from *SecurityFocus.com*, the ISN (InfoSec News) list from *Attrition.org*, and *The Register's* daily newsletter, to which users can subscribe for up-to-date security news. (See Appendix C.)

Remaining informed of new system vulnerabilities is one thing; acting on them is another, and users often neglect this important chore. Fortunately, Windows and the major packaged Linux distributions offer online update features that make patching easier. However, bad patches do occasionally get released, so there is some risk in relying on *automatic* updates. They are absolutely inappropriate for mission-critical systems, but for home users, the benefits of prompt patching may outweigh the risks. Still, *manual* online updating is better, so long as one remembers to check for new patches regularly. It is never a good idea to permit a software vendor to decide what code should be installed on your machine, and when.

When we compare security vulnerabilities affecting Windows systems and Linux systems overall, they run basically neck and neck. However, when we look more narrowly at vulnerabilities that require patching the Windows or Linux operating system kernels, we find that Linux is immensely cleaner. It's rare for a patch affecting the Linux kernel to be released, though it's common for Windows due to the interdependent nature of the system. In other words, with Windows, the majority of vulnerabilities affect the kernel, whereas with Linux, they rarely do. As we noted in the Introduction, kernel-level patches stand a greater chance of breaking things than application-level patches. Furthermore, Linux system vulnerabilities tend to affect services that can be disabled to achieve a temporary workaround, whereas Windows services often cannot be disabled without negative consequences. Security-minded users should give careful thought to installing Linux in place of Windows. In Chapter 6, we will look in depth at the advantages and disadvantages of migrating to Linux.

Application Vulnerabilities

All software applications contain significant vulnerabilities that must be dealt with in addition to operating system vulnerabilities. Microsoft packages a number of useful applications with Windows, but many other applications must be obtained either from Redmond or from secondary sources, called independent software vendors (ISVs). Windows is essentially an *à la carte* computer system. Your office suite, your graphics and image-manipulation programs, many of your multimedia applications, PC games, third-party clients, and utilities are distributed separately and must be patched with software provided by the individual vendors. These applications will *not* be patched when the Windows online update is run, so users must remain aware of security alerts and the availability of new patches for all of their third-party software. Microsoft is not responsible for third-party applications and utilities. It can be difficult to keep up with all the vulnerabilities as they emerge, but again, subscribing to a security news e-mail list like ISN or *The Register's* daily newsletter is a good way to stay on top of them.

Because of the licensing advantages in open source software, the major Linux distributors like SuSE and Mandrake can package virtually every application a computer user might need, and these *will* be patched during online updates. Linux users enjoy more comprehensive updates from their vendors than Windows users. However, software packages not included in the distribution and installed separately will not be updated, so these must be monitored for new vulnerabilities and patched as needed. Still, Linux users who stay with the packages shipped in their distribution can be confident that the online update feature will keep their systems patched with a minimum of bother.

Vulnerable Services

A *service* is a background process running on a system that supports other processes and applications as needed. Generally, the user doesn't access or invoke a service directly; rather, an application or a utility will do so. In addition, one machine can offer services to other machines across a LAN or the Internet. For example, *Samba* and *SMB* are services that provide file and print sharing over a network. *Kerberos* is a service that provides network authentication. *Bind* is a service that enables an Internet server to translate domain names, such as `TheRegister.co.uk`, into an IP address, such as 123.1.2.3. (Machines use IP addresses to communicate, but of course people have a far easier time remembering domain names.) *SSH* (secure shell) is a service that allows a computer to connect to a remote machine via an encrypted link over the Internet. The actual code that provides a service is called a *daemon* in UNIX parlance and a *system agent* in Windows parlance, and the feature or capability that it provides is called a *service* or a *daemon process.*

All of the services I've just mentioned, and many others not listed, have contained vulnerabilities that have in turn led to system compromises. Therefore, an important bit of security housekeeping involves identifying the services your computer is offering and disabling those you don't need. For example, your PC should not be offering to accept SSH connections from other machines on the Internet unless you actually use this service and know how to set it up properly. For another example, the *RPC* (remote procedure call) service, which enables one computer to execute code on another, is a useful feature for networked machines sharing expensive hardware, such as a printer over a LAN, say. But it's very risky when the computer offering RPC is connected to the Internet. (The MSBlaster worm that struck in the summer of 2003 leveraged insecurities in RPC through another service called DCOM.) Unfortunately, Microsoft has made a number of crucial Windows services dependent on RPC, so it can't be disabled. In that case, prompt patching and firewalling are the only practical solutions. On the other hand, Linux users can shut off RPC without penalty. Later in this chapter, we'll walk through the various services provided by Windows and Linux, and eliminate those that pose the greatest security risks.

"Unsafe at Any Speed"

Many, if not most, home PC users are working with a *single-user* edition of Windows, such as Windows 95, 98, or Me. There are also *multiuser* editions such as Windows NT, 2000, and XP. UNIX and its cousins, BSD and Linux, are also multiuser systems.

The multiuser environment offers several distinct security advantages and should *always* be preferred, even in the home, and even when there is only one user.

The chief weakness of a single-user system is that whoever sits at the keyboard is the administrator, capable of taking any action he pleases. He can install programs and delete files or wipe out whole directories; he can alter system settings with the same privileges as the owner. This is bad in two ways. First, anyone with physical access to the machine can reconfigure it and possibly destroy important data files, whether intentionally or accidentally. Second, when every user is automatically an administrator, any malware that the user might pick up will run with the administrator's level of access—that is, with unlimited privileges. Similarly, any remote intruder will automatically have full system access as well.

However, when we run a multiuser system like Windows XP or Linux, we can limit the level of system access granted to each user, and so limit the impact of malware and malicious attacks. There are other benefits as well: parents can prevent children from altering system settings that restrict their freedom on the Internet, for example. Even if a child is given his own computer, a parent can set up an administrator account on that machine for himself, and a user account for the child with fewer privileges. Similarly, if one wishes to share a computer with housemates but does not want them to access one's own personal files or install software or fiddle with system settings, one can assign them user accounts in which to work.

Even when you are the *only* user, running your computer from an unprivileged account is always safer than running it as an administrator, or as *root* in UNIX parlance. If your machine is compromised, the intruder will likely (though not certainly) gain only your lower system privileges and may therefore fail to assume much control. This is true also when malware is inadvertently installed; it too will have fewer privileges if it's installed under a user account. When you need to perform administrative tasks, such as installing software or hardware or changing the system configuration, you can simply log in as an admin or as root and do whatever you please.

Properly set up, a multiuser system can prevent attackers both remote and local from manipulating files and settings, prevent children from exceeding their privileges, and reduce the effectiveness of malware and remote exploits. The best advice I can offer to readers with single-user systems is that they switch to a full-fledged multiuser environment such as Windows XP or Linux right away. The recommendations offered throughout this book are based on a presumption that readers are working with multiuser systems, because the inherent weaknesses of single-user environments cannot be overcome and will undermine the best efforts of even the most conscientious, security-minded user. A single-user system is "unsafe at any speed," so to speak.

A *New York Times* article from August of 2003 by Ian Austen did a good job of advocating the multiuser environment on grounds that it allows parents to regulate their children's computer activity and permits each user to customize his desktop. But the author failed to grasp the important security implications of the multiuser environment and made a serious blunder, noting that "Windows XP ... allow[s] owners to set up a password-protected account for every user. When a computer has a single user, the log-on feature of Windows XP can be a bit of a nuisance."[1]

It is far from a nuisance. It is, in fact, a significant security enhancement, and it should be exploited as such. Even when you are the only user, habitually logging on to an unprivileged user account will make all of your Web activity safer and reduce the impact of malware and scripts.

Admittedly, a multiuser system is no guarantee against exploitation. There are numerous remote and local attacks against both UNIX-compatible and Windows-based systems with which an attacker can increase his privileges, but we can, and should, at least make him work for it. It's foolish, even negligent, to hand over administrative privileges at the front door. By habitually working from, and accessing the Internet through, a nonprivileged user account, we can frustrate a large number of unsophisticated attacks and a good deal of malware from the start. But just like firewalling, virus scanning, eliminating insecure proprietary software, and patching promptly, a multiuser system is no security panacea, though it is an important layer of defense. However, by assembling these layers and building on them, users can disappoint attackers, even fairly sophisticated ones.

It might seem that talking about vectors of infection and multiuser computing environments in the same chapter is an odd mix, but the two are well connected. This is because the *security context*, or the level of system access, that a user is granted affects the potential of malware and malware vectors such as browsers, e-mail, and IM clients to deliver and execute malicious code. It is generally, though not universally, true that we can limit the harmful impact of malicious code by limiting the *user's* access to the system. This is a basic principle, and an important one, though it's not foolproof. It is, however, a useful rule of thumb to keep in mind: generally speaking, an unprivileged user will run unprivileged malware. This is why even the owner and sole user of a system should always work from a limited-access account, except when performing administrative chores.

Single-user editions of Windows attempt to control code execution with so-called "security zones" for online clients like Internet Explorer and Outlook Express. Since everyone using the computer either already is an administrator or can become one with ease, the idea here is to categorize Web content and software providers and their products as trusted or untrusted. For example, Internet Explorer allows a user to choose Web sites from which content like JavaScript and ActiveX controls will be trusted. Content from untrusted Web sites can be assigned reduced privileges on the machine. Similarly, there are digital certificates testifying to the origins of software, which the user can choose to trust or not. The security zone approach might make sense on a single-user system in lieu of something better, but Microsoft has extended this band-aid approach to its multiuser systems, where it actually undermines the essential benefits of the multiuser environment.

---

1. Ian Austin, "To Each, His Own: Sharing a Family PC," *New York Times*, August 14, 2003.

Windows is designed to grant and deny system privileges to third-party software, and even to outside parties, based on preselected trust criteria. Digital certificates for Web sites and for software are proffered to persuade users that their trust criteria have been met. Meanwhile, the operating system is designed to trust code when Microsoft or the user trusts it or its provider, and this means that even users on a multiuser system can sometimes run or install powerful and potentially destructive code from an unprivileged account.

This approach is wrongheaded from the start. It is the *user* whose privileges should be regulated, not the *provider* of a service or a piece of software. By making it possible for a piece of code to be trusted automatically *by the system*, Microsoft has made it possible for software to exceed the privileges of the user who installs it and scripts to exceed the privileges of the user who runs them. Thus a malicious program, apparently certified by Microsoft with a digital certificate, can be installed by a user and the system will grant it access to the deeper layers of the kernel. Incredibly, not only is Microsoft still clinging to this slapdash security scheme left over from the days of Windows 9x, it's actually *expanding* it in Windows XP and all future versions, and incorporating it into its Web services.

The new regime is called Next-Generation Secure Computing Base (NGSCB), or Palladium, a complicated, hence fragile, trust scheme meant to improve the level of confidence a user can place in a Web service or a piece of software by means of "improved" certification. (Actually, certification will become more complicated, though not necessarily better.) Unfortunately, this approach ignores the fundamental problem of allowing the system to trust code that the administrator has not approved, and even to exceed the administrator's authority in these matters. You can see the problem: even a minor flaw in this scheme could allow malicious code to be trusted and permit it to operate at a low level regardless of who installs it. This completely undermines the security benefits inherent in a multiuser environment. It means that your security will only be as good as Microsoft's grand trust scheme makes it, and considering Redmond's history in this area, I wouldn't put much faith in it.

Users should not be expected to know whose content can be trusted and whose can't, or what code is safe to run and what isn't. There are too many variables for anyone to make an informed decision every time some script is about to execute in a Web page or some program is about to install a plugin or an ActiveX control. The right way to do it is the way Linux does it: keep everyone, including the machine's owner, in unprivileged accounts except when administrative tasks need doing. When the system doesn't trust software or its provider based on preselected criteria, users needn't worry about the origins and security implications of some Web script, ActiveX control, patch, or program file. The worst they can do is make a mess of their own home directories. They can't make a mess of the entire system.

The simple way is often the right way, and this case is no exception. On Linux, if root installs a program, it will be trusted systemwide. If *a user* installs a program, it won't be. Generally, a program installed by a user will have no impact outside his home directory. Similarly, if a user's Web clients execute scripts, they too won't have impact outside his home directory. *That* is the right way to manage permissions. Ideally, nothing a user does, or allows a piece of code to do, in an unprivileged account should affect the guts of the system. Ideally, only root can make decisions with systemwide implications. I say "ideally" because there are ways for attackers and some malware and scripts to get around these restrictions, but this is no reason to ignore the benefits. Even Windows users should take advantage of the security enhancements in a multiuser environment, in spite of the fact that Microsoft's basic security scheme often gives them, and the code they execute, more privileges than they ought to have.

We've already done away with Internet Explorer and Outlook Express in favor of Mozilla, partly because the Windows security zone scheme is a failure. The company remains in denial of this fact because it's stuck with a very old and very poor design reaching back to Windows 9x, which it has been patching and elaborating instead of finding ways to abandon in favor of simpler, and better, solutions. Security zones and trusted content are band-aid approaches to the fundamental problem with single-user systems: the fact that all users are administrators—an extremely foolish design that should never have been chosen in the first place. Microsoft's original approach was bad enough, although, admittedly, there are limited options for controlling code execution in a single-user computing environment. But carrying this model forward into its multiuser systems, which would otherwise be a good deal stronger, and steadily building additional layers on top of a failed scheme that's unsound in its footings, is pure folly that will cripple Windows security for years to come.

Fortunately, there are steps we can take to enhance the security of a multiuser Windows system and leverage its inherent superiority to earlier versions in spite of Microsoft. There is much to learn and much to do, but it can be achieved.

Defense

Now, after considering a number of basic system weaknesses and routes to exploitation, it should surprise no one that our correspondent, Rich, was let down by his firewall and antivirus software. Still, we can control many of the risks that firewalls and AV packages can't. There are two essential elements:

- Disabling unnecessary services to reduce our attack profile

- "Sandboxing" users, or limiting their access to the system so that the code they run will also have limited access

This involves a bit of work, especially for Windows users, but it's not difficult.

NOTE   *In order to make the following Windows configuration instructions and their accompanying screen shots easier for Win-NT and Win-2K users to follow, they will be shown in the default Windows XP theme. Win-XP users should change their Start Menu theme to Classic in order to harmonize their screens with our examples. Simply go to the desktop Start Menu and select Control Panel ➤ Taskbar and Start Menu. A dialog will pop up. Click on the Start Menu tab at the top of the dialog and then choose Classic Start Menu. Click Apply and clear the dialog.*

What follows is a detailed set of instructions for both Windows and Linux users to strengthen security by disabling unnecessary services and setting up a multiuser environment the right way. It may be helpful to owners of single-user systems, but to enjoy the full security benefits, a multiuser system is crucial. Again, I strongly urge users of Windows 3.x, 9x, and Me to install Windows XP, or better yet, Linux.

Windows Services

Both Windows and Linux make numerous services available to applications and to local and remote users. A fair number are superfluous on the typical home system and merely act as potential security holes that may one day be exploited, if they haven't been already. Services are important vectors of exploitation, generally attacked by worms and by the more capable class of malicious hacker.

Unfortunately, with Windows, disabling services can be a tricky affair: there are quite a few dependencies, and you can inadvertently disable desirable functions or even make your system unstable if you get too aggressive. However, unnecessary services are a route to exploitation and a waste of system resources to boot, so it's worth doing away with as many as you can.

NOTE   *All of the Windows-related instructions in this chapter assume that you have already logged in to your administrator account on Windows XP.*

To see which services are running on Windows

1. Go to the Start menu, choose Run, and type in *services.msc.* Click OK.

2. You will now be confronted with an enormous list of running services with obscure names like Application Layer Gateway Service, Background Intelligent Transfer Service, and COM+ Event System (Figure 2-1). Highlight any service and right-click. You will get a menu allowing you to start it, stop it, or view its properties.

3. Use the right-click menu to display the properties of the service you chose above. The Properties dialog will launch (Figure 2-2).

4. You will find four tabs at the top of the dialog: General, Log On, Recovery, and Dependencies. The General tab will show you the service's name, a brief description, the path to the relevant executable file, a drop-down menu allowing you to choose how it should start (i.e., Automatic, Manual, or Disabled), and finally, four buttons allowing you to start, stop, pause, and resume the service.

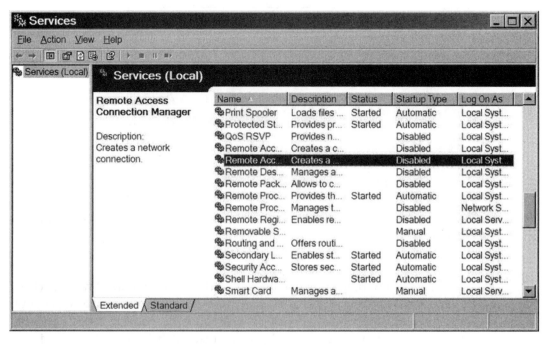

Figure 2-1. The Windows Services menu with the Remote Access Connection Manager service highlighted

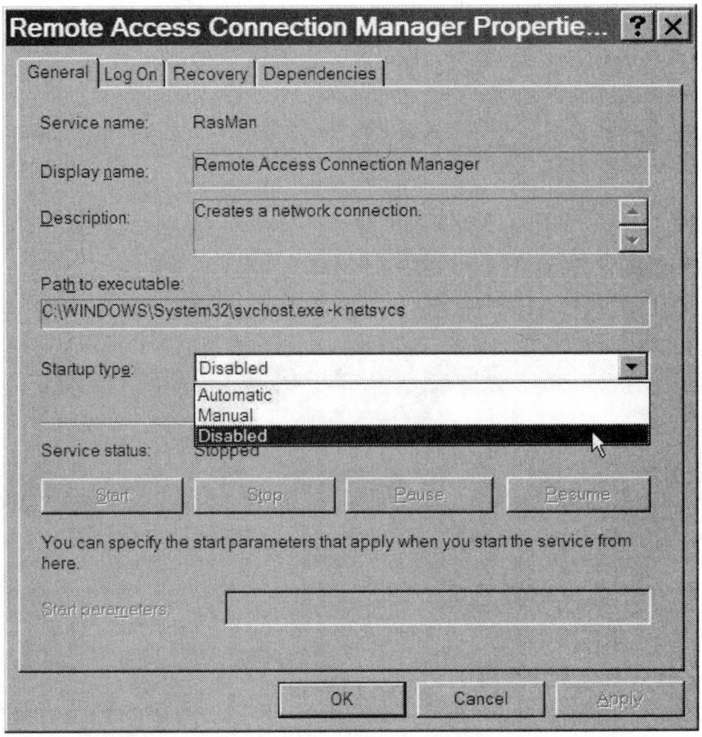

Figure 2-2. The Properties dialog associated with the Remote Access Connection Manager service

You will notice right away that the descriptions tell you little of value, such as how much memory the service uses, how many remote exploits have been found against it, or whether or not you can safely disable it. I'm going to list services with security implications that can usually be disabled safely on a machine that is not providing network services over a LAN but is used for Internet access. Unfortunately, Microsoft enables most of them by default, so disabling all the risky ones will be tedious and time consuming, though it's very important that you press on and get it done. It's best to stop a service using the Properties dialog as described previously, then use the system normally for a while and observe its behavior. You can usually reenable a service if shutting it off causes problems. If nothing untoward happens after a bit of daily use, you can disable it permanently.

Now let's look at the most important insecure services enabled by default on Windows:

Automatic Updates: This service will automatically connect to the Internet, check for available patches, and install them. I recommend running Windows Update manually and choosing the upgrades and patches to be downloaded, unless you like the idea of letting Microsoft decide what code belongs on your system and when it should be installed. Set it to Disabled. (But don't forget to run the update manually on a regular basis. Just click on Start ➤ Windows Update.)

ClipBook: This service stores cut and paste information and allows you to share it with other computers. It multiplies data traces, which complicates the practice of good data hygiene, and also wastes memory. Set it to Disabled.

Error Reporting Service: This service phones home to Microsoft when application errors occur. Set it to Disabled.

Indexing Service: This service essentially maintains data *about* your data (i.e., *metadata*) to speed up searching the local drive and the contents of files. It multiplies data traces, completely undermines the practice of good data hygiene, and wastes a good deal of memory. Set it to Disabled.

Internet Information Service (IIS): This is Microsoft's notoriously insecure Web server. It is usually not installed on XP systems, but if it has been installed it should be uninstalled *with prejudice* unless you're actually using it. If you need a Web server, Apache for Windows is a safer alternative that I recommend. However, you should never install *any* sort of server on a home system unless you need one and know how to run it securely.

Messenger: Often called *Windows Messenger*, this service broadcasts messages on a network. It is *not* the MSN Messenger chat client. It is often exploited to broadcast spam across the Internet but has no other useful function on a home or small business network, though it can be useful on large networks when the administrator needs to broadcast a message to all users. Set it to Disabled.

Net Logon: This service allows logging on to a *domain controller*. This is not required for home and small office networks. Set it to Disabled unless your machine is a member of a domain.

NetMeeting Remote Desktop Sharing: This service permits others to access your computer using NetMeeting. This is a major security hole. Set it to Disabled unless you need it.

Network DDE: This service enables applications on different computers to share data. It's of no use to most home and SOHO users. Set it to Disabled.

Network DDE DSDM: This service manages network shares. It's of no use to most home and SOHO users. Set it to Disabled.

Network Location Awareness: This service collects location and configuration information about networked computers. It's of no use to most home and SOHO users. Set it to Disabled.

Protected Storage: This service saves your login passwords for e-mail, your ISP, and the like. This is not dangerous on a properly configured PC, but I do recommend disabling it on laptop computers, which have a tendency to grow legs. If your laptop is stolen, stored passwords will enable the thief to access your ISP account, VPN, e-mail, etc. Set it to Disabled on laptop computers, and get into the habit of logging in manually.

QoS RSVP: This service provides network traffic information to certain applications. It's of no use to most home and SOHO users. Set it to Disabled.

Remote Access Auto Connection Manager: This service creates a connection to a remote network whenever a program references a remote DNS or NetBIOS name or address. In other words, it's a shortcut for embedded links. Set it to Disabled unless you need it.

Remote Access Connection Manager: This service establishes a network connection when Windows Internet Connection Sharing is in use. Using a router for connection sharing makes this service unnecessary. Set it to Disabled unless you need it.

Remote Desktop Help Session Manager: This service controls the Windows Remote Assistance feature, which allows remote users, such as malicious script kiddies, to connect to your machine and tweak all its settings. I *strongly* recommend against using this service; it is far too susceptible to abuse. Set it to Disabled.

Remote Packet Capture Protocol: This service allows remote users to intercept packet traffic on your machine. This is useful for remote administration, but it is suicidal otherwise. A great boon to malicious hackers and script kiddies: set it to Disabled, with prejudice.

Remote Registry Service: This service allows remote users, such as malicious script kiddies, to tweak your Registry settings to their liking. Set it to Disabled.

Routing and Remote Access: This service allows other computers to dial in to yours through a modem to access the local network. You may need it for some VPN software. Unless you need it, set it to Disabled.

Server: This service permits file and print sharing from your computer, which is a very foolish thing to allow if the computer also connects to the Internet. Unless you are using these features (and preferably on a LAN only), set it to Disabled.

SNMP Service: This is a network monitoring service. It is not necessary on most home or small office computers. Set it to Disabled.

SNMP Trap Service: This service handles messages exchanged between SNMP agents on networked computers. It's of no use to most home and SOHO users. Set it to Disabled.

SSDP Discovery Service: This service enables discovery of UPnP (Universal Plug and Play) devices on your network. UPnP is *very* insecure, easily exploited, and should never be used on a machine with Internet access (see *UPnP* later on this list). Set it to Disabled.

TCP/IP NetBIOS Helper Service: This service provides support for NetBIOS over TCP/IP. However, you should not be using NetBIOS over TCP/IP because it is *very* insecure. Uninstall NetBIOS if you have it (see the instructions that follow), then set this "helper service" to Disabled.

Telnet: This is a *very* insecure mechanism allowing remote users to log on to your computer. Never make Telnet available for any reason. If it is installed, set it to Disabled.

Terminal Services: This is an insecure service allowing remote users to log on to your computer. However, a very useful feature called *Fast User Switching* depends on it. Fast User Switching allows users to move between accounts without ending their sessions. Tasks in one account will remain active while another user is logged in. Unfortunately, Microsoft has made this handy feature dependent on an insecure service. If you disable Terminal Services, your computer will be more secure, but whenever you log out of an account you will have to save all your work because your applications and tasks will be shut down. Choose your poison.

Universal Plug and Play (UPnP): Don't confuse this with *Plug and Play*, which is useful and safe. The UPnP service detects and configures UPnP-compatible devices over a network. It is *very* susceptible to remote exploitation, so set it to Disabled. It works with the SSDP Discovery Service, which should also be set to Disabled (see *SSDP Discovery Service* earlier on this list).

Upload Manager: This service manages file transfers between clients and servers on a network. Very few home users will have any use for it. It also phones home to Microsoft seeking driver information when devices are installed. Set it to Disabled.

WebClient: This service allows Windows and MS applications to modify Web-based content. Some Microsoft applications may need it. If you have difficulty with MSN Messenger or Media Player, you may need to enable WebClient later. However, if you follow my recommendations and substitute more secure Internet clients for the ones Microsoft supplies, there is little chance you will ever need this service. Set it to Disabled.

There's a crucial service that cannot be disabled in Windows, which is unfortunate because it is exceptionally insecure. It's called remote procedure call (RPC), and it allows one computer to execute code on another across a network. This is fine on a LAN, but it is *extremely* risky if the computer is connected to the Internet. Sadly, the roster of services and applications that Microsoft has chosen to make dependent on RPC is enormous. Disabling it can leave your computer unstable, and, in some situations, unbootable. RPC is essentially a security hole that you can't live without. The only practical solution is to set your firewall to block TCP/UDP ports 135–139, 445, and 593. Home users may not be able to configure their firewalls to block specific ports, but a good packet filter or router capable of stateful packet inspection should prove adequate.

It is important to uninstall TCP/IP NetBIOS. This is not a good service to have on any machine connected to the Internet. To remove it, follow these steps:

1. Go to the Start menu and choose Settings ➤ Network Connections or ➤ Control Panel ➤ Network Connections. Click on your network connection device, then on the Properties button.

2. A dialog will launch. Under the General tab you will find your installed network protocols, services, and clients. If your PC is used for Internet access and does not require additional networking capability, you should uninstall *everything* except Internet Protocol (TCP/IP). Get rid of File and Print Sharing, NetBIOS, Client for Microsoft Networks (unless you use PGP), and the rest of these superfluous whistles and bells. TCP/IP is the *only* component you need for an Internet connection to work.

3. After uninstalling all the unnecessary networking components, left-click on Internet Protocol (TCP/IP) to launch its Properties dialog.

4. Click the Advanced button and another dialog will launch, labeled Advanced TCP/IP Settings. Choose the WINS tab at the top (Figure 2-3).

5. Choose the option labeled *Disable NetBIOS over TCP/IP* at the bottom. You will need to reboot for all of these settings to take effect.

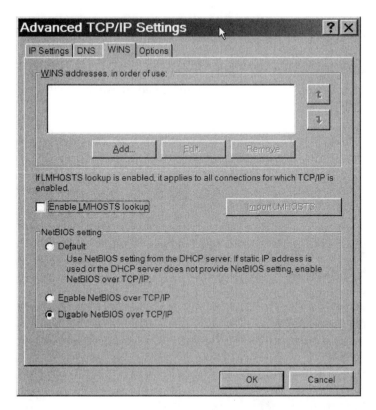

Figure 2-3. The Advanced TCP/IP Settings dialog with proper WINS settings

There is one more notoriously insecure service that we need to disable on Windows, called DCOM (Distributed Component Object Model), which enables software components to communicate directly over a network. It is quite unnecessary for home users, terribly obscure, and the particular service that enabled the MSBlaster worm to attack the Windows RPC service. Power users can open the Registry and alter the key HKEY_LOCAL_MACHINE\Software\Microsoft \OLE\EnableDCOM with a value of *N* and reboot. Novices should disable DCOM thus:

1. Go to the Start menu, choose Run, and type in *dcomcnfg*. Click OK, and the Component Services dialog will launch.

2. In the left pane, choose the menu item Component Services and expand the tree below it. Next choose Computers, expand the tree again, and choose My Computer.

3. In the left pane, right-click on My Computer and choose Properties from the drop-down menu (Figure 2-4). The My Computer Properties dialog will launch.

4. Choose the Default Properties tab on the My Computer Properties dialog and *clear* the checkbox in front of the option *Enable Distributed COM on this computer* (Figure 2-5). You will need to reboot for the change to take effect. If the option is not available, you'll need to use the Registry hack mentioned earlier.

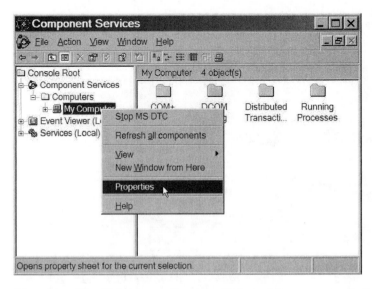

Figure 2-4. The Component Services dialog with tree expanded, right-click menu activated

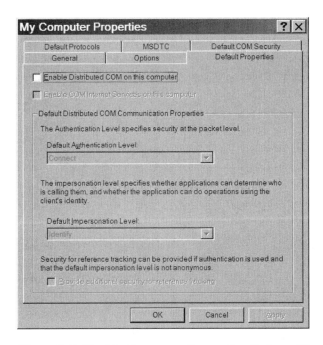

Figure 2-5. The My Computer Properties dialog with proper DCOM settings

By disabling insecure services, not only do you shut off many vectors of attack and exploitation, you also create a second line of defense in case you miss an important security patch. This is not to say that you should get careless with system updates, but it's good to know that if you should miss an important security fix, there's at least a decent chance that the vulnerable item will have been disabled and the problem therefore will not affect you. Disabling unnecessary services is a good proactive step that can protect you from new exploits, viruses, and worms before they become widely known and before patches become available. For example, if you had disabled DCOM before the Blaster worm struck, you would have been blithely unaware of it.

Linux Services

For Linux users, disabling superfluous services is a good deal easier. There are fewer to worry about and far fewer dependencies among them. For example, Linux users can disable RPC without negative consequences, and they should do so unless they need it for NFS (Network File System) or NIS (Network Information Service). Home network users and home business users are unlikely to be using these services, so it's almost always good to disable RPC.

Unlike Microsoft, most Linux vendors will not install many superfluous services and Web applications by default. But it is important to check the following list in case you're running a service that you don't need. If you're using a major, packaged distribution, it's likely that only a few of these services will have been enabled by default.

There are numerous ways to disable services in Linux, though these depend on the particular distribution you're using. For this reason, it will not be practical to provide screen shots. Essentially, you want to halt the daemon, ensure that the system continues to work normally, and then disable it permanently. An easy way to do this is via a GUI admin interface, but of course these vary by distribution. Usually, there will be an admin utility allowing you to select runlevels for various components, where your services or daemon processes will be displayed and can be enabled, disabled, started, and stopped. Linux is usually very tolerant of having services disabled, but you should stop the daemon first and see how the system behaves before making a commitment. If your machine continues to function normally, you can remove it from all runlevels, and even from your /etc/init.d directory so that it can't start again if you reboot.

Here are the main ones you should look out for:

Apache: This is a fine Web server. Most Linux distributions are filled with more packages than any person could possibly use, and sometimes, due to this embarrassment of riches, servers like Apache can be installed without the user's realizing it. If you don't need a Web server or don't know how to run one securely, you should uninstall it promptly.

Berkeley Internet Name Domain (BIND): This service translates domain names to IP addresses. Unless you are operating a server, you have no use for it. Disabling it will not affect your Internet clients: your ISP will provide BIND or DNS services for you. The daemon is called *named* and should be disabled.

File Transfer Protocol (FTP): This is a file server. Few home users will have any use for it. The daemons are called *wuftpd* and *proftpd;* get rid of them unless you need to make FTP available and know how to secure it.

Line Printer Daemon (LPD): This service allows users to connect to a printer across a network. It is *exceptionally* insecure and should be disabled with prejudice.

Nessus: This is a vulnerability scanner that runs a daemon process. It's not terribly dangerous, but there is no point leaving it running when it's not in use, lest others connect to it. I recommend enabling and disabling the nessusd daemon from the command line and leaving it out of your runlevels.

Network Information Service (NIS): This service allows networked machines to share a common interface. It is not so much vulnerable in itself but it requires RPC, which is. Home users should not have any use for it.

Network File System (NFS): This service provides remote access to shared file systems across a network. As with NIS, it is not so much vulnerable in itself but it requires RPC, which is. Home users should not have any use for it.

Postfix: This is a fairly reliable mail server. Few home users need a mail server or know how to run one securely, so this should be disabled, but not uninstalled. Some mail clients may require it to be present, though not running.

Remote Procedure Call (RPC): Sometimes called *sunrpc* or *portmap*, this should be disabled except when NIS or NFS are in use. Any daemon with *rpc* or *portmap* in the name is a good candidate for disabling.

Rlogin: This service accepts remote logins. It is only slightly more secure than Telnet and should be disabled. Use SSH or Webmin if you need to log in to your machine remotely.

Samba: This is a file and print sharing service that offers Windows compatibility. It's unnecessary on most home machines. Computers used primarily to contact the Internet should not be offering such services unless they have to, though Samba can be quite useful in an office if you know how to run it securely.

Secure Shell (SSH): This service accepts remote logins. You should disable the SSH daemon (sshd) unless you need to connect remotely to your computer. If you do connect remotely, SSH is the most secure method and should always be preferred to Telnet and rlogin. Disabling the SSH daemon will not cause any problems when using an SSH client.

Sendmail: This is a mail server. You probably don't need a mail server, so uninstall it. If you do need a mail server, you should *still* uninstall Sendmail and replace it with Postfix, which is more secure. Some e-mail clients may require Postfix to be installed, though not running, so disabling it is better than uninstalling it.

Simple Network Management Protocol (SNMP): This service allows for configuring devices over a network. Home users should have no use for it. There are plenty of exploits against it, so disable the snmpd daemon unless you really need it.

Squid: This is a proxy server, and a fine one, but it's a security issue if you don't need it and don't know how to secure it. If you don't know what a proxy server is, then you absolutely don't need one. Uninstall it if you find it's been installed.

Telnet: This is a *hopelessly* insecure service that permits remote logins. Disable it; remove it from /etc/init.d; exorcise it.

Webmin: This is a fairly trustworthy server for remote administration. However, if you don't need it, uninstall it. If you're not going to use it, there's no point making it available to others on the Internet, like malicious script kiddies.

Ypbind: This daemon supports Network Information Services (NIS). There have been exploits against it. Again, as with any service, if you don't need it, disable it.

Power User Tip

Linux power users can prevent their X server from listening on the Net by editing the relevant configuration file. Depending on your distribution, the file might be found in one of these locations: /etc/opt/kde3/share/config/kdm/Xservers, /etc/X11/xdm/Xservers, /usr/X11R6/lib/X11/xinit/xserverrc, or /etc/X11/xinit/xserverrc. Find the line starting with *:0 local* [*etc...*], and without altering it otherwise, add *-nolisten tcp* at the end. The X server's TCP access is not considered a menace, but this will keep you safe from a new or unknown exploit.

Becoming a User

If you're the owner of a Windows machine—even if you're the only person who uses it—the surest step that you can take toward improved system security and user privacy, after installing Mozilla and disabling unnecessary services, is to set up an individual user account with limited privileges for yourself and everyone else who uses the computer.

Before you begin, it's necessary to set your file display characteristics and permissions so that you can control them yourself. Windows defaults to a condition called simple file sharing, which is an obstacle to good security in general, and to setting proper file and directory permissions in particular.

1. Go to the desktop Start menu and choose Settings ➤ Control Panel ➤ Folder Options. The Folder Options dialog will launch.

2. Choose the tab labeled View from the top of the Folder Options dialog.

3. Check the boxes or radio buttons next to the items labeled *Display the contents of system folders* and *Show hidden files and folders* (Figures 2-6 and 2-7).

4. Next, *clear* the checkbox next to the item labeled *Hide protected operating system files (Recommended)*. You will be warned against clearing this box, but you need to know what's on your system if you want to make it more secure. Ignore the warning (Figures 2-6 and 2-7).

5. Finally, *clear* the checkbox next to the item labeled *Use simple file sharing (Recommended)*. Click Apply and finally OK (Figures 2-6 and 2-7).

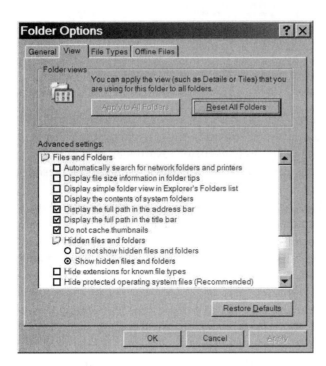

Figure 2-6. The Folder Options dialog with recommended settings

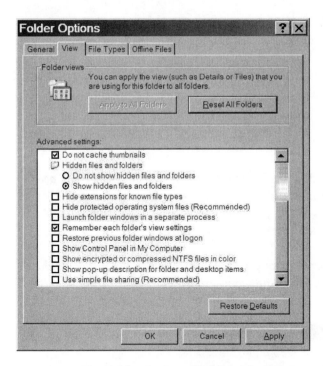

Figure 2-7. The Folder Options dialog with recommended settings, continued

Now, if you didn't choose an Administrator password when you installed Windows XP, do this first. Incredibly, Microsoft permits users to run XP as a single-user system, defeating its inherent security advantages, and permits the creation of accounts without password protection. However, there's no reason for you to follow a bad example.

If you're installing Windows XP, it's best to set an Administrator password when the opportunity is presented so that you won't have to bother with it later. Windows makes setting an Administrator password after the installation more complicated than it ought to be, but if it hasn't been done, it definitely needs doing. So let's get it out of the way.

1. Go to the desktop Start menu and choose Run and type in *compmgmt.msc*. Click OK, and the Computer Management dialog will launch.

2. In the left pane, select Local Users and Groups, expand the tree, and choose Users.

3.   You will see several users listed in the right pane, such as the Administrator, Guest, and the name you chose for yourself when you installed Windows, which is also an administrator (Figure 2-8). Windows XP sets the person who installs the system as *an* administrator, but not *the* Administrator. What's the difference between *the* Admin and *an* admin? Basically, *the* Admin is an inbuilt account coded into Windows, whereas *an* admin is whoever installed the system, plus any other users he decides to nominate for the honor. Let's concern ourselves first with *the* Admin, or the built-in account.

4.   Highlight the Administrator account and right-click. The drop-down menu allows you to set or reset the password. If you've already set a password but think it might be weak, then you should reset it with a better one, using the instructions that follow.

     Make your password a difficult one, combining uppercase and lowercase letters, numerals, and special characters like the dollar and pound signs. It should be at least eight characters in length, though when it comes to passwords, longer is always better. I recommend using a short phrase that makes no sense, like "sleazy bricks." Use some uppercase and some lowercase letters, and substitute characters that resemble a few of the other letters so it looks something like this: sl34ZybR1@k$. Note that we've substituted numbers and special characters that, at least vaguely, resemble the letters they're standing in for to make the password easier to memorize. You can write it down and keep it in a secure place until you're sure you've memorized it. A password like this will be practically impossible to brute force or crack with a dictionary attack.

     When you set the Admin password, you will receive a warning that numerous problems might arise. Ignore it.

5.   Once you've pass-protected the built-in Administrator account, set a strong password for yourself as *an* administrator, associated with the username you chose when you installed Windows XP. You can use the same password for both accounts with little risk, so long as it's a tough one according to our guidelines. It is usually safe for home users to disable the remaining built-in accounts provided by Microsoft, except the Guest account, which may prove useful. Personally, I would disable every account except *the* Admin, *your* admin account, and the Guest account at this point (unless you've already added users, obviously).

6.   To enable or disable an account, select it in the Computer Management dialog, use the right-click menu, and choose Properties. In the Properties dialog, under the General tab, find the checkbox next to the option *Account is disabled* (Figure 2-9).

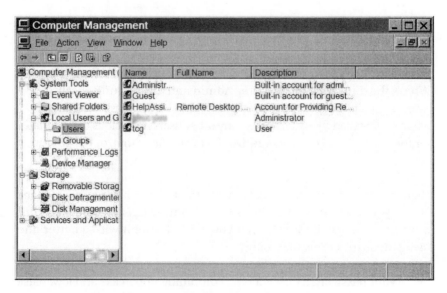

Figure 2-8. The Computer Management dialog with Users selected

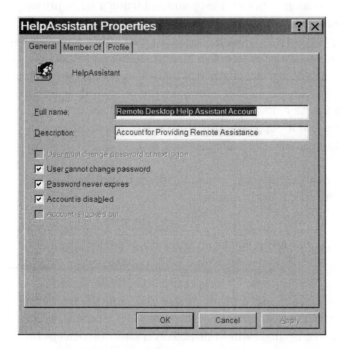

Figure 2-9. The Computer Management Properties dialog with default MS "Help Assistant" account disabled

If you haven't established a user account for yourself or added any other users, you should do so now. But you can close the Computer Management dialog at this point; things will get easier from here.

Now it's time to add users, and this means *you too*. You'll remain an administrator, of course, but you're going to set up and start working from an unprivileged account except when admin access is needed for altering system settings or installing software, just like any security-savvy person. This is not difficult:

1. Open the Start menu and go to Settings ➤ Control Panel ➤ User Accounts. A window will open, most likely reminding you that you are the system administrator.

2. Create a user account for yourself. Choose *Create a new account*, and then choose a login name. Choose *limited* for the account type and click the Create Account button.

3. Now create a password for the account. This is the account you should use at all times, except when you need to perform administrative tasks.

4. Simply repeat the process, choosing limited accounts for each user. You can also activate the Guest account so that occasional visitors and house guests can use your computer without accessing any of the established user accounts. However, the Guest account is not password protected, so *anyone* can use the machine with it. Privileges are low, but this is not a good option if you are unable to supervise use of the computer for extended periods. If you don't set up the Guest account, it will not appear on the boot screen.

Once you've got yourself and every other user working from limited-access accounts, you will enjoy a fundamental security advantage. Malware that you and other users pick up while surfing the Web or from e-mail or instant messaging will have less impact on the system. Scripts and malicious files will have less access to the system. Computer and Internet use by children can be restricted.

Linux does a far better job of sandboxing user accounts from the system than Windows, better limiting the impact of malware and risky behavior. Linux passwords are also more difficult to crack because they're hashed more effectively. However, by taking full advantage of the multiuser features of Windows XP, you will in fact go a considerable distance toward improving security and user privacy.

Linux users have it easier from the start. They are required to set up a root account with a password, plus at least one user account (also with a password), when they install the system. Linux doesn't allow users to make the mistake of running their PCs as single-user systems. Novices who are in the habit of running their computers from the root account should immediately switch to running from a user account. It is rarely necessary to use the root account as a working environment, because virtually all administrative functions are available from your user account. With a command shell, simply enter the command *su* and you will be prompted for the root password and granted root access. Close the shell when you've finished your task, or anyone with access to your machine when your back is turned will have access to a root shell. Alternatively, you can lock the screen if you need to leave your computer while a root shell is open, that is, you can activate your screen saver in such a way that your password is needed to clear it, by choosing the Lock Screen option from the KDE Start menu. If you prefer using a GUI admin interface, such as Mandrake's DrakX or SuSE's YaST, simply select it from the desktop menu and enter the root password when prompted. Make sure that your root password is at least eight characters long and difficult to guess according to the previous example. It's best to hash passwords using MD5, which is stronger than the default. You will find this option in your admin interface under a category such as security and users. If you set up your system with weak passwords, by all means reset them with better ones.

Read, Write, Execute

Permissions for limited user accounts can be fine-tuned beyond the default levels of access afforded by Windows and Linux, which may be too permissive in some situations. However, tweaking file and directory permissions is not trivial and can cause problems if done carelessly.

The three basic file and directory permissions are *read*, *write*, and *execute*. Such permissions are usually granted, in varying levels of authority, to *groups* such as users or administrators. However, it is possible in both Windows and Linux to choose individual directory and file permissions for particular users. This enables the machine's owner to set up a user account for himself with fairly liberal permissions, and to set up another user account for a child, say, or a housemate, with more restrictive ones. This way, people sharing your computer can be kept from opening (i.e., reading) files and directories with sensitive data, from altering (i.e., writing to) program configuration files, and from activating (i.e., executing) programs you choose not to make available to them.

However, altering permissions *recursively*, that is, applying access restrictions that affect all of the contents in a directory, can result in unpleasant surprises. A directory, or a subdirectory within it, may contain program executables or configuration files needed by applications. If these files are unintentionally restricted with recursive changes, a user might be unable to launch programs that he is otherwise authorized to use.

Applying permissions is a good deal more complicated in multiuser versions of Windows than it is in Linux, but Windows allows more granular control, which is good for experienced administrators, though it presents a challenge to home users. The procedure may seem confusing, but basically, you will first choose the directory or file to be restricted, then choose the users to be permitted or denied access. To restrict individual users from running particular programs or browsing certain directories in Windows, do the following:

1. Log in to your administrator account and left-click on the My Computer desktop icon.

2. Under Hard Disk Drives, click on Local Disk (C:). You will see a list of top-level directories such as Program Files, WINDOWS, etc. (Alternatively, you can launch the Windows Explorer file browser; the procedure is the same.)

3. Let's assume that you have a user called tcg with an account on your machine and you want to disable access to the system directory for him alone. Navigate to the WINDOWS\system directory.

4. Highlight the directory, right-click, and select Properties from the right-click menu (Figure 2-10).

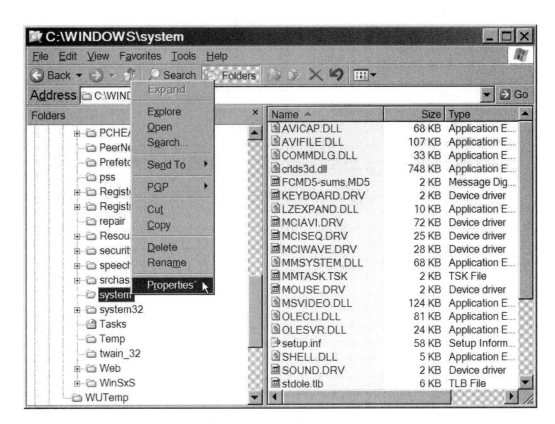

Figure 2-10. Selecting properties for the system directory

5. When the Properties dialog pops up, choose the Security tab. There will be two fields: at the top, a list of user groups, and below, a list of possible permissions. However, if you apply restrictions to a group such as Users, then every user will be denied access. To specify an individual user, click on the Advanced button (Figure 2-11).

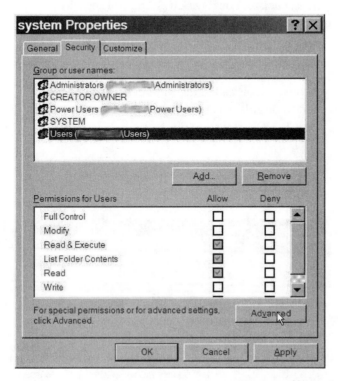

Figure 2-11. Choosing the Advanced user permissions dialog

6. This will bring up the advanced security settings dialog. Again, you will see Users listed as a group. Click the Add button and enter the desired username, tcg, manually in the lower field under *Enter the object name to select* (Figure 2-12). Click OK.

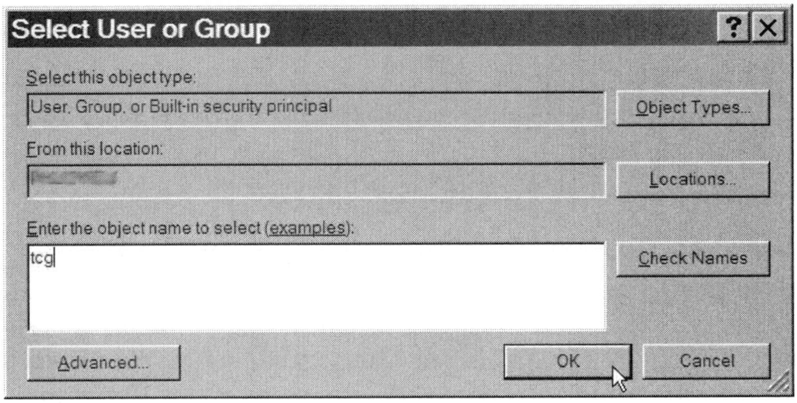

Figure 2-12. Choosing a user instead of a group

7. You will then get another dialog showing the user you chose associated with the system directory. You can now choose the user's permissions for that directory. Unfortunately, there is a plethora of options. To make it simple, choose Deny in the top line labeled Full Control to remove the user's permission to view or launch files in the system directory. This will change all of the options at once (Figure 2-13).

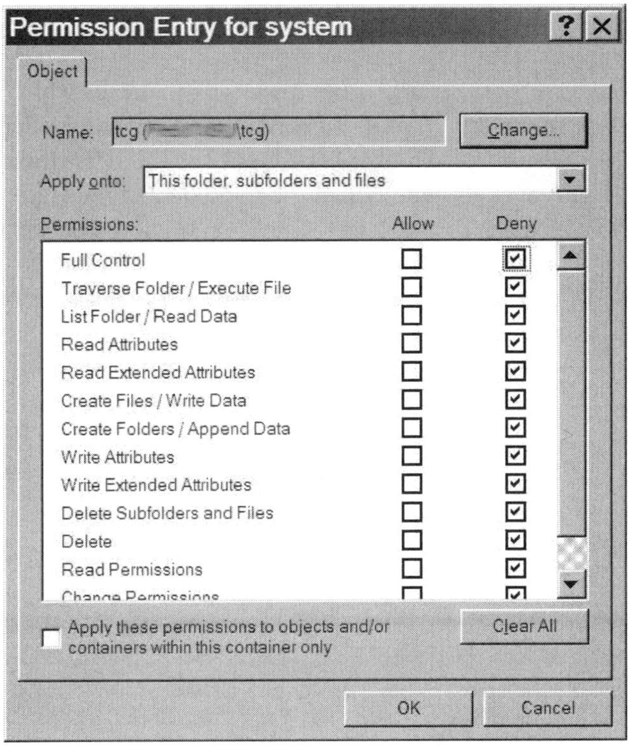

Figure 2-13. Denying a user access to the system folder

8. Click the OK button; you will return to the advanced security settings dialog. Click Apply.

9. You will see a new line with the word *Deny* followed by the username. Click OK and close the system directory Properties box. The user you chose will not be able to view or activate any files in the system directory.

You can use this basic procedure to fine-tune file and directory permissions for each user. You could, for example, deny a small child permission to use a chat client like ICQ or an e-mail client on his own. But remember, if you apply limits to the Users group, *all* users will be kept from the directory or program file chosen. To specify users for particular file and directory restrictions, you must bring up the advanced security settings dialog and apply the restrictions individually as just described.

This technique can be used to keep children from applications and directories that parents don't want them to access without supervision, even when they've been given their own computers. A parent simply needs to set up an administrator account for himself with which to maintain the machine and assign user accounts to each child. Children can be granted different levels of access depending on their ages, regardless of whether they use their parents' computer, share one among themselves, or have their own machines. This way, young children can be kept from e-mail, browsers, and chat clients, while older children can be allowed to use them in their own accounts. This can help ensure that the very young will not be exposed to online content unless an older sibling or a parent is around to supervise them. Even when each child has his own computer, a parent can still administer it and decide which programs can be accessed. Thus, multiuser systems like Windows XP and Linux offer significant advantages for parental control regardless of whether children use their parents' computers, each others', or their own. Because a good deal of malware installs itself to the C:\WINDOWS\System, C:\WINDOWS\System32 and ~\Startup directories, it's not a bad idea to restrict write access for all users following the preceding instructions. This way, if a user encounters a bit of malware, it will not be able to install itself to these directories. This will not prevent all malware from installing itself, but these are popular destinations, so disabling write access is worth the effort. Simply navigate to the ~\System and ~\System32 directories and disable write access for the entire group Users. You should deny the actions Write and Modify in the Properties ➤ Security setup field. You will still be able to write to these directories from your administrator account, which may be necessary when you're installing new software or hardware.

NOTE *The tilde (~) can indicate two things: a shortened directory path or a directory whose name would vary on different computers. Thus, C:\Windows\Temp might be shortened to ~\Temp, and /home/username/ Documents might appear as /home/~/Documents.*

Unfortunately, there is a separate Startup directory for each user, and write access must be disabled for each one individually. The Startup directories are located in C:\Documents and Settings\~\Start Menu\Programs\Startup, that is, C:\Documents and Settings*username*\Start Menu\Programs\Startup.

1. Navigate to the Startup directory for each account, including your administrator account and the accounts All Users and Default User, and deny write access to these directories for the group Users.

2. It may be necessary to add the group Users with the Advanced button in the Properties ➤ Security dialog.

3. You should deny the actions Write and Modify in the setup field. This is not at all difficult, but it is tedious, though worthwhile.

You will still be able to add startup programs to any user account and install software from your administrator account.

Linux goes about things differently. An unprivileged account under Linux is better controlled than one under Windows: users have a harder time getting into mischief or mucking up the system because there's not much damage they can do outside their home directories to begin with. Thus, malware is far less likely to affect the system overall.

NOTE *Setting up the /home directory alone on a separate primary partition will further enhance the system protection inherent in the Linux user sandbox.*

On Windows, it's often easier to work with *users*, whereas on Linux it's often easier to work with *groups*. When you wish to restrict users on a Linux system from directories or program files, a simple approach is to raise the level of privilege needed, then increase the privileges of users to whom you wish to grant access by adding them to a group with greater privileges. (You can do this on Windows, too, but with so many options it can become confusing.) For example, on Linux you might confine the ICQ (licq) program file to access by the group *trusted*, and then add yourself, your spouse, and your older children to that group. Young children would remain in the group *users* only, and not be able to access the ICQ binary from their accounts. The other users would belong to two groups, users and trusted, and so be permitted access by virtue of their membership in the trusted group.

The easiest way to change file and directory permissions is by using a GUI file browser like Krusader or Nautilus, because if you have a lot of files to deal with, making these changes at the command line will be tedious. You can certainly make these changes from a user account with a root shell if you understand the commands *chmod, chuser,* and *chgroup* (well worth learning, by the way), but if you want to use a GUI method, you'll have to log in as root. Simply navigate to the files you wish to restrict, right-click, and pull up their properties. You will find a simple dialog for setting permissions. The options are *read, write,* and *execute.* If you want only one user to have access, then clear the checkboxes on the lines labeled Group and Others. If you wish to allow a group to access it, simply check off the permissions you intend to grant on the line labeled Groups and then specify the group in the field below. If you wish to allow every user to have some access, check off the permissions you intend to grant to members of additional groups on the line labeled Others.

In Figure 2-14, the user tcg is the only one permitted to view, enter, or write to his /home/tcg/Documents directory. Root has free access to the entire system by default, but fellow members of the group to which tcg belongs (users), and all others, are denied access.

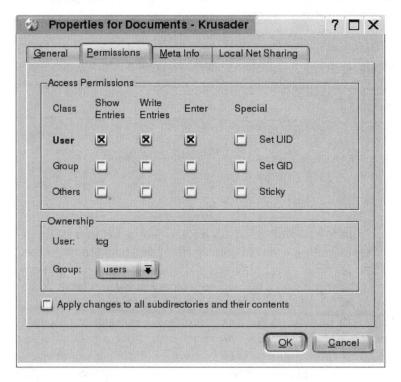

Figure 2-14. Setting directory permissions with Krusader

Because permissions are simpler on Linux than on Windows, it's easier to work with groups than with individual users. If you wish to grant file or directory access to some but not all users, you can assign a directory's or a file's access rights to a more privileged group, such as trusted, then add only the users you choose to that group. And that's all there is to it. Linux makes this procedure quite painless.

You can do permission tweaking with directories, but the earlier cautions about recursive changes apply. If you overprotect a directory, you may block user access to program files or configuration files that you wish to make available. It's also very easy to edit group permissions in terms of the system services available. Small children can have Internet access disabled, for example, by raising the permission level needed to access the service and then denying them membership in the group authorized to do so.

So, if you've carried out the instructions in this chapter, you'll have hardened your machine significantly according to the first two of our trio of principles: *prevention*, *resistance*, and *tolerance*.

And neither your firewall nor your antivirus software had a thing to do with it.

CHAPTER 3

Social Engineering

THOSE WHO PICTURE hacker legend Kevin Mitnick seated before a computer, tirelessly picking apart application code and exhaustively probing remote networks for weaknesses, have got the wrong idea. While perfectly capable of such attacks—at least against the software and network paraphernalia in use before his five years of federal detention—he rarely had to bother. Mitnick is a master of *social engineering* (SE): tech slang for "persuading people to act against their own interests." In the real world, we run across social engineers every day, only we call them *con artists*.

During his days as America's most infamous überhacker, Mitnick managed to persuade employees of major tech corporations to FedEx him the engineering specifications and source code for new products, to grant him user access to company networks, and even to set up voice mail accounts for him. He impersonated workers, managers, sysadmins, and business partners, and in these guises he repeatedly manipulated insiders. He was truly gifted, able to size up a victim over the phone in a matter of seconds. He offered help to the ignorant; he solicited help from the learned; he assumed airs of commanding authority or innocent vulnerability as his instincts guided. Only rarely did he have to resort to the sort of exploitative attack against a hardware or software system that we typically associate with hacking. His victims usually gave him whatever he wanted, even eagerly.

"The human side of computer security is easily exploited and constantly overlooked," Mitnick said in testimony before the Senate Governmental Affairs Committee in March of 2000, shortly after his release from federal lockup. "Companies spend millions of dollars on firewalls, encryption, and secure access devices, and it's money wasted because none of these measures address the weakest link in the security chain: the people who use, administer, and account for computer systems that contain protected information."

Mitnick should know. He detailed for the Committee how, in the mid-1990s, he'd breached security at the Internal Revenue Service and the Social Security Administration simply by hacking humans instead of boxes. "I called employees within these agencies and used social engineering to obtain the name of my target computer system and the commands used by agency employees to obtain protected taxpayer information," he explained. "Once I became familiar with the agency's lingo, I was able to successfully social-engineer other employees into issuing the commands required to obtain information from it, using as a pretext the idea that I was a fellow employee having computer problems.

"I obtained confidential information in the same way government employees did, and I did it all without even touching a computer. I was so successful with this line of attack that I rarely had to go towards a technical attack."

Government and corporate employees with access to protected information are being manipulated with social engineering exploits every day, despite all the policies, procedures, guidelines, and standards in place, Mitnick warned.

"In my successful efforts to social-engineer my way into Motorola, I used a three-level attack to bypass the information security measures then in use. First, I was able to convince Motorola Operations employees to provide me, on repeated occasions, the pass code on their secure access device, as well as the static PIN. The reason this was so extraordinary is that the pass code on their access device changed every 60 seconds: every time I wanted to gain unauthorized access, I had to call the Operations Center and ask for the password in effect for that minute.

"The second level involved convincing the employees to enable an account for my use on one of their machines, and the third level involved convincing one of the engineers who was already entitled to access one of the computers to give me his password. I overcame that engineer's reluctance to provide the password by convincing him that I was a Motorola employee and that I was looking at a form that documented the password he used to access his personal workstation on Motorola's network—despite the fact that he'd never filled out any such form. Once

I gained access to that machine, I obtained Telnet access to the target machine, access which I had sought all along."

During the presentation, which I covered for *The Register*, I noticed that several Committee members were gradually warming to Mitnick. He's a charming fellow, which I know for a fact because I've had the pleasure of socializing with him, and he was using his skills to charm the Committee as any gifted speaker would do. He wanted to get his message across and he knew exactly how to package it. I've covered scores of these hearings, and many witnesses—particularly bureaucrats—tend to deliver mountains of dry material compiled by an armada of analysts and PR flacks in an enervating monotone. I've seen Members' eyes glaze over during witness testimony more often than it would be polite to mention, but not this time. The Committee *enjoyed* listening to Mitnick. They followed everything he said. They asked questions off the cuff, and with obvious interest. Before the meeting ended, they would be elbowing each other aside to flatter him.

Then-Committee Chairman and character actor Fred Thompson (Republican, Tennessee) called the presentation "short but very powerful."

"As I sit here and listen to you ... if one individual can do what you have done, what in the world could a foreign nation do with all the assets that they would have at their disposal?" Thompson fretted. Mitnick said it would be trivial for a foreign government to plant employees in US government agencies and private corporations who could compromise operating system and application code with back doors, or compromise existing security measures on a network.

The affable Mitnick engaged in lighthearted banter with Thompson, Ranking Member Joseph Lieberman (Democrat, Connecticut), and Member Susan Collins (Republican, Maine), who, recalling his former exploits, observed that he'd "paid a pretty heavy price for the crime."

There was an unmistakable tone in her voice. *Too heavy*, she was thinking. As they were wrapping up, Thompson asked Mitnick a question: "How much time did you actually serve?"

"Fifty-nine months and seven days," he replied.

"Fifty-nine months," Thompson repeated, slowly shaking his head. "Well, you know, if to get your excitement you'd raised millions of dollars for political campaigns, you'd have got probation," he remarked with a chuckle.

Mitnick had hacked the Committee.

Serving Hackers with a Smile

Since paying his debt to society, Mitnick has exchanged his black hat for a white one that he wears as a consultant for Defensive Thinking and as the author of a fascinating book called *The Art of Deception*. Both the consulting outfit and the book are primarily concerned with social engineering, which Mitnick believes is the single most neglected threat in the entire realm of computer security. He may be right, but it's equally possible that SE is brutally effective not because it's neglected but because it is the most difficult type of attack to defend against. The entire game is based on the premise that victims should never suspect they're being manipulated.

When a remote attacker is attempting to gain unauthorized access to a system via the Internet, he must go through several steps to assess or *enumerate* the target, search for vulnerabilities, and pursue an attack strategy. Much of this activity is unusual and can therefore be detected, recognized, and logged. Tools called IDS (intrusion detection systems) automatically monitor networks for signs of attack and alert the admins that some activity resembling one or more known attack profiles might be going on. Even when an attacker is using a novel approach, his activity might well be odd enough to arouse suspicion among sharp admins. Furthermore, good system design and data hygiene can reduce the threat from a remote compromise. Not everyone is as cautious or as proactive as they ought to be, certainly, but there is much that can be done to thwart remote attacks and to limit their impact.

Network intrusion involves some degree of abnormal activity; social engineering attacks don't. They're designed to appear normal, indeed to *be* normal. Sometimes a scenario will involve a set of exceptional circumstances, but the attacker's request or offer of assistance always makes sense within that context. If the victim accepts the attacker's premises, the conclusions will seem reasonable, even inevitable.

The best attacks involve the routine. For example, in August of 2003, two men posing as computer technicians walked into the Sydney International Airport Customs Center and signed in at the security desk with false identification. They then walked, unaccompanied, to a secure mainframe room where they spent approximately two hours dismantling two servers, which they then "put on trolleys and wheeled out of the room, past the security desk, into the lift and out of the building," the *Sydney Morning Herald* reported. The thieves were never challenged. The airport security staff apparently thought nothing of two men wheeling sensitive machinery out of the building and "into the shop" for a bit of maintenance. The machines they took belonged to the Customs Service and may have contained sensitive, even classified, data related to law-enforcement investigations with national security implications, though the Australian government vehemently denies this (as one would expect it to do). According to the government, the stolen machines contained no sensitive data, but considering the care with which the attack was planned and executed, this is unlikely to be true.

The thieves knew which contractor the Customs Service used for computer maintenance, Electronic Data Systems, and impersonated its workers, probably with the right kit, uniforms, badges, *et cetera*. They may have produced a phony work order on EDS stationery. They knew where the mainframe room was located. They apparently knew which machines they wanted to steal. Either they had inside help or they did excellent background research. They asked no questions and aroused no suspicion during the attack. They looked and acted like two techies on a routine service call, so that's how they were treated.

It's debatable whether there are effective countermeasures and policies that could have prevented this attack, but there's no doubt that it could have been made more difficult. A simple system of work-order verification would burden the social engineer. The security desk could keep copies of work orders issued and verify that the vendor's employee had a matching copy. Of course, a good SE hacker would be able to get a work order issued to spec, so that's hardly foolproof, but each layer of security—each obstacle—increases the chance that the hacker will expose himself. A service contractor might issue employee badges with an electronic verification system that their clients could check conveniently with a smart-card reader, say. Again, this is hardly foolproof, but it adds complexity to the attack and therefore increases the chance that the hacker will stumble along the way. A few layers of simple and inexpensive security of this sort can go a long way toward discouraging attacks. Whether it can eliminate them is something I personally doubt, but it is inexcusable to make stealing sensitive equipment as easy as the Sydney Airport's security officers made it.

The problem with countermeasures and security protocols—even smart ones—is that the social engineer directs his efforts not toward defeating them directly, but toward sidestepping them or toward persuading his mark to waive them voluntarily. People will substitute their own judgment for policy when confronted with an exceptional situation. This is human nature, and it's impossible to control.

Social engineers use tactics in a fluid manner. They create scenarios in which their marks are encouraged to believe that they're helping someone in need or that they're doing something that will ease the burden on another employee, especially a superior. To avoid arousing suspicion, they may solicit only a small bit of information from each person they contact in an organization as they work their way toward a goal. Each bit will seem harmless in itself, and each request will fit naturally into the scenario. A competent attacker will research his target thoroughly, familiarizing himself with a company's patents, projects, staff, and published material. Company brochures, SEC filings, white papers, conference schedules, press releases, staff directories, even e-mail news lists—any of these can become a gold mine of information. A clever attacker with good research skills can learn more about a company than most of its employees know, often by using sources available to the public. This knowledge is all he needs to assume airs of familiarity that let him pose realistically as an employee or a business partner.

One rich source of information comes from automated "out-of-the-office" e-mail replies. An attacker might find a directory of employee contact information including everyone's phone extensions and e-mail addresses, perhaps by dumpster-diving, perhaps simply by searching the Web. He can learn who's away by regularly e-mailing the staff and noting the automatic replies he gets, or he might simply discover the company's e-mail naming convention and send a mass mailing from an anonymous account. He may do this periodically to keep tabs on who's on holiday, hoping to attack the assistant or temporary substitute of someone in charge of a project of interest. This forms the basis of a very common attack in which a social engineer claims to have unfinished business with an absent employee, whose replacement is naturally eager to demonstrate his ability to handle matters independently, and so gives the attacker whatever he requires.

Such attacks may be conducted in very small increments involving innocuous queries. For example, an attacker might ring a receptionist at a large company claiming to be a business partner whose usual contact, Jack Jones, is on holiday. A little light banter will help to create a smoke screen while the social engineer fishes for a simple item of data: the person substituting for Jones in his absence, Jill Smith.

With this innocent bit of information, a good social engineer can then approach Smith in the guise of a business partner needing assistance. The attacker will have done his research on Jones and will be prepared to speak about him with assumed familiarity. In this case, he's learned that Jones is a member of a popular anglers' club after searching the Web and locating a number of postings Jones made to the club's online bulletin board.

An exchange might go like this:

Jill: "Hello, Jack Jones' office."

Attacker: "Hello, is this Jill Smith?"

"Yes, this is Jill. How can I help you?"

"Hi, Jill. I'm Joe Jackson from TeknoSolutions. I'm in charge of documentation for the CommerceServer software. Jack was supposed to send us the latest release candidate before he took off on vacation, but I guess it slipped his mind. He seemed pretty eager to get up to Hyannis while the blues are still biting."

Jill laughs. "Oh, our Jack's a devoted fisherman, all right."

"Well, he certainly knows what he's doing. What is it he says? 'Ten percent of the fishermen catch 90 percent of the fish?'"

"Yes, he does say that. Every day, in fact," Jill recalls with a chuckle.

"Well I hate to trouble you Jill, but I've got a few deadlines coming up, and the delay here is becoming a bit of a problem. Is it possible you could help me?"

"Sure ... what is it you need again?"

"I need the source code for the latest release candidate of the CommerceServer software. Jack should have a copy of it on his workstation. I just need you to put it on the FTP site for me so I can grab it."

Jill senses she's in over her head at this point. "Gee, I don't know ... I'd better call Jack about it and have him get back to you."

The attacker doesn't struggle with her but instead gently reinforces the illusion that he and Jack are close, and offers a simple solution: "Well, OK Jill, maybe that's best ... but, you know, I'd sure hate to interrupt his vacation. I can just picture him on the boat, partying on deck and reeling in a prize blue right now, the lucky devil. I'd really feel awful if I interfered with something that important, heh heh. But, you know, I could help you to find the file and upload it without bothering him, if you like."

Jill's thinking. "Well..."

Now she needs just a bit more reassurance: "You can check out our Web site at TeknoSolutions.com," the attacker suggests. He can hear her typing the URL. "That's *teknosolutions*, one word," he adds.

"OK, I have it now," Jill says.

"As you can see," the attacker says, "we've been working closely with your company for quite some time."

Jill clicks on a few links and finds her own company's logo on the Partners page. She notes that Joe Jackson is listed as the managing director and that the Web site makes numerous references to producing software documentation.

All she needs now is a gentle push: "I mean, it's fine if you'd rather leave it to Jack, but we're really falling behind schedule over here and it would be a huge relief if we could get this sorted out now. And I'm sure Jack would appreciate it, too."

And so the deal is closed. "All right," says Jill. "How do I get this file, and what am I supposed to do with it?"

The attacker walks Jill through the process of finding the file and posting it to the company's FTP server. While this is going on, he chats her up lightly to keep her from dwelling on any doubts that might be brewing beneath the surface.

When it's done, the attacker twists the knife a bit. "Thanks so much, Jill. I'll be sure to tell Jack how helpful you've been when he gets back from Hyannis next week."

Jill is left with the impression that she's just done a fabulous job of solving a problem and expediting an important piece of business on her own. She'll be in for a rude awakening when her boss returns, but in the meantime she'll savor the accomplishment with satisfaction.

Analysis

Jill missed several opportunities to avoid being manipulated. Her most obvious omission was failing to authenticate the hacker's presumed identity. This would have required her to consult a company database of employees, vendors, and partners and their authorized contact people. Any company that doesn't make current information of this sort available to *bona fide* employees for quick verification is asking for trouble. Of course, making it available and ensuring that it's used are two different things. The first is easy, the second not quite so. But it is crucial that employees verify the identities of people who contact them before divulging any sensitive information. Thus, a database of legitimate contacts, along with their e-mail addresses and phone numbers, is essential, so long as it's protected from access by unauthorized users. If there's any doubt about the person calling, the employee should ask to ring them back on one of their established phone numbers. Social engineers have a number of ruses to deal with this sort of obstacle, chief among them the old "I've been called away from the office on urgent business and I'm using my cell phone" con, but employees must hold firm. If the caller asks to be rung on a number that isn't on the authorized contact list, the conversation needs to stop there and then.

Even an internal phone number is not to be trusted. Kevin Mitnick tells the story of how he once persuaded a company administrator to set up a voice mail account for him on the internal system. The person he later manipulated took that as evidence that he was a fellow employee. In fact, it was evidence of nothing except Mitnick's extraordinary talent and resourcefulness.

Jill's second opportunity to avoid trouble would have been to verify the attacker's implied relationship with her boss. She missed that one, too. There is *no* reason to believe that one person is acquainted with another merely because he seems to know a good deal. The Internet and the commercial privacy invasion industry have made research into people's personal lives enormously easy. The attacker was being clever when he referred to Jack's motto about a few fishermen pulling in the lion's share of the catch. It's a very common expression and *most* fishermen like to say it, though to Jill it seemed like a detail that only a personal acquaintance would know. Too bad she wasn't an angler herself.

There is no such company as TeknoSolutions (though there is a Tekno-Solutions.com based in Luxembourg). Jill did a quick Web search for it, but the attacker was prepared for that. He'd simply registered `TeknoSolutions.com` anonymously. It's not difficult to register a domain while obscuring one's true identity: indeed, using a stolen credit card makes it a snap. The attacker then ran up a quick Web site on his domain for deceptive purposes. The site made much of the fake company's experience in producing software documentation; it listed the attacker's alias, Joe Jackson, as the primary contact; and it advertised Jill's company as a partner, along with several others for appearances' sake. Simply finding a site on the Web is not an adequate means of verification; *anyone* can put up a Web site.

Let Me Help

At the H2K security conference in New York in 2002, I and about 500 other audience members listened as Eric Corley, a.k.a. Emmanuel Goldstein, publisher of the *2600* hacker 'zine, manipulated an employee at a local Starbucks over the phone. Corley impersonated a technician "from network operations" and within minutes convinced the employee that there was a problem with the store's credit card terminal that required him to read back the last two transactions, including the card numbers, cardholder names, and expiration dates. The "network technician" needed to know if the last several transactions had been processed. The employee was pleased to be of assistance. He didn't question the technician: he didn't ask for proof that he was who he claimed to be; he didn't wonder why some network geek would need names and credit card numbers when the dollar amounts of the last few sales would suffice to indicate whether or not the transactions had gone through.

Corley was personable but authoritative, subtly establishing himself as a fellow employee who outranked his victim. He used a fair bit of technical doubletalk that sounded plausible on the surface but didn't quite add up. In this way, he showed the audience that the targets of SE hacks will often cooperate even when the logic behind the manipulation doesn't hold up to scrutiny. The Starbucks victim didn't stop to verify anything he was told or to question any of Corley's requests because he wanted to cooperate and help a fellow employee—especially one who seemed to know a good deal more than he did.

The Servility Olympics

Why are people so compliant? Because they're paid to be. Let me digress briefly: about a year ago, I received a phone call from my bank. I was asked if I might reply to a questionnaire meant to improve customer service. Since I have a personal stake in my bank's quality of service, I agreed to participate in the survey. The questions that were asked, and more importantly, those that weren't, revealed several peculiar assumptions the bank had made about its customers' priorities. Nearly every question was meant to solicit my judgment as to whether, in my daily dealings with the staff, my bum was being kissed adequately.

Do the employees at my branch recognize me and address me by name? Am I greeted properly at the door? Do they smile sincerely? Are they helpful? Do they make me feel welcome? And so on. None of this interests me at all, but it appeared to be the bank's sole basis for evaluating itself. I was never asked if I thought the bank gave good value for money, for example, or if I had ever discovered clerical errors in my monthly statements. The bank seemed only to want assurance that its employees were prostrating themselves before me whenever I condescended to present myself at the local branch.

After giving the staff high marks on all these irrelevant criteria, I was asked which service-related issues concern me personally. "The increasing cost of doing business with the bank, the numerous 'service charges' for just about everything I do, and accuracy and efficiency among the people who handle my money," I replied. "I don't go to the bank to socialize, enjoy tea and biscuits, get my neck massaged or my ego stroked. I go there to sort out my finances. When I want to be surrounded by people who've been paid to flatter me, I'll go to a massage parlor. . . ."

The interviewer laughed, leaving me with the impression that several customers had likewise ridiculed the bank's quest of capturing gold in the Servility Olympics. But this is a major element of modern commercial culture. Companies reward their staff for being cooperative and accommodating. Whether employees keep their wits about them at all times is not always such a high priority.

In the corporate world, we're expected to be team players, obedient to those in authority and cooperative with our peers when the company's interests are at stake. Employee evaluations emphasize such qualities as a positive attitude, leadership abilities, and a professional appearance. Rarely do we find employees lauded heartily for, say, their robust sense of self-respect and personal dignity or because they can detect the merest whiff of sophistry a mile away or because they adhere courageously to the principles of moral theology. On the contrary, the typical corporate evaluation boils down to something like this: "Bob is a model employee—a well-groomed eunuch who believes everything senior management tells him. Bob follows complex instructions without supervision, meets deadlines with pluck, and conducts himself with obsequious courtesy at all times. He is a devoted team player utterly devoid of doubt, personal flair, or independent moral reasoning."

In the commercial world, and especially in fields such as retail marketing and the restaurant, hotel, and tourist industries, an employee's servility toward customers is generally valued more than his competence. Of course, no human resources manager actually tells prospective employees that the company is looking chiefly for obedience and bland conformity in its staff, but the system of rewards and punishments in the business world generally favors the accommodating and the gullible. Cynics are rarely at an advantage in the promotions process.

We are all trained to be cooperative in an increasingly service-based economy. People at work simply have got to cooperate if anything is to be accomplished. Thus, the pressure to conform and to subvert our sense of reality to an organization's "mission" and "culture" is constant and inescapable. Even the strongest among us are affected by it, and this is one reason why social engineers get the better of us every day.

"I Send You This File in Order to Have Your Advice"

Social engineering plays an indispensable role in many kinds of attack. It can be as complex as some meticulously scripted *Mission Impossible*–style sting involving several people, during which an outsider infiltrates a company and makes off with valuable intellectual property, or as simple as the wording of an infected e-mail memo encouraging recipients to activate a malicious payload.

"I send you this file in order to have your advice," the popular SirCam e-mail worm announced to potential victims. In spite of its awkward phrasing, which we might call a good example of bad social engineering, the worm was highly successful. Its success was due in part to a different bit of social engineering that worked better: using the Outlook and Outlook Express address books found on infected hosts to spread itself further. When SirCam arrived, it often appeared to come from a contact known to the victim, who was then more likely to activate the infected file attachment in spite of its somewhat clumsy subject line. There was also a bit of good technical engineering: using its own SMTP (Simple Mail Transfer Protocol) engine to propagate as a background process, without drawing attention to itself.

Another reason why it succeeded is the fact that many Internet users speak English as a second language and don't immediately recognize subtle defects in grammar, spelling, and syntax. English may be the *lingua franca* of the Net, but only a minority of Netizens know it as their mother tongue. People who speak English as a second language are, naturally, easier to take in with poorly composed e-mail inviting them to open an attachment or log on to a malicious Web site, especially when they recognize the sender. Still, SirCam became a burden to networks throughout North America, the British Isles and Ireland, and Australia and New Zealand, so the odd phrasing didn't attract suspicion as often as it should have among native Anglophones. Even the FBI's crack team of elite cybersleuths at the National Infrastructure Protection Center (NIPC) managed to infect their own networks with the worm, much to the security community's amusement.

There are other forms of social engineering used in malicious e-mail every day. One popular tactic for virus spreaders is to mass-mail an infected memo in which a malicious file is presented as a system patch or an antivirus update. One that recently turned up in my inbox offers to immunize me from the Klez e-mail worm with an attached file called FixKlez.com and claims to come from Japanese AV outfit Trend Micro, though a check of the header shows that it originated from an ISP in Kuwait. Still, most users don't bother to check e-mail headers or trace the originating IP, and this one might have fooled a lot of recipients with its return mail address, "Trend Micro av_patch@trendmicro.com," which is all that most recipients would see. That much of the social engineering was good; the rest was laughable.

The body of the memo read: "Klez.H is the most common world-wide spreading worm. It's very dangerous by corrupting your files. Because of its very smart stealth and anti-anti-virus technic, most common AV software can't detect or clean it. We developed this free immunity tool to defeat the malicious virus. You only need to run this tool once, and then Klez will never come into your PC."

The memo's pidgin English sends up a warning flare to any native Anglophone, but remember, only a minority of Netizens *are* native Anglophones. We would expect the Tokyo-based Trend Micro to be slick enough to communicate in English, and quite good English at that, but those who know the language only from textbooks are unlikely to see that the wording here is outlandish. Millions of users might well be taken in by our Kuwaiti script kiddies.

There are virus e-mails, and then there are hoaxes. Several times a year, some script kiddie sends a hoax e-mail purportedly from America Online CEO Steve Case to millions of AOL users and directs them to confirm their billing details on a malicious Web site where passwords and credit card details will be harvested. Usually there are idiomatic blunders and spelling mistakes and bad punctuation to tip off the recipients, but these will be ignored by at least a fraction of them. The sheer improbability that the CEO of a company the size of AOL would busy himself with minor clerical details is likewise ignored. Some people will click on virtually anything presented to them. If a few million such e-mails are sent out, perhaps a few thousand victims will respond, however bad the social engineering might be.

As for the hoax Web sites, these are painfully easy to create. It's trivial to design a malicious site that looks exactly like the original by copying the HTML source and images from relevant pages and uploading these files, with slight modifications, to a different server. Even the URL can be crafted to give an impression of authenticity by obtaining a domain such as `www.aol-acounts.com`, if no such domain happens to be registered. URL redirection can also be employed. A simple page with the right layout and logos inviting victims to log in and "update" their billing information is all that's needed. The data entered can be forwarded automatically to an e-mail *dead drop* for later retrieval by the scammer.

eBay and its PayPal subsidiary are also constant targets of such e-mail hoaxes. Users are advised that their accounts are about to expire or have been misused by others, or that some database glitch has led to the loss of customer data that must be restored immediately by following a link handily provided. Usually there is poor spelling and punctuation, and awkward, un-idiomatic phrasing, but still these ploys bear fruit. One shudders to think what a professional copywriter fluent in commercialese might accomplish with such an approach.

Instant messaging provides another friendly environment in which amateur social engineers flourish. Networks can be flooded with phony alerts from Microsoft, other software vendors, or even an ISP urging that a system patch be downloaded and installed immediately. It should be clear to most Netizens that companies *do not* launch security bulletins via IM and never send patches or requests for billing information via e-mail, but novice users and children are sometimes taken in by these ploys. Another concern is that someone you chat with regularly and perceive as friendly may decide to send you an infected file, trading on trust. Remember, instant messaging and IRC are a vast, electronic masquerade, and should be enjoyed as such. Never forget that people can pretend to be anyone they choose. Unless you know the person you're chatting with in real life and have reason to trust him, you should assume that you don't know him at all. All files from IM chat and IRC companions should be scanned before being activated. It makes no difference what the file extension is or appears to be. It makes no difference how long you've known the person offering it. Unless you're chatting with a real-life friend, you really have no idea who you're dealing with.

Spammers tend to be a good deal more sophisticated than script kiddies when it comes to social engineering. One particularly clever spam e-mail comes from a Web site called Word-of-Mouth.org, which trades in gossip and entices victims to spend 20 dollars to learn what's being said about them.

The bait is usually an e-mail "alert" claiming that "someone has just performed a search for Word-of-Mouth Reports about you at our Web site. Please see the link below to view the search results."

Another version of the spam message reads: "An acquaintance of yours recently conducted a search on your e-mail address in our online community, Word-of-Mouth.org. It could be a friend, a family member, co-worker, business associate, or someone else who's interested in learning more about you."

A more recent version of the same memo comes from WOMC Support support@womexch.org, claiming that "someone has just begun to research your background via our Web site. This email has been automatically sent to you so as to make you aware that your background is being looked into."

The Web sites purportedly help people locate gossip written by acquaintances whose identities are hidden. It's natural for us to be curious about what gossip is being spread about us, so this is a fairly sophisticated attack. The Word-of-Mouth site (now, apparently, the womexch site) doesn't actually host any of this information; instead, it compiles "reports" indicating that someone claims to have information to share and sells access to a "secure e-mail system" that enables users to request the info from one another without revealing their identity. This is smart, because it appears to confer legitimacy: it makes sense to suggest that the system works best when all parties are anonymous to each other. The "reporter" is protected from retaliation, and the "subject" is able to request information that the reporter might resist providing if they knew who was asking.

The Web site operators avoid libel suits by not hosting the actual information advertised, and they avoid prosecution as cheats by not promising anything more than access to an e-mail system and the pseudonymous e-mail addresses of those who are whispering behind one's back. The 20 dollars does in fact buy something. But the anonymous "reporters" aren't obliged to reply to a query, obviously, so the scammers can't be held liable for failure along those lines. Of the people taken in by this ploy whom I've been able to locate, not one has ever received a satisfactory reply from a contact claiming to have information about them. It's likely that the site operators are the ones generating the so-called "reports" and that no further information exists. However, the operators will be difficult to prosecute, since it must be proven that they *know* that no such information exists. Clearly, a good deal of thought went into this little social-engineering scam.

Good social engineering can boost the effectiveness of almost any computer-based or Internet-based attack. A couple of years ago, a group of whitehat hackers conducted an SE sting against online pedophiles. Legal pictures of naked girls—not pornography under most legal definitions but material attractive to pedos—were placed on a free Web site. This was the bait. Also on the Web site were links to several "lolita" bulletin boards and one particular link to a malicious Web site operated by the hackers, where privacy and anonymity tools were reportedly on offer.

Offering legal pictures—so-called lolita or "loli" images with no sexual content—shielded the hackers from running afoul of rather Draconian laws meant to discourage the kiddie porn trade. In most jurisdictions, images that don't sexualize children are legal even if they involve nudity. (If this weren't the case, innocent family snapshots of children bathing would become contraband.) But the hackers knew that pedophiles would be attracted to the nonsexual photos they offered, and they were confident that many visitors would check out the links on their page.

The link to the malicious site was buried among several others so as not to stand out in any way. Pedophiles are a paranoid lot, being universally reviled, and tools promising anonymity and privacy would undoubtedly attract a number of those who had visited the "bait" site. The malicious site was nondescript, offering links to numerous anonymity services and several file downloads, one of which was infected with a rootkit.

The social engineering was good; the hackers didn't try to influence their victims. Rather, they allowed them to stumble upon a malicious file by following a series of links. While this meant that a certain percentage of visitors would never become infected, they also knew that any effort to push them toward a particular download would raise suspicion among characteristically paranoid and cautious pedophiles.

It gets better. The infected file was a copy of Moosoft's utility called The Cleaner, a program that locates and disables hundreds of Trojan rootkits. The Cleaner was infected with a copy of the SubSeven server. Making it work was simple; the hackers used an old version of The Cleaner and infected it with a new version of SubSeven. The Cleaner version they distributed was unable to detect the SubSeven version with which it had been infected. Yet The Cleaner would install and work normally (except for that one crucial omission), which helped to allay suspicion.

The SubSeven servers were configured to alert the hackers in an IRC channel they'd set up for the sting. As infected victims connected to the Internet, they automatically and unknowingly joined the channel, and the hackers began rooting their machines. They would search for hardcore kiddie porn, and, if they found any, search for the computer owner's personal details. Most people have at least a résumé stored on their machines, so it wasn't difficult to get detailed information on each pervert—name, address, date of birth, place of business, and the like. This information, along with evidence of the contraband, would then be forwarded anonymously to law enforcement authorities near the victim's place of residence. In some jurisdictions, evidence obtained illegally by private citizens can be presented in court even though the same evidence, were it obtained by the authorities, would be inadmissible.

Whether the sting resulted in any prosecutions is unknown. Not even the hackers involved can say because they used anonymous e-mail services to communicate with law enforcement. The bait or "loli" site they created may have been barely legal, but breaking into people's computers is a serious crime, and they needed to keep their distance from the authorities. Whether it succeeded or not, it's an example of effective social engineering, as well as an example of hackers using their skills to attempt something worthwhile, though it involved illegal activity.

The P2P Hustle

Sometimes social engineering can be extremely subtle. In Chapter 2, we considered several privacy and security problems associated with P2P file-sharing utilities such as Morpheus and KaZaA. The vendors of these applications encourage users to act against their own interests in setting up the software. For example, the KaZaA utility from Sharman Networks installs itself with unlimited bandwidth use and super-node status enabled by default. These features are unsafe, exposing users to possible retaliation from the RIAA for copyright violation and from one's own ISP for exceeding bandwidth use limits. But it is very much in Sharman Networks' interests that users leave these settings enabled, because they help make the KaZaA system work for everyone: they improve the collective user experience. However, it is definitely not in *your* interest to leave these features enabled. While the KaZaA options dialog permits users to change the settings, they are located under the Advanced tab in the options dialog, at the top of which is a warning that reads: "Only change these advanced settings when you know what they mean." The purpose of this bit of fake wisdom is to discourage tinkering. It's no doubt hoped that novice users will assume that altering these settings can cause harm. Actually, *not altering them* can cause harm. This is a classic social engineering attack, quite gentle and seemingly harmless.

The Unknown Unknown

Social engineering carries risks and threats that are difficult to anticipate, hence difficult to prevent. Often, we can make educated guesses about the threat and risk levels of most attacks and deploy countermeasures to reduce them. But the fluid nature of social engineering attacks makes them particularly resistant to prediction: they only work when they're not detected until the damage is done. Sometimes they're never detected at all. A home user who's installed a piece of spyware that also functions as a handy utility is unlikely to realize that his computer is leaking data. A company whose trade secrets have fallen into a competitor's hands may never figure out how it happened. An IT manager may suspect that a network penetration occurred when in fact an employee innocently cooperated with someone they thought was a network engineer.

There are four sorts of vulnerabilities, often categorized as follows:

- The *known known:* We know RPC is vulnerable and we know that we have RPC running.

- The *known unknown:* We know we're vulnerable to undocumented vulnerabilities.

- The *unknown known:* There are some known vulnerabilities on our system that we haven't yet identified.

- The *unknown unknown:* Vulnerabilities we haven't spotted and that we would not recognize as such if we did spot them.

In one of the previous examples, we postulated that a receptionist innocently told an attacker whom to contact in Jack Jones' absence. It's unlikely that such a mundane occurrence would ever be documented, so it's unknown in the sense that only the receptionist is aware that it happened. But even if it had been documented, it would hardly arouse suspicion. In that sense, it's unknown, or unrecognized, as a vulnerability. Of course, it provided an attacker with the basis for an effective ruse full of sympathy for the vacationing Jones. Social engineers specialize in exploiting the unknown unknown.

There are other things we don't know about SE hacks: most importantly, the actual threats and risks associated with them. Risks and threats are two different things, and they need to be understood, and managed, separately. Let's look briefly at how they differ.

Mad Cows

A *threat* is a bad thing that can happen. A *risk* is the likelihood that a bad thing will happen. Let's consider a few real-world examples that illustrate the distinction.

In 2003, it was revealed that at least one head of cattle in Canada and at least one in the United States were infected with BSE (Bovine Spongiform Encephalopathy), a disease that can cause a deadly illness in humans called vCJD (variant Creutzfeldt-Jakob disease). In this case, the *threat* is catastrophic: certain death. vCJD, unfortunately, has a mortality rate of 100 percent. But the *risk* is something else altogether. In fact, you can eliminate the risk by eating no meat if you can tolerate it (animals infected with BSE are believed to be the only vector of vCJD), or you can reduce the risk by eating meat from animals fed on a vegetable diet if you can afford it. (Animals that don't eat meat or meat by-products are believed unlikely to contract BSE.)

In this case, you cannot manage the threat at all: vCJD *will* kill you. There is nothing you can do to make it less lethal. The *threat* of certain death from vCJD is entirely out of your hands, but the *risk* that you'll contract it is something you can manage quite well.

We find the inverse situation in car safety. There, we can manage the threat of bodily injury from crashes by using seat belts and air bags and by reducing speed. All of these steps will reduce injury during a crash, and so reduce the *threat* of a crash. Unlike vCJD, car crashes can indeed be made less lethal. Thus, the threat can be managed.

However, seat belts and air bags have no effect on the *risk* of a crash, and reducing speed only some effect (driving more slowly improves the chance of avoiding a collision). Safety equipment like seat belts and air bags don't affect risk, which in this case is a function of your driving skills and relative fitness to drive (e.g., eyesight, fatigue, drunkenness, etc.), other motorists' actions and their fitness to drive, road conditions, traffic density, weather, visibility, your car's mechanical condition, and scores of other factors. Assessing risk is different from assessing a threat, and mitigating the risk in this case has nothing to do with air bags and seat belts, though mitigating the threat does.

When you decline to drive on a snowy night because visibility and traction are poor and your car is getting old, you're performing a risk assessment whether you realize it or not. You're deciding that whatever you stand to gain from driving isn't worth the risk of a collision under those conditions. But the threat hasn't changed: it remains suffering or causing bodily injury. That threat is exactly the same when you drive casually to the market on a sunny afternoon. However, the *risk* of a collision will have changed considerably.

Both risk assessment and threat assessment depend on reliable information. For example, experts believe that BSE is rare in North America, but we don't actually test many cattle. (In the U.S., only so-called "downers," or animals too sick to stand, are currently tested before being slaughtered.) We don't test more aggressively because we don't believe the risk is significant. But it's possible that we don't believe the risk to be significant *because* we don't test. In other words, we're not finding it because we're not looking for it. Incomplete or weak information makes an assessment equally incomplete and weak. Since there is no such thing as perfectly comprehensive information, but only better or worse information, we can only make educated guesses and choose sensible compromises.

Safety and security compromises depend on many variables: the value of the asset to be protected, the potential of the threat to cause harm; the risk that the threat will emerge; the cost in money, time, and convenience of securing the asset or avoiding the threat; and one's own sense of risk tolerance. Such compromises often come down to very personal choices. For example, I don't know how serious the risk of contracting vCJD in North America happens to be. I do know that BSE exists in cattle, but until a more aggressive testing regimen is instituted I can't estimate the risk that I might encounter it. So I've made a safety compromise based on personal criteria. For me, going without meat would be intolerable. My solution is to play the odds conservatively, buying and cooking meats primarily from animals fed on a vegetable diet. Meat that I buy and cook at home accounts for about 80 percent of what I consume, so I can control that much. The rest comes from the kitchens of restaurants and friends. I'm accepting an unknown risk from this 20 percent of meat that I consume, knowing that it might come from animals fed on meat products, which is riskier. I accept the risk because I'm unwilling to limit my choice of restaurant to those serving meat exclusively from grass- or grain-fed animals, and I'm equally unwilling to make dietary demands on people who've invited me to their table or to treat with suspicion a dish that someone has gone to the trouble of preparing for me. And I cheat, too. When my local supermarket runs a discount on meats, I stock up regardless of what the animals might have been fed. I'm not going to pass up a good sale.

My goal is to *reduce* my exposure to meat cut from animals fed on animals, that is, to reduce the risk of contracting vCJD, but not to eliminate it because that would require compromises I'm unwilling to make. Thus, I've accepted a compromise in food safety because I'm unwilling to make other compromises affecting my social life and my household budget. Security and safety always involve such compromises. At some point, each of us has got to make an individual decision based on an equally personal evaluation of the threats, the risks, and the costs.

If better information about BSE were available, I might alter my compromise, making it more liberal or more restrictive as the data suggest. For example, if rigorous testing were implemented and I learned that only one in 30 million cattle showed signs of BSE, I might take no precautions at all. On the other hand, if I learned that one in 50,000 cattle were affected, I would be tempted to emigrate. But for now, given what I know and what I don't know, I'm comfortable with the compromise I'm making. The point here is not to discuss my diet, but to illustrate that each of us has got his own, individual sense of risk tolerance that affects thousands of choices we make every day. In response to BSE, you might make no adjustments in your diet or you might make more restrictive ones than I would choose to make. And that's as it should be.

Using, maintaining, and relying on a computer system involves threats and risks too, and these need to be appreciated separately and assessed individually, always on the basis of good information. But we must always accept compromises between security and convenience. A computer locked in a vault with no Internet connection is quite secure, but it's tremendously inconvenient to use and certainly no fun. In order to enjoy your computer and use it productively, you will have to accept risks and, in so doing, expose yourself to threats. The goal of good security is to mitigate both threats and risks without making the whole affair more trouble than it's worth. Security, then, involves the art of making informed, sensible compromises in which personal criteria play a significant role.

That's tough enough, but social engineering operates outside the realm of risk assessment and informed compromise. The threat can be anything from installing an irritating but nondestructive virus to the involuntary sharing of a decade's worth of R&D with a competitor. The risk is similarly unknown. What is the chance that someone will attack you in this manner? Might they use an insider for assistance? Might they be able to pass themselves off as an employee? A contractor? A business partner?

What would be the attacker's motive? Revenge? Politics? Profit? There are so many variables that one can never anticipate them. Security professionals recommend awareness training for staff, but it's debatable whether such training is effective against any but the more mediocre social engineers. Remember, the social engineer is a chameleon, and his job is to convince victims that no danger exists and that caution and suspicion are therefore unnecessary. If he's good at it, he'll likely have his way in the end.

Countermeasures

To defend against the unknown unknown, we can only hope to establish *security protocols* that will draw the attacker into a situation that exceeds his own risk tolerance without inconveniencing ourselves or spending too much money. After all, it makes no sense to spend $1000 to prevent the loss of $500.

Unfortunately, good social engineers attack in so many creative ways that the threat must be assessed as the worst that can happen. This means that when the assets needing protection are valuable, overspending on security is difficult—sometimes impossible—to avoid. For example, gambling casinos typically spend more to prevent cheating than they actually lose to cheats, but if they didn't, their losses would soon become crippling. Casinos have no choice but to overspend on security, because the threat of heavy financial losses to cheats and the risk of being cheated are both high. The slightest weakness will be exploited immediately, ruthlessly, and repeatedly. Fortunately for the casinos, their profit margins easily accommodate security excesses, though few others in business enjoy such luxury.

Defending against a social engineer is very much like defending against a casino cheat. It's impossible to predict the threat (how much money can we lose?) or the risk (how many cheats can beat us undetected?), so it's almost impossible to be too secure.

Of course, the more complicated an attack needs to must be, the greater the attacker's risk of being foiled or caught. At some point, the risk to him becomes too great in terms of the value of the accomplishment or the asset sought. But where is that point? It varies according to the value of the assets you're defending and the motives of the attackers you're likely to attract. When it comes to SE attacks, it's virtually impossible to estimate this accurately. It's tempting, perhaps even necessary, to err on the side of overprotectiveness.

A wary home user is likely to foil the majority of SE hacks directed at him because most will come from script kiddies and spammers and will involve hoax e-mails from Bill Gates and Steve Case, and malware spread via e-mail, IM, and P2P sharing. The home user usually has assets that are moderately to barely valuable; no serious hacker is going to spend his time stealing a couple of credit card numbers off a PC. That's the stuff of script kiddies. However, if an attacker has a personal motive, he could be quite determined against even a home user and might be willing to assume some risk to get his point across.

In the business world, the best defense is for employees to remain aware that they may be manipulated at any time. This means that security protocols have got to be followed, *especially* when good reasons are given to waive them. The social engineer is an expert at persuading people to circumvent security protocols on his behalf.

It's up to everyone to verify the identity of those seeking information, even when the request seems innocent or the reason seems compelling. It's up to management to make it easy for staff to do this. Company directories should be accessible to all *bona fide* employees for a quick search and should contain the e-mail addresses and phone numbers of all fellow employees, contractors, and partners. Anyone not on the list, or anyone who claims to have an e-mail address or a phone number different from what's on file, should be treated as an outsider. Obviously, it's crucial that any such database be updated regularly to prevent unnecessary delays in handling legitimate requests. It must also be protected from access by outsiders. If access can't be regulated effectively, then the database becomes another weapon in the social engineer's arsenal.

Vendors, contractors, and partners should be expected to provide some measure of security at their end so that people claiming to represent them can be identified with a reasonable level of confidence. There's no magic bullet here, but a verification scheme for visitor identification will make the social engineer's job more complex and difficult, hence more risky. So will mandatory digital signatures for e-mail correspondence. Again, it's virtually impossible to come up with any sort of metric, but, generally speaking, increasing the attacker's level of risk reduces his level of encouragement. The difficulty comes in anticipating the actual method of attack, which, in the realm of social engineering, is limited only by the hacker's imagination and resourcefulness.

Return on investment is always difficult to calculate for security. Nothing bad may happen for quite some time, yet you can't determine whether that's because your security is working or because you've been lucky. Social engineering makes this even more difficult. Something bad may well happen at the hands of an expert SE hacker, yet you might never discover it.

Inexpensive, common-sense defenses on the job include being extremely stingy with information over the phone, via e-mail, and even face to face with people whose identities have not been established. People wandering the halls should be challenged regardless of their dress: an attacker might look like an executive, a repairman, or even a security guard. The proper accoutrements, whether a Brooks Brothers' suit or a Federal Express uniform, are *no* indication of a stranger's identity. A well-controlled system for issuing visitor badges comes a lot closer to the mark, though it's hardly foolproof because badges can be lost, stolen, or forged.

At home, the social-engineering threat is lower, and so is the risk. It's unlikely that the typical home user will become the target of an elaborate SE attack. The most common concerns are being manipulated by a contact known only through instant messaging, IRC, or Internet forums, and being taken in by a hoax e-mail or a bogus security alert.

However, there are home users who make very handsome targets for sophisticated attackers. Former CIA Director John Deutch should know. He stored an incredible 17,000 pages of classified intelligence data on his home computers, according to a report by the Office of the Inspector General (OIG) released in February of 2000.

Adversaries could simply have broken into his house and stolen the machines, though that would have aroused considerable alarm. More easily, attackers could have bamboozled his domestic servant, who typically remained in residence while the family was away, with the sort of technicians-on-call scam used recently against the Australian Customs Service.

"Such an entry operation would not have posed a particularly difficult challenge, had a sophisticated operation been launched by opposition forces," the OIG report noted.

The data improperly stored on Deutch's computers included CIA budget information, confidential communications with the President, and details of secret military and paramilitary operations. Deutch later appeared before a closed session of the Senate Intelligence Committee to explain how this sensitive information found its way onto his home PCs. Meanwhile, OIG doubted it would be possible to estimate the damage to national security from this little snafu, as Deutch deleted considerable data from his computers once he realized he was under suspicion for mishandling classified information.

So it is indeed possible that a person known to handle valuable data on the job might be targeted by sophisticated attackers at home. The average Netizen won't be, but people in government, academia, and industry who have access to sensitive information or who are involved in research can become targets. Defense is difficult because an attack can come from almost any direction, possibly involving tradesmen, guests, or even a housekeeper, tutor, or nanny. Even those who normally act with caution in the workplace may drop their guard at home, where they naturally feel safe, leaving themselves more vulnerable than usual.

A former Director of Central Intelligence did just that, although he, more than anyone, should have known better. Stealing classified data from Deutch's office at CIA headquarters in Langley, Virginia, would have been the social engineering attack of the century. Stealing it from his home computers would have been an acceptable challenge for a group of talented SE hackers with a modicum of patience and a bit of money to spend on uniform rentals and fake ID cards.

If social engineering sounds more like espionage than computer hacking, it should. It's hardly a coincidence that SE grandmaster Kevin Mitnick's mobile phone rings with the theme music from *Mission Impossible*.

CHAPTER 4

From Newbie to Power User

So far, we've learned about the most common methods of attack and the system weaknesses most often exploited, and we've taken steps to improve security: installing Mozilla on Windows, disabling unnecessary services, removing or replacing insecure clients, and setting up a multiuser system with sensible permissions. These steps are meant to simplify our systems so that during an attack or under the influence of malware, fewer things can be made to go wrong. We've been relying on *passive defense*: narrowing our target profile and removing unnecessary features that attackers and malware can leverage against us. But there is more to security than denying assistance to attackers; there are, in fact, a number of deliberate steps we can take to monitor our systems, investigate suspicious behavior, and take action. In this chapter, we'll learn about tools of *active defense* that we can use to enhance security and thwart attacks.

For example, setting a tough password on a Web-mail account is a passive defense; with it, we reduce the risk that some script kiddie will gain unauthorized access with a dictionary attack. But this is a step we take once and forget. There's nothing further to be done; it simply helps, and the tougher the password is, the more it helps. However, there is an active defense that goes hand-in-hand with Web-mail security: we can use an encryption utility like PGP or GnuPG (GPG) so that if the account should be compromised, the attacker will be unable to read any of the memos we've chosen to protect. Encrypting e-mail is an example of an active defense: it's something you do deliberately each time you compose a memo. It's not something you do all the time, of course. Some of our correspondence isn't worth encrypting, though a fair portion of it certainly is: medical, financial, and proprietary business information and intimate personal details all need to be encrypted when they're sent via e-mail.

NOTE *Many privacy advocates and security professionals recommend encrypting all e-mail and local documents as a matter of routine to avoid revealing to attackers and snoops which items are especially valuable.*

E-mail is not private. A memo is bounced around the Internet, passing through numerous routers, servers, and proxies, until it reaches its destination. Along the way, any sysadmin whose equipment it happens to pass through can read it. E-mail works on the Internet the way a postcard works in the physical world. A postcard is handled by several people along its route, any of whom is welcome to read it. Indeed, e-mail is *less* private than a postcard because it indicates who sent it as well as who's to receive it, whereas a postcard rarely has a return address. The sender of a postcard is anonymous by default; the sender of an e-mail is not. Anyone handling an e-mail memo along its route can read the text and identify both its sender and its intended recipient. Encryption makes it impossible for third parties to read it in transit.

Another example of an active defense is running a packet sniffer, such as Ethereal, or a simple network monitor, like Netstat, on your network or Internet connection occasionally to observe inbound and outbound traffic. Netstat will report all of your connections, and Ethereal will reveal the contents of every packet crossing your network interface. In Chapter 2, we learned about several passive defense measures to reduce the number of routes by which unauthorized network or Internet traffic can be sent and received. But this sort of defense, while an essential element of security, can protect us only when the system and the threats to it remain static. Unfortunately, both are constantly developing: new vulnerabilities and methods of attack are continually being discovered and malware is constantly being introduced, while our systems are regularly being updated with hotfixes, patches, new versions of software, and firmware that may undo steps we've taken to simplify the system. Sometimes changes are performed in the background automatically without the owner's knowledge, as with automatic updates; sometimes a patch will make changes in an unexpected area; and sometimes a virus or other malware concealed in a software program will reenable insecure services that you've disabled.

Suppose you've just upgraded an Internet client such as an IM program, but, unknown to you, the new version is infected with adware. Or suppose you've disabled file sharing on your Windows machine as I've recommended, but later you encounter malware like the recent Swen worm that reenables it and uses it to propagate. A network-monitoring tool will alert you to these changes.

Of course, you do have to activate the tool and interpret its output, which is why it's an active defense, but doing so from time to time is the best way to detect network-related changes made without your knowledge by new software, patches, or malware. Network monitoring will also tell you which ports to block or which services to disable when unexpected and undesirable changes occur. Unfortunately, unexpected changes happen all too often as computer systems grow increasingly network-centric and interconnected. Even high-profile, trusted vendors may make undocumented changes to your system that turn out to be in their interest, not yours, and raise security and privacy concerns.

For example, in April of 2002 I reported in *The Register* a deceptive "critical update" from Microsoft designed to make Windows Messenger difficult to remove, and even to replace it on machines from which it had been eliminated. Microsoft wants all Windows users to be plugged in to its MSN Messenger and Passport services whether they wish to or not, because some in the company have identified Web services, not software, as the best long-term source of revenue.

The so-called critical item in this case was the Windows Messenger 4.6 Connectivity Update. It was presented via Windows Update as an important, and broadly beneficial, system patch. Microsoft "strongly recommends that you download the update *even if you don't use Windows Messenger*" the description said [my emphasis]. It's that last bit, claiming that the patch is critical even for those who don't use Messenger, that qualifies this as a social engineering attack. Reading that line, one would naturally believe that the fix was good for everyone using Windows.

A related Microsoft Knowledge Base article further assured users that "to improve connectivity and system performance, *even if you do not use Windows Messenger*, Microsoft recommends that you install this update."

Again, the patch was touted as generally beneficial. It was designed to "improve connectivity and *system performance*." Naturally, most users would be persuaded to download and install it, thinking, innocently, that they might get a faster computer or a more reliable Internet connection as a result.

Unfortunately, no one who trusted Microsoft actually got better connectivity or system performance. The only thing the critical update did was reinstall Messenger on machines from which it had been removed, update Messenger on computers still running it, and integrate this new version into the Outlook Express e-mail client. *That* is what Microsoft meant by "improving connectivity and system performance." The wording was patently deceptive, and the patch entirely self-serving.

Ironically, the critical update, which offered no value to people who don't use Messenger (in spite of Microsoft's assurances to the contrary), actually caused *performance degradation* on machines whose owners later dared disable Messenger. In that case, Microsoft's "performance enhancement" would cause Outlook Express to load very, very slowly. Apparently, Outlook Express insists on exhausting all possible means of loading Messenger before launching itself. Disabling the new version of Messenger gave it fits.

Even the most trusted household names in computing can make undesirable changes to your system without your knowledge or permission. Microsoft didn't sneak the Messenger update onto people's computers (though it has the ability to do this). Instead, it used social engineering to make it appear desirable and so persuaded users to install it themselves. The purpose of the update was to promote Messenger and further Microsoft's agenda in expanding and interlinking its Web clients and networking components. It certainly had nothing to do with "improving connectivity and system performance." This is a good example of software from a trusted source containing hidden, even undesirable, features, urged on users without informed consent. It is also a good example of a software vendor making unauthorized configuration changes to a user's system. Judging from the MS boilerplate, one would not expect the patch to reenable Messenger if the user had deliberately disabled or removed it. One would expect one's configuration choices to be respected.

NOTE *There is a simple tool for safely removing Messenger posted to the Downloads section of the Apress Web site.*

So, where does active defense fit in? Soon after Microsoft decided to make Windows Messenger difficult to disable or remove, a spam outfit called DirectAdvertiser found a way to torment Windows users with advertising popups exploiting Messenger. The DirectAdvertiser application uses the Windows RPC weakness to send millions of spam popups across the Internet and activate Windows Messenger on the victim's machine to display the spam. I learned of this when *Register* reader Mike MacNeill sent me a screen shot of a Messenger popup he'd received, offering him the university diploma of his dreams with "no required tests, classes, books, or interviews," in the classic manner. I installed Windows XP on a test computer, then downloaded and installed an evaluation copy of the DirectAdvertiser utility and ran Netstat and Ethereal while experimenting with it. I found that it sent packets destined for ports 135 (DCE/RPC), 137 (NetBIOS name service), and 138 (NetBIOS UDP) on the victim's machine. Disabling those services or setting a firewall to block access to those ports would eliminate the problem.

I was using the DirectAdvertiser utility and observing its behavior from an attacker's point of view. However, if I'd been a victim of this popup spam, I could as easily have used Netstat or Ethereal to find out where the unwanted traffic was coming from and which ports on my machine it was targeting. The same tools would have served me well in either case. Also, if I had removed Messenger from my Windows machine and then innocently installed the Microsoft critical update to "improve connectivity and system performance," not realizing that it would reinstall and reenable Messenger behind my back, I would have been able to detect Messenger's activity with periodic network monitoring. Thus, I could have disabled Messenger before the popup spam began circulating.

In this chapter, we'll learn to work with several security tools appropriate for the home and SOHO environments. The owners of high-value targets deploy expensive, time-consuming security measures that include sophisticated network monitoring, real-time intrusion detection, and system auditing. Fortunately, home and SOHO users don't need this sort of elaborate defense because the systems we're defending rarely attract determined, elite attackers. Indeed, one of the fundamental goals of this book is to help users to harden a system adequately without investing a great deal of money or constantly tweaking and fussing. A well-configured home or small office system should not require much attention; even so, there are times when active security is appropriate, such as when software has been installed, updated, or patched, or when we wish to communicate privately via the Internet. Some of the tools explained below will help us to thwart attacks. Some will alert us to security and privacy weaknesses, and some will help us to protect our data and to communicate securely. Linux users will be pleased to know that most of the tools are free and likely to have been included in their distribution already. Windows users will have to obtain most of them separately and in some cases shell out a bit of money, so for them, the costs need to be balanced against the benefits. To the extent possible, we'll consider free, open-source tools that run on Windows as well as Linux.

Network and Internet Monitoring

In November of 2002, I received an e-mail from *Register* reader Jody Melbourne, who had discovered that the Windows XP Search Companion (also called the Search Assistant) was establishing a connection to a remote machine at Microsoft, even though he was merely searching his own hard disk.

"I did not give Microsoft permission to know what files I am searching for on my local hard drive," Jody wrote. Fair enough; I set out to learn what data MS was pulling off Windows XP computers. I connected an XP box to the Net, started the

Ethereal packet sniffer, and launched the Search Companion. Sure enough, the computer immediately connected to the remote address, sa.windows.com, and fetched a number of *XSL (Extensible Stylesheet Language)* files. But thanks to Ethereal, I could see that it didn't send any data to the site beyond comparing my locally stored versions of those files to the ones hosted on the Microsoft server. That is, the Search Companion didn't inform Microsoft of what I was searching for on my hard drive, as Jody had suspected. However, when I performed an *Internet* search using the Windows Search Companion, it sent my search terms to the Microsoft Web site and dropped a session cookie on my machine.

After discussing these findings with several engineers at Microsoft, I was persuaded that the company was collecting information without invading users' privacy. In the first case, MS was updating files on the local machine to improve Search Companion performance without collecting any identifying data. The XSL files were updated with associations between file extensions and file types, to make searching more productive. In the second case, MS was doing a bit of research on users' search habits, but without IP logging. Microsoft "does not record your choice of Internet search engine, and does not collect or request any personal or demographic information. Information collected by the Search Companion cannot be used to identify you individually, and is never used in conjunction with other data sources that may contain personal data," the company said.

At the time, it appeared that there was nothing for users to worry about. But there is a question about MS playing with people's Internet connections, modifying files on other people's personal computers, and studying user behavior without obtaining informed consent before doing so. The *ability* to violate your privacy in a stealthy manner is there, coded into Windows. The *right* to do it is there as well, coded into the *End User License Agreement (EULA)* that we all click Yes to without reading whenever we install Windows or a Microsoft patch. All that's preventing widespread abuse is the company's self-restraint and goodwill toward users, neither of which has been a traditional Redmond strong suit.

Network or Internet connection monitoring is the only certain way to find out if the company has since decided to exploit its ability to install software, modify files, and spy on users without their knowledge. But let's not single out Microsoft here. The company takes a lot of flak because its installed user base is immense. When Redmond blunders or pulls a fast one, it affects many millions of people: thus even a small infraction becomes a major story. Other makers of proprietary software can be even creepier and more aggressive, but because their user base is smaller, their creepiness rarely becomes news.

It's unfortunate but true, especially for Windows users, that the software we run often grants system privileges to outside parties such as software vendors, advertisers, spammers, Web sites, and ISPs. But there's no reason why we should tolerate such abuse. Now let's learn to install and use the tools that help us recover control over our systems.

> **NOTE** *It's often necessary for Windows users to log in to their administrator accounts before making changes to system settings or using the tools and commands that follow. Linux users can usually stay in their user accounts and either open a root shell, or launch their GUI admin interface and supply the root password when prompted. Windows requires us to switch between admin and user accounts a good deal more often. Therefore, the Windows-related instructions to follow assume that users have already logged in to their admin accounts.*

Netstat

This simple tool allows users to identify the network and Internet connections their machines have established. Almost everyone with a computer has already got it installed. It runs from a command prompt on both Windows and Linux, though some of the command options are different on those two systems. It's an excellent tool for discovering spyware that your antivirus software has over-looked.

Netstat will tell you what your computer is connected to on the Internet, revealing the active ports on your system, the IP addresses of each remote service, and the remote ports accepting the connections. The numbers representing IP addresses are separated by periods and end in a colon, and the port in use follows the colon thus: 123.1.2.3:80. Once you know the remote port in use, you can usually infer which service is active. There is a table of standard ports in Appendix B to help you get familiar with them.

Netstat won't capture packets or show you what data is being exchanged. Still, it's useful whenever you want to make a quick check to see if anything odd is going on. For example, suppose you run Netstat and find that you have a connection to a remote server on its port 6667. This would indicate a connection to an IRC server. But let's say that your IRC client is inactive at the time; then it's likely that your machine is infected with malware. Or suppose you find that your port 31337 is actively listening. In that case, it's likely that you're infected with the Back Orifice Trojan rootkit. Or perhaps you've uninstalled NetBIOS as recommended in Chapter 2, but Netstat reports that TCP port 139 and UDP ports 137 and 138 on your computer are active. It's possible that some piece of new software or some "critical update" has managed to reinstall NetBIOS behind your back.

When using Netstat, it's important to consider the connections you've chosen to make and eliminate them so that you won't be alarmed by normal activity. For instance, if you have a browser window open, it should not distress you to find that you have several connections to remote servers on port 80 (HTTP). However, if you have *no* browser window open, yet Netstat reports a connection to a remote server on port 80, that's worth looking into. It's likely that some other application is reaching out to an ad server via HTTP without your knowledge.

An easy way to use Netstat is to eliminate the connections you know you've made with your various Internet clients. Any extra connections should be investigated. In Appendix B you'll find a table of ports associated with various types of malware.

It's also very easy to detect spyware with Netstat simply by running it with *no* networking clients active. When your e-mail client, browser, chat clients, and the like are all closed, your PC shouldn't be making connections to any remote addresses on the Internet. If it is, you've probably got a rootkit or some form of spyware installed on your machine. Many antivirus scanners and malware detection utilities do a good job of detecting these infections, but if they're closed source, you can't be certain what they do and what they don't do. The infected version of The Cleaner mentioned in Chapter 3 should make it clear that there are limits to how far any piece of software can be trusted. Tools like Netstat and Ethereal will alert you to problems that an antivirus utility may be unable to detect, or even be designed to ignore.

Windows users can access Netstat by going to the Start menu and choosing Programs ➤ Accessories ➤ Command Prompt. I recommend creating a desktop icon for the Command Prompt for convenience's sake. Linux users can open a shell, and if they wish, log in to the shell as root to see every connection. The command for both operating systems is *netstat*. To see a list of Netstat commands and options, enter *netstat -help*.

There are two command options that are most often used. The first is *netstat -a*, which will show all of your connections and attempt to display them as domain names, and the second is *netstat -an*, which will show all connections but display them as IP addresses. The *a* switch stands for *all* and the *n* switch stands for *numerical*.

Using the *-a* switch, you'll get output in this format, where your local address is to the left and the remote address is to the right:

On Linux: `linux.local:1026`   `theregister.co.uk:http`
On Windows: `username:1026`   `theregister.co.uk:http`

When the *-an* switch is used, the output will look like this:

On Linux: `192.168.1.2:1026`   `63.219.179.140:80`
On Windows: `192.168.1.2:1026`   `63.219.179.140:80`

The local port, 1026, is simply the first port a computer will try to use; yours may use another. It's not a port that's been preassigned to any particular service, and there are many other such ports that are up for grabs and used as needed. There are also many ports that have standard assignments, such as 21 (FTP), 22 (SSH), 23 (Telnet), 25 (SMTP), 80 (HTTP), 110 (POP3), 443 (SSL), and so on. In time, you'll become familiar with the most common ones and be able to tell at a glance which service is active just by noting the port number.

Netstat will list your local connections and remote connections in two columns. Figure 4-1 is a screen shot from a Windows computer with a single browser session active.

```
⌨ Command Prompt                                              _ □ ✕
                                                                ▲
Active Connections

  Proto  Local Address          Foreign Address        State
  TCP    0.0.0.0:135            0.0.0.0:0              LISTENING
  TCP    0.0.0.0:445            0.0.0.0:0              LISTENING
  TCP    0.0.0.0:1049           0.0.0.0:0              LISTENING
  TCP    0.0.0.0:1051           0.0.0.0:0              LIST⬚NING
  TCP    0.0.0.0:1052           0.0.0.0:0              LISTENING
  TCP    0.0.0.0:1057           0.0.0.0:0              LISTENING
  TCP    0.0.0.0:1058           0.0.0.0:0              LISTENING
  TCP    0.0.0.0:1063           0.0.0.0:0              LISTENING
  TCP    0.0.0.0:1066           0.0.0.0:0              LISTENING
  TCP    0.0.0.0:1067           0.0.0.0:0              LISTENING
  TCP    127.0.0.1:1026         127.0.0.1:1025         TIME_WAIT
  TCP    127.0.0.1:1048         0.0.0.0:0              LISTENING
  TCP    127.0.0.1:1048         127.0.0.1:1049         ESTABLISHED
  TCP    127.0.0.1:1049         127.0.0.1:1048         ESTABLISHED
  TCP    192.168.1.4:139        0.0.0.0:0              LISTENING
  TCP    192.168.1.4:1029       212.100.234.54:80      TIME_WAIT
  TCP    192.168.1.4:1030       212.100.234.54:80      TIME_WAIT
  TCP    192.168.1.4:1051       212.100.234.54:80      ESTABLISHED
  TCP    192.168.1.4:1052       212.100.234.54:80      ESTABLISHED
  TCP    192.168.1.4:1057       212.100.234.54:80      ESTABLISHED
  TCP    192.168.1.4:1058       212.100.234.54:80      ESTABLISHED
  TCP    192.168.1.4:1063       216.239.51.104:80      ESTABLISHED
  TCP    192.168.1.4:1066       212.100.234.57:80      ESTABLISHED
  TCP    192.168.1.4:1067       212.100.234.57:80      ESTABLISHED
  UDP    0.0.0.0:445            *:*
  UDP    192.168.1.4:137        *:*
  UDP    192.168.1.4:138        *:*
                                                                ▼
◀                                                            ▶
```

Figure 4-1. Netstat at a glance

The far left column shows the network protocol, such as TCP or UDP. To the right of that is the local address, and farther to the right the remote address. Finally, the status or *state* of the connection is listed: ESTABLISHED, WAIT, LISTEN, and so on. Note that UDP does not have a state. It's a *stateless* protocol, which means that packets do not record or exchange any information about what occurred previously between the two machines involved.

The first thing you might notice is that the computer is listening on TCP port 135, a port used by remote procedure call (RPC). This port can, and should, be blocked by a firewall, but the service can't be disabled on Windows. Below that, we see that it's also listening on TCP port 445, which is used by NetBIOS over TCP/IP, an insecure service. So right away, Netstat has alerted us to a security problem that we might not have been aware of: there's an insecure service running, though it's one that most users can disable without penalty (Figure 4-2). There is a list of common ports in Appendix B to which you can refer when a connection looks suspicious.

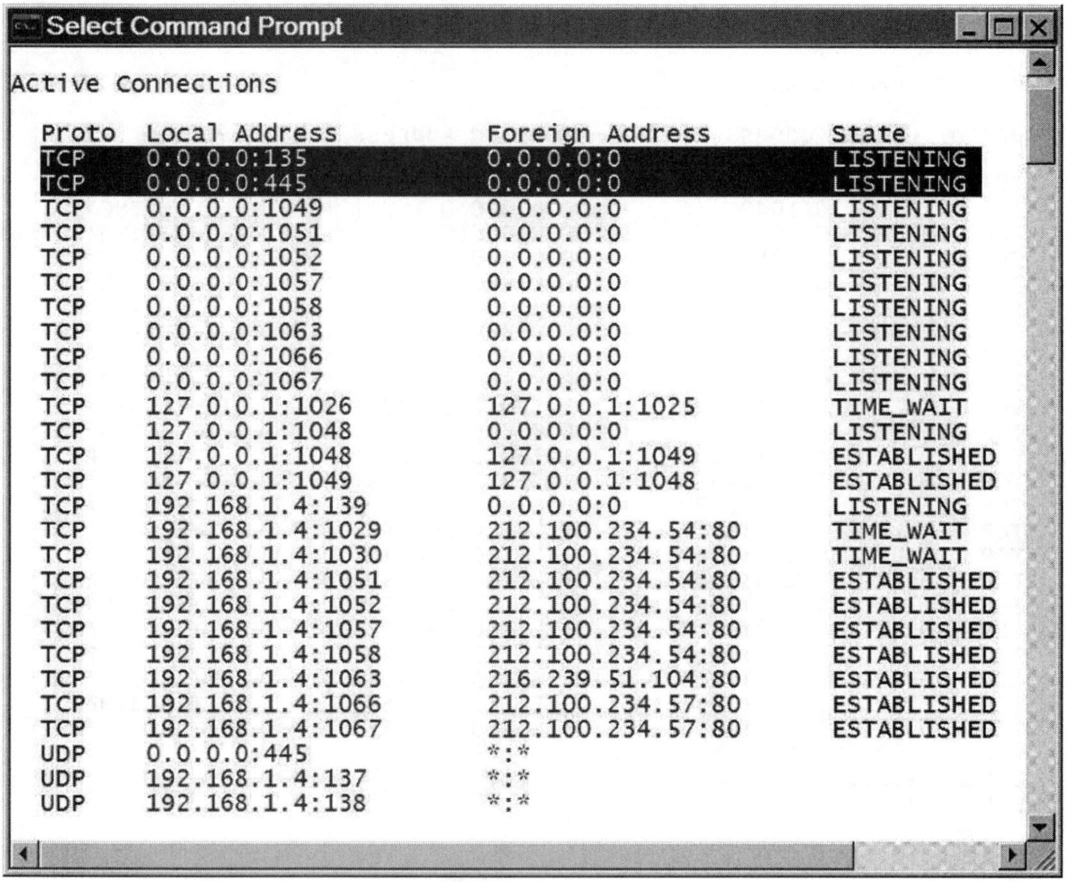

```
Select Command Prompt                                    _ □ ×

Active Connections

   Proto   Local Address        Foreign Address      State
   TCP     0.0.0.0:135          0.0.0.0:0            LISTENING
   TCP     0.0.0.0:445          0.0.0.0:0            LISTENING
   TCP     0.0.0.0:1049         0.0.0.0:0            LISTENING
   TCP     0.0.0.0:1051         0.0.0.0:0            LISTENING
   TCP     0.0.0.0:1052         0.0.0.0:0            LISTENING
   TCP     0.0.0.0:1057         0.0.0.0:0            LISTENING
   TCP     0.0.0.0:1058         0.0.0.0:0            LISTENING
   TCP     0.0.0.0:1063         0.0.0.0:0            LISTENING
   TCP     0.0.0.0:1066         0.0.0.0:0            LISTENING
   TCP     0.0.0.0:1067         0.0.0.0:0            LISTENING
   TCP     127.0.0.1:1026       127.0.0.1:1025       TIME_WAIT
   TCP     127.0.0.1:1048       0.0.0.0:0            LISTENING
   TCP     127.0.0.1:1048       127.0.0.1:1049       ESTABLISHED
   TCP     127.0.0.1:1049       127.0.0.1:1048       ESTABLISHED
   TCP     192.168.1.4:139      0.0.0.0:0            LISTENING
   TCP     192.168.1.4:1029     212.100.234.54:80    TIME_WAIT
   TCP     192.168.1.4:1030     212.100.234.54:80    TIME_WAIT
   TCP     192.168.1.4:1051     212.100.234.54:80    ESTABLISHED
   TCP     192.168.1.4:1052     212.100.234.54:80    ESTABLISHED
   TCP     192.168.1.4:1057     212.100.234.54:80    ESTABLISHED
   TCP     192.168.1.4:1058     212.100.234.54:80    ESTABLISHED
   TCP     192.168.1.4:1063     216.239.51.104:80    ESTABLISHED
   TCP     192.168.1.4:1066     212.100.234.57:80    ESTABLISHED
   TCP     192.168.1.4:1067     212.100.234.57:80    ESTABLISHED
   UDP     0.0.0.0:445          *:*
   UDP     192.168.1.4:137      *:*
   UDP     192.168.1.4:138      *:*
```

Figure 4-2. Suspicious ports active on Windows

Below that, we can see that the computer is listening on ports from 1049 to 1067, which are standard, nonprivileged ports that rarely indicate a problem. A bit farther down, we see that the localhost, 127.0.0.1, is listening on ports from 1026 to 1049 (Figure 4-3). Again, this is nothing to worry about (and we will learn more about the localhost later).

```
Select Command Prompt                                    _ □ ×

Active Connections

    Proto   Local Address          Foreign Address        State
    TCP     0.0.0.0:135            0.0.0.0:0              LISTENING
    TCP     0.0.0.0:445            0.0.0.0:0              LISTENING
    TCP     0.0.0.0:1049           0.0.0.0:0              LISTENING
    TCP     0.0.0.0:1051           0.0.0.0:0              LISTENING
    TCP     0.0.0.0:1052           0.0.0.0:0              LISTENING
    TCP     0.0.0.0:1057           0.0.0.0:0              LISTENING
    TCP     0.0.0.0:1058           0.0.0.0:0              LISTENING
    TCP     0.0.0.0:1063           0.0.0.0:0              LISTENING
    TCP     0.0.0.0:1066           0.0.0.0:0              LISTENING
    TCP     0.0.0.0:1067           0.0.0.0:0              LISTENING
    TCP     127.0.0.1:1026         127.0.0.1:1025         TIME_WAIT
    TCP     127.0.0.1:1048         0.0.0.0:0              LISTENING
    TCP     127.0.0.1:1048         127.0.0.1:1049         ESTABLISHED
    TCP     127.0.0.1:1049         127.0.0.1:1048         ESTABLISHED
    TCP     192.168.1.4:139        0.0.0.0:0              LISTENING
    TCP     192.168.1.4:1029       212.100.234.54:80      TIME_WAIT
    TCP     192.168.1.4:1030       212.100.234.54:80      TIME_WAIT
    TCP     192.168.1.4:1051       212.100.234.54:80      ESTABLISHED
    TCP     192.168.1.4:1052       212.100.234.54:80      ESTABLISHED
    TCP     192.168.1.4:1057       212.100.234.54:80      ESTABLISHED
    TCP     192.168.1.4:1058       212.100.234.54:80      ESTABLISHED
    TCP     192.168.1.4:1063       216.239.51.104:80      ESTABLISHED
    TCP     192.168.1.4:1066       212.100.234.57:80      ESTABLISHED
    TCP     192.168.1.4:1067       212.100.234.57:80      ESTABLISHED
    UDP     0.0.0.0:445            *:*
    UDP     192.168.1.4:137        *:*
    UDP     192.168.1.4:138        *:*
```

Figure 4-3. Usually harmless ports and localhost listening

Now we come to our Internet connections, or *sessions*. There are three different connections to remote HTTP servers: 212.100.234.54:80, 216.239.51.104:80, and 212.100.234.57:80. Yet only one browser window is actually in use. One connection is to the Web site I've chosen to visit; the other two connections are to ad servers (Figure 4-4). There is nothing odd here: most Web sites deliver ads from third-party servers. If you have three or four browser windows open, you could easily be making 10 or 15 HTTP connections. Choosing the Mozilla browser option that blocks images and cookies from third-party sources will obstruct Web bugs and prevent many of these extraneous connections, freeing bandwidth and speeding page loading, and, of course, simplifying your results in Netstat so that questionable behavior is easier to spot.

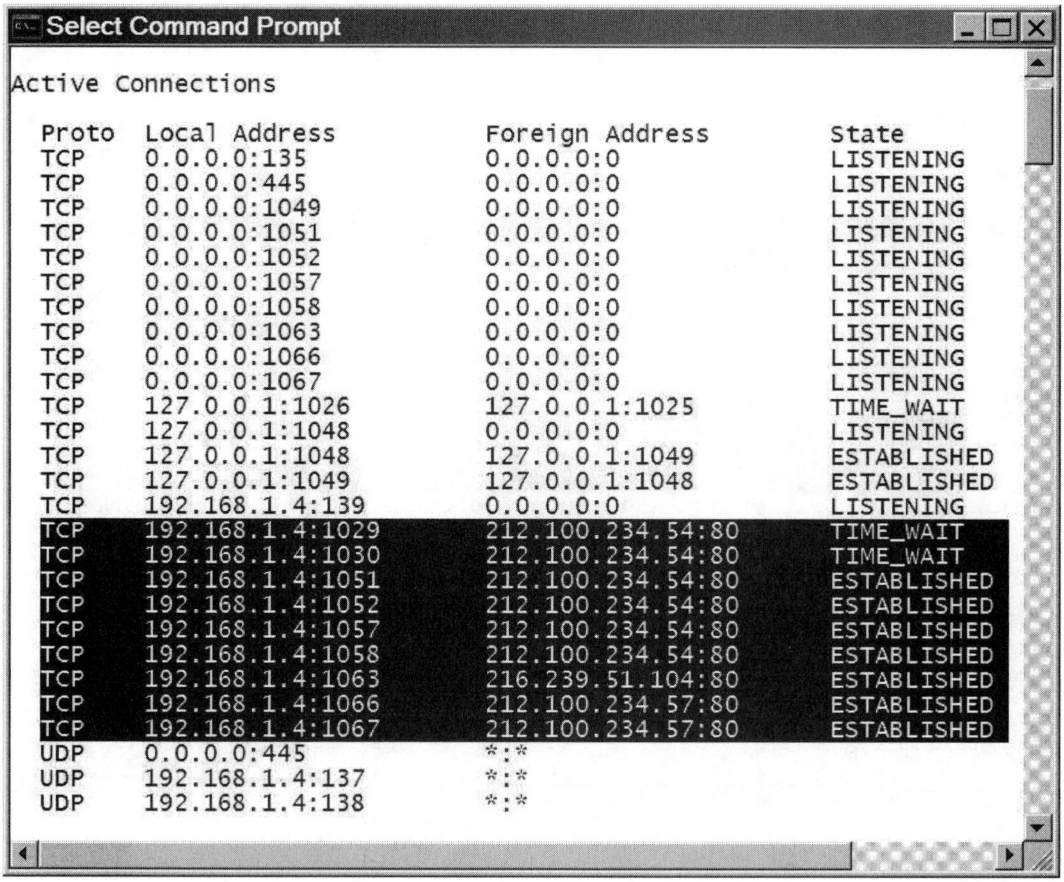

```
┌─────────────────────────────────────────────────────────────────────────┐
│ ▣ Select Command Prompt                                    _ □ ×          │
├─────────────────────────────────────────────────────────────────────────┤
│                                                                       ▲   │
│ Active Connections                                                        │
│                                                                           │
│   Proto  Local Address         Foreign Address        State              │
│   TCP    0.0.0.0:135           0.0.0.0:0              LISTENING           │
│   TCP    0.0.0.0:445           0.0.0.0:0              LISTENING           │
│   TCP    0.0.0.0:1049          0.0.0.0:0              LISTENING           │
│   TCP    0.0.0.0:1051          0.0.0.0:0              LISTENING           │
│   TCP    0.0.0.0:1052          0.0.0.0:0              LISTENING           │
│   TCP    0.0.0.0:1057          0.0.0.0:0              LISTENING           │
│   TCP    0.0.0.0:1058          0.0.0.0:0              LISTENING           │
│   TCP    0.0.0.0:1063          0.0.0.0:0              LISTENING           │
│   TCP    0.0.0.0:1066          0.0.0.0:0              LISTENING           │
│   TCP    0.0.0.0:1067          0.0.0.0:0              LISTENING           │
│   TCP    127.0.0.1:1026        127.0.0.1:1025         TIME_WAIT           │
│   TCP    127.0.0.1:1048        0.0.0.0:0              LISTENING           │
│   TCP    127.0.0.1:1048        127.0.0.1:1049         ESTABLISHED         │
│   TCP    127.0.0.1:1049        127.0.0.1:1048         ESTABLISHED         │
│   TCP    192.168.1.4:139       0.0.0.0:0              LISTENING           │
│   TCP    192.168.1.4:1029      212.100.234.54:80      TIME_WAIT           │
│   TCP    192.168.1.4:1030      212.100.234.54:80      TIME_WAIT           │
│   TCP    192.168.1.4:1051      212.100.234.54:80      ESTABLISHED         │
│   TCP    192.168.1.4:1052      212.100.234.54:80      ESTABLISHED         │
│   TCP    192.168.1.4:1057      212.100.234.54:80      ESTABLISHED         │
│   TCP    192.168.1.4:1058      212.100.234.54:80      ESTABLISHED         │
│   TCP    192.168.1.4:1063      216.239.51.104:80      ESTABLISHED         │
│   TCP    192.168.1.4:1066      212.100.234.57:80      ESTABLISHED         │
│   TCP    192.168.1.4:1067      212.100.234.57:80      ESTABLISHED         │
│   UDP    0.0.0.0:445           *:*                                        │
│   UDP    192.168.1.4:137       *:*                                        │
│   UDP    192.168.1.4:138       *:*                                        │
│                                                                       ▼   │
└─────────────────────────────────────────────────────────────────────────┘
```

Figure 4-4. Connections to three Web sites, two of which are ad servers

Finally, we have UDP ports opened by the Windows RPC and NetBIOS over TCP/IP services. They are not in use; as you can see, there is no foreign address trying to connect to us here. NetBIOS over TCP should be disabled or blocked with a firewall, and RPC, which cannot be disabled, should be blocked with a firewall. Note that UDP is stateless, so the far right column is empty (Figure 4-5).

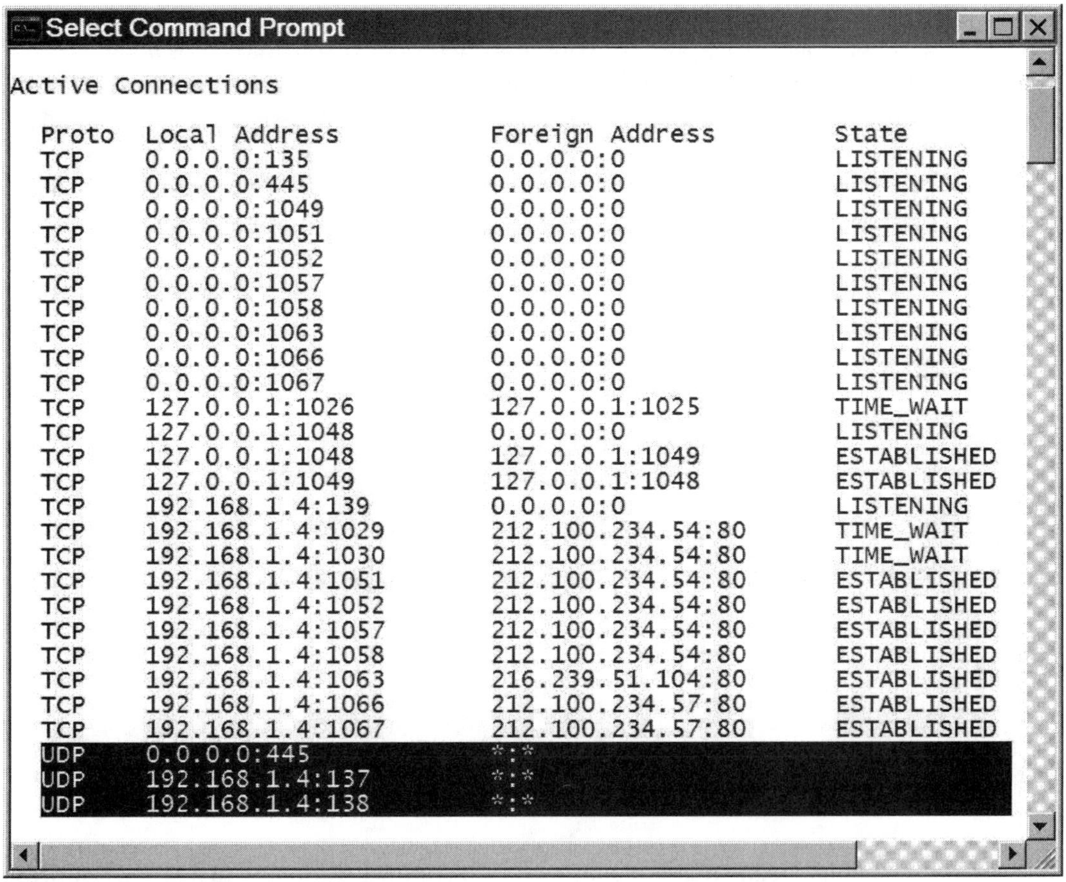

```
 ▓  Select Command Prompt                                          _ □ ×
                                                                         ▲
Active Connections

   Proto   Local Address         Foreign Address        State
   TCP     0.0.0.0:135           0.0.0.0:0              LISTENING
   TCP     0.0.0.0:445           0.0.0.0:0              LISTENING
   TCP     0.0.0.0:1049          0.0.0.0:0              LISTENING
   TCP     0.0.0.0:1051          0.0.0.0:0              LISTENING
   TCP     0.0.0.0:1052          0.0.0.0:0              LISTENING
   TCP     0.0.0.0:1057          0.0.0.0:0              LISTENING
   TCP     0.0.0.0:1058          0.0.0.0:0              LISTENING
   TCP     0.0.0.0:1063          0.0.0.0:0              LISTENING
   TCP     0.0.0.0:1066          0.0.0.0:0              LISTENING
   TCP     0.0.0.0:1067          0.0.0.0:0              LISTENING
   TCP     127.0.0.1:1026        127.0.0.1:1025         TIME_WAIT
   TCP     127.0.0.1:1048        0.0.0.0:0              LISTENING
   TCP     127.0.0.1:1048        127.0.0.1:1049         ESTABLISHED
   TCP     127.0.0.1:1049        127.0.0.1:1048         ESTABLISHED
   TCP     192.168.1.4:139       0.0.0.0:0              LISTENING
   TCP     192.168.1.4:1029      212.100.234.54:80      TIME_WAIT
   TCP     192.168.1.4:1030      212.100.234.54:80      TIME_WAIT
   TCP     192.168.1.4:1051      212.100.234.54:80      ESTABLISHED
   TCP     192.168.1.4:1052      212.100.234.54:80      ESTABLISHED
   TCP     192.168.1.4:1057      212.100.234.54:80      ESTABLISHED
   TCP     192.168.1.4:1058      212.100.234.54:80      ESTABLISHED
   TCP     192.168.1.4:1063      216.239.51.104:80      ESTABLISHED
   TCP     192.168.1.4:1066      212.100.234.57:80      ESTABLISHED
   TCP     192.168.1.4:1067      212.100.234.57:80      ESTABLISHED
   UDP     0.0.0.0:445           *:*
   UDP     192.168.1.4:137       *:*
   UDP     192.168.1.4:138       *:*
                                                                         ▼
 ◄                                                                    ►
```

Figure 4-5. UDP ports on Windows that should be disabled or blocked with a firewall

When you have a question about a particular Internet client, it's helpful to close all your other Internet applications to observe it singly. This way, if it's reaching out to an ad server on port 80, you won't confuse this behavior with normal Web browser activity. It's also wise to run Netstat occasionally with *no* Internet client applications running. This will tell you if any unknown programs are accessing the Internet automatically in the background. It will also alert you if services and daemons you've disabled have been reactivated by a recent software installation or system update.

Figure 4-6 is a screen shot from a Linux computer. The far left column shows the protocol, in this case TCP. To the right are metrics for Recv-Q and Send-Q, which do not appear in Windows versions of Netstat. These metrics are used for troubleshooting a connection and are not relevant to security.

Just to the right is the computer's IP address, 192.168.1.2, similar to the local address shown in the previous Windows screen shots. Note that this is *not* the IP address assigned by my ISP. That's because I'm using an Ethernet card and NAT (network address translation): my router has acquired the ISP-assigned IP address and created a series of internal IP addresses distributed among the several machines that I've got connected to the router. If you're using Ethernet and NAT, your computers will have similar internal IP addresses, following the format 192.168.*x.x*. These addresses aren't publicly routable and protect you from a number of remote attacks: only your router knows where on the Internet your computers are actually located.

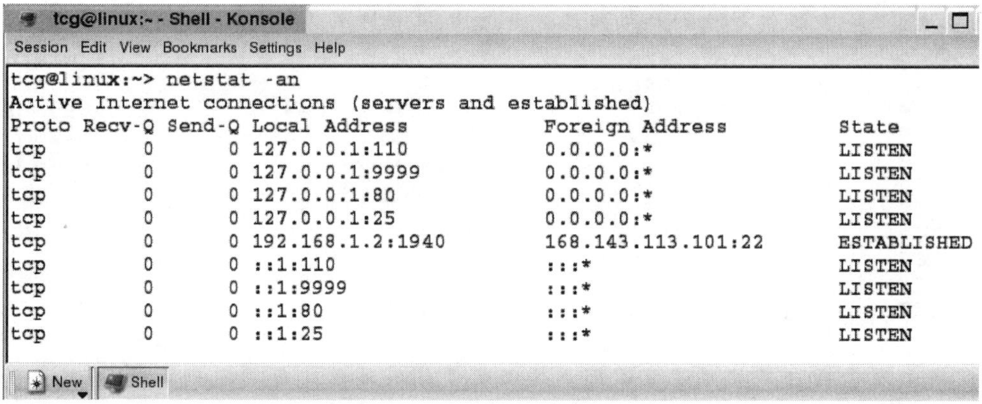

```
tcg@linux:~ - Shell - Konsole                                          _ □
Session  Edit  View  Bookmarks  Settings  Help
tcg@linux:~> netstat -an
Active Internet connections (servers and established)
Proto Recv-Q Send-Q Local Address          Foreign Address        State
tcp        0      0 127.0.0.1:110          0.0.0.0:*              LISTEN
tcp        0      0 127.0.0.1:9999         0.0.0.0:*              LISTEN
tcp        0      0 127.0.0.1:80           0.0.0.0:*              LISTEN
tcp        0      0 127.0.0.1:25           0.0.0.0:*              LISTEN
tcp        0      0 192.168.1.2:1940       168.143.113.101:22     ESTABLISHED
tcp        0      0 ::1:110                :::*                   LISTEN
tcp        0      0 ::1:9999               :::*                   LISTEN
tcp        0      0 ::1:80                 :::*                   LISTEN
tcp        0      0 ::1:25                 :::*                   LISTEN

  New    Shell
```

Figure 4-6. Netstat on Linux

If you're using a dialup connection, your local address will be the IP address assigned by your ISP. Dialup users should not be concerned that they are more exposed on the Internet than broadband users; a personal firewall or packet filter will do much to conceal your computer. Furthermore, in the SSH section below, and again in Chapter 5 with a bit more detail, we'll be learning how to conceal our IP address in all of our Internet traffic so that remote attackers will be unable to locate our machines from the information contained in e-mail headers, server logs, and the like.

NOTE *If you're using Ethernet and a NAT router for Internet access, and Netstat displays your actual IP address—that is, the one assigned by your ISP—in the Local Address column, then you haven't set up NAT correctly. See Appendix B for tips on NAT setup.*

You can see that my PC has no apparent HTTP connections but is connected to another machine at 168.143.113.101 on port 22, the SSH port. That's a proxy server maintained by Anonymizer (www.anonymizer.com). My machine, 192.168.1.2, is using its outbound port 1940 to connect to the proxy server located at

168.143.113.101, which is accepting the connection on its port 22. This indicates that an *SSH session* has been established (Figure 4-7).

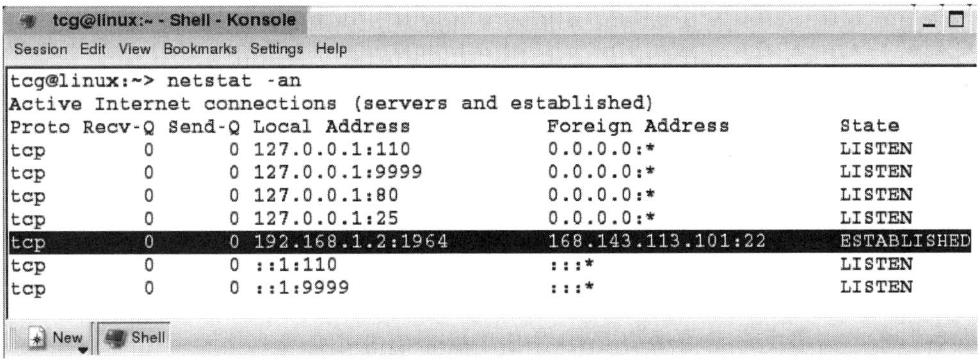

```
 🗗  tcg@linux:~ - Shell - Konsole                                          _ ☐
 Session Edit View Bookmarks Settings Help
 tcg@linux:~> netstat -an
 Active Internet connections (servers and established)
 Proto Recv-Q Send-Q Local Address          Foreign Address        State
 tcp      0      0 127.0.0.1:110           0.0.0.0:*              LISTEN
 tcp      0      0 127.0.0.1:9999          0.0.0.0:*              LISTEN
 tcp      0      0 127.0.0.1:80            0.0.0.0:*              LISTEN
 tcp      0      0 127.0.0.1:25            0.0.0.0:*              LISTEN
 tcp      0      0 192.168.1.2:1964        168.143.113.101:22     ESTABLISHED
 tcp      0      0 ::1:110                 :::*                   LISTEN
 tcp      0      0 ::1:9999                :::*                   LISTEN

 ⊕ New   🐚 Shell
```

Figure 4-7. SSH in use

You can also see that 127.0.0.1 (localhost) is listening for HTTP traffic (port 80), POP3 traffic (port 110), and SMTP traffic (port 25). These ports are not listening on the Internet; they're listening locally instead. The localhost is a *loopback* address that doesn't cross the network interface. Thus, my computer never makes a TCP connection except via SSH (secure shell). It may not be apparent to you yet, but this arrangement allows a user to grab Internet traffic from the localhost, via SSH. This scheme is called *SSH tunneling,* and we will learn about it in detail later in this chapter. The loopback interface allows a computer to make connections to itself so that it can act as both a host and a client. The concept is a bit odd, but it can be illustrated if you imagine sending a packet *from* your computer *to* your computer without accessing the Internet or any local network. The packet's route is entirely internal. This is useful for testing applications whose effects are unknown without disturbing the network. It can also be used to make Internet connections more private, as we will see in the SSH section to follow (Figure 4-8).

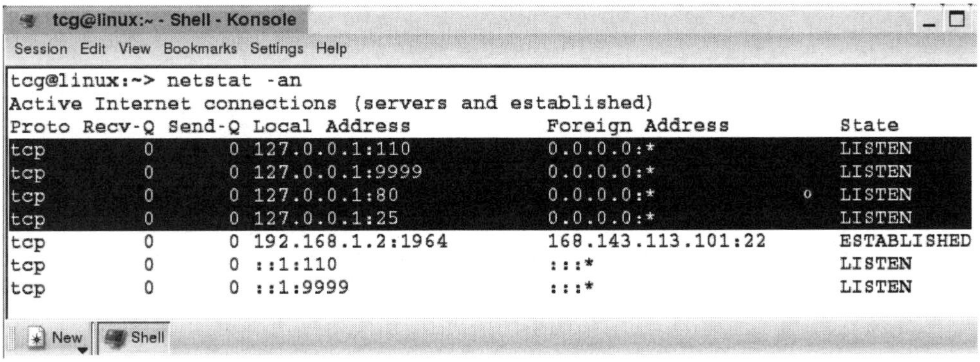

```
 🗗  tcg@linux:~ - Shell - Konsole                                          _ ☐
 Session Edit View Bookmarks Settings Help
 tcg@linux:~> netstat -an
 Active Internet connections (servers and established)
 Proto Recv-Q Send-Q Local Address          Foreign Address        State
 tcp      0      0 127.0.0.1:110           0.0.0.0:*              LISTEN
 tcp      0      0 127.0.0.1:9999          0.0.0.0:*              LISTEN
 tcp      0      0 127.0.0.1:80            0.0.0.0:*           o  LISTEN
 tcp      0      0 127.0.0.1:25            0.0.0.0:*              LISTEN
 tcp      0      0 192.168.1.2:1964        168.143.113.101:22     ESTABLISHED
 tcp      0      0 ::1:110                 :::*                   LISTEN
 tcp      0      0 ::1:9999                :::*                   LISTEN

 ⊕ New   🐚 Shell
```

Figure 4-8. SSH tunneling: the computer is listening for traffic from the SSH client, not the Web

Ethereal

When Netstat reveals Internet connections that can't be attributed to known clients, it's time to investigate. There are three things you'll want to know:

- Which services are involved

- With whom the IP traffic is being exchanged

- What data is involved

Netstat can answer the first two questions, but to answer the third, a packet sniffer is required. Ethereal is a free, open-source tool for Windows and Linux that I recommend.

When you have a questionable connection, the first thing to look at are the ports in use by both the local and remote machines. This will give you an idea of which services are in use. If the port or the service is unknown to you, check it against the list of common malware ports in the appendix. If malware is suspected, a virus scanner or adware/spyware removal tool might take care of it easily. Use the tool, then run Netstat again to verify that the mysterious connection is no longer being made. If it's gone, then your problem is solved; if it persists, then you'll have to explore a bit further.

First, you should try to discover who is at the other end of the suspicious connection. If you run Netstat with just the *-a* switch, it will attempt to resolve the remote IP address into a domain name. If it can't, then you may have to look up the remote IP address in a *whois database*. For this, you will have to use a third-party database available on the Web, such as those available at `SamSpade.org`, or install a whois client on your system. There are several freeware whois clients for Windows, but these should be checked for adware once installed. Most Linux users can simply open a shell and type the command *whois* followed by the IP address at the command prompt, as a whois client is part of most standard distributions and will likely be installed already. Finding out the domain name associated with an unexpected connection can help you determine whether the connection is a threat, a mere annoyance, or perfectly harmless. If the domain name is new to you, perform a Web search using Google and find out what other people have to say about it.

Finally, you should find out what data is being transferred. This is where Ethereal comes in. A packet sniffer captures *everything* that crosses the network interface, so it makes no difference whether you're concerned with traffic coming in or going out. In either case, it will tell you what data is being exchanged, where it's coming from, and where it's going. The drawback is that users are confronted with mountains of data that can be difficult to interpret. Ethereal is a tool suitable for power users, developers, and network geeks, useful for hard-core troubleshooting. As such, it tells basic users a *lot* more than they need to know. Still, people can use it without getting bogged down in the arcane details of network transport. The trick is to use Netstat to identify the questionable remote address first, and then to scroll through

Ethereal's display looking only for packets related to that connection. As you become more proficient with the tool, you will learn how to filter its output to show you only what you want to see.

Figure 4-9 is a screen shot illustrating Ethereal's user interface.

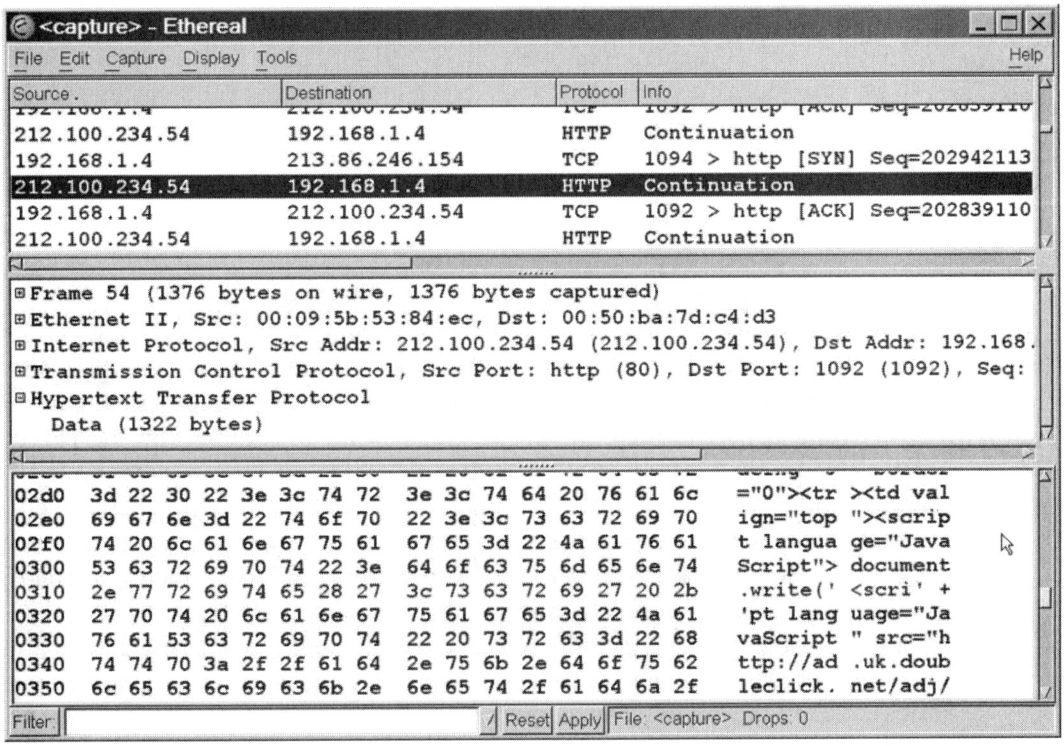

Figure 4-9. The Ethereal screen

There are three fields. The top field is the list of incoming and outgoing packets and their origins and destinations; the middle shows the various packet layers, such as the header and the message body with an expandable tree that you can open and close as you please; and the bottom shows the content of each layer in hex and plain text. Presumably, you would already have used Netstat to identify a remote host that concerns you. With Ethereal, you can scroll through the upper field to find packets going to and coming from that host and examine the contents. The output and user interface are the same on both Windows and Linux. Ethereal's interface is intuitive, and its basic functions are easy to implement. It will seem confusing at first, but after a few minutes' tinkering you'll be well on your way to using it productively.

Windows users can get Ethereal from www.ethereal.com. You will first need to install a library called WinPcap. There is a link to WinPcap on the Windows download page at ethereal.com. Install WinPcap first, then install Ethereal.

Linux users running one of the major distros will likely have Ethereal installed on their machines. If not, you can probably locate it on your installation CDs and install an RPM package built for your system. The ethereal.com Web site also has links to RPMs built for most major distributions, and these will likely be newer than the ones in your original CDs. Ethereal must be run as root, so it's easiest to open a shell, enter the command *su*, supply the root password, and start Ethereal from the command line. Always remember that when you log in as root, anyone can stop whatever process is running with Ctrl+C and have open access to a root shell. Always close the root shell or lock your screen before leaving your machine when others might use it in your absence.

System Monitoring

In previous chapters, we learned a good deal about keeping malware off our computers by shutting down services and other routes to exploitation, by setting file and user permissions to restrict program installation and code execution, and by preferring open-source to closed-source applications and utilities. Still, from time to time it's necessary to monitor system behavior and examine the local hard disk for evidence of viruses, spyware, and undesirable changes to settings brought about by file downloads, software installations, updates, and patches. A well-configured Windows computer or network shouldn't need much attention, but it is wise to scan your hard disk every couple of months, and more often if you tend to download files or install software, updates, and patches frequently.

Once you've simplified and hardened your system, the less you change, the less you'll need to worry about. Unfortunately, new exploits and existing vulnerabilities are discovered every day, so our systems need a great deal of patching and are therefore changing constantly. As illustrated by the previous example concerning the Windows Messenger patch, steps we take to enhance security can be undone later without our knowledge or consent.

Adware/Spyware Detection

The roster of Windows utilities and programs infected with adware and spyware reaches well into the thousands—far beyond the ability of any user to keep track of. There are commercial software utilities available to detect and remove a broad range of these pestilent programs, ranging in price from $10 to $70 and averaging around $40.

Fortunately, free tools such as Ad-aware from Lavasoft and Spybot Search & Destroy by Patrick Kolla do a good job, and you can use more than one free utility to ensure that everything is caught. The pay products will claim in their advertising copy to have some unique mechanism (or "advanced technology") that makes them worth the expense, but such assertions are rarely true. My advice is to use two or even three different free utilities so that one will catch what another misses.

And if any of these tools should contain adware of its own, the others will likely pick that up as well.

It's a good idea for Windows users to run an adware detection utility immediately after installing any new software, patch, or update. Linux users needn't worry about this because it's impossible to conceal spyware or adware in source code that anyone can examine. Occasionally, a Linux program will be infected with malware and posted to a public board, but this sort of thing is usually discovered promptly.

Antivirus Software

Computer viruses have been a godsend to the New Economy, generating billions in revenues for a handful of wealthy companies that distribute antivirus Band-Aids. Just like drug companies that profit mightily from the fact that no one has yet cured the common cold, these companies would be out of business in a heartbeat if the virus problem were ever solved. Fortunately for them, and unfortunately for us, there are about 60,000 Windows viruses and perhaps 50 or so Linux viruses known. Of these, only a fraction are in circulation, and only a fraction of those are destructive, but the active, harmful strains do quite enough damage as it is.

The big players are Symantec, McAfee, and Trend Micro, all of which make antivirus software for home users. F-Secure (www.f-secure.com), Sophos (www.sophos.com), and AVG (www.grisoft.com) make lesser known but very high quality products. For home users, these utilities will cost in the $50 range, and every Windows user should invest in at least one of them. One may resent the need, but that's no excuse for *denying* the need. Computer viruses are a fact of life, much like the common cold, and no one selling symptom relief is interested in finding a cure. Unfortunately, Windows users are stuck in their role as patrons of the antivirus cartel, and will be for the foreseeable future.

Most antivirus products will scan individual files for the presence of malicious code and will also scan an entire hard disk for malicious files. A complete disk scan should be performed every few months as a matter of basic security housekeeping. Meanwhile, *all* files downloaded from the Internet or received via instant messaging, P2P, or e-mail should be scanned for malicious content before they're activated, even with a viewer. *Never* activate any file until it's been scanned. It makes no difference what the file extension appears to be or who's offering it or sending it. File extensions can be concealed or otherwise manipulated, and even your best friend who you think knows computers intimately can make a mistake. And keep in mind that many e-mail worms propagate automatically, appearing to come from a known contact so that you'll be more likely to accept them.

Keep in mind also that antivirus tools intentionally overlook a number of extremely malicious programs and files. Keeping an eye on Netstat and running a spyware detection utility now and again will provide a needed backup against these deficiencies.

Linux is not plagued by viruses for several reasons. The most obvious is that Windows has been installed on more systems and so offers a more attractive target for virus writers. Another reason is that it's simply more difficult to attack a Linux system. Users are discouraged from running their systems as root, which helps limit the potential of malware to do serious damage, and user accounts in Linux are better restricted or sandboxed than user accounts in Windows. Services can be disabled without compromising system functions, which means that worms have few footholds available on a well-configured machine. And Linux e-mail clients like KMail simply won't execute the kinds of dangerous scripts that Outlook and Outlook Express insist on running automatically.

There have been Linux viruses and worms, though they're comparatively rare and few of those circulating are destructive. Patching regularly, managing user permissions properly, disabling unnecessary daemons, using a firewall or packet filter, and keeping an eye on Netstat now and then affords plenty of protection against the occasional bits of malware that Linux users might encounter. However, Linux users who run a mail server or fileserver *do* need to concern themselves with viruses, if for no other reason than to protect vulnerable Windows clients. Trend Micro, F-Secure, Sophos, and Central Command offer several packages for these situations, and there is a free, open-source virus scanner for Linux called AMaViS available from www.amavis.org, but it is not a tool for novices. In any event, Linux home users needn't bother with antivirus products.

Malicious Processes

On both Windows and Linux, it's easy to discover what processes are running and check them against a list of malicious ones. This is your last line of defense against malware. If your computer is misbehaving and your spyware or antivirus scanner fails to identify the problem, you should have a look at the processes running on your machine and verify that none is malicious. Because malware is constantly being developed and discovered, the best way to learn about a suspicious process is to perform a Web search on it. There is a list of common Windows malware processes and common safe processes in Appendix B, but because of the rate of malware development, it will be somewhat out of date before this book goes to press.

To see what's running on Windows

1. Go to the Start menu and choose Run.

2. Type in *taskmgr* and click OK. The Windows Task Manager dialog will launch.

3. The first two tabs at the top, labeled Applications and Processes, are the ones we're concerned with.

Figure 4-10. The Windows Task Manager Applications dialog

Under the Applications tab (Figure 4-10), you should find only those applications that you've launched yourself or added to your startup directory. If there's an application listed that you don't recognize, don't be alarmed, but investigate it with a Web search. Chances are that once you learn what it is, you'll recognize it. But if not, or if you gather that it might be malicious, you will need to kill it and remove it.

First, you will have to find its related executable file. Right-click on the application name and choose the option Go To Process (Figure 4-11). In this example, we are going to kill Mozilla.

Figure 4-11. The Windows Task Manager: Go To Process

This will bring up the processes list with the executable file highlighted. Kill the process by right-clicking and choosing the option End Process Tree from the drop-down menu, which will kill the primary process and each child process it invokes in one go (Figure 4-12).

The best way to rid yourself of unnecessary or suspicious applications is to use the Windows Add or Remove Programs utility. So long as you've killed the process tree as just described, you can go to the Start menu and choose Settings ➤ Control Panel ➤ Add or Remove Programs. Your applications should all be listed, and you can uninstall a questionable one easily with the Change/Remove button. If this is impractical, or if it fails, you can manually delete or wipe the executable file, and even the directory in which it's located, so long as you've killed its related process tree. To remove it manually, note the process name, search your hard disk for the executable file or the program directory, and wipe it—so long as you've confirmed that you don't need it.

Under the Task Manager Processes tab, you'll find a complete list of executable routines running on your computer. There will likely be a large number of them, and they can have very arcane names that give little indication of what they actually do. If you followed my advice about eliminating unnecessary Windows services in Chapter 2, the list will be a good deal more manageable.

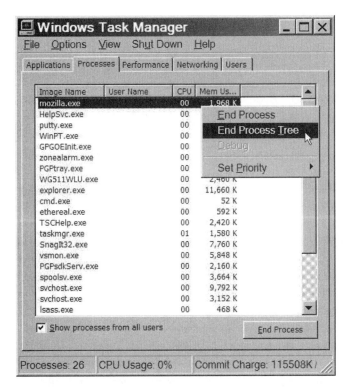

Figure 4-12. The Windows Task Manager: End Process Tree

Malware authors like to give their malicious executables names that resemble normal Windows processes so that you'll be likely to ignore them. Thus, the process *svchost.exe* is normal, while the processes *scvhost.exe*, *svchosts.exe*, and *svshost.exe* are malicious; *system* is normal, but *system.exe* and *system32.exe* are malicious; *services.exe* is normal, but *service.exe* is malicious; *explorer.exe* is normal, but *explore.exe* is malicious; *iexplore.exe* is normal, but *iexplorer.exe* is malicious; and so on. It's important to pay careful attention to a service's spelling before researching it to avoid undue alarm from a simple typo. Take your time and look into it before you act. If you kill the wrong process, your machine might blue-screen or even reboot itself.

When you find a process that arouses suspicion, check it against the list in the appendix and also perform a Web search on it, because the list is not comprehensive. If you're confident that it's not a legitimate system process, feel free to kill it by right-clicking on it and choosing the option End Process Tree as illustrated previously. Once the process is killed, you can use the system normally for a while to ensure that you haven't accidentally disabled anything useful, then search your hard disk for the executable file and wipe it, along with the directory or directories in which you found it.

> **NOTE** *The Performance tab in the Task Manager dialog will bring up a monitor of CPU activity. If your computer is not running applications and other tasks, yet the demand on the CPU is high, it might indicate malware. It's not a bad idea to look at the Performance dialog from time to time, especially when the computer is idling. The Networking tab also can tip you off to odd behavior. If your computer is exchanging data when your networking clients are inactive, you should look into it further with Netstat or Ethereal.*

For Linux users, there is no handy GUI tool for monitoring and killing system processes, but this is easy to do at the command line. There is essentially no malware to be concerned about so long as you're not running any servers and have disabled unnecessary services as outlined in Chapter 2. Most Linux viruses and worms affect systems with servers of one sort or another. However, if a home system suddenly becomes sluggish or an application hangs, this can indicate a runaway process that can easily be killed and restarted.

Let's practice on a nonessential process:

1. Open a few instances of the Mozilla browser.

2. You will need root access to see all of the system processes and kill them. Open a shell, type in the command *su,* and supply the root password. Now type the command *ps ax.*

3. You will see a list of running processes with their corresponding Process IDs, or *PIDs*, and the paths to the relevant binaries.

4. To kill a single process only, enter the command *kill* followed by the PID. To kill the process and all of its child processes, enter the command *killall* followed by the process name. The *killall* command is similar to the End Process Tree option in Windows.

5. Enter the command *killall mozilla-bin.* All of the mozilla instances you started and all of the child processes they invoked will be killed in one go.

The *kill* and *killall* commands are handy and easy to use, but the same cautions for Windows users apply. If you're logged in as root, you can kill a crucial system process by mistake and you might have to reboot your machine to recover. If you're only concerned with processes you started as a user, then you should use the *ps ax* and the *kill* and *killall* commands as a user. This way, the worst you can do is kill your own applications or your X session. You won't be able to interfere with system processes or other users' processes. Attempts to kill important system processes from a user account will fail, and the shell will report "operation not permitted."

Of course, root is at liberty to stuff up the entire system at any time. Linux users have less authority than Windows users, but root has more authority than a Windows administrator. This is a fundamental security advantage of Linux: it's *your* computer and no one has more authority than you've got when you're logged in as root, yet the user account will prevent you from making a mess of things by mistake. On Windows, it's really not your computer; *Microsoft* has more authority than the administrator, yet users are given enough power to turn it into a virus- and spyware-infested morass.

But then, Redmond has always entertained very quaint ideas about computer security.

Encryption

No piece of personal technology is more controversial than strong encryption. Ever since a programmer named Phil Zimmermann created a crypto application for ordinary computer users called PGP, or Pretty Good Privacy, it's become highly politicized, the frequent object of strenuous and heated debate, lauded by human rights advocates and denounced by police and intelligence agencies the world over. Even the enlightened governments of North America and western Europe, which rarely miss an opportunity to tout themselves as paragons of democracy and liberty, have either imposed Draconian restrictions on encryption already or are considering imposing them in the future.

Americans who've been using the Net for a few years will recall that downloading the Netscape or Internet Explorer browser used to involve pledging that the products would not be brought into another country. That's because, at the time, the encryption implemented by SSL (Secure Socket Layer) was regulated as a deadly munition. Military and national-security agencies engaged in overseas spying didn't wish to see adversaries and competitors in possession of such technology. Nevertheless, the export restrictions were lifted in 2000, over the vehement objections of law enforcement agencies, intelligence spooks, and tough-on-crime legislators.

Some people believe that the export regulations were eased after the U.S. National Security Agency (NSA), a military support organization that intercepts electronic communications abroad and performs cryptanalysis, became confident it could break most commercial crypto products. A more realistic theory is that the cat had by this time got so far out of the bag that the restrictions were obsolete.

Governments hate encryption. They use it, all right, for protecting sensitive documents and communications, but the idea of the average citizen getting his hands on it gives them fits. Governments like to monitor, even regulate, what their citizens may read and write and say. Citizens, on the other hand, feel that there are a number of things that government has no right to know and some activities it has no right to regulate. Tensions are unavoidable.

There are a few minor downsides to encryption. Fifty-three criminal cases slipped through the FBI's hands because their (apparently quite overrated) technicians were unable to access computer files that had been encrypted by suspects, former FBI Director Louis Freeh explained in testimony to the Senate Appropriations Subcommittee in February of 2000, just as the export restrictions were about to be lifted. Freeh was, and remains today, one of the developed world's most aggressive opponents of private encryption. He, like many in his line of work, feels that anything with the potential to make law enforcement more difficult should be regulated, regardless of the good it might do.

During their tenure, Freeh and his boss, former U.S. Attorney General Janet Reno, repeatedly called for crypto regulations along lines preferred by such neurotic governments as Iran, North Korea, and the United Kingdom. They proposed mandatory key escrow, a scheme whereby the government would be given a copy of each citizen's private encryption key so that the police would be able to decrypt any file for which they obtained a search warrant. The so-called Clipper Chip, touted by the Clinton Administration but finally abandoned under a withering barrage of public ridicule, was based on a similar approach. The implementation was badly flawed and ripe for official abuse. Meanwhile, the UK's dreaded Regulation of Investigatory Powers (RIP) Act of 2000 passed through Parliament and now imposes prison sentences of two years on any citizen who refuses to reveal his private key to the authorities on demand, and *five years* if he should dare reveal publicly that his key has been demanded. (This is no surprise; *embarrassing* an authoritarian regime is typically a more serious offense than quietly defying it.)

All governments hate personal crypto because it allows people to communicate in a private manner that cannot be violated if the crypto application is implemented properly. As PGP creator Phil Zimmermann has said, "Two hundred years ago, all conversations were private. If someone else was within earshot, you could just go out behind the barn and have your conversation there. No one could listen in without your knowledge."[1]

But things are vastly different today. "With the coming of the information age, starting with the invention of the telephone, all that has changed. Now most of our conversations are conducted electronically. This allows our most intimate conversations to be exposed without our knowledge,"[2] Zimmermann points out.

Throughout virtually all of human history, government has been unable to eavesdrop secretly on citizens' conversations. A nosy third party—a snitch—was always needed. Since the telephone age it has had this capacity, and it's grown to like it very much. Phone calls, faxes, and data passing over an Internet connection can all be monitored secretly and easily.

---

1. See www.philzimmermann.com/essays-WhyIWrotePGP.shtml.

2. Ibid.

Data interception is an inherent feature of the Internet. Unless you take positive steps to prevent it, every byte of data that you exchange is logged and can be traced to you and whomever you exchanged it with. Cryptography makes data interception unproductive. It can't prevent it, certainly, but the fruits of interception are worthless if they're encrypted robustly. Thus there are vocal opponents in every government denouncing personal encryption as a tool of child molesters and terrorists.

But crypto does enormously more good than harm. It secures intimate personal details against disclosure, protects sensitive business and financial data, and ensures that privileged communications between people and their doctors, lawyers, clergy, and the press will remain privileged. It enables relief workers and human rights advocates to communicate securely and to protect documents from disclosure in countries where what they say can get them imprisoned, tortured, even killed. The good it can do in the hands of millions far outweighs the harm it can do in the hands of a few. We feel the same about such items as fertilizer and box cutters, which is why they're still legal in spite of having been leveraged by terrorists in recent years to kill and maim thousands. They're simply too useful to be restricted.

Citizens should not feel obligated to make life easy for lazy or incompetent police officers by supporting the passage of laws that regulate strong encryption for personal use. We should not surrender our collective privacy merely because the FBI or MI5 bungles an investigation now and then. Personal crypto products are the last means of secure, and private, electronic communication left to us today. If we lose control over them, then the only possible scenario for private communication becomes the heart-to-heart behind the barn—assuming we're not the subjects of video surveillance at the time. Personal crypto is our last remaining hope of closing a door on government that it can't open at will.

Unfortunately, personal crypto products aren't as easy to use as they might be. A study entitled *Why Johnny Can't Encrypt,* by Alma Whitten of the Carnegie Mellon University School of Computer Science, cites poor and confusing user experiences with personal crypto products and low success rates among novices. For this reason, we're going to spend a good deal of time explaining this crucial security tool.

Basics

Encryption uses mathematics to scramble data and to unscramble it. There are four basic components:

- *The algorithm:* The mathematical routine with which data is scrambled

- *The cryptosystem:* The basic architectural scheme with which the algorithm is put to use

- *The application:* The computer program that makes all this easy for people to use

- *The key:* The mechanism for scrambling data and unscrambling it later in a controlled fashion

In Chapter 1, we talked about hashing, which is a one-way scrambling function. Good hashing means that the original input should not be recoverable. That's one type of cryptosystem. Personal encryption is different; what's scrambled needs to be unscrambled, albeit in a very tightly controlled way. This is another type of cryptosystem.

When you access a Web site via SSL, indicated by a URL starting with HTTPS, you're using encryption whether you realize it or not. The data transferred between your browser and the Web server is encrypted and decrypted on the fly at its points of origin and destination. Thus, any secondary Web server through which the data passes *en route* will receive only a lot of meaningless characters. Your ISP may log your Internet traffic and can easily determine what Web sites you're connecting to and when, but it can't read the contents of SSL traffic.

PGP and GnuPG are crypto applications that enable computer users to encrypt and decrypt data stored on their machines or sent via the Internet whenever they please. These applications use an asymmetrical paired-key cryptosystem. It's called *asymmetrical* because one key scrambles the data, while a different key (and *only* that key) unscrambles it. No one should be able to decrypt a file or a message except the owner of the key pair. Anyone can use the encrypting key, but access to the decrypting key is controlled with a strong password. Thus, if you encrypt a file on your computer using your own encryption key, only you can decrypt it using the corresponding decryption key *so long as you are the only person who knows the password*. If the password is shared, then the person you reveal it to can decrypt the file, as can anyone with whom he or she shares it in turn, assuming they can obtain local or remote access to your computer. Similarly, if the password is weak, then another person may be able to guess it or discover it with a dictionary or brute-force attack.

This process of paired-key encryption is easy to picture in a situation such as protecting a file on your computer. You have an *en*cryption key and a corresponding *de*cryption key created as a matched pair just for yourself. You use the first key to scramble the file, and the second key to unscramble it. No other decryption key will work because the keys are created as a key pair. The pair only works together; therefore, if you should accidentally delete your decryption key, you will *never* be able to decrypt a file encoded with its corresponding encryption key.

That's fairly simple, but it gets confusing when two people are exchanging encrypted messages and we now have four keys to worry about, not two. Think for a moment—how would you encrypt an e-mail memo so that only I could decrypt it? If you use your own encryption key, then only *you* would be able to decrypt the memo: I would need your decryption key to read it. And of course, if I had your decryption key, I would be able to decrypt *anything* you'd encrypted. So that certainly won't work.

The solution is for us both to share our *en*cryption keys, but jealously guard our *de*cryption keys. That is, to send me a memo that only I can read, you would encrypt it with *my* encryption key, not yours. Unless you also encrypt a copy of the memo with your own encryption key, then even you won't be able to decrypt the message you've sent me, and neither will anyone else. If you use only my encryption key, then only I will have the corresponding decryption key, protected with a strong password that only I know. When I reply to your memo, I would encrypt my reply using *your* encryption key so that only you can decrypt it with its corresponding decryption key, presumably protected by a strong password that only you know.

Thus we call the *en*cryption key our *public key*, and the *de*cryption key our *private key.* When you use an encryption program initially, your first step will be to create a key pair. Your public, or encrypting, key can be published so that others can use it in communicating with you securely. Your private, or decrypting, key is stored on your computer, protected by a very strong password or passphrase. In order for us to exchange encrypted e-mail, we first have to share our public encrypting keys with each other.

You encrypt e-mail with *my* public key, and *I* encrypt e-mail with *your* public key. Except, of course, when you're encrypting files on your own computer. In that case, you encrypt with your own public key and decrypt with your own private key. If you should accidentally encrypt a file using someone else's key and delete the original, then only they will be able to decrypt it. So you normally encrypt your own files with your own keys, except when you wish to send an e-mail memo with an encrypted file attachment. In that case, you'd encrypt the attached file with the recipient's public key, or they would be unable to decrypt it. You can encrypt a file with more than one public key. You could send a copy to me encrypted for me, and retain a copy encrypted for yourself so that you can access it later. Finally, to confuse everyone further, there is the issue of *digitally signing* a memo or a file so that the recipient can verify that you, and no one else, sent it. In that case, you sign it using your *private* key, and the recipient verifies the signature with your *public* key.

If you find this confusing, don't get discouraged. According to the usability study by Alma Whitten, a majority of users asked to encrypt and digitally sign an e-mail memo with PGP 5.0 remained unsuccessful after 90 minutes of trying. Many were confused about which key does what. Another problem, Whitten found, is that common metaphors, such as *key* and *signature,* can be misleading to novices.

Summary

Because there's so much confusion associated with personal encryption, let's summarize the main points for future reference:

1. You *en*crypt personal files on your computer with your own public key and *de*crypt them with your own private key. If you send these encrypted files to someone else, they will be unable to decrypt them. Only you can decrypt these files. If you wish to make an encrypted file available to someone else, you must encrypt it with their public key as well as your own.

2. You *en*crypt outgoing mail with the recipient's public key and they *de*crypt it with their private key. You *de*crypt incoming mail that someone else has encrypted using your public key, by using your own private key.

3. You digitally sign an outgoing e-mail memo with your *private* key, and the recipient verifies the signature with your *public* key.

4. You encrypt a file that you wish to send via e-mail or IM with the recipient's public key. Take care that your encryption program is not set to delete the original automatically when you do this, or you will be unable to decrypt the file yourself. Fortunately, most encryption programs allow you to encrypt a file with more than one public key. Thus, you can encrypt it with the recipient's public key and your own, so that both of you can decrypt it later.

5. Your public key may be shared freely, even published on a *key server*; but you must protect your private key with a very strong password or passphrase that only you know. Because people use encryption for their most sensitive files and correspondence, your crypto passphrase is the most important of all and should be created with special care. Even if someone gets root on your computer, they won't be able to read your encrypted files and correspondence so long as the passphrase is strong. I recommend no fewer than 12 characters with a mixture of numerals, uppercase and lowercase letters, spaces, and special characters. And longer is *always* better. Write down your passphrase and store it securely until you're confident you've memorized it. Then destroy the record. But before you do, be *certain* that you've memorized the passphrase. If you forget it, everything you've encrypted will be permanently unavailable.

6. You should create a backup copy of your key pair (also called a *keyring*) on removable media and store it in a secure location as soon as you've created it, in case of computer problems. Otherwise, if your private key is lost, you will be unable to decrypt messages or files encrypted with its corresponding public key. Once your private key is gone, it's gone forever. There's no way to re-create it, so you must back it up on removable media. If you should lose your private key, you will have to generate a new key pair and send your new public key to your contacts. It is not necessary to save backups of your keyring each time you add someone's public key to it. They can send you their keys again if you lose them. Only your original pair must be backed up. If you create additional key pairs for different aliases you might have, they all need to be backed up as soon as they're created.

Readers who are still a bit uncertain can take heart. In the following sections, we're going to install PGP and GnuPG, and then generate and use a key pair, step by step. Linux users may profit from skimming the PGP section, as it contains a few general tips.

PGP

Pretty Good Privacy (PGP) is a semi-closed-source encryption tool for Windows. It costs between $50 and $70 for full-featured, personal-use versions and can be purchased from www.pgp.com. The company also makes a free version available, but with less functionality. The pay version of PGP is a good choice for Windows users, but not for Linux users. However, the free, open-source GnuPG program works beautifully with Linux. It can also be used on Windows, though not with ease.

PGP for Windows is not ideal; it does not have a plugin for Mozilla Mail, which I recommend, and it requires Client for Microsoft Networks, which I don't recommend. Unfortunately, GnuPG for Windows is still under development and is appropriate for more advanced users, so novices are stuck with PGP. And they're stuck with Client for Microsoft Networks, which is a bit of a security risk for an Internet-connected machine.

The good news is that PGP is easy to set up and can be mastered by a novice. It features a graphical installer and user interface, plugins for several clients, a secure file-wipe utility, and a feature allowing a disk volume to be encrypted, which can be useful for theft-prone laptop computers that contain sensitive or proprietary data. However, once the encrypted disk volume is mounted, it's decrypted, so if the laptop grows legs while the PGP volume is open, its contents will be available to the thief. In some cases, it may be safer to encrypt crucial files individually and decrypt them only as needed.

To begin, first download the current version of PGP that suits you. The pay versions are available at www.pgp.com, the free version at www1.pgp.com/products/freeware.html. The free version lacks the plugins for ICQ, Outlook, and the like. Without the plugins, it's necessary to compose an e-mail memo, then encrypt it with the intended recipient's public key using the Encrypt Current Window feature. If you choose a pay version of PGP, it will be a bit easier to encrypt e-mail, but you will have to use Microsoft's insecure clients to enjoy the convenience, and I would urge you not to do so.

If you followed my earlier advice about uninstalling Client for Microsoft Networks, you will have to reinstall it to use any version of PGP. To do this, follow these steps:

1. Go to the Start menu and choose Settings ➤ Network Connections.

2. Click on the icon corresponding to your network connection, and a status dialog will appear. (The name will depend on what sort of connection you make.)

3. Choose Properties, and a connection Properties dialog will appear.

4. Click on Install.

5. The Select Network Component Type dialog will appear asking you what to install; choose Client and click the Add button.

6. Finally, the Select Network Client dialog will appear, in which you should specify Client for Microsoft Networks. Click OK and clear the dialogs.

You will have to reboot Windows after installing PGP, so it's wise to save any work you have open before you begin.

Now you can unzip the PGP file and activate the installer, a typical GUI wizard. After clicking through the welcome and license screens, etc., you will be asked if you have an existing keyring or if you're a new user. Next you will be asked to choose a directory for the program or accept the default. Either is fine. The next screen offers you several plugins. (The plugins won't work if you're using the free version.) Next the wizard will install several files and prompt you to reboot, which you must do before using the program.

When Windows restarts, you'll have to launch PGP and create your key pair. There should be a new tray applet with a little padlock icon that launches PGP. Bring it up and select the PGPkeys feature. (Or go to the Start menu and choose Programs ➤ PGP ➤ PGPkeys.) A dialog will pop up, called PGPkeys, allowing you to create your own keys and to add or import other people's public keys to your keyring.

Now it's time to create your first key pair:

1. Using the menu bar at the top of the PGPkeys dialog, go to Keys ➤ New Keys. Another wizard will start, to simplify creating them.

2. On the first screen, type in your name and e-mail address, or your alias and a corresponding e-mail address. (You can repeat this for as many e-mail accounts and aliases as you own.)

3. On the next screen, you will choose your passphrase. Make it a good one. There is a little progress bar that indicates the passphrase quality. Shoot for somewhere past the halfway mark. Write it down if you need to and keep the record secure; destroy it only when you're confident that you've memorized it. It is crucial that you not forget this passphrase, or anything you encrypt will be impossible to decrypt later.

4. Once that's done, the program will generate your new keys. When it's finished, clear the wizard and you should find the keys listed in the original dialog. If there are no error messages or warning symbols, you're done (Figure 4-13). But leave the original PGPkeys dialog open until we've finished.

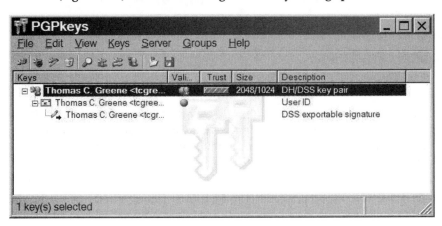

Figure 4-13. The PGPkeys dialog with a new key pair illustrated

You're now ready to encrypt and decrypt files on your computer. Let's give it a quick try:

1. Open Notepad, type in a brief message, then save the file as test-pgp.txt.

2. Open the Windows Explorer file browser and find the file. You'll see, as you right-click on the file, that PGP is now integrated with Windows Explorer. Use the right-click menu and scroll down to PGP (Figure 4-14). You'll be able to encrypt, sign, decrypt, or wipe the file.

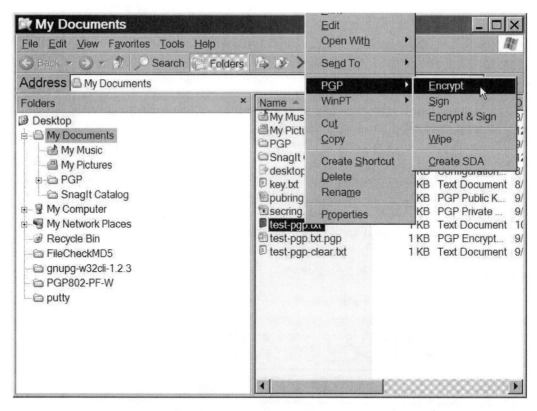

Figure 4-14. The PGP right-click menu

3. Choose Encrypt. A second dialog will appear, listing the Recipients in the top field and yourself in the bottom field. Since we haven't added any other people's public keys, the upper field will be blank (Figure 4-15). Once you've added other public keys, your contacts will be listed in the upper field, and you can drag them to the lower field if you wish. The lower field lists the public key or keys to be used for encryption. If you should add others later, PGP can encrypt the file so that these people will be able to decrypt it as well.

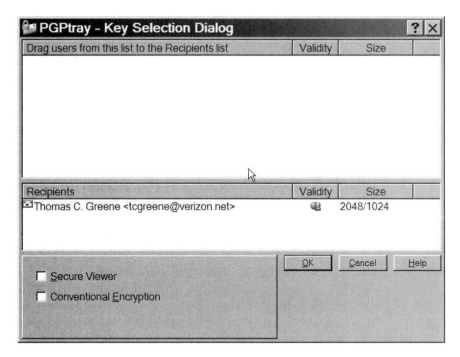

Figure 4-15. The PGP Key Selection dialog with one recipient selected

4. For now, only you should appear in the lower field. Since this is a test, make sure that the option Automatically wipe on delete is *not* selected in the bottom left field of the PGP Options dialog (Figure 4-16). Just click on OK, and in a moment you'll find that you have two files with the same name, your original and one encrypted (indicated with a little padlock icon), named test-pgp.txt.pgp.

5. To decrypt the file you just created, simply left-click as if to launch it. You will be prompted for your passphrase. Enter the passphrase, and a dialog will appear. A decrypted version of the encrypted file will be created. Call the decrypted version test-pgp-clear.txt and save it.

6. Now you can verify that your original file, test-pgp.txt, and the decrypted file, test-pgp-clear.txt, are identical. To see the contents of the encrypted file, right-click on it in Windows Explorer and choose Open With ➤ Notepad. The encrypted version will be a lot of meaningless characters. Now that you've verified that PGP is working properly, you can decrypt this file again whenever you please. It's safe to wipe both the original file and the decrypted file so that only the encrypted one remains.

7. To wipe your original file and the decrypted file, select them in Windows Explorer, right-click, and choose PGP ➤ Wipe. This will not merely delete the files but will actually obliterate them, so that only the encrypted file remains.

Next, let's create, sign, and send an encrypted e-mail memo. Since you haven't yet added anyone else's public key to your keyring, you can only send it to yourself, encrypted for yourself. But that's fine; this is merely a test.

1. Open Mozilla Mail and choose Compose. Enter your own e-mail address in the To field. Now type in a brief message.

2. Go to the PGP tray applet and select Current Window ➤ Encrypt & Sign. The Key Selection dialog will pop up so that you can choose the key or keys to use. Your key will already be chosen, so just click OK. You'll get a password prompt, and after a moment the text in the e-mail memo will change to a lot of gibberish.

3. Now send the memo and wait for it to return. When it comes back, it will still be a lot of gibberish. Return to the PGP applet, choose Current Window from the menu, and select Decrypt & Verify.

4. In a moment, a password prompt will appear. Enter your passphrase. A text editor will pop up, showing the memo contents in clear text and informing you that the signature is valid. Digitally signing e-mail is useful when you want a recipient to be confident that a memo appearing to be from you actually *is* from you. E-mail is ludicrously easy to forge.

What you've just done is encrypt a memo using your public key, decrypt it using your private key, sign it with your private key, then verify the signature with your public key, though it all happened automatically.

If you wish to send an encrypted memo to someone else, you will first have to add their public key to your keyring. If you want another person to be able to verify your digital signature, you will have to send them your public key. You cannot verify the signature of, or encrypt a memo for, someone whose public key is not in your keyring. Similarly, a person who hasn't got your public key in their keyring can't verify your signature or encrypt a memo for you. So if you want to use PGP for e-mail, you've got to exchange public keys with your correspondents.

If these two tests have been successful, everything is working as it should and it's time to back up your keyring and adjust a few options.

1. First, choose a backup medium such as a blank, formatted floppy disk or CD and put it into its related drive.

2. Return to the PGPkeys dialog, which should still be open. From the menu bar, choose Keys ➤ Export. You'll get a Windows dialog allowing you to save the keys wherever you wish. Choose the appropriate disk drive and make sure that the checkbox labeled Include Private Key(s) is checked. Save your key pair, and store the disk in a secure place.

If your computer ever crashes hopelessly, you can restore your keys from the disk later using the PGPkeys Import feature. Again, you needn't save your keyring on external media each time you add someone's public key, but you *do* need to do it each time you generate a fresh key pair for yourself.

The PGP default options and settings are all sensible, but let's go over a few that are important to understand. Using the PGPkeys dialog, go to Edit ➤ Options. Another dialog will launch with a row of tabs at the top (Figure 4-16). We're not going to deal with each tab or all the available options, but only those that need reviewing.

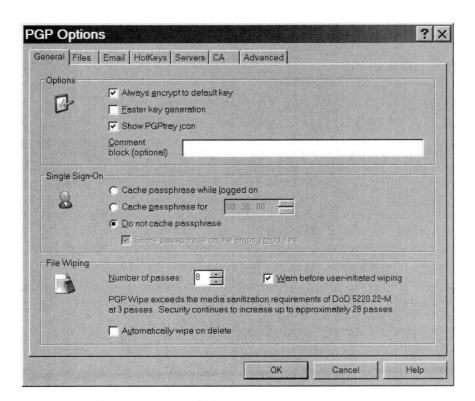

Figure 4-16. The PGP Options dialog

Under the General tab, I recommend the option *Always encrypt to default key* for most users. This way, whenever you encrypt a file or a memo with someone else's public key, you'll retain a copy of it encrypted with your own key so you can access it later. If you don't choose this option and you also choose to wipe the original file automatically after encrypting it, you could end up encrypting one of your own files so that only someone else can read it. Your recourse then would be to ask the recipient to decrypt it, reencrypt it with *your* public key, and send it back—assuming they haven't wiped it in the meantime.

The next set of options under General concerns the Single Sign-On feature, which allows your passphrase to be cached in memory. Home users who don't share their account with others can select the first option, which keeps the passphrase in memory for as long as they're logged in. You will enter your passphrase once and not need to again until you log out of your account or reboot Windows. People in a nonhostile but busy computing environment can choose the second option, which caches the passphrase for a set period of time. The default is two minutes, and this is reasonable for those who work with encrypted files but are frequently called away from their workstation. A home user or a business person with a private office might safely choose one or two hours. People in a hostile environment, where others might attempt to spy on them, or who work with extremely sensitive files, should choose the third option, no memory caching, which requires a passphrase every time an encrypted file or memo is accessed.

Finally, there is the File Wiping option for data destruction. This deletes a file and overwrites it with random characters several times so that the original can't be recovered. The default is three passes, which is good enough for most purposes.

Under the Advanced tab, there is a checkbox at the bottom enabling you to back up your keyring each time PGPkeys closes. The default is to save it to your keyring folder. This is a good feature that will keep your keyring current as you add other people's public keys to it. But it's important to know that this is *not* the same as saving your key pair on removable media for safekeeping. Backing it up on your hard drive is not adequate; if there's a major computer breakdown, your backup will be lost along with the original.

There are other things you can do with the PGP program, such as encrypting the clipboard contents, key signing, document signing, exporting your public keys to a keyserver, importing others' public keys from a keyserver, encrypting disk volumes, creating key revocation certificates, and so on. If we were to explain each one in detail, this chapter would never end. But you now have both a theoretical and a practical grasp of the basics and are ready to learn the rest on your own. Once you become a PGP power user, you'll be able to help your friends and correspondents set it up on their computers, though they may need a bit of urging.

You can obtain other people's public keys from keyservers and publish your own to a keyserver, if you wish. I personally believe that keyservers are better in theory than in practice. Many people, myself included, have tested PGP or GPG and created and published several test keys, many of which are no longer in use. Most keyservers are cluttered with defunct keys, which can make finding the right one difficult. It's easier to exchange keys with your correspondents or publish yours (and even theirs) on a personal Web page, where they can be changed easily whenever a new one is created to replace an old one.

Windows users who don't like paying for closed-source software, or who resent installing a potentially insecure service merely to use encryption, can use the free, open-source GnuPG with Mozilla Mail on Windows. As with PGP, it's necessary to compose a memo and then encrypt it with the Current Window feature. GPG on Windows is more secure than PGP because it permits users to uninstall Client for Microsoft Networks. It does, however, need a bit of tweaking.

The best GnuPG tool available for novices is WinPT (Windows Privacy Tools), available from sourceforge.net/projects/winpt. The look and feel is similar to PGP for Windows. It's a work in progress that still has a few bugs. However, it's under constant development, and by the time this book goes to press a better version may be available. I tested version 0.7.96rc1 and found that the directory paths needed to be harmonized. Specifically, the options file had been placed in a directory different from the one indicated in the setup interface by default. The application was searching the wrong path. This was easy to correct by searching for the options file and inserting the correct path into the setup interface. If you're comfortable tinkering with these sorts of settings, then WinPT should not give you any trouble. If you're not, then you should visit Sourceforge and see if a more recent version has been released. It certainly won't hurt you to download it try it out. If you find a version that works well for you, you can switch from PGP to WinPT and un-install Client for Microsoft Networks, which I recommend.

GPG

GnuPG (GPG) is a free, open-source encryption tool for Windows and Linux. On Windows it's not as user friendly as even the free version of PGP, but it's worth learning if you're comfortable with a bit of tinkering. For Linux users, it's actually easier and more convenient than PGP on Windows; it can be imported to Mozilla Mail and KMail quite conveniently, features a GUI frontend, and doesn't require any insecure services to run.

There are several frontends available: Seahorse and GnomePGP for the Gnome desktop, KGpg for the KDE desktop, and GPA (GNU Privacy Assistant) for pretty much all Linux desktops. They're all good and offer more or less the same features, but because this book is chiefly for novices, we're going to choose the simplest example for illustrating GPG: the KDE 3.0 and later desktop for Linux with GPG and KGpg installed. There are numerous free desktop environments available for Linux and several good crypto frontends, but we can't possibly cover them all. Still, the explanation that follows should prove useful to those using other desktops and GPG frontends. There are more similarities than differences among them. I've chosen KDE because it's easy to use, has a look and feel much like Windows, and is a good starting point for Linux newbies, especially those just migrating from Microsoft products.

Recent versions of the KDE desktop are equipped with the KGpg frontend as part of the kdeutils package. Users of earlier KDE versions can download it separately. KGpg is simple and intuitive enough for any novice. It handles key generation, signing and importing, and browsing files with Krusader or Konqueror that can be encrypted or decrypted with the right-click menu. It can be used for verifying MD5 checksums and includes a tray applet that makes it a snap to access GPG at any time and to encrypt the contents of the clipboard. It has an editor that takes the place of PGP's Encrypt Current Window feature. A KGpg version capable of encrypting whole directories in a single operation is in development at this writing and may be available by the time this book goes to press. Importing keys to KMail also could not be easier. While I recommend Mozilla Mail to Windows users, my first choice for security-minded Linux novices would be KDE's KMail. However, recent versions of Mozilla Mail for Linux have a feature called Enigmail (not available in the Windows version at this writing) that simplifies encryption and signing, making GPG as easy to use with Mozilla as it is with KMail, and considerably easier than using GPG or PGP on Windows. And even without Enigmail, the KGpg editor can create an encrypted file that you can send as an attachment with any e-mail or IM client.

If you're using a recent version of a major packaged distribution like SuSE or Mandrake, GnuPG and KGpg are probably installed on your system already. If they're not, GPG and its several frontends are available from www.gnupg.org, where you can get both GPG and KGpg, either as source packages or binaries according to your preference. You can also download and install a recent KDE version from www.kde.org if you wish. Alternatively, if you're using a packaged distro, you can go to your vendor's Web site and download up-to-date RPMs for KDE, GnuPG, and KGpg built specifically for your system.

The great thing about Linux is the extraordinary level of individual control it gives users over their systems. This makes Linux far easier to configure for security than Windows, which often prevents users from making commonsense changes. But this flexibility also makes it difficult to offer detailed instructions that will work identically across the various distros. It's one thing to explain how to install PGP on Windows XP. It's quite another to explain it to Linux users who may build from source or use RPM, who may obtain software from the developer's Web site or from their vendor's, who may install from their vendor's supplied disks using the command line or with a GUI administrative interface, and who may prefer different desktop environments. So we will have to assume that you already have GPG and KGpg installed. Novices should try to obtain RPMs built by their Linux vendor. These may not always be the latest packages, but they will be configured to work on your system without bother.

KGpg will install a tray applet with a key manager and an editor. Go to the applet and select Open Key Manager from the menu (Figure 4-17). If you already have keys, it will search in /home/~/.gnupg for them. If they're not located there, go to the menu bar, choose Keys ➤ Import Key, and browse to the directory where your keys are located. Be sure to check the option *Allow import of secret keys* when you're importing your own keys. You can also use this same procedure to add other people's public keys to your keyring.

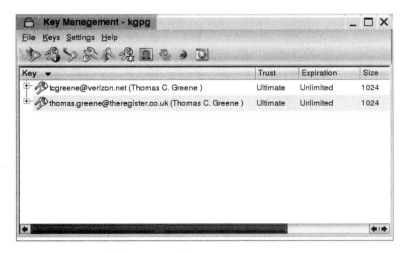

Figure 4-17. The KGpg Key Management dialog

If you have no keys, it's time to create them. From the Key Manager menu bar choose Keys ➤ Generate Key Pair. Another dialog will pop up, prompting you for your name and e-mail address. The defaults for Key Size and Algorithm are perfectly adequate, but you can change them if you wish. The Advanced button will open a shell so that you can use the standard, interactive GPG setup, but novices can use the Key Generation dialog in GUI mode without worry (Figure 4-18). You will then be prompted to supply a passphrase, and the keys will be generated. While this is going on, you will be asked to do things with your computer such as launching programs to create *entropy*. Linux generates random numbers from system "noise" caused by device drivers and the like. This noise is gathered and stored in an *entropy pool*, which helps improve the randomness of numbers generated.

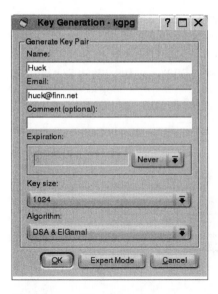

Figure 4-18. The KGpg Key Generation dialog

> **NOTE** *KDE is to be commended for prompting users to generate a crypto key pair as soon as they've set up their accounts, and for making this easy to do. However, if keys are generated immediately after a system has been installed, the entropy pool may be too small to generate strong keys. It's better to use a newly built (or recently rebooted) system for a few hours, activating peripherals, doing a few hard-disk searches, and so on, before generating keys.*

Once your keys are generated, you should test them. Let's start by importing them to KMail:

1. Open KMail and go to Settings ➤ Configure KMail. The KMail Configure dialog will launch (Figure 4-19).

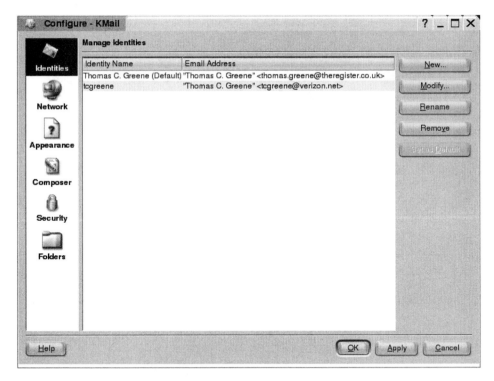

Figure 4-19. The KMail Configure dialog

2. Choose Identities from the left menu and highlight the e-mail account corresponding to the key pair you just created.

3. Click the Modify button and the Edit Identity dialog will launch. From the tabs at the top, choose Advanced.

4. In the middle of Advanced dialog, there will be a line labeled Open PGP key (Figure 4-20). If your new key appears along that line, skip to step 7.

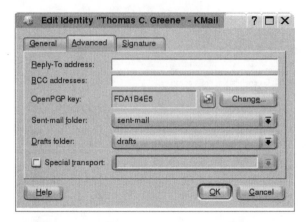

Figure 4-20. The KMail Edit Identity Advanced dialog

5. If your new key doesn't appear, verify that the Security dialog (Figure 4-22) option *Select encryption tool to use* is set to *GnuPG – Gnu Privacy Guard* as illustrated. Then return to the Edit Identity Advanced dialog and click the button labeled Change. Another dialog, labeled Your Open PGP Key, will pop up, showing your key pair (Figure 4-21). If the pair *still* is not listed, click the button at the bottom labeled Reread Keys. Your new key pair will now appear in the window.

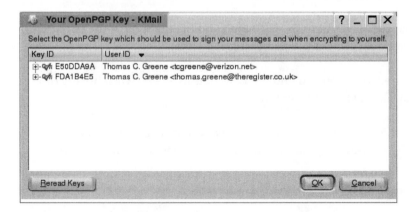

Figure 4-21. The KMail Open PGP Key dialog—notice the button labeled Reread Keys

6. Select your new key pair in the Open PGP Key dialog and return to the KMail Edit Identity Advanced dialog. Your key will be listed in the line labeled Open PGP key. Click OK.

7. Next, choose Security from the left-hand menu in the KMail Settings dialog, and click on the OpenPGP tab (Figure 4-22). Here are your basic options for using GPG. I recommend *not* choosing Keep

passphrase in memory, unless you trust all of the people who might have unsupervised access to your machine while you're logged in to your account. I do recommend choosing the option Always encrypt to self, so that you will be able to read the messages you've sent to others. The remaining options are chiefly a matter of personal preference. Now you can close the KMail Settings dialog.

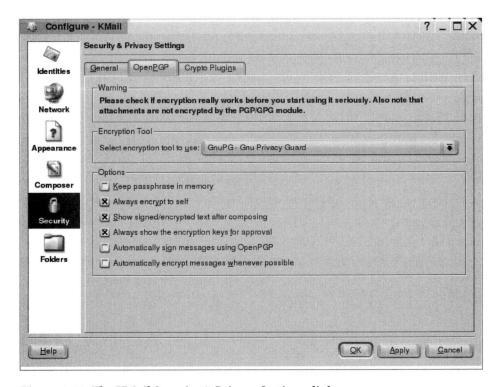

Figure 4-22. The KMail Security & Privacy Settings dialog

You can create a key pair for each of your e-mail accounts and aliases, and import public keys from all of your correspondents. KMail will automatically select the correct key for the identity you choose whenever you compose a memo. It will also automatically choose the public key for each recipient, so long as you've added their public keys to your keyring and indicated that you trust the keys using the Key Manager ➤ Edit Key feature. This way, you can easily send an encrypted memo to several people in a single operation.

Now it's time to create an e-mail memo addressed to yourself. Open a new message and type in a few sentences, then go to the menu bar and choose Options ➤ Encrypt Message, and Options ➤ Sign Message. Send the message, and you will be prompted for your crypto passphrase. Enter it, and the memo will be sent immediately or the encrypted text will be displayed, depending on the options you've chosen. When the memo returns, you'll be prompted for your passphrase.

Enter it, and the memo should be decrypted and indicate that you've signed it. If you don't enter your passphrase, only the encrypted text will be displayed.

Now let's try the KGpg editor. Open the KGpg tray applet and select Open Editor from the menu. Type in a brief message, then click on the Encrypt button. A dialog will pop up, asking which key to use. Select your key and the text will change to something like the example in Figure 4-23.

Figure 4-23. The KGpg Editor with a short phrase encrypted

With most versions of KGpg, you can use the editor to encrypt the text, sign it using the Sign/Verify button, and paste it into an e-mail memo or IM client. If you do copy and paste the encrypted text, be sure to include the opening and closing lines -----BEGIN PGP MESSAGE----- and -----END PGP MESSAGE-----.

You can also save the message to your hard disk and send it as a file attachment later. From the KGpg Editor menu bar, choose File ➤ Save, or File ➤ Save As. The standard KDE dialog will launch with your /home/~/Documents directory as the default location. Name the file and save it, and then attach it to an e-mail memo if you like. The editor is also quite handy if you wish to type out a brief note and save it locally or on removable media as an encrypted file.

Encrypting files on your local hard disk is easy. There are two ways to go about it. First, you can use the KGpg Editor, and from the menu bar choose File ➤ Encrypt File, or File ➤ Decrypt File. You will be able to browse to the file you wish to work with. Second, on later versions of KDE, KGpg integrates itself with the Konqueror file and Web browser and the Krusader file browser, allowing you to select a file, right-click, and encrypt or decrypt it from the right-click menu. This ability to select and encrypt or decrypt files easily is important because KMail doesn't automatically encrypt file attachments. You'll need to encrypt them separately, which you can do conveniently with the KGpg Editor or the right-click menus in Konqueror or Krusader.

Here's how to test this feature:

1. Open Konqueror or Krusader and navigate to a file you'd like to encrypt. Right-click on it and find the options Encrypt and Decrypt in the menu. (If the options are unavailable, you may have to update your version of KDE or KGpg.) Now choose Encrypt.

2. You will be prompted for the key you wish to use. When the key selection dialog pops up, you can choose more than one encryption key by using the Shift key with the mouse to select them. If you're encrypting the file with someone else's public key, be sure to select your own key as well.

3. The encrypted file will have the extension .asc and receive a little padlock icon, indicating that it's a GPG file.

4. Now you can decrypt it, again using the right-click menu. The decrypted file will have the same name as the original, so you will be warned that decryption will overwrite it. To keep the original, simply change the proposed name of the decrypted file and click the Rename button.

5. Next, enter your passphrase. The file will be decrypted and the renamed output file can be compared with the original input file. If everything is working, you can right-click on the two clear-text versions and choose Shred or Wipe from the right-click menu. This will obliterate the files by wiping them several times with random data so that only the encrypted file remains.

The KGpg editor also allows for convenient comparison of MD5 checksums (See the following MD5 section for more information.):

1. First, copy the checksum supplied by the vendor to the clipboard. Then open the KGpg Editor, and from the menu bar choose Signature ➤ Check MD5 Sum. A file browser will launch.

2. Navigate to the file you wish to check and click on it.

3. The file's MD5 sum will be displayed in a dialog box. There is a button labeled Compare MD5 With Clipboard that you can click to compare the file's sum against the sum you copied to the clipboard to see if they match. A green radio button will appear to let you know that the sums are the same.

Once you've verified that GPG is working as it should, it's time to back up your key pair to removable media for safekeeping. The easiest way is simply to copy your /home/~/.gnupg directory to a CD or floppy. You should do this whenever you create a new key pair for yourself. Backing up your correspondents' public keys is a good idea as well, but it's not crucial because you can always ask them to send the keys again if your computer should suffer a major malfunction. Your own private keys, however, can never be recovered if they're lost.

Again, there are other things you can do with KGpg, such as encrypting the clipboard contents, key signing, document signing, exporting your public keys to a keyserver, importing others' public keys from a keyserver, creating key revocation certificates, and so on. But you'll have no trouble learning them on your own, now that you've got the basics.

Crypto Snafus

Now for some caveats. PGP and GnuPG use extremely powerful cryptosystems that create files virtually impossible to crack. If a third party were to intercept a properly encrypted message or file, it's inconceivable that they would ever be able to decrypt it. The computational burden of doing so is beyond the reach of all but perhaps a handful of the world's military intelligence outfits. You can remain quite confident, unless you're a head of state, a high-ranking spook, military officer or diplomat, a captain of industry, or a notorious international terrorist, that no such agency is going to waste its time trying to crack your encrypted e-mail. Disappointing news to the tinfoil hat chorus, but there it is.

However, when someone gains access to your computer, either in person or by a remote attack, they might gain access to your private decryption key. In that situation, *encryption is only as strong as your crypto passphrase*. So choose a unique passphrase of at least 12 characters, combining upper- and lowercase letters, numerals, spaces, and special characters. If you're in frequent possession of very sensitive files, especially on a laptop computer that's only begging to be stolen, you should use a passphrase in the 20 to 25 character range. *Never* use dictionary words or phrases that have any meaning in any language.

If someone installs a keystroke logger on your computer, the game is over. They will obtain your passphrase in plain text simply by intercepting your keystrokes. It makes no difference how robust the encryption is or how tough the passphrase. There are a number of (reputedly) sophisticated loggers used by law enforcement and intelligence services, and they may come in either software or hardware forms. But even the SubSeven script-kiddie rootkit contains one. A number of commercial spyware programs, like eBlaster, do too. It's ironic to consider the effort that's gone into making personal crypto products unbreakable by even the world's top mathematicians, and then to realize that some 13-year-old cretin with a rootkit can defeat them with ease. This is why I say there's no security without privacy, and no privacy without security. They are the twin sides of a single coin. Hardening your system will make it a lot more difficult for someone to attack your machine with a rootkit and violate your privacy.

PGP Wipe, and the free Linux utilities Shred and Wipe, are appropriate for everyday data destruction. Earlier, I recommended three passes as an adequate setting for PGP Wipe. However, there are sophisticated forensic techniques for recovering data that can yield traces of files wiped in this manner. Of course, such techniques are expensive both in terms of equipment and effort and therefore rarely used. If you're wiping a file with, say, national security implications, or one that can get you sent to jail for several years, 20 to 30 passes is a safer bet, but this is overkill in all but the most exceptional cases. Admittedly, if the KGB or CIA or MI6 is apt to snatch your hard drive, then they're apt to apply the best techniques available in rooting it, so a 20-pass wipe is appropriate if this is a danger for you. (An oxyacetylene torch is even more appropriate if this is a danger for you.) On the other hand, your spouse's divorce lawyer, armed with a subpoena for your computer files, is likely to be thwarted with a three-pass wipe. Ditto for the local police department. You can achieve quite adequate data destruction with these utilities, so long as you also learn to control the *duplicate data traces* that accumulate in other regions of the hard disk, explained in Chapter 5.

MD5

MD5 is a hashing algorithm that can be used to generate password hashes or create a *checksum* for a file, which is rather similar. That is, the file itself can be used as input and hashed, and a brief numerical checksum (also called a *message digest* or *fingerprint*) can be created. The fingerprint is unique; it's highly unlikely (though not impossible) that two different files would create the same one. When you first install a system from trusted media, you can generate MD5 sums for important program files and check them later to verify that they haven't been tampered with by other users, remote attackers, or installed malware.

When a developer makes a file or a program available for download from a Web site, he may generate a message digest from his original file and post that as well. When you download the file, you can also generate a message digest or checksum from whatever file eventually ends up on your computer. If the checksum you create matches the one the developer created, you can be confident that it's the same file.

Now, this hardly guarantees that a file is safe. Anyone can put a malicious file on a Web site along with its accompanying MD5 sum. When you download the file, you can generate a sum and check it against the sum created by the author or developer (or hacker). If the sums match, then the file you downloaded is the same one the author posted. This is called an *integrity check*. If the file has been tampered with since being posted or during the download, you'll know. But this merely guarantees that you've received what you believed you were downloading.

If the file is malicious, the MD5 comparison will only verify that you've got an authentic rootkit.

This has been an occasional problem. For example, in March 2003, an attacker gained root access to the Free Software Foundation's gnu.org download site, a huge repository of open-source software. It's not believed that any of the software had been tampered with, but it could have been. With root access, the attacker could have replaced any of the thousands of files offered for download with malicious duplicates, and could easily have calculated and posted the correct MD5 sums for the malicious files.

The Free Software Foundation (FSF) had to establish the validity of all its software with older, trusted MD5 checksums that predated the intrusion, which was a considerable task. The admins couldn't trust any checksums posted to the server after the breach occurred, because they could have been changed. Fortunately, the attacker "was interested primarily in using gnu.org to collect passwords and as a launching point to attack other machines," the organization explained.

Because a malicious file can be posted with a valid checksum, I find the security value of MD5 verification for downloaded files to be rather limited. It's certainly easy enough for you to do, but I wouldn't put much faith in its ability to reduce the spread of malware. It can protect you from some attacks, such as when a download is redirected, but it's not much of a security measure overall.

The most practical use for MD5 fingerprinting is performing an integrity check of files on your own computer, so long as they were installed from trusted media such as your software vendor's original installation CDs. Fingerprinting can alert you when a file is replaced with malware or manipulated in some way. For example, some rootkits and viruses replace common binaries or executables with malicious ones. If you detect unusual system behavior, one way to verify the infection is by comparing the MD5 sum of the suspect file on your computer against the sum published by the vendor or the sum you established when you installed it. If the sums matched when you installed the file but fail to match at a later date, you can infer that someone or some program or update has tampered with it in the meantime. Of course, *you* may well be the culprit here: whenever you install system updates, patches, and hotfixes, you will change the MD5 checksums of many files. And whenever Windows boots, it makes changes to hundreds of files, which in turn makes this sort of auditing quite tedious. You will have to update your MD5s whenever you update software from a trusted source. If you generate MD5 fingerprints for your executable system files when you install your system and update these fingerprints whenever you perform a software or system update, you can compare your established fingerprints to current ones at any time, possibly spotting an infection that your AV software missed.

Most personal computers are loaded with tens of thousands of files, and the number of malicious ones circulating is at least in the thousands. There are more convenient ways of detecting malware, such as using an antivirus scanner. Unfortunately, AV scanners don't detect all malware. Some powerful commercial rootkits like eBlaster, SpyAnywhere, NetVizor, and the like are deliberately overlooked by the antivirus industry. (Apparently, so long as someone is earning a profit from malware, it ceases to *be* malware.) MD5 checking is a useful trick to know for those situations when you can't trust your antivirus software.

Windows users can download a number of different utilities. I would recommend the free FileCheckMD5, available from `www.brandonstaggs.com/filecheckmd5.html` and from the Downloads section of the Apress Web site, for its speed and ease of use. Simply download the file, unzip it, and it's ready. It works by creating a text file containing MD5 sums of the contents of directories you choose. This file will be stored in the directory scanned. To scan the contents of a directory, simply click on the tab Create Checkfile, navigate to the directory of your choice, and click Go. The files will be scanned, and another file called FCMD5-sums.MD5 will be created, which contains the fingerprints of all the files in that directory. To verify them later, simply choose the tab Check Files and choose Open Checkfile. Now navigate to the MD5 checkfile you wish to verify, and load it. The utility will scan the current MD5 sums against those recorded in the checkfile and alert you to those that have changed.

I'd suggest scanning the C:\WINDOWS directory, C:\Program Files directory, and C:\Documents and Settings\All Users\Start Menu\Programs\Startup directory and checking the sums of executable and library files occasionally. To avoid being alarmed by harmless changes, it's a good idea to rescan these directories after installing updates and patches, so long as you trust the source.

This sort of fingerprint checking is similar to what your antivirus scanner does, but manual MD5 checking gives you control over what's to be scanned and what isn't, and lets you decide how important an unexpected change might be. It's not a substitute for virus scanners, which search for specific checksums, other data, and even system behavior indicating malware (all jealously guarded by the antivirus cartel so that you *have to* buy their products). MD5 auditing is a second-line defense that can catch changes to system files that your AV software misses or is designed to ignore. It's that second category—the malware and rootkits that AV scanners won't alert you to—that makes occasional MD5 integrity checking an important bit of security housekeeping. Unexpected changes to executable (~.exe) and library (~.dll) files should be investigated. Do not concern yourself with changes to configuration files such as ~.ini files, log files, or the Registry, as Windows writes to these files whenever it boots. Although it's true that some malware will alter these files, Windows plays fast and loose with them as well, and you can easily go mad trying to stay on top of these changes.

For Linux users there is a free, open-source version of the Tripwire utility, but this is a command-line application not suitable for novices. There are easy-to-use pay versions of Tripwire available for most operating systems from `www.tripwire.com`, but these are too expensive for home and SOHO users. Unfortunately, at this writing there isn't a free, open-source utility capable of doing recursive MD5 sums and integrity comparisons with a simple, GUI frontend appropriate for Linux novices. The KGpg utility will do quick comparisons of individual files, but it can't (yet) be used for recursive checking. However, if you're comfortable with command-line applications, I would recommend the free version of Tripwire, available from Sourceforge at `sourceforge.net/projects/tripwire` or from your Linux vendor. It's actually a quite powerful tool capable of a lot more than comparing MD5 fingerprints, and well worth learning if you're motivated.

Finally, MD5 is a good algorithm for hashing passwords. It's an option for Linux computers that I recommend. Of course it isn't foolproof, just better than most. All passfiles can be cracked; the only question is how difficult and time consuming doing it will be. MD5 does a good job of making it both difficult and time consuming, which is all you can expect.

SSH

Secure shell (SSH) is one of the most useful security and privacy tools ever devised. Essentially, it encrypts Internet and network traffic between two computers so that any traffic intercepted can't be deciphered. The Internet is a profoundly insecure network where traffic can be intercepted with ease. SSH doesn't prevent interception; it makes the fruits of interception worthless. It's a bit like PGP for your Internet connection.

SSH has several applications: you can use it to log in to your computer securely from a remote location, or you can use it to log in to a proxy server. It's even possible to encrypt all of your Internet traffic with it, including e-mail, Web browsing, and chat sessions, with a feature called *SSH tunneling*. SSH is a separate Internet protocol, just like HTTP, FTP, SMTP, and so on. But it can be used to carry and encrypt data that travels via other protocols. This practice of enclosing, say, an HTTP packet inside an SSH session is called *tunneling*. It's rather like enclosing a postcard inside an opaque, sealed envelope so that it can't be read as it travels through the post.

If you're on the road and using a laptop from a convention center, hotel, or other place where Internet connectivity is provided, you can log in to your workstation at the office, your computer at home, or a proxy, with SSH and conceal the entire session from whoever might be monitoring the traffic.

Anyone who provides a network connection can monitor it. Consider the broadband cable conveniently located in your hotel room. The hotel will let you use it for about $20 a day. You plug one end of the cable into your laptop computer's NIC (network interface card), but you have no idea what the other end is connected to.

It's connected to some sort of computer, router, or switch—that's certain. But where is this equipment located? In the hotel, or elsewhere? Who has access to it? Are the admins qualified, and have they passed adequate background checks? What other gear is connected to this unknown equipment at the far end of that cable in your hotel room (or airport, or convention center, or Internet cafe)? Perhaps you're being connected to a name-brand ISP motivated to behave responsibly because it has a national reputation to protect. Even so, you have no idea what machinery lies between that handy broadband cable and the ISP.

What's the threat here? That your Internet traffic, especially your passwords, will be intercepted by a third party about whom you know nothing. What is the risk? Pick a number between zero and a hundred percent, because your guess is as good as mine. You're dealing with a known unknown: a known threat and an unknown risk. You could ask the hotel manager to give you a detailed briefing on precisely how and by whom this convenience is provided, but chances are his guess will be as good as yours. He'll likely tell you that it's been looked at by experts and judged very secure, and that the hotel takes its clients' privacy very seriously. But then, that's what he's paid to say.

Obviously, we need a solution that's portable and gives us some control over our IP traffic. SSH is the simplest answer: it will encrypt your IP traffic so you needn't worry about who may or may not be in a position to monitor your comings and goings on the Internet. For this you need two things: a client and a server.

The SSH client is a small software program, in this case running on your laptop computer. It allows you to make an encrypted connection to an SSH server. Everything that passes between the client and server is encrypted, regardless of what equipment lies between them. This type of connection is called an *SSH session*. By taking advantage of the tunneling feature, you can send and receive *all* of your IP traffic through the SSH session. The server can be your own desktop computer at home, so long as it's switched on and connected to the Internet and is running the SSH server daemon. Between your home computer and your laptop are the ISP that your laptop is connected to and the ISP your home computer is connected to, and this involves a whole series of routers and switches administered by God knows who. But the IP traffic moving between the two machines will be encrypted end to end. From your hotel room, you can connect to your home PC via an SSH session and use the home machine as a proxy server forwarding all your IP traffic and returning only encrypted data to your laptop.

If it's not convenient for you to leave a home computer available for such purposes, you can subscribe to a service like the one offered by Anonymizer, which provides an SSH-enabled proxy server to which you can log in from anywhere. Essentially, it's a public SSH server that anyone can hire. Wherever you are, you can establish an SSH session with the Anonymizer proxy. The proxy will fetch all your Web, e-mail, IM traffic, etc., and encrypt it before forwarding it to you. Whatever equipment happens to lie between your computer and the proxy is irrelevant; all the data passing between them is protected. The service costs about $100 per year, but it frees you from having to set up an SSH server of your own and keeping a computer available for remote connections. It's very handy for people who travel frequently and use Internet connections from numerous providers, but who prefer not to leave a home computer running. Such a service is necessary for people who own only one computer and obviously can't set up their own SSH server.

Let's look at an SSH connection from Netstat's point of view.

```
tcg@linux:~ - Shell - Konsole                                      _ □
Session  Edit  View  Bookmarks  Settings  Help
tcg@linux:~> netstat -an
Active Internet connections (servers and established)
Proto Recv-Q Send-Q Local Address         Foreign Address        State
tcp        0      0 127.0.0.1:110         0.0.0.0:*              LISTEN
tcp        0      0 127.0.0.1:9999        0.0.0.0:*              LISTEN
tcp        0      0 127.0.0.1:80          0.0.0.0:*              LISTEN
tcp        0      0 127.0.0.1:25          0.0.0.0:*              LISTEN
tcp        0      0 192.168.1.2:1940      168.143.113.101:22     ESTABLISHED
tcp        0      0 ::1:110               :::*                   LISTEN
tcp        0      0 ::1:9999              :::*                   LISTEN
tcp        0      0 ::1:80                :::*                   LISTEN
tcp        0      0 ::1:25                :::*                   LISTEN

  New      Shell
```

Figure 4-24. Many Internet clients but only one remote connection

You can see that my PC is connected to another machine at 168.143.113.101. That's the proxy server maintained by Anonymizer. My machine, 192.168.1.2, is using its outbound port 1940 to connect to the SSH proxy server located at 168.143.113.101, which is accepting the connection on its port 22.

This shows an example of SSH tunneling and *port forwarding* to the proxy. This funnels all of my IP traffic through the proxy, which in turn prevents my ISP from reading any of my Internet traffic and prevents others who receive my traffic from obtaining my actual, or ISP-assigned, IP address. I can log in to this proxy from anywhere, using my own laptop or even someone else's computer, and my traffic will be protected. (However, if I don't own the computer I'm using, I must still be concerned with the data traces I might leave behind and any malware that might be loaded on it.)

Fellow Linux users will notice that I have no daemon processes or servers running on my home machine and that I've prevented my X Window server from listening on the Internet. Even identd is disabled because the proxy will handle it: a remote server will get a valid ident reply if it needs one, but from the proxy, not from me. The *only* remote TCP connection my machine *ever* makes is to the SSH proxy, and all the IP traffic exchanged between the two is encrypted.

This is an example of a secure and private Internet setup for a home or small business network taking advantage of NAT and SSH tunneling. But it's also quite simple to set up and largely maintenance-free. Because the NAT router performs stateful packet inspection (SPI), I have no use for a packet filter or personal firewall; because I use Linux, I have no use for antivirus software. Unnecessary daemon processes are disabled. An occasional file integrity check with Tripwire is all I need to protect myself from malware. *All* of my clients—my browser, e-mail client, chat clients, FTP client, and the like—connect to the Internet through an encrypted SSH session with the Anonymizer proxy. Of course, all of this traffic has to pass through my ISP along the way, and its admins can easily monitor it, but because SSH encrypts the data, they'll see only a lot of meaningless characters. And because, from the ISP's point of view, I only make one connection to a single proxy using a single port, there is no way for its admins to determine which Web sites I'm visiting or where my e-mail is going. The Anonymizer proxy is designed to provide privacy with SSH, but it's also designed for *anonymity*, which is entirely different. We'll get into that in Chapter 5.

In the previous section dealing with Netstat, we learned that 127.0.0.1 (local-host) is a loopback interface that bypasses the local network and the Internet, and exchanges packets internally, within the local machine. You can also see in Figure 4-24 that 127.0.0.1 or localhost is listening for and accepting HTTP, SMTP, and POP traffic. How is this so? It's done with a trick called port forwarding, which SSH makes possible. In a virtual sense, all of these ports are "forwarded" to the proxy via SSH. The Internet traffic between the Anonymizer proxy and my local machine is passed to and from the Internet clients on my PC via the loopback interface, or localhost. Therefore, only one port on the computer is actually open to the Internet: port 22, or the SSH port. The other ports are "open" only in an internal sense. They're not facing the Internet; they're facing the internal loopback interface, or localhost. The idea is a bit hard to grasp, but in practical terms it means that all TCP traffic, going in both directions, is tunneled through port 22, regardless of the protocol it would normally use.

For example, when I fetch a Web page with my browser, it uses the loopback interface (localhost) to communicate with the SSH client installed on my machine, *not* the Internet. That is, the browser sends its request to port 80 through the local-host, where the SSH client picks it up, encrypts it, and forwards it to the proxy, or SSH server. The proxy decrypts it and then forwards it to the remote Web server I'm trying to contact. From the Web server's perspective, the request has come from the proxy, *not* my machine. The Web server then sends the data I've requested back to the proxy, which encrypts it before sending it back to me. Data returning to my machine comes from the proxy to the SSH client. The SSH client decrypts it and passes it to the localhost, where the browser grabs it on port 80—although this is an internal process. The browser never accesses the Internet. The SSH client *alone* makes contact with the Internet. All the other clients make contact with the internal loopback interface, or localhost, where the SSH client responds either by sending or fetching the data requested.

Port forwarding and SSH tunneling can be used with all IP clients: e-mail, FTP, instant messaging, IRC, and the like. The ports they use can be forwarded to the SSH server. The clients can be configured to communicate with the localhost; and their traffic, while it may require a different protocol, can be tunneled through an encrypted SSH session.

An SSH server can fetch your e-mail, or send it, and prevent your ISP or local network admin from reading it or even knowing where it's being sent. But it's not a substitute for encrypting e-mail. Whoever provides your e-mail service can read your mail because it resides on their servers. And if the provider is your ISP, then they can read it too. SSH tunneling prevents *outsiders* from reading packets in transit. For example, if you use Hotmail, SSH will prevent your ISP from reading your mail as it passes through their system on its way between your computer and the MSN servers, but the admins at MSN can read all they wish because they're hosting it. Encryption utilities like GPG and PGP are still necessary whenever privacy is imperative.

There are numerous software packages available to implement SSH on Windows, but most are closed source and costly, such as VShell and SecureCRT from VanDyke (client and server sold separately) and F-Secure SSH from `www.f-secure.com` (client and server sold separately). There is a free, open-source SSH client for Windows called PuTTY, available from `www.chiark.greenend.org.uk/~sgtatham/putty/download.html`. The file you'll want is putty-*x.x.x*-installer.exe, where *x.x.x* is the current version number. This file will install the OpenSSH client in a single operation and includes a GUI frontend.

Linux users probably have OpenSSH installed on their machines, but if not, it's available from `www.openssh.com`. As the name implies, it's open-source and free, and includes both a client and a server. There is a GUI frontend for the client included with the KDE desktop, called Kssh. However, to use SSH tunneling it's necessary to forward the associated local ports, and on Linux, ports below 1024 can't be forwarded without root access. Kssh doesn't allow you to log in as root from a user account. So in this case, SSH must be run from the command prompt as root. To forward a privileged port from your user account, open a shell and enter the command *su*, then supply the root password. Then use the command *ssh* followed by the option *-L* (for local ports), and the numbers of the local ports you wish to forward in this format: *-L 80:sshserver.net:80.*

Here, we're forwarding our local ports 110 (POP), 25 (SMTP), and 80 (HTTP) to an SSH server at `sshserver.net`. The command is *ssh*; the option *-2* tells OpenSSH to use the more secure SSH-2 protocol; and the uppercase *-L* stands for local port. The destination, *sshserver.net*, is at the end:

ssh -2 -L 110:mail.sshserver.net:110 -L 25:smtp.sshserver.net:25 -L 80:sshserver.net:80 sshserver.net

You will be prompted for your username on the SSH server, and then your password. This will log you into the SSH server or SSH proxy with the desired local ports forwarded, but you must set up your browser and Internet clients to use localhost as their network interface for SSH tunneling to work properly.

There is a lot that SSH can do, but the basic functions, like logging in to a remote machine, or IP tunneling and port forwarding, are quite simple. Two screen shots follow, showing how PuTTY on Windows would be configured to log in to `sshserver.net` (Figure 4-25) and tunnel browser traffic by forwarding your local port 80 to the SSH server (Figure 4-26).

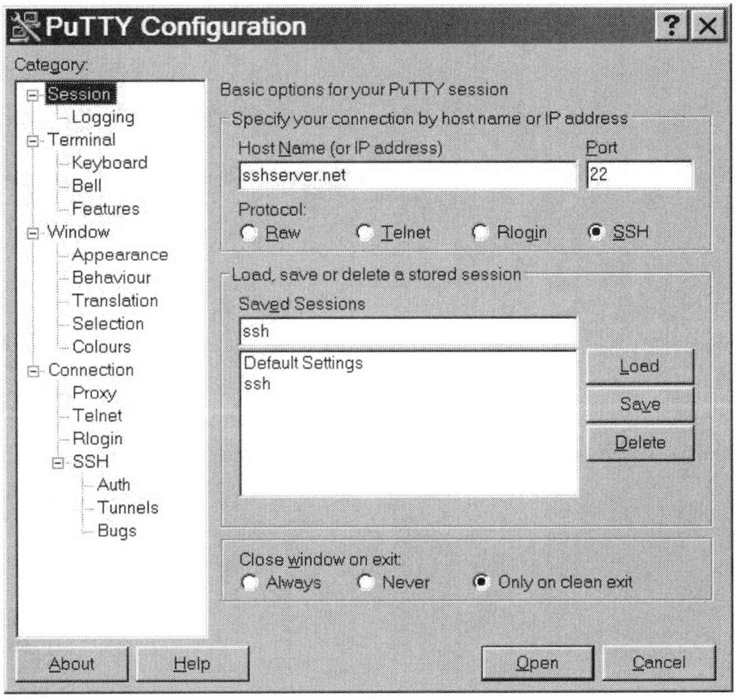

Figure 4-25. Logging in to SSH with PuTTY

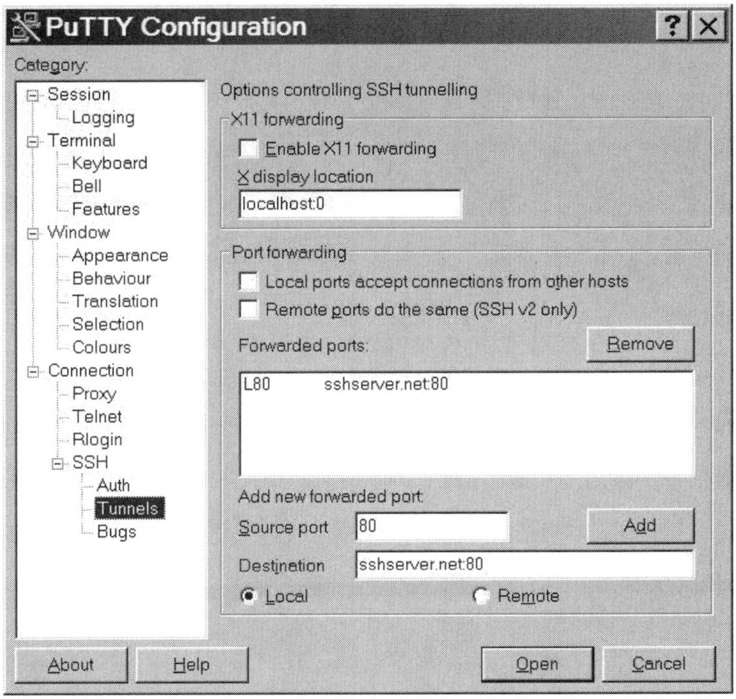

Figure 4-26. Local port forwarding with PuTTY

And Figure 4-27 shows an example of how to set the Mozilla browser to exchange Web traffic, including HTTP, SSL, and FTP, with the localhost, using forwarded local ports.

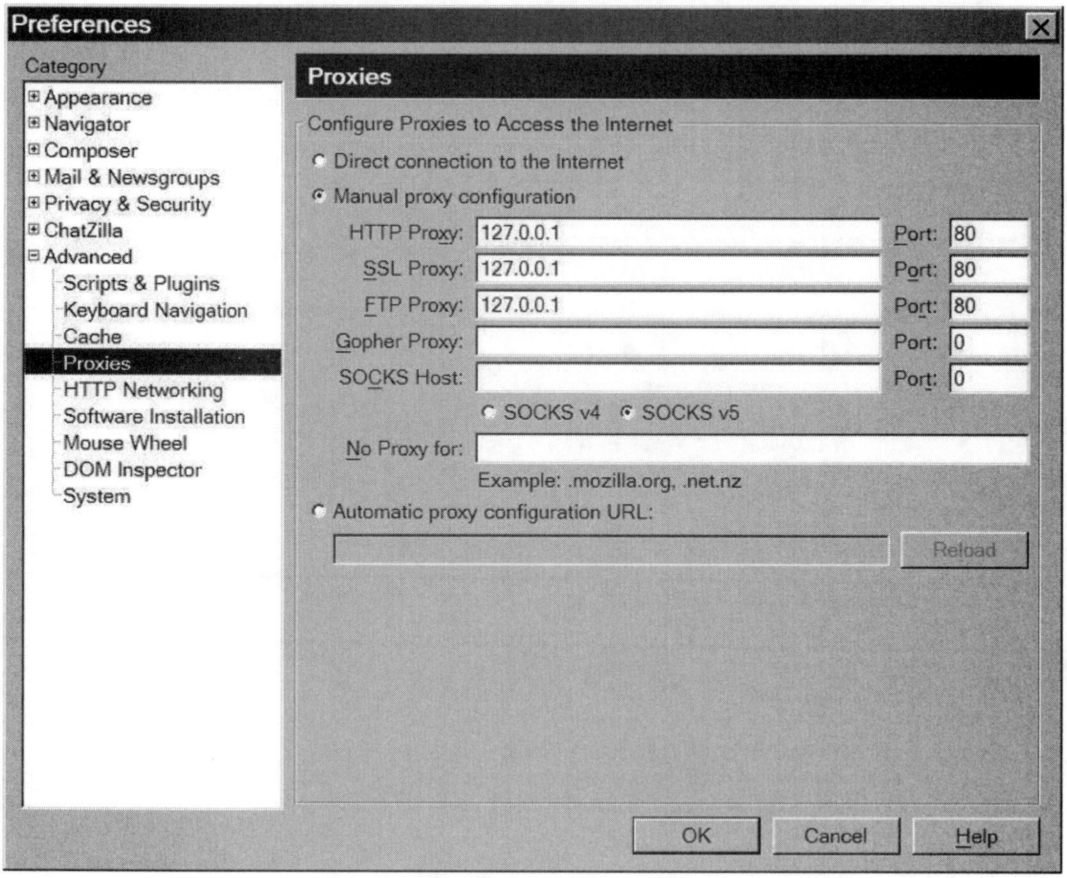

Figure 4-27. Mozilla configured for SSH tunneling

The setup shown in Figure 4-27 is a generic model of how to tunnel your browser sessions through the localhost with SSH so that all the data passing between your computer and the SSH server will be encrypted. This same basic procedure can be repeated for other TCP clients. You simply forward the related local port to the SSH server and configure the client to use localhost as its network interface.

SSL

Secure Socket Layer (SSL) is an encryption standard familiar to nearly everyone who uses the Internet. It's indicated by a URL beginning with HTTPS rather than HTTP, often with a little padlock icon visible in the browser's status bar. It's most often used for secure transactions such as credit-card purchases and online banking. Unlike SSH, it encrypts and decrypts data between a Web server and a browser end to end. Encryption and decryption happen at the terminal points of the connection. One of the limitations of SSH tunneling is that data passing between the SSH server and an upstream Web server will not be encrypted, unless SSL is also in use. Data passing between the SSH server and your computer is encrypted, but any data upstream of the SSH server or proxy is not. This means that passwords and other data can be intercepted. On the other hand, SSL encrypts end to end, but it can't conceal your IP address from the Web server or from anyone monitoring your IP traffic. A weakness in SSL is that a third party, such as your ISP, can determine which Web sites you've visited and when, though the data itself can't be read. So SSH and SSL are not substitutes for each other. They both have strengths and weaknesses, though the two can be used together, one compensating for the other, with very nice results in terms of privacy.

Any SSH session between a local client and an SSH server is secure. You can send anything over such a connection safely. But when you use SSH tunneling, your communications don't terminate at the SSH server; they will be going upstream to another server. Beyond that boundary, communications cease to be encrypted, though their true origins can't be determined: the SSH server appears to be the point of origin. The SSH tunnel completely conceals the traffic inside it. The packets, including their headers, or address information, are enclosed so that no one can tell which protocol is being tunneled and what the final destination is. The part of the stream that your ISP can monitor can't be deciphered at all, and the upstream part that can be monitored by third parties can't be associated with you. Furthermore, the destination Web site can determine only the IP address of the SSH server or proxy; it can't determine your computer's IP address.

The contents of an SSL session are encrypted end to end, but your ISP can see what protocol you're using and what Web sites you're visiting. And the destination Web site can determine your actual IP address because your Web traffic is coming to them straight from your browser.

Thus, SSH tunneling gives you greater privacy than SSL, but only for part of the virtual journey. SSL gives you some privacy for the entire journey, but your comings and goings can be observed by third parties. However, when you use both, you get the benefits of both: SSL traffic can be concealed within an SSH tunnel as well as any other protocol. This combination ensures a fully encrypted SSL link that protects packet contents at all times, and an encrypted SSH tunnel that protects packet contents and header information between your computer and the SSH server or proxy.

Only a fraction of Web sites support SSL, and those that do usually reserve it for login prompts, shopping carts, and the like. Obviously, you can't use SSL unless the destination Web site is also using it. For this reason, the Anonymizer service offers the option of surfing the Web with both SSH tunneling and SSL, which they provide in case the destination Web site doesn't support it. This security overhead can result in a slow connection, so one wouldn't use it for everyday Web surfing (SSH tunneling alone is adequate most of the time). But when you're sending passwords or identifying information, or viewing content that can bring legal trouble (such as a Tibetan might risk when looking at Web content from Amnesty International, say), the combination of SSH and SSL is the way to go.

SSL has other uses. The licq ICQ client for Linux uses it to encrypt chat sessions, so long as both parties are using licq or another SSL-enabled ICQ client. It's also used in connection with some VPNs (virtual private networks). However, it is not a service that the average user would implement for himself; it's more a tool for programmers and developers. OpenSSL is a free, open-source suite with both client and server components, and there is even an SSL tunneling tool called *stunnel,* but SSH is more user friendly and better adapted to do-it-yourself security.

WEP

Wired equivalent privacy (WEP) is a must for anyone using a wireless or WiFi Internet connection in a populated venue such as a public hotspot, hotel, conference center, or even at home in an apartment building. Wireless home users will have observed that their access points transmit over a fair distance and through obstructions like ceilings and walls. While it's nice to wander freely about the house with a laptop computer connected to the Internet without wires, there are security and privacy implications.

Wireless networking uses the *802.11 standard* and involves two basic components: an access point that provides a link to the Internet, and a wireless NIC (network interface card) for each of the PCs using it.

Intercepting a wireless signal is trivial. The chief factor is one's distance from the access point: the greater the distance, the weaker the signal. A user whose house is a few hundred feet from his nearest neighbor has little to worry about, but an apartment dweller may be inadvertently sharing his Internet connection with several grateful neighbors.

Some attackers are opportunists who just happen to be near enough to take advantage of someone else's WiFi access point. Others make a game of locating access points by driving or walking about with a laptop computer and a bit of homemade gear to extend the range of their wireless NICs. For this they need an antenna or signal amplifier to find an access point at a distance, and a directional apparatus enabling them to close in on the target. Any radio hobbyist can modify a wireless NIC to accommodate an antenna, and a disused Pringles canister makes a handy directional device. Software such as Netstumbler and Airsnort makes an access point easy to exploit.

In addition to attracting connection freeloaders, a poorly protected wireless link can provide a gateway for malicious intruders to access a LAN. A signal can be intercepted and monitored for content. The best solution for home users and small offices is to employ WEP, a signal encryption scheme that offers a decent, if not great, level of protection. There have been exploits against WEP, and it does impose a bit of overhead that slows a connection, but it is currently the best solution for WiFi users. Better alternatives are in development, fortunately.

CHAPTER 5

Treasure Hunt

YOU MAY NOT KEEP a diary, but your computer does. For as long as you've used it, your PC has been faithfully preserving data that you likely know nothing about, and would wish to be rid of if you did know. Nuggets of potentially sensitive information scattered about your computer include bits of deleted files, parts of documents created or opened, leftovers from chats in IRC or IM, temporary files, browser pages, URLs and cookies from Web sites you've visited, documents printed, online search results, and more. Meanwhile, much of what you've done via the Internet is also logged on remote machines. Your ISP may log your Web activity, including e-mail and chats; the servers you contact may log your IP address and the data you've exchanged with them, as might the various routers, switches, and servers your Internet traffic passes through from point to point. IRC and instant messaging servers log your chats. When you post a message to an Internet bulletin board—even if you use an alias—it can be traced to your computer because IP addresses are usually logged. Your outbound e-mail is stored locally on your PC and remotely on other people's computers and on mail servers, and may well be recorded for posterity. You can't type a sentence, print a file, install or launch a program, view a Web page, chat with a friend, or send a memo without creating a record of it locally, remotely, or both. Our data traces are literally scattered everywhere. This is because computers and networks do a fine job of storing and sharing data, and a wretched job of controlling it. For users, asserting control over this data is difficult because software and hardware engineers have done little to facilitate it.

In this chapter, we'll learn to practice *data hygiene*: the art of controlling the many data traces we leave behind, both on our local computers and on the Internet. If you share a computer with people whom you don't trust fully, or if you use a public computer at a library, Internet café, or copy shop, data hygiene is important. Laptops need data hygiene because they're often stolen. People living in countries where free expression is regarded as a threat to state authority need it if they document their views on a PC or publish them via the Internet. Anyone who visits controversial Web sites or whose chats or e-mail contains sensitive information needs it. Those whose children might be scandalized or whose spouses might be outraged by the contents of their PC need it. Anyone who might one day confront a court order for the contents of their hard disk needs it.

You may not keep a diary, but your computer and the Internet both do: your electronic life is an open book, and it's important that you learn what's being written in it. So let's have a look.

Local Stealth

We'll begin by cleaning up the data traces constantly accumulating on our computers and configuring them to record less duplicate data in the future. As with many security procedures, Windows users can expect to have a somewhat harder time with data hygiene than Linux users. Nevertheless, a Windows system can be made cleaner and made to run cleaner, though more work is involved. But the benefits are real: if a laptop is stolen, if a PC is hacked, if another user gains access to your account, if the authorities seize your machine, data hygiene will make your computer *tolerant* of such attacks.

Virtual Memory

All computer programs require memory in order to function, and every year they seem to demand more. Unfortunately, physical RAM (random access memory) modules are expensive, and as a result, most computers have less memory installed than today's applications need, especially in a multitasking environment like Windows or Linux where four or five memory-hungry applications may be running simultaneously. An important feature of all modern operating systems is their ability to address this shortfall by supplying *virtual memory* in place of physical memory. The way it works is simple: when an application requests access to more memory than happens to be available as RAM, the operating system permits it to write data to, and read it from, the hard disk instead. While swapping data to the disk is slower than reading and writing to memory, hard-disk capacity is immensely cheaper than RAM. Today, a 200-GB hard drive can be had for about $130 on sale; that amount of RAM, even with a generous volume discount, would cost in the tens of thousands of dollars. Naturally, most computers have a good deal more disk space than they need, and a good deal less physical RAM than they need. By leveraging this relatively inexpensive hard-disk capacity, virtual memory makes personal computing affordable, even as the memory demands of applications continue to soar.

It's a fabulous thing, but it's also a privacy nightmare. Virtual memory requires that a section of the hard disk be reserved for memory swapping. Instead of writing data to RAM, where it would be destroyed whenever the system is powered off, the system writes it to the local hard disk, where it can remain for years. On Windows we call this virtual memory region the *paging file* or the *swap file*; on Linux we call it the *swap partition*. Whatever it's called, it preserves data in ways that we can't easily control, and that's a problem.

Imagine that you've created a Word document with sensitive information that you intend to encrypt, thereby limiting access to it. Unfortunately, Word requires a good deal of memory and will usually need to write data to the swap file in order to run properly. That swapped data may well include your original, unencrypted text. When you finish composing the document, you might encrypt the resulting document file, but the original, plain-text version could be mirrored in the swap file. Later, you might even *wipe* the original plain-text document, and *still* a trace could remain in the swap file. Text that you copy to the clipboard can end up in the swap file. So can files you've downloaded, the contents of e-mail memos you've written or read, Web pages you've visited and images you've viewed, and chats you've had in IRC or via IM. Pretty much anything you do with your computer or encounter on the Web can be mirrored in the swap file.

> **NOTE** *Whenever you open an encrypted file, your encryption program should protect the decrypted text from ending up in the swap file. That is, when you decrypt a file or memo, the resulting clear text shouldn't be swapped to disk if the crypto program is designed properly. But this offers no protection when you first compose a memo with a word processor or a text editor and encrypt it later. To control data traces while you're composing a memo that you intend to encrypt, use your encryption program's own text editor, which should be designed to prevent virtual-memory swapping while you're using it.*

On most computers, the virtual-memory swap file or paging file will be quite large, in the range of 128 MB to 1 GB. Obviously, it can hold a tremendous amount of data. On Windows XP, it's called pagefile.sys and it resides in the C:\ or root directory. If you can't find it with the Windows Explorer file browser, you will have to change your file view settings to enable the display of system files, as explained in Chapter 2:

1. Go to the desktop Start menu and choose Settings ➤ Control Panel ➤ Folder Options. The Folder Options dialog will launch.

2. Choose the tab labeled View from the top of the Folder Options dialog.

3. Check the boxes or radio buttons next to the items labeled Display the contents of system folders and Show hidden files and folders.

4. Next, *clear* the checkbox next to the item labeled Hide protected operating system files (Recommended). You will be warned against clearing this box, but you need to know what's on your system if you want to make it more secure. Ignore the warning.

5. Finally, *clear* the checkbox next to the item labeled Use simple file sharing (Recommended). Click the button labeled Apply and the one labeled OK.

You'll now be able to use Windows Explorer to find the Windows swap file, C:\pagefile.sys. (On other versions of Windows, the file may be named 386spart.par or win386.swp.) The swap file can't be deleted or wiped while Windows is running. Users can wipe the swap file by booting to Windows protected mode or booting to DOS. Power users can also cause Windows to delete the swap file whenever the system is rebooted or powered off by editing the Registry thus:

1. Open the Registry editor and navigate to HKEY_LOCAL_MACHINE\ SYSTEM\CurrentControlSet\Control\Session Manager\Memory Management.

2. Select ClearPageFileAtShutdown from the list on the right.

3. Right-click on it, select Modify, and change the value to 1.

This Registry trick will not wipe the swap file securely, but if the file is deleted and re-created frequently, its older data traces will eventually be overwritten. However, this will not help when the swap file size is set to dynamic, because data traces will be scattered across the hard disk. There are two basic options for the Windows swap file: dynamic and fixed. A *dynamic* setup allows Windows to decide the file's size according to shifting memory needs, from 0 bytes to the entire amount of unused disk space available, called unallocated disk space. This is the worst possible setup for data hygiene because the swap file's contents will be left in unallocated disk space each time it shrinks. For example, suppose that at one point the swap file reaches 500 MB, but when you go to wipe it, it has shrunk to 256 MB. When you wipe it, only the 256 MB it's using will be erased; the 256 MB that it had been using previously have become unallocated disk space in the meantime and any data collected there will remain. Therefore, a dynamic swap file's data traces can end up anywhere on the disk and be very difficult to remove.

A far better setup is to create a permanently allocated swap file and give it a fixed size so that swapped data will be written to a particular part of the disk in a consistent manner. The swap file can be destroyed periodically with a file-wipe utility, simplifying data hygiene. To change your swap file settings in Windows XP

1. Go to the Start menu and choose Settings ➤ Control Panel ➤ System.

2. The System Properties dialog will pop up. Click the tab labeled Advanced. On the Advanced dialog, in the field labeled Performance, click the Settings button (Figure 5-1).

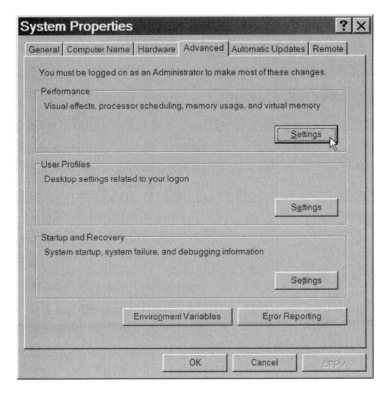

Figure 5-1. The System Properties dialog

3. The Performance Options dialog will pop up. Again, choose the Advanced tab and click the Change button in the field labeled Virtual memory (Figure 5-2).

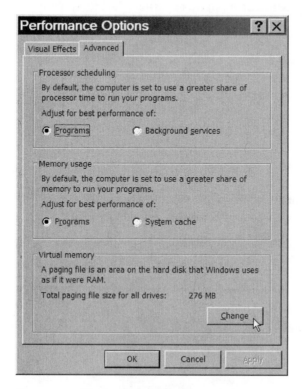

Figure 5-2. The Performance Options dialog

4. The Virtual Memory dialog will pop up. Choose Custom size and ensure that the fields labeled Initial size and Maximum size have the same value (Figure 5-3). A popular rule of thumb for Windows is to choose a swap-file size equaling twice the amount of RAM you have installed. For example, if you have 128 MB of RAM, you might choose 256 MB for both the Initial and Maximum sizes of your swap file. (Opinions differ on the optimal size for a swap file; my example is simply a common one. It's most important that the Initial and Maximum sizes be the same.)

Once you've changed your swap file to a single, fixed size, you will need to reboot. You can then use a wipe utility to clear unused disk space, eliminating the old data traces created by the swap file.

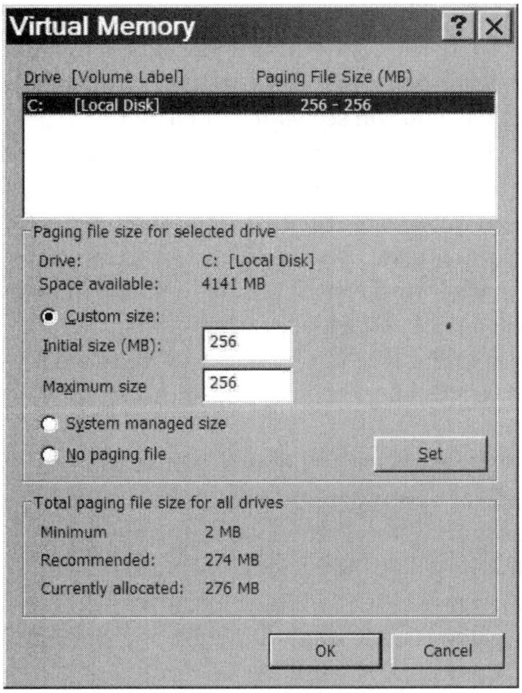

Figure 5-3. The Virtual Memory dialog

Windows will no longer scatter data traces carelessly about the hard disk, but will instead store them in a single location. You will be able to destroy the swap file periodically with a file-wipe utility such as PGPWipe, BCWipe, or Norton Wipeinfo. It's important to use these utilities periodically to wipe unused or unallocated disk space and to destroy the swap file. How often is a matter of personal choice that depends on what you do with your computer (and who else is interested in what you do with your computer). Once every few months is a reasonable schedule for most people. Access to the swap file will be denied while it's in use; consult your wipe utility's documentation for a workaround. Booting to Windows protected mode is usually good enough to get the job done, though you might have to boot to DOS and run a DOS version of your wipe utility. Once you've destroyed the swap file, you should reboot normally: Windows will re-create it automatically when you start your machine again.

It's possible to do without virtual memory altogether if you've got enough physical RAM, but some applications might demand it regardless of how much memory is installed and possibly crash or run poorly when they try to access the missing swap file. Doing without it is a good security measure, but this may not be appropriate for everyone. If you have at least 256 MB of RAM, it's worth trying. You can always reenable memory swapping if your applications balk. If you have less than 128 MB, Windows itself might balk and might even fail to boot. To find out how much RAM you have, go to the My Computer desktop icon and right-click. Select Properties from the drop-down menu. The System Properties dialog will launch. Under the General tab, you will see your RAM listed.

Linux also uses a swap partition for virtual memory. It can be either a primary partition or a secondary, or virtual, partition, depending on choices you made when you installed Linux and partitioned your hard disk. At the moment, there is no file-wipe utility that will eliminate the contents of the Linux swap partition, but I have a free shell script called wipeswap.sh posted to the Downloads section of the Apress Web site that will detect and wipe it with random values using /dev/urandom for entropy. If a running application has written data to the swap partition and later tries to retrieve it, it may crash, so you should close your applications before running the script.

The penalty for going without a swap partition is the same: some applications might not run properly regardless of how much RAM you have. I have no swap partitions on my own Linux boxes and I've never encountered any problems, but this is hardly a guarantee that you'll get away with it on your system. It's certainly worth trying if you have at least 256 MB of RAM installed.

Linux's chief weakness in data hygiene is the current difficulty of ensuring reliable data destruction. The Linux Wipe and Shred utilities do a good job on individual files, but it is difficult to wipe whole directories or large swaths of unused disk space, though the Wipe utility can be used recursively from the command line. I have a few other free shell scripts available that address this, but they are not capable of wiping file *slack space* (see the next section). However, Linux offers numerous advantages over Windows in preventing duplicate data traces from accumulating in the first place. There are far fewer hiding places to worry about, and directories and configuration files that tend to collect data can easily be emptied and write-protected so that nothing will be written to them in the future, an approach that's often impractical with Windows.

File Slack and Unallocated Space

When you install, save, or create a file, your operating system allocates disk space for it to reside in and maintains a record of its location. However, the area of disk space allocated to a file will usually be larger than the file itself, much as a parking space will be larger than most cars parked in it. A public parking space may be allocated to accommodate anything from a Beetle to an Escalade. If someone parks a Beetle in it, there is going to be a lot of unused space. Your computer's operating system allocates disk space in file blocks, or virtual parking spaces, of a fixed size. If a file is too big for one block, even if it's only slightly too big, it gets two blocks, and so on. Suppose your system allocates file blocks of 512 bytes, and you create a file that's 1025 bytes, or just over two blocks in size. When you save it, it will have to occupy three blocks, or 1536 bytes of space. Nearly all of the third block is what's called *file slack space*. This may seem wasteful, but there is a minor performance payback: if a file outgrows its allocated area and is saved again, it will have to be broken up and scattered about the disk, which then makes reading it and writing to it more time consuming. This condition is called *fragmentation*, and if it becomes widespread, it degrades hard-drive performance. Slack space allows a file to grow a bit before being fragmented. That's all well and good, but slack space can contain data from files previously stored in the same spot and since deleted.

Let's return to our example of a file 1025 bytes in length occupying three blocks, or an area of 1536 bytes. Let's say that previously, a file 1535 bytes in length resided there. When the new file is saved, it will overwrite 1025 bytes of the previous file's data; thus there will be 510 bytes from the previous file remaining in the slack space. Now, multiply this by the hundreds of thousands of file blocks, or "parking spaces," on a hard disk, and you can see that a great deal of data can accumulate in the slack space, left over from files that have been deleted, changed, or moved. Thus, it's important to wipe the disk's file slack whenever you use your wipe utility for periodic maintenance.

File slack space is *allocated*, but *unoccupied*, disk space. There's another region of the disk we need to worry about, called *unallocated* space. This is space that hasn't been assigned to a file or space created when files are deleted. On some computers, unused or unallocated space can account for most of the disk. It's "unused" or "unoccupied" by definition, but it may have been occupied in the past and it may well contain data. All the data it contains will remain until new data is written over it. Thus the words "free," "unused," "unoccupied," and "unallocated" do *not* mean "empty of data." These words indicate disk space that is not currently assigned to a particular file. There is often a good deal of data in these regions that can be read with a simple disk-editing utility.

When you delete a file, you don't erase it. All that happens is this: the file blocks that had been allocated to it are recorded as unallocated, leaving them up for grabs. The data contained in a deleted file may or may not be overwritten when a new file is saved. Because there is such a large amount of unallocated space, or free space, on most hard disks, a deleted file's data might never be overwritten through normal use. That's why it's important to wipe all of a disk's unallocated disk space deliberately from time to time. That's also why it's crucial to prevent the Windows swap file from operating dynamically, which gives it indiscriminate access to this potentially huge region of the disk for memory swaps. Most of the popular Windows wipe utilities are easy to use and have simple options allowing both unallocated space and file slack space to be wiped securely. It's important to wipe both as a matter of routine system maintenance.

> **NOTE** *The journaling NTFS filesystem for Windows is more difficult to wipe securely than FAT-16 or FAT-32. Wipes on NTFS may not be as effective as users expect. For improved data hygiene on Windows, use FAT-32. The same is true with Linux: journaling file systems like ReiserFS, ext3, XFS, and JFS may not be cleaned adequately. For superior data hygiene on Linux, use the ext2 filesystem.*

For Linux, again, secure data *destruction* has not been a great priority among developers because data *accumulation* is easy to control. In addition to the wipeswap.sh utility I've made available, there is also a script called wipefree.sh that will wipe unallocated disk space. Unfortunately, it won't wipe file slack space, though it can be used while you work with your computer, whereas wipeswap.sh requires that applications be closed to prevent crashes. I've also prepared a script called wipeall.sh, which will perform a fairly secure wipe of an entire hard disk. Obviously, you would have to save all of your data on removable media before using it, and then rebuild your system afterward. Performing a complete disk wipe is a serious inconvenience when slack space is all that one is concerned with. However, if you're already planning to rebuild your system, it's a good idea to run the wipeall.sh script beforehand to eliminate data traces from your previous disk image.

Because it's easy to control data traces on Linux, a user who takes care to use the Wipe or Shred utilities to destroy individual files should not have a problem with file slack and traces in unallocated space. A Linux system without a swap partition using the ext2 filesystem will be very easy to administer for good data hygiene. Shred and Wipe ought to overwrite the entire file blocks used by the target file, not just the file's data, so there should not be many slack traces to worry about when sensitive files are habitually wiped rather than merely deleted.

Shadow Data

A file has been wiped properly when fresh data has been written over it several times. In theory, it's gone without a trace; in practice, it isn't. A disk drive is a mechanical device with less-than-perfect manufacturing tolerances. In addition to *file blocks*, which we might think of as parking spaces, there is also the concept of *disk tracks*, which we might think of as the lanes in a highway, only arranged concentrically. As the disk spins, a mechanical arm with a magnetic device at the end called a *head* follows these tracks, or lanes, attempting to read the data we've asked for. When we save a file, the arm moves into position and the head writes it to file blocks in these tracks while the disk spins below it. Both the arm and the disk are susceptible to minor vibration, which means that the tracking will always be less than perfect. When you save, or write, data to a particular track on the disk, the alignment between the head and the track may vary slightly each time. Thus, when you overwrite a file with a wipe utility, there's no guarantee that the new data will cover it perfectly, because you can't be certain that the head will be positioned over the track exactly as it was during previous passes. You can overwrite a file repeatedly, yet some of the old data might remain in the outer fringes of the track.

Another problem is the disk's surface, which is coated with a granular magnetic substance. We've all seen how a hand-held magnet can realign iron filings on a surface even without touching them. Just so, the hard drive's magnetic head realigns particles on the disk's surface when it writes data. There can be a bit of "bleeding" when it does this. Think of spray-painting on a bed of sand with several coats of different colors. You can brush away the top layers and still find evidence of the deeper, or older, ones. This is another type of shadow data. The first type we might think of as "overspray"; the second as "layers" built up over time. To address shadow data, file-wipe utilities make numerous write-passes so that the entire area that *should* be covered *will* be covered with new data. It's a good strategy, but it's never perfect.

Modern, high-speed hard disk drives are less susceptible to shadow data because their manufacturing tolerances have got to be tight. On the other hand, outdated drives, and floppy and Zip disks that are sloppily made, wobble a great deal and can produce a lot of shadow data. You can use a software wipe utility on them, but it won't be nearly as effective as it would be on a fast, modern hard disk. However, floppies, Zip disks, and CDs are cheap and very easily destroyed by incineration.

I would emphasize that recovering shadow data from a high-performance, up-to-date hard disk drive is *extremely* expensive in terms of equipment and man hours. The target disk has got to be valuable enough for someone, or some agency, to invest significant time and money in forensic data recovery, and not many disks are worth it. Very few users will need to protect their data against this sophisticated level of attack and can remain confident in disk-wipe software. However, if you're in the minority, the best way to "declassify" a hard disk is by using a software wipe utility with a generous number of passes, and following that up with physical destruction.

The Windows Registry

A great obstacle to data hygiene on Windows is the Registry, a vast, poorly documented database that few people in the world understand fully. The Registry contains configuration data and provides information for programs and device drivers to run properly and interact with each other. It contains tens of thousands of entries in confusing forms such as: HKLM\Software\Microsoft\ Windows\CurrentVersion\Explorer\Advanced\Folder\HideFileExt.

This is simply the Registry path to an option indicating whether the Windows Explorer file browser will hide known file extensions or display them.

The string is called a *key*, and below this one are several subkeys, or values, that you would have changed if you followed my advice about configuring Windows Explorer to display hidden and system files. If you like, you can open the Registry by going to the Start menu, choosing Run, and typing *regedit*, and then navigate to this key and its values. But the main point here is that whenever you or a piece of software you're installing makes even the simplest change to the system, it's almost always reflected in the Registry. Not *everything* ends up there, but *anything* might.

Entire books have been written to explain the mysterious functions of just this one system database. Scores of software utilities have been created to help users sort through it and correct errors in it. Many thousands of Web pages are devoted to divining its peculiarities. A Google search on the phrase *windows registry* returns over 300,000 hits.

The chief problem with the Registry is its obscurity: most users have no idea what it contains or how it functions. System transparency promotes security because we can see what's going on and change what we don't like or don't trust. System obscurity, on the other hand, is a constant obstacle to security. The Windows Registry is labyrinthine and confusing and even contains encrypted entries. We can only trust that the encrypted sections don't contain any data we wouldn't want them to contain. The Registry also cannot be read with a simple text editor, but requires one of two proprietary tools from Microsoft: regedit.exe and regedit32.exe. It's about as user-unfriendly as it can be, yet it is crucial to Windows.

Among the data traces it contains are URLs that you type into the Internet Explorer address bar, the names and locations of files you've accessed recently, and the names of files you've searched for with the Windows Search Companion. Download managers may use it to record the files you've downloaded. Software you've installed and later uninstalled may still be listed there. Internet clients may stash data related to your Web activity in the Registry. Any application on your Windows machine is welcome to store any data there that it pleases.

Unfortunately, there isn't much one can do to defeat the Registry's appetite for obscure bits of data. It's a black box that can contain virtually anything, but it's crucial, so it can't simply be wiped the way unused disk space can. You can do serious harm to your system by making changes to the Registry, so it's important that you know exactly what you're doing before attempting to edit it. The only practical approach to controlling traces of your Internet history, short of combing through the Registry for days on end searching for revealing tidbits, is to use the Mozilla browser, which stores user data and Web activity records in ordinary Windows directories that can be emptied, and even write-protected, at any time. Relying on open-source Internet clients will also help reduce Registry data traces related to Web activity, but not absolutely. Still, it's always better to use software that can be examined freely, because this promotes system transparency. Proprietary software can easily be loaded with secret functions and can use the Registry to stash data that the user knows nothing about. The Registry is a drawback to using Windows: it can't be done away with, and there isn't a convenient, effective way for users to control the data that it tends to accumulate. Using open-source applications and clients will ease the problem, but there really is no cure.

Windows Indexing Service

According to Microsoft, this feature indexes the contents of your hard disk, and the *contents of your files*, to make searching faster. The service creates and then consults a number of index catalogs, or databases. These catalogs contain data about your data, and therefore seriously undermine the practice of good hygiene. In Chapter 2, I recommended disabling the Windows Indexing Service for this reason. But let's review briefly. To disable the Indexing Service

1. Go to the Start menu and choose Run.

2. Type in *services.msc* and click OK. The Services dialog will launch.

3. Right-click on the Indexing Service to bring up the Properties dialog, and click Stop if the service is running. Then select Disabled. Click Apply and close the dialog.

To prevent the service from being reenabled

1. Activate the My Computer desktop icon. Next, select (Local Disk C:) under Hard Disk Drives.

2. Right-click on the (Local Disk C:) icon and choose Properties from the right-click menu. The Local Disk Properties dialog will pop up. Near the bottom you will see the option Allow Indexing Service to index this disk for fast file searching. (The option will not be available on all systems, so don't worry if you don't see it.)

3. *Clear* the checkbox, click Apply, and select the option Apply changes to C:\, subfolders and files. Click OK.

Once the service is fully disabled, it should not be difficult to delete any remaining index files (*.idx, *.idq, *.ida, and *.htx), if they exist. You will have to set Windows Explorer to display hidden files and system files, as described previously in this chapter and in Chapter 2, in order to find them. You can then locate any stragglers with the Search Companion (also known as the Search Assistant) using *.ida, .idx, .idq,* and *.htx* as terms. When you use the Search Companion's

Search all files and folders option, be sure also to include the options *Search system folders, Search hidden files and folders,* and *Search subfolders* from the Companion's *More advanced options* menu. It's not likely that you will find many of these files, especially on a home system, but it's important to look for them. Deleting, or better yet, wiping them may be tedious, but you will only have to do it once so long as the Indexing Service remains off. The catalog files, if any should exist, will appear in the right-hand pane of the Search Companion window. You can right-click and use your wipe utility to destroy them.

For an added bonus, disabling the Indexing Service will free up some processor power and RAM, so while indexing may make searching faster, it degrades overall system performance. It's foolish to devote system resources to speeding up a service that you might use only occasionally. If you normally spend a great deal of time searching for files or for strings of text within your files, you might wish to use the Indexing Service, but it makes data hygiene impossible. It creates what amounts to an obscure, shadow volume of your data, and your wipe utility will probably fail to erase these related traces when it erases a file. If you want your computer to be clean and as much of your data under your control as possible, the Windows Indexing Service has got to go.

Related to this are several important files, all named *index.dat*, that you'll find in numerous locations. These are, essentially, mini-databases cataloging the contents of sensitive directories related to your Internet behavior. Your cookies, your Web history, and several other peculiar items are recorded for posterity. You can delete the contents of these directories, but you can't easily delete the index.dat files that record their contents. Index.dat files maintain records of other files that you open, cookies you accept, and URLs you follow. Oddly, Microsoft does *not* want you to play with these index files, so if you attempt to delete them, access will be denied, even to an Administrator. Some wipe utilities can override the limits on Administrator privileges that Microsoft has built into Windows; others cannot. To eliminate these tattletale files, open the Search Companion and enter *index.dat* as a search term. Each one will be listed in the right-hand pane. Right-click and use your wipe utility to destroy them. If access is still denied, you will have to restart your machine with a DOS boot disk or a Windows CD, and remove them manually with the *del* command or the *erase* command, or by using a DOS version of your wipe utility if one is available. But before you boot to DOS, you should use the Search Companion and note the path to each index.dat file. It will be tedious, but these files are a serious obstacle to data hygiene.

Now for the bad news: even if you wipe these files, Windows will re-create them as soon as you reboot and continue storing data in them. I recommend that you wipe each one, reboot, and then write-protect all of them. It's also important to search for them occasionally because Windows may create additional index.dat files as you use your machine. There are numerous utilities available that claim to remove these files while Windows is running. If you wish to check them out, perform a Google search using *index.dat* as a term, and you'll find links to several such tools.

If you followed my advice in the Introduction about installing and configuring the Mozilla browser and e-mail client, you will not have to worry much about index.dat files. You'll only have to wipe them once. They'll be re-created, but if you use Mozilla they will no longer record details of your Internet behavior. All of the directories that Mozilla uses, and all the files it saves, can be wiped easily and securely or emptied and write-protected. You will need to keep Internet Explorer in order to use Windows Update (because of its support of ActiveX Controls), but you needn't, and shouldn't, use IE for any other purpose. Once Mozilla is installed and configured, you can destroy all of your index.dat files once, write-protect them, and not worry about them in the future.

System Restore

This is actually a useful Windows feature. It creates snapshots of the system at periodic intervals called *restore points*. If the system is damaged by malware or a bad software installation, users can roll back their systems to a previous restore point when it was known to be working nicely. Obviously, this is bad for data hygiene, though it is a real convenience. Ideally, the system contents backed up to the C:\System Volume Information_Restore directory would be limited to the Registry, library files, drivers, and configuration files. However, with Microsoft one can never assume that there won't be a few unpleasant surprises. The company has a well-earned reputation for undocumented functions, and I would be reluctant to trust the feature. It is also possible for viruses to remain in the _Restore directory when infected files are inadvertently backed up, defying removal by antivirus products. When you restore the system, you'll restore your viruses and malware as well. You will have to decide if the convenience is worth the risk and choose your poison. If you wish to disable System Restore, follow these steps:

1. Go to the Start menu and choose Settings ➤ Control Panel ➤ System to launch the System Properties dialog (or right-click on the My Computer icon and choose Properties).

2. Choose the System Restore tab at the top of the System Properties dialog and check the box on the line reading Turn off System Restore. Click OK.

3. Next, go to the Start menu, choose Run, and type in *services.msc* to launch the Services dialog. Find the System Restore service, stop it if it's running, and set it to Disabled. To activate System Restore, the Task Scheduler and Event Log services must also be enabled.

Temporary Files

There might be hundreds, even thousands, of temporary files on your computer. Most are deleted automatically when you shut down Windows, but whenever a power interruption or a system crash occurs, they will be left behind. They're created for scores of different reasons. Most are harmless, but it's impossible to predict what a temporary file might contain. For example, a word processor will periodically create temporary versions of documents you're working on so that if your system goes down, you'll be able to recover a recent version and very little work will be lost.

But suppose you had been composing a document that you intended to encrypt: a temporary version of the original clear-text file might be created and stored in your documents directory. If the system goes down, the temporary file will remain. We've already seen how memory swapping can cause data to be preserved in the swap file, and how the Indexing Service can record file contents. Temporary files are another source of potentially revealing data traces. On Windows, most such files are located in directories named ~\Temp, and most temporary files have the extension .tmp. From time to time, you should destroy the contents of all your ~\Temp directories and wipe all of the files on your computer with the .tmp extension. This is quite easy using the Search Companion and a wipe utility. First you would use *temp* as a search term and find all the Temp directories. Most of them should be empty, but check each one and wipe anything you find in it. There will also be several directories called Temporary Internet Files. Wipe the contents of those while you're at it. Next, use *.tmp* as a search term and wipe every file that the Search Companion lists. Do this every few months, unless you have reason to be paranoid. In that case, do it as often as you please. If you do it often, fewer files will have accumulated in the meantime, so destroying them will go a lot faster.

NOTE *The tilde (~) can indicate two things: a shortened directory path or a directory whose name would vary on different computers. Thus C:\Windows\Temp and C:\Program Files\Temp might be shortened to ~\Temp, and /home/*username*/Documents might appear as /home/~/Documents.*

Linux users should check the /tmp, /usr/tmp, and /var/tmp directories occasionally. Most applications are designed to clear their own temporary files, but you should have a look to make sure nothing untoward has been saved. If you do find it necessary to clear the /tmp, /usr/tmp, or /var/tmp directories, you can use the Wipe or Shred utility on any file, or simply delete the directory's contents and then run the wipefree.sh script to eliminate any leftover data traces. If you're using an office suite, temporary files will probably be saved in your /home/~/Documents directory, or in another directory specified by the application, so these need to be checked periodically as well.

E-Mail Traces

E-mail memos and attachments are usually not saved individually on your computer, though KMail does save them that way. Often, the memos and attachments contained in a particular e-mail directory, such as your inbox or sent-mail directory, are saved together in a single, large file which your e-mail client presents to you as if it were a directory. Mozilla Mail works this way. The inbox looks like a directory because your client interprets it that way, but it's actually just a big file in which mail and attachments are collected. This makes it difficult to wipe an individual memo securely; you can delete it using the Delete button, but its traces may remain. Of course, the files in which your mail is stored are constantly changing in size as new mail comes in and old mail is deleted, so it's likely that traces of older, deleted memos will be overwritten through normal use.

Still, it's easy to wipe these traces indirectly, especially because memos and attachments are stored together. Wiping the directory files manually might seem the most direct route to cleanliness, but doing so may cause difficulty and may require you to reinstall your mail client when you're done. A better method is to use your mail client to delete the memos you want to be rid of, then run your wipe utility or the wipefree.sh script to clean the free space on the hard disk. When you delete unwanted e-mail memos, the associated directory file will shrink, and the wipe utility will vacuum up the crumbs, so to speak. Mozilla Mail appends file attachments to the directory files. With Mozilla, whether on Windows or Linux, deleting a memo deletes its related file attachment. So if you regularly clean out your inbox, sent mail, and trash directories using your mail client's Delete button and stick to a regular schedule of wiping disk free space, you should have little to worry about from e-mail data traces.

If this approach isn't good enough for you, then you will have to navigate to the directory that your e-mail client uses to store mail and wipe each directory file manually. But as I said, this approach can cause problems when the client searches for files that no longer exist, and you may end up having to reinstall the client. This is a technique better suited to power users. And remember, if you perform a manual wipe, *all* of your e-mail archives will be destroyed, unless you've deliberately saved copies of important memos in a different directory.

KMail on Linux offers several advantages. It saves memos and attachments as individual files that can be wiped manually without difficulty and without destroying the whole lot. You can wipe individual memos manually in the /root/Mail and /home/~/Mail directories. KMail is very tolerant of aggressive wiping; you can wipe the entire contents of /root/Mail and /home/~/Mail and then delete the top-level Mail directories. The next time you run KMail, you will be prompted to create a Mail directory, which KMail will do automatically for you.

KMail automatically saves e-mail attachments in subdirectories just below /tmp/kde-root and /tmp/kde-*username*. It's a good idea to check the contents of these directories occasionally. If you delete or manually wipe a memo with a sensitive attachment, you should verify that there's no copy of the attachment remaining in a temporary directory. If there is, you can wipe it manually and securely. KMail makes doing manual, secure wipes of individual e-mail memos and their related attachments easier than Mozilla Mail and is generally better for Linux users. Mozilla Mail is a big improvement over Outlook Express on Windows, but KMail is better than Mozilla Mail on Linux.

Print Spool

Spool stands for simultaneous peripheral operations on line. Spooling is a means of holding several jobs in a *buffer*, or a *queue*, where a device can access them whenever it's ready to perform the assigned task. When you print a document, it's saved in a disk buffer called a *print spool* until the job is complete. Once it's done, the spool files are deleted automatically. However, if a computer loses power or crashes while a print job is pending, the spool files may remain. The print spool can preserve traces of files you've printed and subsequently wiped. To clear these traces, open Windows Explorer, navigate to C:\WINDOWS\system32\spool\printers, and wipe any leftover files.

On Linux, you can open a shell and enter the command *lpc*, followed by the command *clean*. This will delete (though not wipe) any leftover files. However, if you're using CUPS (common UNIX printing system), the *clean* command may not work. In that case, you can use Krusader or Nautilus and navigate to /var/spool/cups and /var/spool/lpd to wipe any leftover files.

Additionally, portions of print jobs might be swapped to virtual memory when system resources are low, leaving traces in the swap file or swap partition. This is another reason why the swap file should be wiped periodically.

Clipboard

The clipboard is a convenience that allows you to copy and paste objects such as images and text. When you select and copy an item, it's stored in memory. You can then paste it into several documents with ease. The basic Windows clipboard is simple: each time you copy something, it replaces whatever had been copied before. The Windows clipboard can be cleared by copying something harmless into it, thereby replacing whatever you wish to clear.

The MS Office Clipboard and the KDE clipboard (Klipper) on Linux are more functional, allowing you to copy several items and then select the one you wish to paste from a list. This is hardly a threat to security, but if you've copied something personal or otherwise sensitive, be aware that the clipboard's contents might end up in the swap file when system resources are low. Both the Office Clipboard and KDE's Klipper have buttons or menu items enabling you to clear them easily. PGP for Windows and KGpg for KDE allow you to encrypt the clipboard's contents as well, which you might do if you want to leave your computer while keeping something private in clipboard memory until you return. It's important to disable the Klipper option allowing its history to be saved.

Because the clipboards are easily cleared, and because the data held in them is constantly changing, they aren't a security concern so long as you remain aware of them. The real problem here is the swap file or swap partition, which might preserve traces of clipboard contents. Again, regular destruction of the swap file is important. If this is beginning to sound bothersome, it's perfectly reasonable to try doing without a swap file. However, Windows users should be careful before disabling virtual memory; if you haven't got enough physical RAM, your machine may not boot. You might also have problems with some applications that expect a swap file to be present. With Linux there's little danger of disabling your machine when you disable memory swapping, but some applications might balk.

Recently Accessed Files

The Windows Start menu contains an item called Documents, which is a list of files you've opened recently, with direct links to them. This list can easily be viewed and activated by anyone with access to your computer. Unfortunately, there is no off switch and no easy way to clear the list. It's a convenience when you want to open a recently used file quickly, which is why it's there, but there ought to be a simple way of clearing it and eliminating it. Unfortunately, you will have to hack your Registry to clear the list and disable it. Registry tweaking can be dangerous for novices and should only be attempted by users who are comfortable hacking their systems.

First, navigate to HKEY_CURRENT_USER\Software\Microsoft\Windows\ CurrentVersion\Explorer\RecentDocs and clear the list by selecting its contents in the right-hand window and deleting.

Then, navigate to HKEY_CURRENT_USER\Software\Microsoft\Windows\ CurrentVersion\Policies\Explorer, create a DWORD value called NoRecentDocsHistory, and set the value to one.

So many Windows applications will save this sort of information in the Registry that covering them comprehensively would require a separate book. However, there are quite a few hacks for clearing data traces associated with applications such as MS Word, Windows MediaPlayer, and many others as well. The WinGuides Network for Windows Web site has a good series of articles covering useful Registry hacks at www.winguides.com/registry and offers several tools for controlling this mystery database. A Google search on *registry tweak windows* will lead you to thousands of Web sites and tools that may help you to edit your Registry for improved privacy and data hygiene. I must point out, however, that a user can become proficient with Linux in a fraction of the time needed to gain control over the Windows Registry alone.

On Linux with KDE, one can simply use Krusader or Konqueror and navigate to the /home/~/.kde/apps/share/RecentDocuments directory. If you wish to clear and disable the Recent Documents menu item, wipe everything in the ~/RecentDocuments subdirectory and then write-protect it (i.e., change its permissions to "read only"). You will never have to worry about it again. Merely using the KDE Control Center to hide the Documents tab in the Start menu will not prevent the ~/RecentDocuments subdirectory from accumulating data: it only hides the menu item. Wipe the directory's contents and write-protect it instead.

This technique can be used throughout KDE to prevent recently accessed files lists associated with applications, and a great deal of other data, from being written to the hard disk. There is no Registry in Linux, so when you clean out your home directory and set your write permissions for proper data hygiene, things will remain that way: Linux patches, unlike Windows patches, do not override your configuration choices.

KDE stores configuration files conveniently in subdirectories under /home/~/.kde/share/apps, /home/~/.kde/share/cache, and /home/~/.kde/ share/config. Any subdirectories or files that are gathering data traces can be emptied and made read only to protect your privacy. Normally, you won't be wiping an entire subdirectory or changing its permissions (though ~/favicons and ~/RecentDocuments are exceptions), but you will instead look for configuration files that contain data traces. I'd be most concerned with files in these subdirectories: ~/kbear, ~/kcookiejar, ~/favicons, ~/konqueror, ~/krusader, and ~/noatun. For example, in the ~/konqueror subdirectory, you'll find several configuration files, such as ~/faviconrc and ~/konq_history. You certainly don't want to write-protect the ~/konqueror directory; you only want to locate the files that contain data traces, empty them of traces, and write-protect them. To do this, open the file in a text editor, select the offending text, delete it, then save the file and set it to read only. By the way, konq_history also appears in home/~/.kde/ share/config. This version contains your typed URLs. Do a search for konq_history so you won't miss either one.

Because Linux uses simple, plain-text configuration files, you can easily edit ones that might gather data traces used by each application. Such items as IRC or ICQ logs, bookmarks and saved URLs, and recently accessed files in word processors and media players can easily be controlled. But it's best not to delete directories or entire configuration files. Many of them may be re-created by the associated application when you next launch it. It's better to purge the file or subdirectory of data traces and then write-protect it. Keep in mind that some files may have to be present for an application to run properly. Here again, deleting the file's contents and write-protecting is the better way to go.

There's one caveat: by making a configuration file read only, you also make it impossible to update the related application's settings. You will have to remove the file's write protection before making configuration changes, then restore it. You might also have trouble installing a new version of an application whose config file you've write-protected, so be sure to change the file's permissions before doing so.

Most KDE applications store configuration files in the /home/~/.kde/share/config subdirectory. One of the more common types of data held in these files is the recently accessed files list associated with each application. It's quite easy to open the configuration files and delete the lists, then write-protect the files, leaving the rest of the configuration data unchanged. You might do this with your media players, archiving utilities, download managers, and the like. Virtually all KDE applications store their configuration files in the /home/~/.kde/share/config subdirectory. You should browse the directory and open the files to see what's being stored in them. It's easy to purge them of traces while preserving the configuration data, then write-protect them. With these steps, you can dramatically reduce the amount of personal data your computer collects.

> **NOTE** *Take care that your text editor isn't set to back up files automatically when you save them, or the original version will remain as a backup.*

This direct approach is not practical on Windows because the Registry contains, or mirrors, much of this data, and because third-party software stores data in too many unpredictable locations.

Browser Traces

The traces of your Web activity dutifully preserved on your hard disk by Internet Explorer are difficult to eliminate, and even when they are eliminated, they begin accumulating again. There is a URL history that lists the sites you visit by following hyperlinks or bookmarks, and another one that lists the URLs you type into the browser's address bar. (Sometimes, the address bar history will contain passwords when people log in to remote services with a URL in this form: `ftp://username:password@ftp.server.net`.) There is a record of the files you've downloaded and the locations you downloaded them from. There are cookies containing surprising amounts of data that can remain for months, even years, and be updated continually. Originally, cookies were a solution to the stateless nature of HTTP; something had to be done to maintain state information during a session. Cookies solved the problem, but it didn't take long for the privacy-invasion industry to turn them into a marketing and profiling tool capable of tracking Netizens individually and observing their behavior. Companies like DoubleClick specialize in this sort of commercial surveillance. There are also favicons, little site-specific icons that appear in your bookmarks and elsewhere that keep a record of where you've been in cyberspace. And finally, there is your browser's cache of Web pages. The browser cache speeds up surfing, but it creates a local copy of everything you've looked at on the Web.

Fortunately, there's Mozilla. It records these items as well, but it gives you complete control over them. Nearly all of your data traces can be controlled from the browser's Edit ➤ Preferences menu, except your download history. That one has to be dealt with manually. To do this on Windows

1. First, open the Windows Explorer file browser, navigate to C:\Documents and Settings\, and choose the subdirectory associated with your username.

2. Now go to ~\Application Data\Mozilla\Profiles. Drop down to your Mozilla profile, which could be named "default" or your username.

3. Drop down again to the directory just below (the directory name will end in .slt) and find a file named downloads.rdf. (Or simply search for downloads.rdf.) This is your download history.

4. Open downloads.rdf with Notepad, delete all the text, save the blank file, and then write protect it (i.e., using Windows Explorer, right-click on the file and choose Properties ➤ Attributes ➤ Read-only).

The rest of your Mozilla data traces can be controlled from the browser's Edit ➤ Preferences menu. If you followed the Mozilla setup instructions in the Introduction, then your browser is already configured to prevent many data traces from accumulating.

On Linux, navigate to /home/~/.mozilla and find your profile name, which could be "default" or your username. Drop down to the directory below (the directory name will end in .slt) and find the file named downloads.rdf. (Or search for downloads.rdf.) Open it with a text editor, delete all the text, save the blank file, then write-protect it. As with Windows, the rest of your Mozilla data traces can be controlled from the browser's Edit ➤ Preferences menu. Again, the setup recommendations in the Introduction will prevent many data traces from accumulating.

When accessing controversial Web sites, even ones you visit regularly, it's a good idea to search for them via Google and follow the link provided rather than bookmark them. This prevents the site name and URL from appearing in your bookmarks list. Of course, your search terms might be preserved in the cookie that Google drops on your machine when you use the service, but setting cookies to expire with each browser session, as I recommend in the Introduction, will prevent the Google cookie from swelling and storing your comings and goings over time. Whenever you shut down Mozilla, the Google cookie will be deleted, along with many others. Traces of your Internet search history will not accumulate, and advertisers' cookies will not be able to track you over time.

The browser cache is important; it can store immense volumes of your surfing history, including images, some of which may be forbidden in your jurisdiction. Thus, you should restrict the size of the cache to the smallest amount of disk space that you can get away with in terms of system performance. If the cache is small and you empty it regularly, its contents will be overwritten frequently and it won't maintain a long-term history of your Web activity. If you have a fast Internet connection and a good computer, you can do without a browser cache, which I would recommend to anyone who can afford it performance-wise. In that case, you can disable the browser cache in the Mozilla Edit ➤ Preferences ➤ Advanced ➤ Cache menu by setting its size to 0 MB and use the Clear Disk Cache button to empty it. Or, if you prefer, you can wipe its contents manually and write-protect the directory so that data can't be written to it in the future. To do a manual wipe

On Windows, navigate to C:\Documents and Settings\~\Application Data\Mozilla\Profiles\default\~.slt\Cache, or ~*username*\~.slt\Cache.

On Linux, navigate to /home/~/.mozilla/default/~.slt/Cache, or ~/*username*/~.slt/Cache.

Once the cache contents have been wiped, you can right-click and change the Cache directory attributes to read only. The cache will no longer record your surfing history, and you can clean up any remaining data traces with routine wiping of the disk's free space.

Bash

Linux users have a handy feature called the *bash history,* which records commands entered in the shell and saves them from session to session. This lets you use the keyboard arrow keys to find frequently used commands stored in history and enter them at the command prompt without bothering to type them. This is especially convenient when you have long directory paths to remember.

But there's a problem: if you ever get distracted and carelessly enter your root password or a password to a remote service at the command prompt, instead of at the password prompt, it will be saved in the bash history in clear text. When you receive a password prompt in the shell, the password will not be saved, but anything you enter at the command prompt will be. On KDE, you'll find the history files in /root/.bash_history and /home/~/.bash_history. You can open them with a text editor and remove any important traces, then save them. But again, take care that your text editor isn't set to back up saved files automatically, or the original will remain. You could write-protect the bash history files, but this is a bit of overkill. Alternatively, you could allow the history files to fill up with a good number of frequently used commands, then write-protect them. But it's easy enough to check them occasionally to ensure that you haven't recorded any passwords in them by mistake.

The Wibbly Wobbly Web

For all the utility and personal enjoyment it offers, the Internet remains the largest and most insecure network ever devised. Those who trust it do so at their own risk. There is no privacy, there is no anonymity, and there is no security inherent in an open system of networked machines relaying billions of data packets every day. Privacy, anonymity, and security are goals that you must achieve by deliberate effort. Such efforts need not represent a great burden—after all, it makes little sense to put more time and money into defending something than it's actually worth to you. As we've noted before, the value of security depends on our individual sense of risk tolerance and the value of the asset we're trying to defend. Sometimes, an asset such as a computer file can be defended simply by duplicating it and keeping the duplicate in a location separate from the original. If one copy is lost or accidentally destroyed, the duplicate will work just as well. Other times, the simple fact that someone else has gained access to a file might diminish its value to us or create other difficulties. In that case, we would be more concerned with preventing unauthorized access.

On the Internet, the asset we want to defend is, of course, our privacy. This is not something we can duplicate. It's finite and fragile: once it's gone, it's gone for good. Protecting our privacy ought not to be terribly difficult, but unfortunately there is a large and well-heeled industry devoted to learning everything it can about each of us. You and I have a natural desire for privacy, but there are people with billions of dollars to spend who earn their living by invading it. And of course money talks: their ability to invade it far exceeds our ability to protect it. With the exception of dramatic steps like dropping out of society, even the most diligent defensive efforts will yield only a modest improvement over the status quo.

There is a popular myth, propagated by conservative legislators and law-enforcement officials, that the Internet allows Netizens in general, and criminals in particular, to hide behind aliases and to evade justice through some property of anonymity inherent to the Internet. This is absolutely false. But consider their agenda: detecting and tracing cybercrime is difficult and time consuming, requiring a good deal of legwork. Many local police departments lack the budgets to hire qualified technicians and often rely on self-taught officers and inexpensive, even donated, investigative tools of dubious quality. (If you make an inferior product, donating it to a resource-strapped PD is a good way of generating publicity. The dysfunctional face-recognition gear given to several American PDs since 9/11, and later abandoned, illustrates this marketing tactic.) Naturally, the police would like their jobs to be easier, as anyone would. They would very much prefer that the Internet be even more transparent than it already is. They'd be delighted if they could simply press a button and have instant access to all the information they need to conduct a cybercrime investigation from the comfort of their cubicles down at headquarters. And who wouldn't? It's a perfectly natural desire. Remember, cops are people too: many work very hard and appreciate a shortcut as much as anyone. Of course, good criminal justice and police short-cuts are a bad mix, but the desire for convenience is universal.

As a result of aggressive lobbying from the law-enforcement community, many jurisdictions have enacted, or are currently debating, mandatory data-retention laws for ISPs and other telecom providers. Such a scheme would make cybercrime investigations more convenient and cut down on legwork by establishing a record of each user's Internet history and an easy, standard method of data access. But it also places a significant financial burden on the service providers (which will inevitably be passed on to consumers) and puts them in the legally awkward position of doing law-enforcement support work. Such a scheme might also represent a serious assault on the privacy of citizens, depending on how access to this data is controlled and audited.

In spite of the anonymity myth—a persistent law-enforcement preoccupation—the minute you venture onto the Net, your computer begins leaking data about you in prodigious quantities, fetching images and advertisements and taking cookies from secondary and tertiary sources too numerous to mention. Passwords often go out in clear text, and the majority of data packets, regardless of the protocol used, can be read in their entirety.

As I mentioned in the Introduction, all Internet clients and servers break large chunks of data into packets that are reassembled at their destination. For example, when you send someone an e-mail memo, it gets broken into data packets. The mail server that you are using forwards your memo to the mail server your correspondent is using, through the numerous routers and switches that lie between them. The receiving mail server then reassembles the packets and stores the memo until your correspondent downloads it. During the trip between servers, these packets may take any number of routes, depending on network conditions. Because traffic conditions are constantly shifting, the packets may not arrive in the order they were sent, but they don't have to: each is given a sequence number that establishes the correct order for reassembly. This is an example of *packet switching*, and it's the trick that makes the Internet work with reasonable speed. Packets of all types are routed dynamically, according to the path of least resistance. I might send you an e-mail on Monday and another on Wednesday, and the two might take different routes through the Internet. The same is true of all IP traffic. Packets are switched and bounced about according to the best path at the time, and there are literally thousands of parallel routes by which they might be transferred from point to point.

Thus the Internet is said to be *massively parallel*, which is why, theoretically, it can't be shut down. If one route between two machines is blocked by some regional technical failure, the Internet's routing infrastructure will automatically find a way around it. We saw this in the summer of 2003, when the American

Northeast suffered a sudden power blackout stretching from New York as far west as Cleveland and as far north as Ottawa. A great deal of routing infrastructure went off line, yet the Internet continued functioning as it had been designed to do. People without power were forced off line, of course, but the Internet routed traffic around the enormous hole that suddenly appeared in the infrastructure. Just so, mail between England and Spain doesn't suddenly cease flowing because the French post is on strike. The post, too, is massively parallel, like the Internet.

Packet switching is one reason why Internet privacy is so difficult to achieve. A data packet has got to tell any machine that receives it where it came from and where it's going. This is because the two end-points, the origin (e.g., your Web browser) and destination (e.g., a remote Web site), are likely to establish a session and exchange data for a period of time. A Web server half a world away has got to know precisely where your PC is located in order for you to establish an HTTP session and receive the data you've requested. And the eight or ten routers between your PC and the server you're contacting have to know where these packets are coming from and where they're going in order to route them and reassemble them correctly.

A postcard is a one-way, switched packet. It might pass through several post offices along its route, though it only needs to display its destination address and a message. Internet traffic is a bit different: it's open like a postcard, but *reciprocal* like a letter. In order for two machines to establish a session across the Net, the data packets exchanged need both a valid destination address and a valid originating, or return, address. And they're broken into bits, so they also need to advertise the sequence in which they were created to be reassembled correctly. A data packet reveals a great deal more about itself than any postcard. Indeed, the post is quite anonymous and quite secure; it handles billions of items every day, so it's impossible for anyone to monitor these real-world "packets" for content. Valuables can be sent securely through the post: unless you advertise that the contents of a mailed package are worth stealing ("Cuban Cigars—Handle With Care"), the chance of it being intercepted by a third party is the same as it would be for some ghastly fruitcake.

Data packets are different: they can easily be sniffed. It's not difficult to set up a proxy server on the Internet along with a filter that will examine packets for, say, login and password information, and capture interesting ones. Certain keywords can also be set to trigger a capture. It's easy to filter and search for individual packets that contain valuable data. No one working in a post office can do anything of the sort, because they would have to open packages and envelopes and inspect them individually. Data packets, on the other hand, can be inspected automatically.

Let's look at a rather oversimplified packet:

Header:	Source IP address, Destination IP address, Protocol
Header:	Source port, Destination port, Sequence number, etc.
Body:	Data payload, Padding to achieve correct size
Trailer:	Error correction, "The End"

Of course, a packet doesn't really look like this. It's an invisible object, so, strictly speaking, it doesn't look like anything. And there is a bit more to it. But you can imagine it as an electronic postcard where the header contains the address information and the body is the message, or the data being exchanged. Sometimes extra data will be added to make a short packet the right size for the network. The trailer usually consists of a few bits indicating the end of the packet. Sometimes error-correction data is included so that a packet can be re-sent if it's malformed. So a data packet is rather like a postcard, only in this case, the sender as well as the recipient have got to be identified, which makes a data packet considerably less private.

Unless you take steps such as using SSL, SSH, or *TLS* (transport layer security), a packet's body (message content) and header (address information) are readable by anyone whose equipment it passes through. Packets can be filtered automatically for interesting content like passwords or politically controversial text. Most Web sites use SSL for logging in to pass-protected areas, but not all do. When you log in to your ISP or e-mail server, your password will likely go out in plain text. Most Web-mail services use SSL for logins, and that's a good thing. But it's important to keep in mind that the Internet and World Wide Web always default to hopelessly insecure. It's up to service providers and users to employ the tools and techniques needed to make it more private and secure.

Online Stealth

Previously, we learned about SSH tunneling, which allows us to enclose data packets within an encrypted protocol, a tactic rather like mailing a postcard inside a sealed envelope. We also learned about message and file encryption with utilities like PGP and GPG. These tools afford *privacy*, but not *anonymity*, which is another matter altogether. Privacy means that others can't read your online correspondence or any files stored on your computer unless you permit them to, and it means that others can't read the packet content flowing between your computer and other machines via the Internet. Anonymity means that others can't determine who wrote, sent, or created a computer file, and that no one receiving or intercepting Internet traffic can determine where it came from. Privacy obscures the *content* that's being communicated; anonymity obscures the *people* who are communicating.

Let's recall Phil Zimmermann's example from Chapter 4. If you and I hold a conversation in an open, outdoor space, we can ensure our privacy. We can simply stop talking when someone else comes within earshot and resume the conversation once they've moved on. But we're not anonymous. Three people know who took part in the conversation: you, me, and the stranger, though the stranger has no idea what it was about because he couldn't hear it. Thus, the conversation will have been private but not anonymous. When it comes to computers and the Internet, privacy is fairly easy to achieve with tools like SSH, SSL, and PGP or GnuPG. Such tools are crucial for communications security, but they don't represent the whole story. Sometimes, when we communicate, the last thing we want is privacy. Political writing, for example, needs to reach a broad audience; only sometimes, what a person believes or knows or says can get them into serious trouble. In such cases, anonymity, not privacy, is the answer.

> A whistleblower wants to contact a journalist to expose malfeasance at the company or government bureau that employs him.

> A relief worker in a Third World country wants to expose official corruption, ethnic persecution, or police brutality.

> A witness to a crime wants to alert the police without drawing attention to himself.

> A government official wants to leak secret documents that he believes the public is entitled to see.

All of these people would be put at risk if they were identified. They don't want privacy; indeed, they want the information they've got to be disseminated as broadly as possible. What they want is a reliable way to conceal their identity. The Internet might seem an ideal mechanism for putting the word out because it enables an individual to reach millions of others conveniently, but it isn't safe. Dropping the information into a mailbox located in a crowded venue would be far more prudent. Theodore Kaczynski, the Unabomber, understood this, as did the person responsible for the anthrax attacks in 2001. Kaczynski would likely never have been caught had he not published a manifesto that enabled others to recognize him. The anthrax attacker still has not been caught, and won't be unless he's made a similar mistake or has left other clues behind.

Earlier I claimed that the Internet doesn't afford anonymity, and that's true. The Internet was designed to enable the exchange of data, not to protect it or its sender's identity. Pretty much all of our online comings and goings are recorded somewhere and may one day come back to bite us. Anonymity is not a fundamental property of the Net, but that doesn't mean it can't be achieved. It can be, and quite nicely at that, so long as you understand how it works.

Crowds

Nothing promotes anonymity like a big gathering of people. Picture two men in a crowded city rail terminal, sitting on a bench together reading newspapers. They don't interact; yet when they leave, each walks off with the other's briefcase. Perhaps a crime has just been committed; or perhaps one has just been prevented. Either way, no one is going to take any notice of those two men, and certainly no notice of who owns which briefcase. They don't need privacy because they're anonymous. No one knows, or cares, who they are or what they're doing. If they were the only two passengers in the terminal, they might well be noticed and remembered by the staff. But two men among five thousand are practically invisible.

The idea of using a crowd to achieve anonymity can be adapted to the Internet. It's not easy, because the Internet generally works by connecting two machines point-to-point. But it is possible to set up a crowd between a client and a server, and to do it in a way that prevents observers from determining which member of the crowd is responsible for which action. In order to set up an online crowd, it's necessary to set up an intermediate server, called a *proxy*. Proxy servers can be used in several ways. Some store large caches of popular Web pages so they can be fetched more conveniently. This type of proxy helps to speed up Internet surfing and is especially useful for people with dialup connections. Many Web-based companies and ISPs use caching proxies to mirror their content and serve Web pages to more users at once. When you see the words *high-speed dialup,* you can infer that caching proxies are involved. Akamai is one outfit that provides this type of service to other companies. It mirrors Web content on numerous proxy servers so that it can be made available to more users than a single machine could accommodate.

Proxy servers can be used in other ways. They can be set up as a virtual gathering place where a crowd of users can be formed. If this is done right, it's possible to assemble a crowd so that observers can't identify individuals within it. When you, and perhaps thousands of other people, log in to an anonymizing proxy, a buffer zone is created between your computer and the rest of the Internet. Meanwhile, other people are logged in as well, using the same virtual buffer zone. When you and other members of the crowd fetch a Web page or send an e-mail, it appears to an observer that the anonymizing proxy is performing all of these actions.

It's possible for an observer to learn that someone is using the proxy, and it's also possible for an observer to determine what traffic is being sent and received between the proxy and the wider Web. But so long as the proxy is designed properly and a large crowd of people is using it, it's impossible to associate the crowd's collective Web activity with a particular member.

In this case, we're assuming that no one is using encryption or another privacy tool along with the anonymizing proxy. So this system, as we've described it, is not private; it's simply anonymous. There are a couple of caveats here that we need to keep in mind. We obviously need some way of connecting to the proxy so that the traffic we send to it and receive from it can't be read or associated with us personally by our ISP. It is possible for your ISP to see that you're using the proxy, but if you connect via SSH it will be unable to see any of the traffic you exchange with it. For example, the proxy service provided by Anonymizer uses SSH tunneling between the user's computer and the proxy. So long as you establish privacy between your computer and the proxy, you are safely concealed within a large crowd and it's impossible for an observer to associate your Web traffic with you. But it's necessary to *sneak into the crowd*, so to speak. So long as IP traffic between your computer and the proxy is private, traffic between the proxy and the Internet at large will be anonymous.

According to Anonymizer founder Lance Cottrell, the proxy service has been designed so that not even the administrators or staff at Anonymizer can associate Internet traffic with a particular user. Wary subscribers can pay for the service with a money order, so not even the company needs to know who you are. There is also a semi-anonymous POP e-mail service, and a fully anonymous Web-mail service available. The semi-anonymous service is a normal POP mail account that enables you to send and receive e-mail using your Anonymizer username, and to send it and access it via SSH, bypassing your ISP-assigned POP mail account, which can be monitored. But you do have a username that can be associated with you. The fully anonymous e-mail service is a Web interface; it's designed so that it's impossible for the company to determine who sent an e-mail with it, and the message can be encrypted with the recipient's public key for additional security. But this is like sending an anonymous postcard; you cannot receive replies to e-mails sent this way because they all have the same return address: anonymous@anonymizer.com. However, if you send an encrypted message, you can identify yourself either personally or with an alias within the encrypted text so that only the recipient will know who you are, assuming you wish them to know. They could then reply to you using the Anonymizer Web-mail service, and encrypt their message so that only you would be able to identify them. If both parties were to use SSH tunneling and an anonymizing proxy when they access the Web-mail interface and encrypt their memos, their exchange would be both anonymous to outsiders and completely private. This arrangement is probably not foolproof to some metaphysical degree of certainty, but it's as good as it gets.

There have been several attempts to create services that provide Internet anonymity. A company called SafeWeb used to offer anonymous Web surfing for free but was unable to find a decent return on investment and has since discontinued the service. AT&T Labs developed an anonymizing service called the Crowds Project, but that too has been discontinued. A product from ZeroKnowledge Systems called Freedom WebSecure offers a decent level of privacy and anonymity, but it requires a browser plugin and Microsoft Internet Explorer, and does not run on Linux. A German project called the Java Anonymizing Proxy, or JAP, also leverages online crowds: unfortunately, this service cannot be trusted.

Proxy servers are often accidentally left open by careless admins. These proxies can be used by other people surfing the Web, though without invitation. If you connect to someone's proxy by loading it into your browser's proxy setup, any Web site you visit will see the proxy's IP address instead of yours. A lot of people think this is a good way to surf the Web anonymously. There are large lists of so-called anonymous open proxies collected at Web sites such as www.proxys4all.com, tools.rosinstrument.com/proxy, www.stayinvisible.com, www.proxylist.net, and scores of others. Lists of open HTTP proxies are collected by contributors and shared freely on such Web sites. However, there is no guarantee that the proxies listed will be anonymous. While some proxies may have been left open by accident and may offer you a measure of anonymity, some are deliberately left open by people sniffing for passwords. Others are deliberately set up by law-enforcement officials searching for people who are looking for anonymity, on the popular theory that anything a citizen wishes to hide is probably illegal. These proxies are a gamble for novices, and I don't recommend them. There are steps that power users can take to improve their odds, such as tracing the proxy geographically and choosing one in a country where the local authorities probably won't care about them, but this is not foolproof. It is never a good idea to trust a proxy when you don't know who's running it, or why.

For do-it-yourselfers, there is James Marshall's free CGI Proxy, a good product if you have a server to set it up on and know what you're doing. CGI Proxy supports SSL and can be configured to filter images, ads, cookies, and scripts. A group of people who know and trust each other can share the proxy. It doesn't require an executable or a plugin on the user's machine, which in some countries can be incriminating. It's also handy because once it's running, users can access it from any computer they happen to be on. It's useful for people in countries where there are national firewalls to censor Internet content and block access to privacy and anonymity services. (If the local authorities discover the CGI Proxy and ban access to it, it can simply be moved to another server, whack-a-mole-wise.) Marshall says he started the project as a means of defeating national censorship firewalls and that its anonymity features evolved later, in line with popular demand. CGI Proxy is available at jmarshall.com/tools/cgiproxy.

There is an important caveat, however: anyone, including the authorities, can set up an anonymizing proxy or service. Always beware any free anonymizing service that might actually be a *honeypot* set up by the police to eavesdrop on unwitting users. A company that charges for such services has a financial stake in protecting your privacy; if they're careless or corrupt, it will eventually become known and their business will suffer. On the other hand, a free or do-it-yourself service can be set up by anyone for any reason. If you can't determine who's behind an anonymizing service, don't use it. It may well be a trap set by hackers sniffing for passwords, or worse, a trap set by the authorities sniffing for people with something to hide.

A Healthy Contempt for Surveillance

A strong desire for privacy and anonymity on the Internet hardly indicates paranoia or unsavory intentions. If someone tells you that only criminals have something to hide, ask to install a wireless video camera in their bedroom and see how they react. Privacy is a fundamental human need. It's absolutely natural and absolutely right; it needs no justification. There is no reason why your ISP needs to know what you do on the Web. There is no reason why it should know whom you correspond with via e-mail or what you have to say, which Web sites you visit, what files you download, or what you search for using Google. Yet it can monitor all of these things if it wishes to. Of course, all it really needs to know is how much to bill you for the services you're using. It's quite easy for your bandwidth use to be metered without your ISP knowing what data that bandwidth actually contains. Used correctly, privacy tools and anonymizing services will ensure that your personal business remains personal.

There is also no reason why marketing outfits need to know who you are or where you live, and they certainly don't need to know anything about your children. You are under no obligation to cooperate with them or advance their agenda. Privacy and anonymity are your best defenses against the intrusions of marketers, spammers, data miners, social engineers, stalkers, overzealous police officers, sexual perverts, and other Internet parasites.

Anonymity provides a very important defense against censorship as well. Sometimes Internet censorship is accomplished with firewalls and filters, but sometimes it's accomplished through intimidation. Speech can be chilled quite effectively by the looming threat of retaliation. Free-speech laws are fine, but they can change, be riddled with exceptions, or simply not be enforced. The musical group the Dixie Chicks paid a price in 2003 for criticizing U.S. President George W. Bush, and they will no doubt think twice before voicing controversial opinions again. Radio stations, especially those under the control of ClearChannel Communications, cut the group's airtime in retaliation for exercising their First Amendment rights, costing them royalties. The group finally had to issue a groveling public apology to get their music back on the air. Speech was chilled in that case, though no law was broken. The Bush administration couldn't shut them up, but Big Business sympathetic to the administration could, and did.

Many Web sites endure almost constant intimidation for posting content inconvenient to large corporations. The usual tactic is to threaten a copyright-infringement or trademark-infringement lawsuit. A blogger, independent Web site operator, or Internet hobbyist is unlikely to be able to afford a defense, and will often give in to corporate extortion rather than sink vast amounts of money into a lawsuit that's stacked against him from the start. Sometimes companies will threaten the ISP or hosting company, which will often pull the plug on an offending Web site rather than risk an expensive legal challenge from a major corporation on behalf of some small-potatoes customer.

An important recent struggle involves Diebold Election Systems, a company criticized for numerous security snafus in its computerized, touch-screen voting machines that could compromise election results, and the Independent Media Center (www.indymedia.org), a San Francisco Web publisher that has been spreading the bad news. In a letter dated 10 October 2003, Diebold's lawyers threaten to sue on copyright grounds if Indymedia should persist in providing Web links to an archive of unflattering company memos.

"You appear to be hosting a Web site that contains information location tools that refer or link users to one or more online locations containing Diebold Property .... The Web page you are hosting clearly infringes Diebold's copyrights by providing information location tools that refer or link users ... to an online location containing infringing material," the company's legal beagles warn.

At this writing, the forbidden memos have been mirrored by numerous university and news Web sites, most of which have also received nastygrams from Diebold's legal squad. Sadly, a number of colleges and universities have since been cowed into removing the material. Speech has again been chilled with financial intimidation, though in this case, the documents raise questions about the security of a national balloting system and are therefore of paramount concern to the public. Doubts about ballot systems and election results attack the very roots of democracy. In an ideal world, it would be impossible for a company to suppress inquiry into matters of such grave public importance with any conceivable justification, but the world we live in is far from ideal.

We live in a world dominated by corporate principalities where "free speech" is a beloved incantation, yet a rare privilege enjoyed chiefly by those who can afford to be sued. Financial intimidation may be perfectly legal and far from violent, but it's no less effective in chilling speech than the torture rack. Today, those of us living in the advanced democracies of western Europe and North America have little reason to fear being beaten senseless by the police for expressing an inconvenient idea, but we have a great deal to fear from impeccably groomed lawyers with posh accents and Brooks Brothers' suits.

It's as true today as it was in the Dark Ages: anonymity is the only shield capable of defeating censorship and enabling free speech. The American Bill of Rights, while a good model for civil liberties, can't protect speech in the private sector because it's merely a check on government power. On the street, things are very different: anyone who can afford to outspend you in court can shut you up. And they don't have to win a judgment; they can force you to abandon your defense because it's too expensive to fight. A well-heeled opponent can be entirely in the wrong, yet win easily by financial attrition. It happens every day.

Anonymity alone guarantees you a voice. It has always been so and it will always be so. The *desire* to escape observation is fundamental to human nature, and the *ability* to escape observation is crucial to any realistic notion of human liberty. There's nothing remotely unsavory about it.

Notice: You Have No Privacy

If hundreds of millions of people are communicating over an insecure global network, it stands to reason that Big Commerce will find a way to exploit the situation for financial gain. And indeed, privacy invasion has become a multibillion-dollar industry in today's information economy. Marketing outfits are growing rich by cross-referencing, packaging, and reselling every scrap of personal data they can find. Because the Internet is essentially open to all and very transparent, it should surprise no one that it's also a veritable gold mine of personal data and consumer behavior. Marketers often know which Web sites you visit, what you buy on line, what you download, what you read, and even your name, age, occupation, and where you live. It is not difficult to associate your online aliases with the real you. For example, most Netizens have filled in scores of online marketing surveys in exchange for discounts or free products and services, and these surveys are a very powerful mechanism of privacy invasion. They often seek what's called *aggregate data*, meaning data that locates you within a group and doesn't identify you personally. That would be fine if it were as far as it went, only it's quite easy to associate this aggregate data with an individual. Web sites may claim that they never associate aggregate data with identifying data, but they also have policies that are invariably "subject to change without notice."

Web sites offering services that require them to know who you are in real life may collect detailed profiles and share them with anyone they please. Often, a Web site's "privacy policy" is nothing more than notice that you have no privacy. Most of these electronic documents are long, confusing masterpieces of legalese that appear to affirm user privacy but actually warn you of the reverse in obscure language. As songwriter Tom Waits has wryly noted, "the large print giveth and the small print taketh away." Because these policy statements are written by legal people trained in the high art of putting readers to sleep, most users never reach the part where they're told that any notion of privacy they may have harbored is fictional. The privacy policy always starts out with an assurance that Company X is "deeply committed to protecting its customers' privacy at all times," but this will be followed by several thousand unreadable words that eventually boil down to the simple phrase, "except when we choose not to protect it."

Speaking at a cybercrime conference in 2003, eBay executive Joseph Sullivan boasted that his company has the weakest privacy policy in the industry.

"When someone uses our site and clicks on the *I Agree* button, it is as if he agrees to let us submit all of his data to the legal authorities," Sullivan bragged to an audience made up largely of law enforcement officials. "Which means that if you are a law enforcement officer, all you have to do is send us a fax with a request for information, and ask about the person behind the seller's identity number, and we will provide you with his name, address, sales history, and other details, all without having to produce a court order. We want law enforcement people to spend time on our site."

Forget about due process and troublesome affidavits sworn in the presence of snippy judges; any busybody with a badge, or any fraudster with a fax machine and a fake badge, is welcome to conduct whatever sort of unauthorized fishing expedition he pleases against any Netizen, and eBay will be only too happy to accommodate them.

Sullivan, who left the U.S. Department of Justice to join eBay in 2002, claimed that he "didn't know another Web site that has a privacy policy as flexible as eBay's." Information available for the asking includes users' auction activity, real-life identity, credit card data, and posts to the eBay forums.

The company also owns the PayPal online banking service, another gold mine of personal information that eBay is eager to disseminate far and wide. "If you contact me, I will hook you up with the PayPal people. They will help you get the information you're looking for," Sullivan trilled.

The hands-down global champion in *commercial* privacy invasion is the United States, but it's hardly alone. The associated technology is powerful and widely deployed. RFID (radio frequency identification) transponders can be hidden in virtually any consumer product, and soon will be if the retail industry has its way. In time, these will develop into the real-world equivalent of browser cookies, only stuck to people, not disk drives. GPS (Global Positioning System) transponders are being incorporated into mobile phones so that users' locations can be pinpointed remotely to within feet. Many automobiles are already equipped with GPS gear, and more will be soon. Electronic and plastic financial transactions can be monitored in real time and on a mass scale. A phone call to almost any company's customer service department involves monitoring or recording "for training and quality-control purposes." (Read, "for preparation in case a legal dispute should emerge.") Millions of people are under constant video surveillance in the workplace, and companies are increasingly given to monitoring employee e-mail, Web surfing, and even phone calls. The average citizen can't walk around the block without becoming the subject of video surveillance from several sources. And databases, both public and private, are now converging in ways that would astonish even Kafka and Orwell.

Today, privacy invasion is a constant, inescapable feature of daily life. In Europe, it's more likely that government will be doing the surveillance and eavesdropping, as there are fairly tough data protection laws restricting private-sector snooping. In America, the watchful culprit is more likely to be a commercial entity. However, this is starting to change in the political aftermath of the September 11, 2001, atrocities. In July of 2003, the President's Commission on the United States Postal Service recommended that the U.S. Department of Homeland Security "explore the use of [mandatory] sender identification for every piece of mail." Anonymous mail, for centuries a lone guardian of free speech, may soon be forbidden on national security pretexts.

Government is beginning to harness the awesome surveillance powers of American commerce and its vast databases with numerous schemes for aggressive data mining. Children are being trained to accept remote surveillance as a normal part of life, as video cameras increasingly turn up in school corridors and even classrooms. The American surveillance and data-mining infrastructure, while it remains largely in private hands, is more powerful and more comprehensive than any created in human history, including those belonging to such deeply unhealthy nations as North Korea and the former Soviet Union.

It is also immensely profitable. Data collection, mining, and packaging are crucial elements of modern commerce. In the commercial world, every human being is seen as a potential consumer, though what one consumes will shift according to a vast range of variables. Thus, people are categorized according to complex consumer profiles involving income, education, geographical location, cultural background, and purchasing history.

Marketers know more about you than you might imagine. Demographic data, like average household income, rates of house ownership, car ownership, fertility, and mortality, are readily available for geographical areas, down to the fine-grained level of individual neighborhoods. A marketer who knows only your street address and age is already equipped to make several reasonable assumptions about your personal interests and patterns of consumption. But things can get a lot more personal. Consumers can be fitted into profiles based on information they willingly divulge, and credit cards and supermarket loyalty cards create records of our individual spending histories.

One element of marketing involves matching an individual to the consumer profile most likely to reflect, and predict, his behavior. Everyone's spending habits are observed and referenced with demographic and personal data to create these profiles. The marketer's job is to determine which consumer profile you come closest to matching, so he can pitch products and services to you that you're likely to want, need, and be able to afford. But in order to fit you into a profile, marketers need to learn as much about you as they can. When you fill out a survey or questionnaire, you can be sure that a marketing outfit is trying to match you with an established profile, and possibly find out who you are and where you live.

On the Internet, marketing surveys are a common requirement for so-called "free" services like Web-mail and products like software. Actually, you're exchanging very valuable information for these goodies, so don't imagine that you're taking advantage of anyone. And when it comes to Internet adware and browser cookies, profiling can go from personal to positively intimate. Your entire Internet surfing history can be analyzed to drive advertisements to your desktop and browser, tailored to your online habits. Setting your cookies to expire with each browser session and rejecting cookies from third parties, as recommended in the Introduction, will go a long way toward frustrating this sort of surveillance. My advice for defeating online marketing surveys that can't be avoided is simply to supply a fictitious name, address, and phone number. You can maintain several anonymous Web-mail accounts and supply these e-mail addresses instead of the one associated with your ISP, which might identify you.

(This kind of e-mail account is also handy for keeping some distance between yourself and contacts you've met through online chat services.) Hotmail and Yahoo! Mail are both good for establishing aliases.

Of course, if you intend to do business with an online company, it makes no sense to mislead them or hide from them. But when you're confronted with some survey that you need to fill out for access to a one-off download or service, you should feel free to lie creatively. You are hardly under oath in these situations. You should never reveal your name, address, age, phone number, or ISP-related e-mail address to anyone on line except those with whom you have either a personal or a business relationship in the real world. No one else is entitled to this information.

Wired Sprouts

Children are a major target of the marketing establishment. Even the very young, who have no discretionary spending power, can be conscripted to nag their parents into a purchase. McDonald's, for one corporation, has been brilliantly successful at harnessing the toddler "nag factor." Disney, Mattel, Oscar Mayer, Kellogg, and Kraft Foods are equally good examples of corporations that deliberately reach out to small children. Older children have allowances and part-time jobs, and, unless they're unfortunate, their incomes are 100 percent disposable. They've become a potent force in commerce, as the intellectual and aesthetic content of creative products like movies, television programs, magazines, and popular music clearly illustrates.

But children are unprepared to deal with the immensely slick and inherently dishonest business of mass marketing. They have little choice but to trust adults, and for this reason there are potent social taboos against taking advantage of children's naïveté or physical weakness. Misleading, cheating, or manipulating a child for gain is universally considered loathsome, although Big Commerce is absolved for using these tactics because enormous profits are at stake.

Children have no choice but to rely on their elders and trust what they say. Yet we allow well-educated, cynical adults with huge corporate budgets to conduct focus groups, to manufacture desire in young minds, to establish the standards of coolness, and then sell the expensive gear needed to achieve it. Children are no match for the slick machinery of modern marketing. It would not be wise for parents to underestimate the manipulative genius of an industry that's managed to persuade generations of boys to play with dolls by marketing them as "action figures."

Because they tend to take things at face value, children are particularly susceptible to commercial propaganda and marketing surveys in the guise of online opinion polls and contests. They can very easily be tricked into giving up personal information. In 1998, the U.S. Congress passed the Children's

Online Privacy Protection Act (COPPA) in hopes of protecting young sprouts from marketing manipulation and privacy invasion via the Internet. The law deals only with children under the age of 13 and is administered by the Federal Trade Commission (FTC), a regulatory body renowned for nothing so much as its timidity in the face of corporate interests. The Act requires parental consent before children may divulge personal details, but contains numerous exceptions and indulgences no doubt inserted by retail-industry lobbyists. In many cases, a mere e-mail memo pretending to come from a parent or legal guardian is all that's needed to grant permission. The COPPA is a nice piece of legislative window-dressing enabling members of Congress to express their deep concern for the welfare of children, but it's not to be trusted. It's essential that parents take an active interest in their children's comings and goings on the Net. Parents should talk frankly about the dangers of privacy invasion with their older children, while small children should never be allowed to venture onto the Internet alone, but should always be supervised by a parent, teacher, sitter, or older sibling while using any Internet-related software.

The Internet is adult space, like a bar, casino, or nightclub. We wouldn't allow small children into these places any more than we would allow them to play on the freeway. There are many places in life where children simply don't belong unless they're under adult supervision, and the Internet is definitely one of them. Numerous legislative steps have been taken to make it more child-friendly, such as the Child Online Protection Act (COPA) of 1998, but these efforts have been unsuccessful and would cause more harm than good if they ever were to succeed. An earlier attempt, the Communications Decency Act (CDA) of 1996, was struck down by the U.S. Supreme Court for burdening adult speech. The COPA has twice been ruled unconstitutional in federal district court on the same grounds. The problem here is that Net censorship would diminish the level of adult discourse, dialogue, and inquiry to that which is suitable for the eyes and ears of children, a step that would obliterate the Internet's value as an open public forum. We certainly wouldn't try to make the interstate highway system safe for children to play on. Motorways are adult space, and must remain so in order to be of any value to society. The Internet is very much the same.

Rather than pressure Congress to transform the Internet into a virtual "Sesame Street," parents should take more practical and effective steps toward protecting their children from pornography, hate speech, tasteless humor, profanity, marketing come-ons, and sexual predators. There are two technological approaches: Internet filtering software and family-oriented ISPs.

Filtering programs such as CyberPatrol, NetNanny, or CyberSitter can be quite helpful. They work by preventing Internet clients from accessing certain Web sites and servers, but they're hardly foolproof. One problem is that they may overfilter and prevent children from accessing Web sites that their parents don't mind them visiting. Internet filters are not intelligent devices; they rely on keywords that indicate objectionable material. A popular example, often repeated, of how they fail is by blocking the word *breast* to prevent access to pornographic

Web sites. Of course, the forbidden word appears in quite innocent contexts such as breast cancer, breast feeding, and so on. Filtering software can interfere with research along these lines. It will also block e-mail that contains forbidden keywords. But there again, *stripping* and *caning* might indicate sadomasochism, or furniture restoration. *X-X-X* might indicate pornography, or hugs and kisses from Gran. The software can't tell the difference.

Another drawback to filtering software is the simple fact that it's proprietary: end users don't know how it works or exactly what it will and will not block. You will have your own ideas about what content is appropriate for your children, but the software may have other ideas. It certainly can be useful, but it's not a panacea and children still have got to be supervised when they're accessing the Internet. Filtering is not a substitute for adult supervision; it is simply a useful tool—a handy backup defense. The primary defense must always be parents educating children about the dangers that exist on line and keeping an eye on their Internet use.

Family-friendly ISPs and filtering proxy services are also available, and they can be a good alternative for Linux users because there is little filtering software available for Linux just yet. Most of these ISPs allow adults to bypass the filtering for their own Web use and offer several options for individual levels of filtering according to the ages of children using the Internet. Many also offer broadband access. Families that don't mind the added expense might consider using a filtered ISP for the children and a standard one for the teenagers and adults in the household.

There is powerful spyware available, such as eBlaster, NetVizor, and the like, and this can be a solution when children are stubbornly disobedient. However, I would not recommend using it unless better measures have failed, because spying on a child can lead to a serious erosion of trust within a family. Education, adult supervision, and filtering are always to be preferred. Of course, children can be willful and incredibly sneaky and deceptive, so if a child insists on defying household rules and puts himself at risk with Internet use, it may be necessary to resort to an extreme measure like installing spyware.

NOTE *Intercepting the electronic communications of a person other than your own minor child without their knowledge and consent is a serious federal offense in the United States, a fact that spyware vendors have been very reluctant to emphasize. Spyware outfits market their tools as a good way for parents to keep track of family members using the Internet, but monitoring your spouse or adult children without their informed consent is a crime. If you install this sort of software, it is not merely a courtesy to let users know that it's there; it's a legal obligation, unless those using the infected computer are your own children or legal wards and under the age of 18.*

Generally, Internet-based threats to children from serious criminals like sexual predators and kidnappers have been grossly exaggerated by parties interested in greater transparency, such as the police, the privacy invasion industry, and child-protective hysterics. The news media also fan the flames because an Internet-related abduction is so absurdly rare that it automatically becomes a story. Thousands of children are abducted by noncustodial parents; or molested by relatives, teachers, clergy, and coaches; or assaulted and even murdered by neighbors, but they don't get much airtime (unless, like JonBenet Ramsey and Elizabeth Smart, they happen to be exceptionally photogenic). Yet on those rare occasions when the Internet is involved in an abduction, murder, or molestation, the story runs for weeks. It's only *because* it's so unusual that the media latch onto it. If we were to gauge the likelihood of events by their news coverage, we would have to believe that there are epidemics of surgeons amputating the wrong limbs, heavily armed teenagers going on murder rampages in the schools, and creepy old ladies living in tiny flats with hundreds of emaciated cats. These things do happen sometimes, but we only hear about them because they're so bizarre.

During the mid- and late 1990s, the media trumpeted the commercial potential of the Internet as if it were the second coming of Christ. Obviously, it wasn't. The media have also trumpeted its deadly potential to lure innocent children to their doom at the hands of bloodthirsty perverts. That, too, is fiction. Your children are immensely safer from molestation on line than they are at slumber parties, in school locker rooms, or at summer camp. There is no reason for parents to be afraid of letting children use the Internet. There is a good deal of content out there that's entirely inappropriate for the young, all right, but this is true everywhere in life. The Internet is *adult* space, not *evil* space. Educating and supervising children, and speaking frankly with them about common dangers, will go a long way toward keeping them safe on the Net, as elsewhere.

And switching off the TV news will help you sleep better while you're about it.

CHAPTER 6

The Open-Source Escape Hatch

IF I WANTED TO HAVE an easy time writing this book, I would have argued that no one except a professional systems administrator should ever use Windows, and focused entirely on Linux. But I know that many people prefer Windows, and it's not my place to dictate anyone's choice of operating system. It would be easy, but shabby, to gloss over the steps required to harden Windows adequately. But it would be equally shabby to gloss over the comparative ease and convenience of hardening Linux. This is an especially important consideration for readers who aren't confident in their ability to tweak system settings in a computing environment as confusing and opaque as Windows.

By now it should be evident that Linux is a better operating system for security-minded users of all skill levels. Windows can, of course, be hardened significantly, but a great deal of activity goes on below the surface, well concealed from users and home administrators. Unless you're a power user or a professional admin, it's difficult and time consuming to make Windows secure, as the preceding pages make obvious. Windows is also less convenient to administer: one often has to log in to the admin account to make system changes, which encourages the risky habit of using the system with full privileges. Linux, in contrast, is less bother to lock down: there are fewer security procedures involved and they're easier to understand. And most administrative tasks are easy to perform from a user account. Thus a *less* technically inclined user stands a *better* chance of getting basic security right on a Linux system. This may seem counterintuitive, since Windows is presumed easier to use, but it's nevertheless true. A power user with an understanding of computer security can deal with most of the challenges of hardening Windows. However, a basic computer user and newcomer to computer security will find Linux a good deal easier to handle. I recommend Linux to computing novices in particular because they can achieve better security with far less effort and worry, and save money while they're about it.

But what, exactly, *is* Linux and why is it better? What advantages and disadvantages does it involve? Can a Windows user step off the Microsoft treadmill, onto Linux, without difficulty? Should *you* migrate to Linux? Let's consider these questions, starting with a brief history.

A Fresh Approach

First, Linux is not UNIX. It's quite similar, certainly, with a basic architecture and user interface familiar to all UNIX aficionados. BSD resembles UNIX in the same ways. Thus we might say there is a UNIX family, of which Sun Solaris, BSD, and Linux are three well-known members. Within that family are several operating systems using the same commands and running the same applications and services, so in terms of the user experience, Solaris (which *is* UNIX), BSD, and Linux are virtually indistinguishable. If you can use one, you can use them all. But the underlying code is different. Linux was built from the ground up, albeit with UNIX as its basic template. People refer to UNIX, BSD, and Linux as *unices* or with the expression **nix,* which is short for UNIX but usually indicates the family in general.

During the 1980s, UNIX was one of the few professional-quality operating systems available, but it was expensive, just like the equipment it operated. UNIX didn't work with the cheap Intel processors that were pouring into the market at the time. Big companies, universities, and scientists in major research outfits used UNIX; mere mortals were stuck with Intel processors and Microsoft DOS, a half-baked operating system designed for Intel hardware and cheap enough to fuel the PC revolution once a handful of office applications, such as word processors and spreadsheets, were created to run on it. But DOS, like its successor, Windows, would never be made any better than necessary to run the applications it supported. They are not professional-quality computing platforms;

they are, rather, application platforms. Microsoft is focused intensely on applications (and, lately, on Web services), and that's where the real development money and talent goes. DOS, and now Windows, are merely system components that make applications work and push consumers toward Microsoft applications and Web services.

During the 1980s, MS-DOS would swiftly become the Model T Ford of the office computing world: cheap enough for anyone to own, reasonably serviceable, and basically shabby. Naturally, it would become a monumental commercial hit. Meanwhile, an American computer science professor teaching in Holland named Andrew Tanenbaum created a simple operating system called MINIX, based loosely on UNIX, essentially as a teaching device. He published the source code—a fairly unusual step in those days—and encouraged his students to learn and take inspiration from his creation. He also maintained a MINIX mailing list, which attracted thousands of fellow programmers and students. A Finnish graduate student in computer science named Linus Torvalds thought MINIX could become a fully functional operating system, but Tanenbaum resisted complicating it because he intended it as a teaching device. Torvalds later began developing a system on his own that he called Linux, which he did from scratch using UNIX and MINIX as his basic templates. He announced Linux on the MINIX mailing list in 1991 and invited other programmers to test the software and contribute to the project. In time, interest in Linux outpaced interest in MINIX, and a new operating system was conceived. It was developed collectively by scores of professional programmers and academicians who wanted to create something inexpensive and portable, yet up to the best professional computing standards. Eventually, Linux would become not only a professional-grade operating system for the Intel-based personal computer, but a popular server and database system ported to numerous hardware platforms. MINIX wasn't abandoned, but it was Linux that evolved into a worldwide, and world-class, computing platform.

As Tanenbaum once put it, "I wanted to keep MINIX small enough for my students to understand in one semester. My consistent refusal to add all these new features is what inspired Linus to write Linux. Both of us are now happy with the results. The only person who is perhaps not so happy is Bill Gates. I think this is a good thing."[1]

During the early stages of Linux's development, Torvalds connected with Richard Stallman of the Free Software Foundation. Stallman was an evangelist for the open-source movement who had devised a licensing scheme called the GPL (GNU General Public License). Stallman had also created an open-source C compiler called GCC (GNU C Compiler) which he distributed freely. GCC was ported to Linux so that users could build and improve their applications and tweak the kernel with a free tool.

---

1. See www.cs.vu.nl/~ast/home/faq.html.

Strictly speaking, Linux is simply an operating system kernel, though most users think of it as a complete system. The major vendors, or distributors, such as SuSE in Germany, Red Hat in the United States, and Mandrake in France, package it with numerous applications and utilities and sell complete computer systems built around the Linux kernel. These full packages are called *distros,* short for distributions. The kernel itself may even be different from distro to distro; the licensing scheme under which Linux is made available allows anyone to alter it and distribute their own version. The major vendors often do tweak the kernel a bit to add value; thus we can speak of the Red Hat kernel, the SuSE kernel, and so on.

Linux is made available under the GPL, which is designed to keep open-source software—well—open. It discourages opportunists from commingling free, open-source code with expensive, closed-source applications. Anyone is welcome to use GPL code in an application they're creating, but if they do, they usually have to release the software under the GPL. Even using a small amount of free GPL code can obligate you to release the finished product under its terms. But this doesn't mean that a developer can't *sell* software under the GPL. Indeed, people are at liberty to use and modify GPL software however they see fit and sell their creations at whatever price the market will bear. You can even take someone else's GPL software and sell it yourself if you wish. For example, you could download the source code of a Linux kernel and several applications, build them, package them using RPM (Red Hat Package Manager) to make them convenient for others to use, and sell them on CDs without violating the GPL. By packaging the software, you're adding value and you're welcome to collect on that. What you're not at liberty to do is withhold the source code from your customers, or commingle GPL code with your own proprietary, closed-source code. This ensures that whenever you profit from GPL code, what you sell will be open to all—available for others to inspect and even to modify and resell—even though you're not offering it free of charge. Thus, it's often said that open-source software is free as in "free speech," not as in "free beer," or, put another way, *libre,* not *gratis.*

Linux, the Free Software Foundation, and the GPL have proved two things:

- First, that open-source software created by people who've *chosen* to create it is inherently better than proprietary software created by people who've been *commissioned* to create it.

- Second, that companies can earn a profit from a product that's open to everyone.

We tend to think of the software business as a zero-sum game where trade secrets must be guarded jealously and where quality products are always expensive and cheap products are always shabby. Open-source software has turned this around, creating cheap products of superb quality while enabling vendors to profit by repackaging the software with value added and offering technical support services.

Caveats

There's a lot to dislike in Windows, including its many undocumented functions, the interdependency of its many components, its tendency to phone home; its eagerness to execute code in unexpected contexts; the difficulty of practicing data hygiene; its long history of severe security flaws and virus propagation; its lack of Internet privacy features; its scheduled, forced upgrade cycle; its usurious licensing scheme; and its notorious tendency to crash. These are all areas where Linux offers dramatic advantages. There are no hidden functions in open-source software: it's simply impossible to conceal anything like a phone-home function in source code that's available for review by anyone who uses it. The features that enable virus propagation, automatic script execution, and remote system exploitation on Windows can all be shut off on a Linux system. Patches rarely cause difficulties because the system is modular in design. Upgrades are not a problem: whereas Microsoft ceases to support or issue patches for older software according to a schedule designed to keep everyone buying upgrades on a regular basis, new versions of open-source software can be installed at any time for free. You may have an old distro that's no longer supported by the vendor, but you can always obtain and install free upgrades for all of your software, including the kernel. There is nothing like the mysterious Windows Registry capturing data traces and God knows what else. And Linux's stability is exceptional. Most Windows users have no idea what it's like to use a computer for months, installing software, starting and stopping services, enabling and disabling driver modules, and tweaking the configuration, without ever seeing a blue screen or needing to reboot. With Windows, there are so many memory leaks and library conflicts that a daily rebooting is actually therapeutic, but the only time you need to reboot a Linux machine is when you've installed a new kernel and want to switch to it.

Linux is indeed better than Windows, but it may not be the best operating system for everyone. The advantages are compelling: it's open source so no one company or group of people can control it. The kernel and most applications are free, and even a full, packaged distribution is half the price of Windows. Linux is easier for users to configure for security, and it can ultimately be made a good deal more secure than Windows. It uses system resources more efficiently. Viruses and malicious scripts are hardly a concern. Services are easy to understand, involve few interdependencies, and can be shut off without penalty. It doesn't phone home. There's no Linux spyware. It's easier, and safer, to patch. Data traces are easier to control. Configuration files can be modified with a simple text editor. The major distros come packed with immensely more applications, programs, and utilities than Windows—indeed, choosing from the overabundance of available packages is the most time-consuming part of a Linux installation. And it's no more difficult to install or to use than Windows, especially with the KDE desktop.

But Linux does demand a couple of sacrifices. Chief among these are PC games, few of which have been ported to it. If you use your PC for games, Linux is not a good choice. However, if you've switched to console games, this won't be an issue.

There are many Linux applications that will undoubtedly work well for most recovering Windows users, including a free Outlook clone called Evolution from Ximian, but there really aren't adequate substitutes for MS Word or Excel. If you've got a lot of templates and macros, you won't want to abandon them to use the open-source OpenOffice or Sun's StarOffice. However, users, and even companies, that want to stay with Microsoft Office can still migrate to Linux and run Office on it with a program from CodeWeavers (www.codeweavers.com) called CrossOver Office, which costs about $70. I wrote this book using Microsoft Word on a Linux computer, and without difficulty. My publisher, Apress, has an MS Word template that it likes authors to use. CrossOver Office enabled me to conform to house specs without resorting to Windows. So Linux is a perfectly reasonable alternative even when Microsoft Office is important to you.

Another caveat is that Linux needs to be installed and set up manually; there are no PCs pre-loaded with it as there are with Windows. Chances are that your PC came with Windows installed, and you may never have performed a manual installation, that is, you may never have set up Windows from scratch. This is important: a complete system installation can be challenging and time consuming. Users have to find, download, and install good hardware drivers, and a great deal of configuration needs to be done. Normally, the PC maker will have done all this for you, and you can usually restore all your computer's features and original settings from a vendor-supplied restore CD (though it will likely destroy all of your data in the bargain). If you feel you'd have a hard time doing a manual installation with Windows, then you'll have an equally hard time doing it with Linux. However, if you feel that you could set up Windows from a common retail package on a naked PC, as opposed to using a PC vendor's restore CD or an upgrade version of Windows over an existing installation, then you can set up Linux just as easily.

There's a popular myth, encouraged by Microsoft's senior staff at every possible opportunity, that Linux is too difficult for the average user to set up and use, and this is why it's "not ready" for the consumer market. This was true as recently as two years ago, but not any longer. The major distributors have put a great deal of effort into making Linux as easy to set up as Windows, with the possible exception of XP, which is a bit easier than previous versions. But Windows 95, 98, and Me were always tough to set up from scratch if you didn't already know your way around them. The default desktop looked disgusting and Redmond's hardware drivers were barely functional. The user always had to find better drivers, whether on his vendor-supplied disks or by going on line to search for them. And there was always a lot of configuration to be done and third-party software to be installed if one wanted a decent-looking, decently functional, Windows desktop. To say that Linux isn't ready is to say that Windows 95, 98, and Me weren't ready either. Of course they *seemed* easy because the PC vendors, or OEMs, did the setup and configuration ahead of time. But because no one is preinstalling Linux on retail PCs these days, if you migrate, you'll have to be ready to do a full, manual installation.

Yet another caveat is that hardware and peripheral vendors don't always provide open-source drivers for their equipment. Many do, but even then, the drivers can be slow to emerge. Video, Ethernet, and PCMCIA support are all very good, and there are sound drivers for most cards. But there are problems with several software modem, or Winmodem, drivers, for example, so it's important to check the availability of open-source drivers for your equipment before migrating to Linux. Users can check the Linmodems.org Web site at www.linmodems.org, which has a good deal of information and numerous links to Linux softmodem drivers.

It's also important for current Linux users to check for drivers before buying a new piece of hardware. The more popular hardware brands provide open-source drivers, but smaller companies may not care about accommodating a user base that represents three or four percent of PC desktops. (Many Mac users complain about their peripheral drivers for the same reason—the vendors don't see them as priority customers.) Linux support for USB devices, scanners, and digital cameras is spotty, but improving. And there are licensing and distribution hassles: TrueType fonts have got to be installed manually because the Linux vendors aren't authorized to distribute them. But there are easy workarounds: if you have a licensed copy of Windows that you're planning to stop using when you migrate, you can copy the fonts to a CD before installing Linux, then reinstall them later using the KDE font installer. KDE has a good, and free, video and DVD player called KMPlayer, and SuSE offers a good video editor called MainActor, but you will have to search the Web for all the necessary codecs and install them yourself because there are several that can't be distributed with Linux due to similar licensing difficulties.

There are also problems with some laptop functions such as suspend and hibernate, because the manufacturers don't always support Linux in the BIOS (basic input–output system). There is APM (advanced power management) and ACPI (advanced configuration and power interface) support for laptop power management in Linux, but it doesn't work on all models because several laptop and BIOS manufacturers don't believe it's important to support Linux fully. Laptop users looking to migrate to Linux can check the Linux on Laptops Web site at www.linux-laptop.net, where there is an archive of anecdotal information covering users' Linux experiences with most laptop makes and models.

LUGs

There is casual, friendly support available through a network of Linux user groups, or LUGs, which are ad hoc clubs of Linux enthusiasts scattered throughout the world. There are a lot of LUGs, so there's a fair chance that there will be one near you. The groups often conduct "installfests," which are free workshops where Linux power users gather to help newbies install and configure the operating system. People bring their PC or laptop to an installfest, where the more experienced members help the novices to get Linux running on it. To find a LUG or an installfest near you, point your browser at www.linux.org/groups. Or search Google with terms such as "linux *mycity* installfest." Making friends at the local LUG is an effective and agreeable way of getting the most out of Linux.

Value for Money

Windows systems are more costly than most people realize. They may not seem so when Windows is preloaded on almost any PC you might buy, but you certainly do pay for it. The OEMs are granted volume discounts by Microsoft, but they guard this financial information jealously, so it's impossible to estimate what fraction of a computer's price involves MS software, though there's no doubt that it represents a significant sum. Additionally, users have got to obtain numerous other proprietary software applications to make a Windows system reasonably useful. Thus Windows can be said to have a high cost of ownership. (Actually, you don't *buy* Windows; you buy a *license* to use it according to terms and conditions dictated by Microsoft.) For a large business, the costs of IT-related "ownership" show up in support contracts with software and hardware vendors and the salaries of in-house administrators who keep the machinery patched and working. Software is rarely the main cost, though licenses can be expensive and assuring license compliance can impose a significant administrative burden. But for home and SOHO users, software is the single largest investment after the hardware, and in some cases, software is the greater investment. When you buy a full-featured Linux package from a big distributor, you get open-source software that would cost many thousands of dollars if it were proprietary.

Based on current retail prices, Windows XP Professional Edition costs $300 and may be installed on a single computer only. Microsoft Works (good enough for most home users) is $100, and Office XP Professional (for telecommuters and SOHO users) is $400 per machine. McAfee Firewall is $40, and its Virus Scan Home Edition is $30. So we have a minimum of $470 in software for a bare-bones home system on one computer. Keep adding if you want to telecommute and need MS Office or want an FTP client, an SSH client, a graphics manipulation suite like PhotoShop, remote-administration software like pcAnywhere, encryption software like PGP, multimedia whistles and bells, jukeboxes, video editors and CD rippers/writers, fax software, encryption software, network monitoring tools, performance and maintenance tools like Norton SystemWorks, or any software development suites. The majority of home users will want only a few of these deluxe items, though for the individual power user or the SOHO user, software costs can easily run into thousands of dollars *per machine*. Merely substituting

Office XP for Works drives up the price from $470 to $770. If you want Adobe Photoshop CS, add $650 for a total of $1,420. And if you should need a database server, heaven help you: a license for Microsoft SQL can run as high as $20,000 per machine for the enterprise edition. Even the standard edition is a whopping $5,000 per machine.

On the other hand, SuSE Linux Professional Edition retails for $100. It has everything the home and SOHO user needs, and then some. It's actually a *deluxe* system for one-fifth the price of a *bare-bones* Windows system. Business and power users will get the Apache Web server, the Postfix mail server, the MySQL database server (a packaged MySQL enterprise edition with technical support can be had for $500), Samba (Windows-compatible file and print server software), the Squid Web proxy/caching software, and the BIND DNS (domain name system) server and domain library. Home users will get the OpenSSH client and server; the GnuPG encryption tools; the GIMP (GNU Image Manipulation Program, a Photoshop substitute); Ximian Evolution (an MS Exchange–compatible Outlook clone); several video and audio editors; several utilities for ripping/burning CDs; several media and CD players and mixers; the OpenOffice and KOffice suites; fax software; several WWWGet clones; an FTP server and client; a file-wipe utility; AIM; ICQ; MSN Messenger and IRC clients and even an IRC server; several P2P applications (without the spyware); a personal firewall; the Webmin remote administration tool; file archive and compression utilities such as Gzip, Bzip, and Zip; free versions of SAINT, Nessus, Ethereal, Nmap, Snort, and Tripwire; free versions of the Adobe Acrobat Reader and RealNetworks RealPlayer; file comparison utilities; and a vast selection of software development tools, including the GNU C Compiler (GCC), Java, Perl, Borland Kylix, various debuggers, and tools for HTML and XML. All of it is clear of adware and spyware. SuSE Pro is a complete IT package for a small business, and overkill for home users, who might prefer the $50 Personal Edition instead. There is basically nothing you need to purchase, or even trade your privacy for. CodeWeavers' CrossOver Office, for those who wish to use MS Office on Linux, is about all that most home, SOHO, or small business users might wish to buy.

When it comes to security, product quality, and value for money, Linux is far and away the best operating system for the home or SOHO user. Consider that the $300 Windows XP Pro fits on a single CD, whereas the $100 SuSE Linux Pro needs five CDs because so much software comes bundled with it (it's also distributed on two DVDs). Consider also that the vendor's online update services will patch *all* of this software for you, not just the Linux kernel.

And thanks to the GPL, the software is effectively yours; with few exceptions, a noncommercial user can install it on as many machines as he happens to own. The choice, then, is between thousands of dollars for Microsoft software licenses and related application licenses sold on a per-machine, *à la carte* basis, or a hundred dollars for a deluxe Linux system that a home or SOHO user can install on several machines. You make the call.

The Sins of William Perfidious

No essay in praise of Linux would be complete without exploring why Windows is so mediocre. Indeed, Linux is outstanding chiefly in comparison to Windows. There are plenty of good operating systems such as Mac OSX, FreeBSD, Solaris, AIX, VMS, and many more, and few people would contend that Linux is dramatically better. Microsoft alone lags behind the pack in terms of quality. There are reasons for this. Some are cultural; others are coldly economical. But it is not an accident. And yet Windows is the most popular operating system in the world. It owes its success not to superior quality, but to a multibillion-dollar marketing apparatus and an incredible stroke of good fortune. We mustn't forget the peculiar confluence of coincidence and sheer dumb luck in the 1980s that propelled a small group of geeks—who, during any other moment in history would have slid silently and irretrievably down the tubes of ignominy—toward world desktop domination. The PC revolution was a paranormal moment in commercial history, and its chief beneficiary is Microsoft. But how has the company repaid the Fates for this dazzling stroke of fortune? Certainly not with the grace one might expect.

Hype and Mud

Redmond likes to point to its vast user base as evidence of Windows' superiority, but the logic here is off the mark. Enormously more people eat McDonald's hamburgers than those served at the Peter Luger steakhouse in New York, but this hardly makes the Big Mac superior. Of course it's admirably cheap, effectively filling, and available virtually everywhere, so it's hardly a wonder that billions have been served. It's also marketed aggressively through advertising campaigns targeting children with clowns and cartoon characters, and side arrangements with shopping malls, highway rest stops, airports, convention centers, and even hospital and school cafeterias.

If MS-DOS was the Model T of operating systems, Windows is the Big Mac: endlessly hyped and promoted, fairly cheap, available everywhere, and rather nasty. But unlike the Big Mac, Windows is force-fed to virtually every computer user in the world.

How can this be? Consider this example: a big hotel will host five or six restaurants from the humblest fast-food joints to mid-level family dining establishments to three-star temples of gastronomy, thereby accommodating the tastes and budgets of most of its clients. But imagine that McDonald's Corporation had established exclusive distribution contracts with all the major hotel chains. Imagine that it could outbid *all* of its competitors with lavish offers of free advertising. A hotel would draw guests because McDonald's would be subsidizing its ad campaign. In exchange, the hotel would serve nothing but McDonald's food: at street level, a food-court McDonald's; in the morning, Egg McMuffins delivered by room service on a trolley; upstairs, a rooftop luxury McDonald's with linen tablecloths, spectacular views, and waiters in black tie ceremoniously carrying a pile of Chicken McNuggets to tables on an ornate salver.

This may sound mad, but it's precisely what Microsoft has managed to do with the major personal computer manufacturers, or OEMs, like Hewlett Packard/Compaq, Dell, Gateway, and the like. Microsoft pumps vast advertising revenues into their coffers. This is why a TV ad for, say, Dell or Gateway computers is as likely to draw attention the Microsoft software preloaded on the machines (or the Intel processors within) as to the machines themselves. Microsoft and Intel are footing the advertising bill, and as everyone knows, he who pays the piper calls the tune. The OEMs don't actually believe that Windows is a superior operating system; they tout it and preload it because they're paid to tout it and preload it. They don't offer other operating systems because Microsoft would withdraw its advertising largesse if they did.

In order for the OEMs to begin preloading Linux on their PCs, distributors like SuSE, Red Hat, and Mandrake would have to reward them as generously as Microsoft does. Unfortunately, none of these companies is sitting on a $45 billion pile of loot, so the chance that they'll be able to compete with Redmond for the affections of OEMs is remote. Only when consumers begin demanding OEM PCs with Linux preloaded, configured, and ready to use will this change.

In the meantime, Microsoft continues to do all it can to impugn the quality of Linux and open-source applications. In a recent PR rant at the Gartner Fall Symposium in Orlando, Florida, company CEO Steve Ballmer dismissed open-source developers as a lot of teenage hobbyists with questionable motives.

"Why should code that may get written randomly by some hacker in China and contributed to some open-source project, why is its pedigree by definition somehow better than the pedigree of something that is written in a controlled fashion? I don't buy that," he said. "The vulnerabilities are there [in open-source software]. The fact that somebody in the middle of the night in China who you don't know, quote, 'patched' it and you don't know the quality of that. I mean, there's nothing per se that says there should be integrity that comes out of that process. At the end of the day, it's *people* who write software. We have a methodology; we have an approach; we have a testing process that we know can lead to a sustained and predictable level of quality." (The Big Mac, too, is renowned for its "sustained and predictable level of quality.")

Few people can pack as much untruth into a brief statement as Steve Ballmer. He's a truly gifted salesman. Here he's implying that open-source developers are a lot of irresponsible "random hackers" in far-off countries not exactly famous for business ethics. But the truth is that open-source software is created by some of the most experienced and talented developers in the world—professionals employed by the biggest names in the IT industry. Open-source projects are the ones these people work on by choice; it's work they *wish* to do as opposed to work they *have* to do. Mozilla, for one example, comes primarily from the Netscape development team at AOL. Mozilla is the browser they'd choose to build if the corporate bean counters at AOL headquarters would stop making demands based on the insights of marketing gurus and pressure from justifiably angry shareholders.

Another important point is that open-source developers have no deadlines, marketing roadmaps, or strategic rollouts to worry about. They never have to rush to market with some half-baked new gimmick designed to boost revenues. They release code when they're ready to release it. Whom would you rather have designing your software? Teams of volunteers drawn from the highest levels of programming and computer science doing things according to their best professional judgment, or Microsoft's regimented legions of McProgrammers doing things the way the marketing department directs?

Ballmer also tried to impugn Linux's security, throwing a few numbers carelessly about at the conference: "In the first 150 days of Windows 2000 we had 17 critical vulnerabilities.... The first 150 days of Red Hat 6—go check the number, just go check the number. It's five to ten times higher than what we are showing," he warbled.

What Ballmer concealed is the fact that each of the 17 vulnerabilities he cited were critical security flaws in Windows itself. The ones reported by Red Hat were spread among the thousand or so packages distributed along with the Linux kernel.

But Windows 2000 and Red Hat 6 are old news. Let's look at a more recent example so we can appreciate the true depths of Ballmer's duplicity. During the 22-month period between 1 January 2002 and 1 November 2003, the SuSE Linux kernel received two—that's right, *two*—security patches. During that same period, Windows XP received 35 security patches ranked Critical and 11 ranked Important.

Ballmer's numbers would have been meaningful if he'd compared the two security patches issued for Linux itself to the *46* issued for Windows (not including vulnerabilities ranked Moderate and Low, which account for an additional 16). As for Linux, its two kernel patches in just under two years represent an enviable record for a bunch of "random hackers in China." To be fair, SuSE did issue 93 security bulletins and patches during that period, but these involved *all* of the software bundled in each of SuSE's distributions. If we were to look at flaws affecting all flavors of Windows along with all of the third-party applications and utilities running on it for a two-year period, the list would reach into the thousands. It's doubtful that Microsoft could afford to remain in business if it assumed responsibility for patching virtually everything on your machine the way a Linux vendor does.

Microsoft has been trying to address its dismal security record with a PR initiative it calls "Trustworthy Computing." One innovation has been to bundle security patches into periodic roll-ups and service packs so that dozens can be installed at once. This is both good and bad. It's good because the frequency with which security holes are discovered and patches issued makes it virtually impossible for users and admins to stay on top of them. Issuing periodic service packs makes this process a good deal simpler and can ensure that critical patches won't be missed in the confusing torrent of monthly Windows debacles involving worms and viruses and remote exploits. But it's bad for two reasons. First, it can leave users vulnerable for extended periods of time: a flaw discovered in January may not get patched until the August roll-up is issued. Second, it allows Microsoft to conceal the number of security flaws in its systems by combining a dozen or so patches in one file. This, in turn, can lead users to trust Windows a good deal more than they should. Still, it will likely do more good than harm to release an occasional megapatch ensuring that nothing crucial has been missed.

As for the Trustworthy Computing initiative, it's chiefly a public-relations gesture, much like McDonald's exhibiting its commitment to good nutrition by adding a couple of salads to the menu. Microsoft's recent bounty of $250,000 for information leading to the arrest of the Blaster and Sobig worm authors, and its establishment of a hacker snitch fund of $5 million, amount to symbolic admissions of failure in the technical realm. If Trustworthy Computing were more than a marketing slogan, we would not expect Redmond to bribe snitches. We would instead expect a company that bleats endlessly about its "great software" to achieve security through the efforts of its putatively brilliant staff of developers. Going after the blackhats themselves is a valid tactic, but it speaks volumes about Microsoft's true pessimism that Windows can ever be made secure. Windows never was and never will be about Trustworthy Computing; it's about being just good enough to run Microsoft applications and drive consumers to Microsoft Web services. It will never be made any better than that. Improving it significantly would be grotesquely expensive and represent a colossal waste of the company's money. Thanks to Microsoft's monopoly position, Windows is selling brilliantly, shabby though it may be.

When they're compared straight up—kernel to kernel—Linux exposes Windows for the overhyped, and overpriced, system that it is. Windows XP does have an exceptionally slick user interface, but beneath the shiny veneer lies a vast heap of sloppy legacy code inherited from decades of inept, hurried programming. One is reminded of Spenser's "sinfull house of Pride," which, we are told

> *...was a goodly heape for to behould,*
> *And spake the praises of the workmans wit;*
> *But full great pittie that so faire a mould*
>
> *Did on so weake foundation ever sit:*
> *For on a sandie hill that still did flit*
> *And fall away, it mounted was full hie,*
> *That every breath of heaven shakèd it:*
> *And all the hinder parts that few could spie*
> *Were ruinous and old, but painted cunningly.*

> —*The Faerie Queene* I, IV: 37–45

But let's let Microsoft Corporation say it in its own words.

Dogfood

In 1997, Microsoft bought Hotmail. At the time of this acquisition, Hotmail had been operating on front-end Web servers running FreeBSD and back-end database servers running Sun Solaris. A Microsoft internal whitepaper from August 2000, obtained by Tamer Sahin of security research outfit SecurityOffice, evaluated the advantages and disadvantages of switching the Hotmail system from FreeBSD and Solaris to Windows 2000, or from an essentially UNIX world to an essentially Microsoft world. The paper concluded that MS software was inferior, but that the company needed to set the right example in public. According to the author, Windows 2000 Server Product Group member David Brooks, MS should, and I quote, "eat its own dogfood."

Among the several observations Microsoft made was a very basic one about security: "A fact about UNIX is that it is easy for an administrator to ensure that there are no irrelevant services running. As well as giving the potential for maximizing performance, it is useful to be sure that there are no random TCP/IP or UDP ports open that could be used as a basis for an attack," the paper explained.

Next there's the persistent issue of stability: "Both the UNIX kernel, and the design techniques it encourages, are renowned for stability. A system of several thousand servers must run reliably and without intervention to restart failed systems," the author notes, and adds that "Apache is also designed for stability and correctness, rather than breadth of features or high performance demands."

Then there's cost of ownership, which MS publicly insists, against overwhelming contradictory evidence, is a Windows strong suit. In private, the company sees it differently: "FreeBSD is free. Although there are collateral costs (it's not particularly easy to set up), the freedom from license costs is a major consideration, especially for a startup."

And it's easy to minimize and simplify a UNIX-based system, Microsoft notes: "It is particularly easy to cut down the load on the system so that only the minimum number of services is running. This reduces complexity [and] aids stability and transparency." Whereas, "a Windows server out of the box is an elaborate system. Although it performs specific tasks well, there are many services that have a complex set of dependencies and it is never clear which ones are necessary and which can be removed to improve the system's efficiency."

Another advantage in UNIX is that everything is out in the open: "It's easy to look at a UNIX system and know what is running and why. Although its configuration files may have arcane (and sometimes too-simple) syntax, they are easy to find and change."

On the other hand, Windows is difficult to configure and mysterious things are often made to happen: "Some parameters that control the system's operation are hidden and difficult to fully assess. The metabase is an obvious example. The problem here is that it makes the administrator nervous; he wants to be able to understand all of the configuration-related *choices that the system is making on his behalf*" [my emphasis].

Another strike against Windows is its dependence on the graphical user interface and its poor scripting support: "GUI operations are essentially impossible to script. With large numbers of servers, it is impractical to use the GUI to carry out installation tasks or regular maintenance tasks."

Microsoft also praises the ease of UNIX administration: "Most configuration setups, log files, and so on, are plain text files with reasonably short line lengths. Although this may be marginally detrimental to performance, it is a powerful approach because a small, familiar set of tools can be used by administrators for most of their daily tasks. In particular ... UNIX versions have evolved a good set of single-function commands and shell scripting languages that work well for automated administration."

We find also that the Windows image size can be a terrible inconvenience on a big server farm: "The team was unable to reduce the size of the image below 900MB; Windows contains many complex relationships between pieces, and the team was not able to determine with safety how much could be left out of the image. Although disk space on each server was not an issue, the time taken to image thousands of servers across the internal network was significant. By comparison, the equivalent FreeBSD image size is a few tens of MB."

Finally, Microsoft reminds us that Windows often needs a reboot when a UNIX admin can simply stop the process in question, edit the configuration file, and immediately restart it with the new configuration. This is a great advantage when upgrades are performed and when things go wrong: "A service may be hung, and rather than take the time to find and fix the problem, it is often more convenient to reboot [a Windows machine]. By contrast, UNIX administrators are conditioned to quickly identify the failing service and simply restart it; they are helped in this by the greater transparency of UNIX and the small number of interdependencies."

Greater transparency and fewer interdependencies. That's the private voice of Microsoft, acknowledging the superiority and cost savings of the UNIX family in numerous situations. The *public* voice of Microsoft, however, tells a radically different story. After failing to bury Linux under thousands of cubic yards of mud, including one occasion when Steve Ballmer ranted incoherently about it as "a cancer," the company has lately begun making more rational PR gestures, commissioning research studies that show a miraculous cost savings for Windows users. Not surprisingly, the several analysis-for-hire outfits performing these studies repeatedly discover precisely what Microsoft pays them to discover. In September of 2003, MS released two such studies in the same week, one from Giga Research and another from Gartner, both finding that Microsoft software is somehow cheaper than free software. A large archive of consumer anecdotes, research studies, and whitepapers claiming that Windows is better than Linux is collected at two Microsoft Web sites dedicated to sales and marketing. One, called "Resources for Competing with Linux," is geared more toward salespeople, while the other, called "Get the Facts," is geared more toward buyers. The collections promise "everything you need to convince business and technical decision makers to build their systems on the Microsoft Windows platform instead of Linux." The so-called independent studies commissioned by Redmond inevitably discover that Windows is truly great software. Articles have such titles as "Competing with Linux: What Everybody Needs to Know" and "Windows Wins Against Linux Every Time" and (without a trace of irony) "Linux Rated Less Secure than Windows"—no doubt because random hackers in China are believed to be designing it.

As my *Register* colleague John Lettice has noted, Microsoft's "obsession with Linux is deeply unhealthy. If we were talking about a person, successful and perfectly normal apart from a compulsion to prove that they're better than another, particular, person, we'd regard it as a case for analysis."[2]

Penguin Nightmares

"Linux is *the* long-term threat against our core business; never forget that!" Microsoft Windows Division Vice President Brian Valentine exclaimed in a November 2001 internal memo obtained by *The Register*. It's hard to believe that software supposedly cobbled together in the middle of the night by Chinese hackers could frighten the Redmond leviathan more than neighboring behemoths like IBM and Sun Microsystems, but apparently it does. Microsoft was once content to ignore Linux as a mere hobbyist phenomenon, but as the open-source user base continues to swell in the enterprise, office, and home desktop arenas, the tactics have changed and the gloves have come off.

Computing exotica like IBM mainframes, Solaris, and Oracle represent the gold standards in the enterprise arena where data integrity, system security, and up-time are mission critical. Not surprisingly, such systems are extremely expensive and often require special hardware also bought at great expense. One way to reduce costs is to replace UNIX on high-end hardware with Linux on inexpensive Intel-based substitutes. Since most of the admins responsible for these systems are already acquainted with UNIX, migrating from, say, Solaris on the expensive Sparc processor to Linux on the inexpensive Intel processor represents a significant savings in software licenses, support contracts, and machinery, and requires no retraining of staff. The Linux/Intel combination is called a *LinTel* system, and the Windows/Intel combination is called a *WinTel* system. Although a number of companies have been migrating from UNIX to LinTel, fewer have been embracing Windows because it would require them to replace all of their applications with MS-compatible ones, and to retrain or replace staff, which is both expensive and risky.

Valentine knows this well: Big companies are "looking to move and they want to migrate to the Intel platform," he observes. "Unfortunately, because Linux is very similar to UNIX, and porting applications from UNIX to Linux isn't

---

2. See theregister.co.uk/content/archive/32739.html.

that hard, we're starting to see customers move their UNIX applications to Linux on Intel platforms. I need you to make sure that these customers continue to migrate off of UNIX, but on to Windows 2000 on Intel."

It makes little sense to migrate from UNIX to Windows when it's safer, easier, and cheaper to migrate to Linux. It's tricky to make a rational case for such a move; hence all the studies, whitepapers, and television commercials for Microsoft server and desktop products promising a new computing Valhalla.

Valentine dispatches his sales force as if they were so many hall monitors, marching them through corporate data centers, searching for open-source contaminants and anything else that dares to breathe Microsoft's air: "If you haven't done it at your customer sites, then do a walk-through of their data centers and take inventory of where you see Sun machines, IBM, etc., and ask them what they are running on those machines. Learn about what they do with those systems; keep that inventory in your back pocket—Hell—tattoo it on your butt if you have to—and go after them. Knock them out one machine, one application, one department at a time. I cannot stress how important this is!"

In a later memo, Valentine talks about the many "independent studies" Microsoft is commissioning to cast Linux in a negative light: "We're approaching this in waves," he explains. "The first wave will attack the perception that Linux is free. To that effect, we'll have an independent analysis commissioned by DH Brown looking at a very popular topic these days—server consolidation.... The DH Brown report will be customer ready and will help your customer understand just how competitive Microsoft is in this arena. The second wave will be a full-blown cost analysis comparison case study between Linux and Windows in a variety of usage scenarios (Web, file and print, etc.) done independently by the analysts for us.... It will be a great tool to help you sell the value of Windows solutions over Linux."

It should surprise no one acquainted with the tactics of modern marketing that Valentine knows in advance what conclusions these "independent studies" will reach. The conclusions are, of course, their starting points.

Microsoft is flailing at Linux because it can't compete with it. Linux is better, cheaper, more secure, and easier to administer. All the company can do is advertise heavily, hype Windows loudly, and harangue, pressure, and bribe customers to stay with MS or to migrate from high-end UNIX systems to cheaper WinTel systems instead of better, and still cheaper, LinTel systems.

The company has also got its tentacles deeply entwined in educational establishments from kindergartens to universities. Redmond offers discounts, organizes donations, and provides other incentives so that "partner schools" will promote its products by acclimating the young to Windows from an early age and throughout their educational careers.

Even academicians have been conscripted into Redmond's anti-Linux jihad. In a recent column in *Syllabus Magazine*, a technology journal for school administrators, Princeton University Technology Strategy and Outreach Manager Howard

Strauss channeled the very soul of Steve Ballmer. Strauss hit all the buttons, first by painting open-source developers as "a smattering of teenagers too young to work at Redmond, hackers, virus creators, and a menagerie of others." He hit the quality-is-always-expensive button as well: "We cannot avoid the high cost of high-quality IT," he warns, and equates open-source software with the famous Nigerian e-mail scam promising riches in exchange for modest investment. "While you are installing your free, open-source software you may want to write [Nigerian scammer] Mrs. Ahmed a check. Her $8.5 million will help pay for the real cost of that free software," he chirps. The article is so palpably doctrinaire that one suspects it of being ghost-written by the Microsoft marketing department.

The Bill and Melinda Gates Foundation is also something of a marketing organ, capturing headlines for its devotion to the world's unfortunates while promoting Microsoft products. For example, in November of 2002, Bill Gates and several senior MS execs made a week-long pilgrimage to India. The Foundation generously pledged $100 million for HIV-related health initiatives over ten years, while Microsoft pledged $421 million, over a mere three years, to support Microsoft-friendly educational initiatives and development centers. India is a nation with a vast population and a comparatively weak economy; not surprisingly, Linux has become quite popular there. Naturally, Microsoft wants to change this and is willing to make a substantial investment in expectation of greater profits in the future. Meanwhile, the *New York Times* ran an incredible *five* vanity puff-pieces that week celebrating Gates's generosity, including one written by the Microsoft PR department and attributed to Gates himself. Interestingly, the *NYT* neglected to mention the Microsoft marketing tie-in and obvious bribe against, and obstacle to, India's rapid pace of Linux adoption. The paper had been falling all over Gates in its eagerness to give him ink, so it's odd that the editors could find no place, among those many thousands of words, for a brief mention of the $421 million in anti-Linux ammunition that Microsoft also delivered to India.

Redmond has additional worries. A growing number of local, state, and national governments have been proposing legislation requiring that open-source software be considered when public money is spent on technology. Microsoft's anti-Linux lobbying arm, called the Initiative for Software Choice—itself an organ of the MS-funded Computing Technology Industry Association (CompTIA)—has been busy denouncing the trend as "anti-competitive," though the proposed legislation rarely *mandates* open-source software, but usually requires only that it be given serious consideration. Evidence that governments are attracted to open-source products is terrifying to the Redmond behemoth because the amount of money at stake is enormous. The customer base is by no means limited to the vast bureaucracies most of us imagine when we think about government: Microsoft, along with several other commercial software makers, is also one of the world's major defense contractors. In most countries, defense and national-security spending often escape challenge from legislators because cynics are too easily branded unpatriotic by their political opponents. For the contractors, defense money has traditionally been easy money. Introducing competition from the open-source community will exert downward pressure on commercial software prices, frustrating vendors for whom government procurement has long served as a lavish gravy train. Such competition is good for taxpayers, and a growing number of legislators now regard encouraging it as part of their fiduciary duty to the public. It's no wonder that Big Business denounces it as "anti-competitive." The reality, of course, is that it's anti–free lunch for corporate giants.

Another horror for Redmond is the recent trend among companies with Linux servers and Windows desktops to harmonize the desktops on Linux. It's expensive to maintain essentially two IT staffs: *nix guys for the server and network gear, and Windows guys for the desktop computers. Now that the Linux desktop can run MS Office, a long-time barrier to office migration, and since Windows emulators like Wine and software like VMware, Samba, and Evolution can run several other Microsoft applications and Windows-compatible clones, there's little reason to keep Windows on the desktop when the rest of the equipment is running on Linux. As Linux turns up on company workstations and office desktops, users will naturally harmonize their home systems with their workplace systems for simplicity's sake. This is what gave Microsoft its unchallenged monopoly over the home PC years ago, first with DOS and later with Windows: many people used these systems at work and naturally wanted them at home. But now the Linux server is driving the Linux desktop in the workplace, and the workplace in turn is driving Linux adoption on the home PC. Microsoft applications will always remain popular, but Windows is no longer a concession that anyone has to make, even where MS applications are preferred.

Microsoft is beginning to panic, and with good reason: it simply can't compete with products that are both cheaper and better. It can only hype itself with sentimental TV ads for software that will somehow "help you reach your potential," flatter consumers by professing to "stand in awe" of them, grease palms in legislatures throughout the world, sling mud at every opportunity, and hope that Linux and open-source applications will be smothered by the blanketing white noise of a media blitz costing billions of dollars and reaching into virtually every sector of commerce, government, education, and charity.

The SCO Sideshow

A company called SCO Group, formerly Caldera International, holds the rights to several flavors of UNIX and has lately been claiming that Linux infringes them. According to SCO legal beagles, computing colossus IBM illegally inserted proprietary UNIX code into the Linux kernel. In July of 2003, SCO began sending nastygrams to commercial Linux users, offering to indemnify them against copyright claims for the bargain price of $700 per server and $200 per desktop, and warning that the price would rise dramatically in the near future, much in the manner of a street gang demanding protection money from neighborhood merchants. Not surprisingly, SCO has repeatedly failed to document its Linux infringement claims, even under court order.

Interestingly, SCO shares have climbed on this news. Investors are betting that SCO's unsupported infringement claims are a secret weapon to haul in vast revenues. Personally, I'd be surprised if it should turn out to be more than an extortion bid enacted with lawyerly intimidation, accompanied by a stock swindle. I would look for company insiders to begin selling shares before the courts force them to show their hand.

In any event, no business should allow SCO's pot-of-gold gimmick to discourage migrating to Linux, and no company using Linux should pay up unless, miraculously, SCO should prevail in court. The company has been burning capital at a furious rate to pursue its legal stunt, against IBM of all adversaries, and may not stay in the game much longer. According to my *Register* colleague Andrew Orlowski, SCO "reported a loss of $1.6 million for [Q-4 2003] on sales of $24.3 million, after excluding a $9 million charge for legal fees. It would have posted a $7.4 million profit otherwise."[3]

And as for investors betting on a miracle—personally, I'd drop those shares like a sack of dirt, lest the company's senior execs beat me to it.

Before You Leap

If you're a home or SOHO user interested in migrating to Linux, you should first take stock of the hardware and peripherals you're using and verify that they're supported. Older hardware almost always is supported, but the "latest and greatest" may not be. Perform a Web search with terms such as *HP LaserJet Linux driver* or *Connexant Winmodem Linux driver,* etc., and verify that drivers are available. You may not have to install them manually: chances are, if you're using a packaged distro, the installation program will detect your hardware and install the necessary driver modules automatically, but it's important to know ahead of time that the drivers exist. (I would recommend replacing an inexpensive piece of hardware if that's all that stands in the way of migrating.) If you're already using Linux, do a Web search before buying a new peripheral or other piece of hardware for your system. Choose gear that has good Linux support. If you wish to install Linux on a laptop, consider first how important the power-management features are to you; not all laptops support Linux in that capacity. If you rarely run your laptop on battery power, this is not an issue. But if you do, check the Linux on Laptops Web site before deciding which one to buy. Similarly, if you're a Linux user thinking of buying a laptop, do some research ahead of time so you'll be able to buy one with good Linux support.

If you're a Linux novice, you should look for prebuilt RPM packages or installation shell scripts (files with the .sh or .run extensions) whenever you look

---

3. See theregister.co.uk/content/4/34639.html.

for software and drivers. If you have to build them from source code, you will first have to learn a bit more about the ins and outs of Linux. Fortunately, all the tools you need to build from source are already on your machine or can be installed easily from your vendor's CDs, so it's worthwhile teaching yourself this useful skill if you're motivated. Installing an RPM application is just as easy as installing software with a Windows wizard. It's not the *same* as using an MS-style wizard, but it's certainly no more difficult. Typically, you'll use a GUI file browser like Konqueror or Krusader and select the RPM file, right-click on it, choose Open With from the drop-down menu, and then Kpackage (if you're using KDE, for example). This will launch a simple GUI installation program. If the package needs to be installed by root, you will be prompted for the password.

I'd be hard pressed to recommend a particular distro; the big three are all good in their own ways. I personally use SuSE Linux on all of my machines; I find that it accommodates beginners and power users equally, and I like the YaST administration tool. Mandrake is superb for novices but it can be a bit limiting for power users. Still, I consider it ideal for first-time Linux users. Red Hat makes a good product, but the company is focused far more on big business clients than retail users. I would *not* recommend Red Hat for a home or SOHO installation. Indeed, the company is discontinuing its line of consumer products, which it never took seriously. There are other excellent distros such as Debian, Slackware, and Gentoo, which are free and have fewer restrictions on the number of commercial desktops they can be installed on, but they may not be appropriate for novices. On the other hand, Xandros Desktop OS is a Debian-based distro designed specifically for ease of use, though not flexibility. Personally, I'm not a fan of Xandros or LindowsOS, which lack the flexibility of the major distros. But they may serve well as transitional products for first-time Linux users to get acquainted with the system.

The big commercial Linux vendors generally distribute the most user-friendly, flexible, and fully loaded systems with good support features like online updates. However, the big three also impose licensing terms that restrict the number of commercial desktop installations and require substantial support contracts. (Some in the open-source community have denounced this trend as a move toward "proprietary Linux.") While licensing and support issues are of little concern to home or SOHO users, they are an important consideration for small to medium businesses (SMBs). With this in mind, a distro called UserLinux based on Debian with unrestricted commercial installation is in the early planning stages at this writing. It's meant chiefly for businesses small enough to be thrifty in their software purchases yet large enough to get stung by the commercial Linux distributors' licensing terms and support contracts. I should note, however, that license compliance with Linux is generally cheaper and easier than it is with Microsoft. Complying with Redmond's licensing regime can impose significant administrative burdens and financial overhead on an SMB.

There is a security-oriented Linux distro for users with a Web presence called EnGarde from Guardian Digital. If you're running Internet servers it's worth looking into; for home users or those with a LAN or Internet connection only, it's overkill. Finally, total security paranoiacs can check out Tinfoil Hat Linux at `tinfoilhat.shmoo.com` and the NSA's SE-Linux at `www.nsa.gov/selinux`. But be warned; these distros don't do much out of the box. By the time you've tweaked them enough to make them useful, you'll have undermined their alluring paranoiac value.

As for desktop environments, KDE is best for Linux novices migrating from Windows because it's similar in look and feel. Sun Solaris uses Gnome as its default desktop, so those familiar with Solaris at work will likely prefer it at home. Of course, the beauty of Linux is that you *always* have plenty of options: you can install both desktops and try each for a while, and several others to boot. Later, you can default to the one you prefer. (But note that with newbie-friendly offerings like Xandros and Lindows, you won't have this sort of flexibility.)

My choice of filesystem, especially for novices, is ext2. It doesn't create a data journal, which means that whenever a volume is not unmounted cleanly it will need checking. The *fsck* utility will be invoked automatically and errors will be corrected. This is an inconvenience because it slows mounting a disk or booting an image, say, after a power interruption. But its advantages are several: ext2 is time proven and rock solid. When you can't take chances with your data, it's the obvious choice. Because it doesn't keep a journal, it makes data hygiene easier and data destruction more certain. And while its speed might not be up to the more performance-oriented filesystems like xfs and jfs, it uses less memory, so there is a payoff. Because of this memory payback, I've found that ext2 performs about as well as jfs, but with greater reliability.

Security is the chief topic of this book, and from that perspective alone I would recommend Linux to just about anyone. Windows can be made fairly secure by firewalling, using antivirus software and adware/spyware scanners, patching regularly, disabling unnecessary services, setting up a multiuser environment, and replacing its Internet client software with open-source equivalents, and this is a perfectly reasonable strategy. But considering Windows' tremendous complexity, hidden functions and inescapable security flaws, migrating to Linux really is the best option, especially for people who aren't entirely confident in their computer skills. Indeed, the *less* confident you are, the *better* Linux will suit you. Migrating alone will make your system harder to attack. The very transparency of a UNIX-based system, recognized by Microsoft, makes it easier to configure Linux for superior security. And Linux does a better job of sandboxing users so that any malware they encounter will have less impact on the system. Add a firewall or packet filter, disable unnecessary daemons, patch regularly, don't go on line as root, and your system will be safe from all but the top two or three percent of potential attackers. If you're a home user, you needn't worry about those people; they're not interested in your computer. The vast majority of script kiddies and virus authors just don't have enough game to deal with a Linux box. Migrating to Linux and following a few, common-sense security guidelines will allow you to enjoy your computer without bothering about all the exploits and malicious scripts and mysterious functions and insecure services and adware and malware and worms and viruses that plague Windows users. You'll be able to relax and just *use* your computer. And the blue screens will go away too.

Most commercial Linux distros cost about $100 for a professional edition with all the whistles and bells, and about $50 for a scaled-back personal edition with fewer packages for Internet servers and software development. You can try Linux for a few weeks, and even if you dislike it, you won't have invested much in the experiment. Fifty dollars represents a small risk when you stand to be rescued from the Microsoft upgrade treadmill. There's a lot to like: Linux can be made more secure than Windows; it supports more users; it's easier to administer; it uses memory and other system resources more efficiently; it's more stable; it doesn't harangue you to sign up for an MSN Passport or Hotmail account; it doesn't run Internet clients like MSN Messenger automatically; it simplifies data hygiene; it doesn't phone home; it's built by volunteers who know what they're doing and love what they're doing—and it's very cheap to own.

Steve Ballmer and Brian Valentine may not see any virtue in Linux, but believe me, you will.

CHAPTER 7

Trust Nothing,
Fear Nothing

THERE IS A GREAT DEAL of mystery surrounding security, and it only gets worse when technology is involved. The combination can be unfortunate: both realms are jealously guarded by self-appointed illuminati and are largely closed to the public, in part due to the complexity involved and in part because public scrutiny is anathema to the many interested parties who have learned to mine rich profits from a vaguely confused, or vaguely worried, populace. Although there are plenty of honest, hardworking people doing serious research and providing quality services, there are quite a few bottom feeders as well. The worst elements of the security establishment don't merely prey on ignorance and fear; they actively contribute to both. They promote myths, exaggerate threats, and overpromise results.

Unfortunately, the honest workaday souls are too busy providing worthwhile services to become performers in the security media circus. When security is in the news, it's the bottom feeders we usually hear from. It's they who establish the terms of public dialogue and fix the boundaries of acceptable public inquiry. And when cybersecurity is in the news, things often go from bad to worse: high technology and hacker mythology add layers of mystery to an already inscrutable subject. Wherever security and technology converge, there will always be far more fiction than truth in circulation and always more Mickey Mouse gimmicks than real solutions on offer.

In this chapter, we'll consider security from a more general, even theoretical, point of view. We'll look at a few instructive security snafus and swindles both in computing and in the wider world beyond. We'll consider the motives of the major players in commerce and government and learn to spot unsupported claims, exaggerated threats, and conflicts of interest indicating that we're being taken for a ride by fast-talking charlatans.

Security is a huge industry spanning many public and commercial sectors. A great deal of cross-pollination goes on between defense, national-security, law-enforcement, and commercial players. Contractors provide spy satellites, military weapons systems, telecommunications gear for intelligence services, bugging devices, computer systems and databases, mercenary forces, military support services, police support services, bodyguards and armored vehicles for governments and wealthy corporations, security guards, and even prisons. Much of this high-dollar activity is funded with public money, yet the industry tolerates little public scrutiny. In recent years, the boundaries between military operations, law enforcement, and private security have eroded dramatically. The security establishments both governmental and commercial have laid claim to some extremely profitable and exclusive territory that few outsiders have explored. Security is a notoriously dark region of commerce and public policy, though there's a saying that "sunlight is the best disinfectant." So let's throw open the curtains and see what's scuttling about in the shadows.

"Depend on Us"

In Chapter 5, I wrote about the importance of online anonymity and mentioned in passing that one anonymizing service, the Java Anonymous Proxy (JAP), cannot be trusted. The JAP story is an instructive tale for anyone concerned with Internet privacy and computer security. It reminds us that things are not always what they seem to be, or are said to be.

The JAP system is a free network of proxy servers that establish online crowds to create an environment for anonymous Web surfing. Based in Germany, JAP is a collaborative effort between Dresden University of Technology, Free University Berlin, and the Independent Center for Privacy Protection Schleswig-Holstein, also called the AN.ON Project. According to the JAP Web site, "no one, not anyone from outside, not any of the other users, not even the provider of the intermediary service can determine which connection belongs to which user."

In August of 2003, I reported in *The Register* that the JAP network had been secretly and willingly infected with a back door by its own maintainers, following a demand from the German federal police. After taking the JAP service down for a few days, claiming that the interruption was "due to a hardware failure," the operators required users to install an "upgraded version" of the JAP software to continue using the service.

"As soon as our service works again, an obligatory update (version 00.02.001) [will be] needed by all users," the public was told. There was not a word about any police business or any back doors.

Fortunately, someone examined the software "upgrade," noticed some suspicious code in it, and posted his findings to an Internet bulletin board. Soon the JAP team replied to the post, admitting that there is now a "crime detection function" in the system mandated by the courts. But they defended their decision.

"What was the alternative? Shutting down the service? The security apparatchiks would have appreciated that—anonymity in the Internet and especially AN.ON are a thorn in their side anyway," the JAP team argued.

No doubt the police appreciated the team's willingness to backdoor the system a good deal more than they would have appreciated seeing it shut down with a warning that JAP could no longer fulfill its stated purpose of protecting anonymity due to government interference.

Admittedly, the JAP team fought the demand in court, but they did comply with it and they did remain silent until a decision was reached on their appeal. They were under a gag order, but of course there are ways around that.

Users were told that the service made it "impossible" for outsiders to observe Web traffic on the system. This is obviously no longer true, if it ever was. And that's a crucial issue, that element of doubt. Anonymity services are useful only if users can trust providers to be straight with them at all times. This means that providers must be punctilious in disclosing every exception to their claims. One doesn't build confidence by letting the police plug in to the network, legally or otherwise, and neglecting to mention it.

There were a couple of ways the group could have handled the situation without sacrificing user trust. It could simply have withdrawn the service until its legal challenge was decided (surely the German police can't force an organization to provide a free service just so they can hijack it). Or the group could have put the word out. If the people involved really are privacy experts, then they ought to know how to send an anonymous e-mail to a journalist, especially one in another country whom the German authorities would be unable to pressure. True, the police would have known who leaked the story, but in an advanced Western democracy like Germany, what the police know is irrelevant: all that matters is what they can prove in court. Real anonymity experts ought to have been able to leak the information without leaving any incriminating evidence behind, and any decent journalist would sooner hang himself than give up a source. The gag order could have been defeated easily and safely.

But the service was not withdrawn and no information was leaked to the press. The group played along with the police, granting a surveillance request that two appellate courts later declared illegal (although the wrangling continues). Users who trusted the JAP network were betrayed, and the rest of us have received an important lesson about putting faith in complicated electronic equipment maintained by people other than ourselves.

Free Internet services should be treated with extra suspicion because bandwidth is an expensive commodity. Banner ads, popups, and adware-infected clients are one way for service providers to generate revenue. Selling user information to data miners is another. Offering a free service as a semifunctional demo, along with a pay (or "premium") service that works a lot better, is yet another tactic, and the least objectionable of the three. Free software is one thing; the developers may donate their time to create it, but it doesn't cost them anything when you use it. An Internet service, on the other hand, costs the provider every time it's used. You *will* be paying for it, one way or another. If it isn't apparent to you how a service is funded, chances are you won't like the business model. In general, security, privacy, and anonymity services to which you subscribe at a fair price are less risky than those offered for free. When you pay for your bandwidth use with a subscription, there's less need for adware, hence less risk that it will be used. When the provider is a business, it has a reputation to defend, hence a financial stake in protecting your privacy. The AN.ON Project was not in a position to lose large amounts of money as a penalty for cooperating with the government. A company that might have lost significant subscriber revenue, on the other hand, would have tried a good deal harder to find a legal loophole or other remedy. Does this mean there's no risk in using a pay service? No, it doesn't; but it does mean that your odds of escaping surveillance are generally better when you pay your way. Bandwidth is expensive, and you'll pay for it one way or another. Paying with cash is better than paying with privacy or security.

In November of 2001, Seattle researcher Marc Slemko discovered a bug in the MSN network that enabled attackers to use Hotmail to hijack the Microsoft Passport and Passport Wallet services. Passport is an authentication system enabling users to log in to numerous Web sites with a single set of credentials maintained by Microsoft. The Passport Wallet manages a user's credit card details in a similar fashion to make online shopping simpler for merchants and consumers, with a gimmick called Express Purchase. It is, therefore, something of a security system, though not a terribly good one. Microsoft suggests that the Passport Wallet offers a security advantage because credit card information is not stored on a user's computer, from which it might be stolen, but is instead held "securely" on their servers.

According to Slemko, "When you are in the process of checking out at a participating merchant, clicking on the Microsoft Express Purchase icon will take you to a Passport server to select what billing and shipping information to send to the merchant. When you submit the form, Passport redirects your browser back to the merchant with the [payment] information you selected."[1]

Microsoft's and the merchant's servers receive the purchase information. It's only the user himself who is blind in the process. Such a lack of transparency always invites security blunders.

And so it did in this case. Slemko devised a Hotmail exploit that enabled an attacker to use a malicious e-mail to obtain a victim's Passport Wallet shopping credentials and use them as if they were his own. The exploit involved stealing session cookies used to authenticate users to the Passport server and other sites that support Passport, thereby impersonating the victim. Session cookies are often used for authentication, and if they're handled right they can be safe and effective. If they're handled badly, an attacker can read them and reuse them to authenticate himself as the victim.

Slemko discovered that whenever a user signed in to Hotmail, they would be allowed access to their Passport Wallet without further authentication for 15 minutes. If someone were to log in to Hotmail, then read a malicious e-mail designed to steal their Passport cookies, the attacker would be able to impersonate them. The threat from such an attack ranges from credit card fraud all the way up to identity theft. It was a very serious design flaw.

Microsoft was in no hurry to fix its broken system, however. In fact, Slemko had to resort to publishing an exploit to motivate the company to act. Once he did, the company took the system down briefly and applied a fix that kept the initial session cookies alive for only a couple of minutes, thereby reducing, though not eliminating, the problem.

In March of 2003, Microsoft finally cancelled the Passport Wallet and Express Purchase programs, no doubt in response to continuing security concerns that prevented the public from embracing it as warmly as Redmond had hoped. It was never a good idea. For one thing, it was unnecessary, and when it comes to information security and privacy, one should never do anything that's unnecessary. Every complication adds several new points of failure. This is why we disable unnecessary services on our machines: anything we don't need is just something that can cause problems. If you need something, fine; but if you get no benefit from it, then the only other thing you can get from it is grief.

Transparency promotes security. Simplicity promotes security. The Passport Wallet was neither simple nor transparent. And no one needed it. Microsoft interposed itself between merchants and shoppers, and created additional points of failure with no counterbalancing benefits. My own suspicion is that this was a pilot

---

1. See `alive.znep.com/~marcs/passport`.

program that the company was testing with an eye toward rolling out a pay service in the future. I suspect that if it had caught on, Microsoft would have begun charging a small handling fee for each transaction, enabling the Passport servers to act as a network of tollbooths on the Internet.

> **NOTE** *The fewer online databases your financial information is in, and the less information is in them, the better off you are. For now, the best security measure is to use a* dynamic account, *which a number of card issuers offer, and never to allow a merchant site to store your credit and purchase information. It's far better to enter it each time you buy something, even if it slows you down a bit. Or you can use the Mozilla Form Manager as described in the Introduction. But never let a Web merchant manage this data for you. If a merchant site doesn't offer you the option of* not *saving your details, take your business elsewhere.*

We might hope that Microsoft's agreements with merchant sites would have included a provision for data destruction, but they didn't. According to the company's Wallet cancellation notice, we can rest assured that the Passport servers have been purged. However, "if you used Passport Express Purchase at a participating site, the site may have stored any credit card or billing/shipping address information that you shared with them," the company explains. Redmond advises us to go and "read the participating site's privacy statement for more information." And good luck to you all.

Public computers are another security disaster in waiting. In July of 2003, one JuJu Jiang pleaded guilty to computer fraud after infecting computers at 13 Kinko's stores in New York City with a commercial spyware program called Invisible KeyLogger Stealth. Jiang had used the software to sniff usernames and passwords related to online banking, and compromised upwards of 450 accounts. He sometimes used his victims' financial information to open new accounts under their names, then transfer money from their accounts into new, fake ones under his control. This scam went on for over a year before being detected. Jiang was eventually caught, though not through the diligence of Kinko's IT staff, as one might hope. A victim detected and logged Jiang's activity on his own home PC. Jiang had sniffed the password that the victim used to administer his machine remotely, which he did one day from a Kinko's store that Jiang was monitoring. Jiang later had the audacity to use the sniffed password to log in to the victim's machine while the owner was using it. The victim contacted the police, and Jiang was soon caught. The remote administration tool had logged Jiang's IP address, which led police to his door. Only after the authorities confiscated and examined Jiang's computers did they learn of the scam.

Our Mr. Jiang was not a clever attacker, which tells you all you need to know about Kinko's security. He didn't cover his tracks well, perhaps because he was overconfident, perhaps because he was ignorant. But in any case, his attack was unsophisticated. Still, for over a year, Kinko's had no clue what was going on under their noses. We can all forgive an occasional blunder confined to a single store, but 13 stores indicates a serious failure, or complete lack, of security protocols. And my advice is *never* to expect better.

Public computers in libraries, Internet cafes, and copy shops must never be trusted. They should be *assumed* to be infected with spyware. When you use one, approach it in just that spirit. Don't use it for sensitive correspondence. Don't use it to log in to any Web site or for any online service that involves banking or finances, or anything of a deeply personal or politically controversial nature. Don't use it to make online purchases. Use it only for casual correspondence, for research on the Web, for printing files and images, for scanning photographs, and the like. Remember, if a key logger is installed, encryption is worthless: everything you type will be captured in clear text. If a *remote* key logger is installed, a spy can monitor you from virtually anywhere. He needn't show up at the scene of the crime again. He can install the program on a computer at Kinko's and monitor it from a computer in the library across the street. I wouldn't say that you should never use public computers, but I would say that you should never use one for any business that you wouldn't eagerly share with a complete stranger—because the chances are good that one will be watching you closely.

On the Job

Depending on where you live, the company that employs you may or may not be permitted to intercept your personal communications. In many European countries there are legal limits to such abuse, but in most Third-World dictatorships and the United States, an employer is essentially a feudal lord and your soul more or less belongs to the company. The U.S. Bill of Rights may be a lovely instrument, but it only prevents *the government* from making you a peon. Pretty much anyone else in a position to do so is at liberty to do so. Workplace surveillance of computer activity is now commonplace, a depraved practice encouraged by company lawyers terrified of the liabilities inherent in allowing adults to communicate freely at work, and potentially irritating others with chips on their shoulders and lawyers of their own.

Needless to say, no one should consider their workplace computer a safe device for personal or otherwise sensitive correspondence. The sysadmin knows all that you do, and any monitoring activity that he can claim is routine will be legal almost anywhere. You might use SSH tunneling from your work computer to your home computer for unauthorized business, but keystroke logging is not unknown in the workplace, and keystroke logging trumps *all* privacy measures.

Wherever you are, and whomever you work for, it's wise to treat your workplace computer as you would a public computer. *Assume* that it's loaded with spyware.

Stupid Software Tricks

The Internet is insecure from the ground up, and any privacy or security you achieve comes from deliberate effort to compensate for its inherent weakness. Software is different; it doesn't *have* to be insecure, but it often is. Security engineering is expensive and time consuming, and product upgrade cycles, a major source of fresh revenue from existing users, often require that new software versions be released before being tested thoroughly. We're all familiar with the upgrade treadmill: a new version is released, often with much promotional fanfare promising a radical breakthrough in information technology, when in reality the product turns out to be little more than a service pack with a few trivial new whistles and bells. Meanwhile, support for older versions is withdrawn on a regular schedule, prompting existing users to upgrade, and thus ensuring that we all keep buying the same products again and again. The need to attract new users from among one's competitors, and to obtain future revenue from existing users, often results in a rush-to-market mentality where features and a slick appearance are emphasized and security is an afterthought.

Even security-oriented software is vulnerable. In late January of 2001, trust authority VeriSign sold two digital certificates, used to verify the origin of software, to a hacker. The vendor named on both certificates was Microsoft Corporation. If the certificates had been used to sign malicious programs or ActiveX controls, the user, on installing them, would have seen a popup dialog claiming that Microsoft was certified as the maker. Although the snafu occurred on 29 and 30 January, the Microsoft security bulletin didn't emerge until 22 March, or eight weeks later.

In November of 2002, a security outfit called eEye Digital Security discovered that a malicious e-mail memo could create a buffer overrun in the PGP plugin for Microsoft Outlook, which in turn could be used to run arbitrary code with the user's level of privilege. At a minimum this could have compromised the user's passphrase and exposed his encrypted messages; at a maximum it could have surrendered control of the victim's machine. File attachments did not need to be activated; merely selecting the malicious message with Outlook was sufficient to launch the attack.

In early August of 2002, it was revealed that some copies of the OpenSSH source code were modified by an intruder and contained a back door. An attacker gained access to the OpenBSD FTP server and inserted the malicious files some time between 30 and 31 July. The admins detected the breach, issued a bulletin, and replaced the malicious files on 1 August, or 24 to 48 hours later.

On 5 November 2003, a backdoored version of the Linux 2.6 kernel was detected almost by accident. An attacker had compromised the server at `kernel.kbits.net` and inserted an extremely subtle bit of malicious code. Had it not been detected, it would have allowed a root compromise. Because of the way development changes are tracked and cataloged, the kernel maintainers saw immediately that something had been altered. Yet two programmers noticed it but were not alarmed (it was, as I said, quite subtle). Fortunately, a third programmer recognized it as a back door and the code was removed before it could circulate. The hacker was clearly a very skilled programmer, but not such a clever attacker. Had he made this change later, to a version posted at a download site, it might have got into circulation and escaped detection for quite some time.

While it's true that open-source products are better for security, they are hardly immune to bugs or attacks by malicious hackers. The security advantages of open-source software are its modular design, which makes fixing flaws easier, temporary workarounds safer and easier to implement, and patches less likely to break other parts of the system; and its transparency, which means that malicious functions can't be concealed within it. However, the fact that something nasty can't be concealed does *not* guarantee that it will be detected. The malicious nature of the changes to the Linux 2.6 kernel quite nearly escaped notice and the backdoor code could have ended up in circulation. It didn't, but it very well might have.

In late November 2003, the Debian Project discovered that it had been compromised by an attacker using what was, until then, an unknown exploit against the Linux 2.4.x kernel. The attacker had been able to log on to the Debian machines as a user and found a way to get root on several of them. This type of attack is called *privilege escalation*. There was no back door involved, only a bit of poor coding that some bright empiricist managed to exploit before anyone else noticed it. But the bug had been circulating for roughly two years before being found. It's not known how often the exploit might have been used before being noticed: perhaps that was the first time, perhaps the fiftieth. On the day when an unknown exploit is first detected, called *zero-day* or *0-day*, it ceases to be unknown and its value diminishes rapidly as users begin patching their systems or applying workarounds. But so long as it remains undetected, it's impossible to defend against; and it's impossible to estimate how many times it might have been used successfully.

So, even the best single piece of advice I can offer for avoiding security difficulties in general, that is, either migrating to Linux or using Windows with open-source clients and utilities, is no guarantee. There are bugs in every product. There are a lot *fewer* bugs in open-source products, they come to light more often, and they get fixed faster, but there is no such thing as immunity. Thus security has got to be applied in layers, with the strengths of one compensating for the weaknesses of another. There is no one scheme or product you can cling to as a panacea. You really can't trust anything.

Disinformation

We live in a media-driven world where mass communication confers tremendous persuasive power on those who can afford access to it. Little of what we hear is the unvarnished truth. Facts are constantly manipulated by skilled players with an interest in altering our perceptions and who often have the money or political connections needed to get their message across. Therefore, whenever someone speaks publicly about safety or security, the question you should ask is, "What might this person gain from persuading me?" More often than not, the answer will be money, power, or the furtherance of a political agenda.

Popinjay Experts

Some readers might be tempted to think that I'm a computer security expert. I'm not. I'm a computer security *specialist*. It's what I cover in my *Register* column, what I research, what I read about, and what I discuss with like-minded colleagues. It's a subject that I'm well acquainted with, certainly, but I don't *do* security. I don't fix other people's broken systems or advise corporate IT managers. I haven't got the day-in, day-out, hands-on experience with scores of different systems that yields genuine expertise. Thus I would *never* call myself a security expert. Unfortunately, there are self-promoters in this field who would, and regularly do, call themselves experts, and an alarming number of them are either mediocre practitioners, incompetents, or outright charlatans. I should know. I've interviewed them; I've met them at industry conferences; I've read their books and heard their talks; I've written about them; I've been unkind to them during press conferences; I've even met them socially on occasion. The worst among them have no training in computer security, use off-the-shelf vulnerability scanners like Nessus and Saint and ISS, and charge high fees for reports that any fool could generate with the same tools. They have no experience in network or system administration, no experience writing and debugging code, and no knowledge of the inner workings of software or hardware. They are, in essence, script kiddies for hire. Only they earn a fine living by advising innocent people who know even less than they do, to whom they really do look like experts. They start their own consulting outfits and hire PR flacks and publicity agents. They talk about the latest Windows viruses and worms on CNN and NBC and in the *New York Times* and *USA Today*. In no time, they develop an unearned reputation as computer security experts—and as their fame rises, so do their consulting fees.

My colleagues in the press play a crucial role in helping the fraudulent gain respect. How many times have you noticed someone you've never heard of quoted in a news article and identified as "a prominent security expert"? (Much like the "terrorism experts" we so often meet on the TV news these days.) Who *are* these people? And how did they become renowned experts in the first place? Have they got advanced degrees in computer science? Have they spent years administering a large, secure network for the military, say? In reality, a fair number of them are former hackers and script kiddies. Quite a few others simply invented themselves to cash in on corporate security budgets and Homeland Defense pork. There is an excellent and entertaining rundown of computer-security charlatans posted to the Attrition.org Web site at `www.attrition.org/errata/charlatan.html`. It's good reading.

Popinjay experts proliferate because there's a lot of money to be made in security and the temptation to pad résumés and embroider reputations is therefore irresistible; because there is no regulatory body imposing minimum qualifications on practitioners; and because the journalists covering cyber-crime and computer security for mainstream newspapers and television news outlets rarely have any real interest in the subject. They don't do their own research; they don't tinker with systems; they often don't even use the software and hardware they write about.

Now, it's true that even a good journalist is rarely an expert on a single topic, but it is possible to specialize in an area of news coverage so that over time one develops a solid grasp of the surrounding subject matter. But this isn't always the way things work in a busy newsroom; quite often, editors assign stories based on who happens to be available.

I know this well. Years ago, when I was a very green, journeyman hack, I covered the pharmaceutical industry. My first solo assignment was to cover a U.S. Food and Drug Administration (FDA) Advisory Committee meeting where an emphysema treatment was being evaluated by a group of Ph.D.s in pharmacology who spoke, it seemed to me, a sort of polysyllabic pidgin English. They liked to say, as they reviewed the study data, that this or that patient had "progressed." They did not appear pleased by this news, though I was thinking—innocently, I now realize—"Well, that's a relief." Hours later I figured out that when medical researchers say that a patient has progressed, they actually mean that the *disease* has progressed, and this is why they were not at all reassured by what struck me as quite cheerful news.

One of the study endpoints was the relative concentration of neutrophils in the lungs of patients. I had never heard of neutrophils. I have a degree in English literature; neutrophils never came up. I didn't know whether they were good or bad, and therefore didn't know whether their presence was good or bad news, but the treatment was said to work or fail according to the number of neutrophils a patient had. At times, neutrophils were spoken of as if they were quite useful; at times they were spoken of as evidence of disease.

The meeting lasted six hours. It was not until the last hour that I managed to noodle out the fact that neutrophils are white blood cells, and indeed very good things to have, but that a high concentration of them indicates a health problem. If a patient had a lot of neutrophils, wonderful though they may be, it meant he was sick. *Neutrophil* is a fancy word for pus. Its presence is good because it means your immune system is working; its presence is bad because it means you're unwell. Had I known this going in, I would have gotten a lot more out of the meeting. But because I spent the better part of six hours trying to figure out the difference between the researchers' definition of *progressed* and a normal, educated person's definition of *progressed,* and what a neutrophil is and how it might be relevant to the success of an emphysema treatment, I failed to grasp most of what was said. As you can imagine, my report was essentially worthless. But it *was* published. I'd been the only reporter available for the assignment. My shallow little story was all we had, so we ran with it. I can only hope that the editors caught all the mistakes I must have made.

When a journalist with little knowledge or experience in computer technology hacks out a story about the latest Windows e-mail worm, he knows only what he's told by the few actual experts, and the vast pool of third-rate poseurs clamoring for publicity, whom he happens to interview for the story. He hasn't got the reporting experience in computer security, or the technical knowledge of computer systems and networks, needed to detect exaggeration, faulty reasoning, or outright fiction. It's all neutrophils to him. All he can do is tell you what he's been told by his sources, the majority of whom will have been flooding the newsroom with press releases offering pithy quotes and expert "perspectives" from the moment the worm struck. To most reporters in this situation, the expert's wisdom and the charlatan's drivel are as one. If they hear roughly the same thing from two or three sources, they'll trust it and pass it along to you. But they won't have been able to *evaluate* it. Or the source, for that matter.

Almost everyone who contacts a news organization offering himself as a source has the same agenda: free publicity. People get their name, their company's name, or the title of their latest book in print, and it costs them nothing. Government bureaus get their agenda, their political spin, their "message" in print, and it costs them nothing. I literally can't count the number of times I've been approached by some PR bunny, some startup's CEO, or some bureaucrat offering me a crucial bit of "inside news" that turned out to be nothing more than a company press release or a desiccated scrap of government propaganda. Everyone in business and government tries to use the media as a forum of free advertising. As a result, much of the news you read and watch on TV has been interlarded with misleading information that some "source" has provided as a service to himself or his organization. And all too often, the reporter passing it along is in no position to detect it.

As consumers of news, it's important that we not put too much credit in what we're told or be too impressed by the fancy titles of quoted sources. Joseph Blow, Chief Information Officer for SemiTech Security Systems, might be the CEO's brother-in-law, and SemiTech may comprise little more than a post office box and a Web site. Mr. Blow might clean up well for his interview on CNN, and he might recite a few industry truisms convincingly, but he may not have the faintest idea what he's talking about. His insight could well be limited to what he's read in the newspapers. He has a simple agenda: free publicity. The retired generals advising Americans on the war in Iraq also have an agenda. Many of them are employed by defense contractors, and in that industrial sector, war is good for trade. So-called terrorism experts are often in business, seeking lush government contracts for Defense Department gimmicks and Homeland Security schemes. No wonder they fret so much about the inadequacy of national counterterrorism budgets. Take it from a journalist: virtually every talking head on the news has an agenda, and your interests rarely figure into it.

Giving You the Business

Cybersecurity is both big business and big news. The media like to detail the latest software bugs and hacker attacks because the subject matter is relatively new and not widely understood, therefore intriguing, and even a bit frightening. News organizations know that the public will listen closely whenever something dangerous or exotic is mentioned. Security vendors, and government bureaucrats concerned with security, also know this and exploit it freely. They've learned that virtually anything that sounds threatening, however far-fetched it might be, will be picked up by the media. Vague warnings propagated via the news result in public uncertainty and do a fine job of selling security and antivirus products. They also help legitimize the ever increasing budget requests made by government agencies. Thus the most plentiful single product of the security establishments, both corporate and governmental, is what's called FUD, or *fear, uncertainty, and doubt*. FUD is the seed stock of the security racket. And it is scattered very liberally indeed.

Keep in mind that hundreds of billions of dollars are at stake. The temptation for people in commerce and government to exaggerate the threats they're supposedly working to reduce on our behalf is natural and compelling. Let's recall a familiar example.

In the summer of 2001, eEye Digital Security discovered a security hole in the Microsoft IIS server that could yield system-level access to a remote attacker. The vulnerability was first reported and described by eEye on 18 June; an exploit script was released on 21 June by a Japanese computer enthusiast called HighSpeed Junkie; and a worm called Code Red, based on the exploit, appeared on 13 July.

The publicity folks at eEye had been hammering the security mailing lists and tech news outlets for days, trumpeting their discovery of the IIS hole and hardselling the fact that their security product, called SecureIIS, protects against it. From the company's perspective, the hole they discovered had validated their product and they wanted everyone to know it. But there is a strange confluence of interests here. Finding a security hole that one's own products protect against, then publicizing the details of how to exploit it, is a bit like a pharmaceutical company engineering a new flu virus, publishing the steps needed to cultivate it, then offering a vaccine for sale as soon as the inevitable pandemic strikes. Still, it would be unfair to single out eEye in this context. Most security outfits put a good deal of effort into finding new bugs so that they can sell us the remedies. This is an established element of the security racket: find a new hole that your product can fix, publish an exploit, intrigue the media with FUD, and watch your sales increase.

Once the Code Red worm began circulating, the news media got involved and, as usual, distorted the public's understanding of what was going on. After infecting a victim, the worm would use the compromised machine to scan for other vulnerable IIS boxes and infect them automatically. This consumed Internet bandwidth, and, more importantly, allowed for a system-level compromise of infected machines. One of the worm's more curious features was its ability to cause some infected systems to send packets to port 80 at Whitehouse.gov, tying up its bandwidth and capacity. This was an insignificant detail in terms of the worm's destructive potential, but it was the media hook that kept the Code Red story alive for months. The worm's true impact was the fact that it yielded system-level access to an intruder, along with some Internet overhead caused by thousands of IIS machines aggressively scanning for new victims. The President was never in any danger.

For weeks, battalions of "security experts" paraded themselves before the press, trotting out their finest doomsday quotes for a shot at 15 minutes of fame. The Net would be overloaded and shut down by the worm's activity, we were repeatedly warned. Legions of clueless journalists eagerly sucked up the quotes and generated absurd headlines predicting that Code Red was about to break the Internet.

While the mainstream press was occupied with business of publishing quotations wholesale, I was criticizing eEye in my column, suggesting that their own PR blitz over the IIS hole (and the fine performance of their SecureIIS product) had made it more likely that Code Red would be developed quickly, before most admins had a chance to patch their systems. I believed that the company had published too many details too early, and it was therefore no surprise that a worm author had been able to get the jump on everyone else. I am not against full disclosure; the public needs to know how exploits work so they can defend themselves. But I am against *incontinent* disclosure, and accused eEye of precisely that. I later had an e-mail exchange with eEye's "Chief Hacking Officer," Marc Maiffret. "The Internet is about to shut down and you're bickering about nonsense," he wrote.

We also got a good serving of FUD from security outfit TruSecure's "Surgeon General," Russ Cooper, who claimed that Code Red–infected machines would scan so aggressively that the Internet would experience "a meltdown."

"If it does slow down as I expect it will, then you won't even be able to get to Microsoft's site to install the patch," Cooper predicted. "I expect that to happen."

It didn't. Over a million users successfully downloaded the patch, and the Internet kept humming along.

Steve Gibson, founder of Gibson Research Corporation (grc.com) added more fuel to the fire, exclaiming in hyperbolic multicolored lettering on his Web site that Code Red's "'growth line' is actually exponential!"

While numbers can increase exponentially, worm infections can't. Code Red spread very rapidly in the early days, but because there were a finite number of IIS machines, the scans soon began hitting already infected or patched boxes. This resulted in a diminishing return, not an exponential increase, as a moment's reflection would have made apparent. Gibson tried to argue that the worm's spread would be immense and sustained. Nevertheless, within a few days, the rate of infection began to decline sharply because the likelihood of finding an unpatched or uninfected target had fallen off—well—exponentially.

Gibson is a classic popinjay expert, well known for hyperbole, innuendo, and speculation, which he passes off as deep insight. Not surprisingly, he's got no background in computer security, but he has got one in advertising and marketing. He's also got a bit of a cult following, as most charlatans do. (The faithful would do well to check out grcsucks.com for a few alternative views.) Yet it didn't take long for veteran PBS tech columnist Robert X. Cringely to get infected with Gibson mania.

"Some experts believe nothing will happen at all but I believe that's just plain wrong," Cringely wrote. "The information I will use to support this assertion was acquired either from those, like Steve Gibson, who have disassembled and examined the Code Red worm or from the officials charged with fighting it, including sources at the CERT [Computer Emergency Response Center] data security coordination center at Carnegie-Mellon University, eEye Digital Security, in law enforcement, and at several very large corporations."[2]

Those would be just about the most self-serving sources possible, and Cringely, a veteran tech journo, should have known better.

"And what happens on the 20th, when the attack cycle begins?" Cringely asked rhetorically. "It depends on the number of infected machines and the nature of the chosen target, but the worst case says the Internet simply comes to a standstill and we go back to watching TV and talking on the phone until the 28th day of the month, and potentially until every 28th day of the month thereafter," he fretted.

Code Red did reappear once a month, but each time there were fewer machines for it to infect. The worm remains in circulation even today, though its effect on the Internet is negligible. This is how worms typically work: they spread automatically, without user interaction, and therefore infect everything they can with surprising speed, but then they taper off as the supply of vulnerable hosts dwindles.

Finally, Carolyn "Happy Hacker" Meinel got a most appalling piece of Code Red FUD published by *Scientific American*, a middlebrow publication that prides itself on its cutting-edge scientific and technical savvy. Naturally, Meinel hit all the hot buttons, from biowarfare to terrorism to cyberwar with China, which she emphasized:

"According to the official Chinese publication *People's Daily*, soon after the mid-air collision was an all-out offensive on Chinese Web sites by US hackers.... By the end of April, over 600 Chinese Web sites had come under fire or totally broke down.... Many hackers' organizations known as China Honkers Union and Hackers Union of China promptly responded in an all-out cyber-war against their

2. See www.pbs.org/cringely/pulpit/pulpit20010730.html.

US counterparts May 1 to 7. Clearly, *People's Daily* was eager for China to take credit for attacks through May 7. But it has been silent on Code Red."[3]

Meinel suggested that Chinese cyberterrorists had something to do with Code Red. She didn't say it, but she clearly wanted readers to think it. Her evidence was limited to the fact that Code Red defaced the default pages of infected IIS servers with the inane motto, "Hacked by Chinese!" Hardly a smoking gun.

Meinel even went so far as to suggest that eEye created and released the Code Red worm as a publicity stunt, but the *Scientific American* editors later, and wisely, retracted it: "An earlier version of this story included a quoted speculation that eEye Digital Security might have been involved in the creation of the Code Red worm. eEye denies any such involvement. We apologize for including that inadequately supported statement in our report," the editors said.

Of course, if the editorial staff at *Scientific American* knew anything about computers, networks, or cybersecurity, they would have apologized for the entire article.

Interestingly, while Code Red was monopolizing the headlines, two concurrent threats to Internet stability went largely unreported. These were the Sircam Outlook worm, which devoured a tremendous amount of bandwidth, and an underground fire in Baltimore that obliterated a large swath of Internet backbone on the U.S. East Coast. So, while Code Red was supposedly bringing all of Christendom to its knees, the Internet was also fighting off Sircam and a major backbone fracture. And it handled all three assaults simultaneously with just the sort of resilience it was designed to have. Not only could Code Red not break the Internet, Code Red, Sircam, and a missing chunk of infrastructure couldn't break it. But this would not discourage the security establishment from talking in positively apocalyptic terms, or the press from validating and propagating the torrents of FUD generated by security vendors and bureaucrats, two groups that always benefit from a confused and worried public.

Code Red, like its predecessors such as Melissa and its successors such as Blaster, was a great boon to popinjay experts. It represented a moderate burden on Internet bandwidth and on system and network administrators, but took its greatest toll in fear, uncertainty, and doubt. Industry critic Rob Rosenberger of Vmyths (vmyths.com) reported that "unbridled fear about Code Red made many US Air Force bases go off-line via a precautionary disconnect. I repeat, *fear* crippled the Air Force, not the worm itself."[4]

A good portion of Code Red's impact probably can be attributed to admins disabling their equipment as a precaution and from the torrents of e-mail exchanged among others needlessly fretting about it. Media hype made it a monster story, but mainstream media attention is never a trustworthy gauge of a story's importance.

---

3. See www.sciam.com/article.cfm?articleID=00033FF0-A329-1C75-9B81809EC588EF21.

4. See related article at vmyths.com/resource.cfm?id=26&page=1.

Code Red was hardly the digital Apocalypse, but judging by the predictions of a sensationalist and gullible press, it certainly sounded like it.

Parasites

Face recognition technology has been in the news lately. It's an interesting technology, quite useful for *authenticating* people, but very poor at *identification*. Let's consider the difference: when you're identified, it means that someone else recognizes you. When you're authenticated, it means that someone else has verified that you are who you claim to be.

In a controlled environment, face recognition can be used for authentication. For example, let's say there's a restricted wing in a building. One way to manage access is to post a guard who will authenticate those wishing to pass. A simpler system would involve a locked door that can be opened automatically by people authorized to enter. But rather than issue keys, badges, or smart cards that can be lost, stolen, lent, or duplicated, we might use a mathematical representation of a person's face instead. A face scanned at the door will unlock it when it generates a valid set of numbers. This is essentially how all biometrics, such as fingerprint and iris scans, work as tokens for authentication.

Authorized people will have their faces scanned to create a reference photograph. The mathematical product of the reference photograph will be recorded in a digital file rather like a passfile. (Note that this is similar to the way password hashing works, and that its essential weakness is the same. Hack the "passfile" and you own the system.)

When someone seeks access at the door, their face will be scanned again. The mathematical product of the authenticating scan will be compared against a list of numbers created by the previous reference scans. If there's a match, the door will unlock automatically. This is convenient, but it's crucial that the reference scans and the authenticating scans be created under virtually identical conditions. Distance to the camera, head angle, camera angle, and lighting must all be consistent for it to work. Face recognition is reliable only in controlled situations, and even then, there is a significant error rate. Under the best possible circumstances, a failure rate of one in 250 is to be expected. For this reason, face recognition is usually backed up with a second biometric, such as a fingerprint or iris scan, to increase its reliability.

Biometric criteria are good for authentication because they are hard to reproduce. They solve the problem of keys and smart cards that can be lost, duplicated, or forged. But they create other difficulties: biometric devices are finicky. Conditions have got to be right for them to work.

Honest companies that develop this sort of gear always use more than one biometric and never pretend that a single one is reliable. And they never claim that face recognition can be used for *identification*, a task at which it is comically ineffective.

Parasites like Viisage and Visionics/Identix, on the other hand, deliberately market face recognition as a means of identifying criminals and terrorists in a crowd, despite the fact that it has repeatedly been proved worthless for surveillance.

Visionics sponsored a public surveillance trial on the streets of Tampa, Florida, with the stated goal of identifying sex offenders and pedophiles, two target groups that no one would rush to defend. The trials of its FaceIt system were a dismal failure, and the Tampa police abandoned it after indulging it for about two years without success. Nevertheless, Visionics has continued to approach PDs and has even played the terror card, offering its FaceIt snake oil for airport surveillance.

Viisage, which earned headlines by scanning crowds at Super Bowl 2000 to no worthwhile effect, is also eagerly pursuing the airport surveillance angle and has "offered the FBI free use of their face-recognition technology to aid in the apprehension or identification of the persons responsible for the terrorism in New York City and Washington," for an added marketing gimmick.

The majority of police departments and airports taken in by these companies have since discovered the hard way that authentication technology doesn't work for identification. In 2003, face-recognition systems installed at Boston's Logan Airport failed to detect volunteers posing as terrorists 96 times during a three-month trial, and stupidly fingered the innocent with comparable frequency. An earlier trial at Palm Beach International Airport also ended in failure, with more than half the people who should have been flagged slipping past undetected. The rate of false positives was also discouraging, at approximately two to three per hour per checkpoint. Obviously, a gizmo that finds a terrorist every 30 minutes would make it impossible for an airport to get a single plane off the ground. Numerous other tests have revealed similar rates of failure, as a damning 2000 report by the U.S. Department of Defense called the "Facial Recognition Vendor Test" makes evident.

The culprit here is the charlatan's trusty tool: the demonstration. Company representatives conduct sales demos meticulously engineered to make it appear that their gadget works as advertised. This generates enthusiasm among potential suckers, but, inevitably, the performance seen under controlled conditions can't be duplicated in the real world. This is because demonstrations and tests are two radically different things. Demonstrations highlight what the vendor wants revealed. Tests uncover what the vendor is trying to conceal.

The security racket is infested with parasites of this sort. Face recognition is a handy example, but there are thousands of other expensive schemes and products that work as poorly, yet are embraced just as enthusiastically by the gullible. Many unscrupulous security vendors bamboozle their customers with technology that the client doesn't understand, hoping to sell him expensive products he doesn't need or that don't even work. It's impossible to judge something you can't quite grasp, and the vendors know it. In the New Economy, we are all at the mercy of people who know more than we do. Compounding the problem is a tendency we all share to trust technology *because* we don't understand it. When the underlying theory makes sense and the actual technology is obscure, we often assume that the technology has bridged the gap between theory and practice. Tellingly, while the Tampa police have chucked their FaceIt system, the Virginia Beach police still cling to theirs after more than a year of failure. Their superstitious faith in the magic of technology has yet to be shaken. Or perhaps their embarrassment at being made fools by technocharlatans forces them to press on with a stiff upper lip. Either way, the citizens of Virginia Beach are being swindled: every police officer fiddling with useless computer equipment is one who's not on patrol.

It's difficult to defend against security parasites. They know more than most of us, and they prey on our ignorance of complicated technology and our natural optimism toward it. But there are always a few clues, chief among them a heavy emphasis on theory, a reluctance to explain a system's nuts-and-bolts functioning in plain English, and a reluctance to encourage independent, unsupervised testing.

Good systems do not rely on demonstrations and always withstand rigorous examination. Honest vendors do not discourage independent testing, and they never require nondisclosure agreements when independent testing is done. Good people do not conceal facts behind obscure polysyllabic words and piles of acronyms. If you don't understand what you're being told, chances are the system in question is snake oil and the people pitching it are parasites.

Hacker-centric Security

Many of the central frauds of the New Economy, or dot-com media circus of the late nineties and early millennium, have, mercifully, been exposed. For example, we no longer believe in supernatural IPOs. We saw too many venture capitalists and investment banks get rich cashing out their IPO allocations, and too many ordinary folks get poor by taking the inflated shares off their hands on the aftermarket while squads of cheerleading "analysts" and "journalists"—many with gross conflicts of interest—talked up the worthless shares on CNBC even as they tanked spectacularly.

We no longer believe that a merely clever idea is actually a multibillion-dollar industry in the rough. We saw enough 30-year-old CEOs doing their venture capital rounds, falling in love with their incredibly bright ideas and the sound of their own voices as they pitched them, and going bankrupt within a year's time.

The dot-com appendage no longer strikes us as an emblem of shamanistic power defying all market rationale. It no longer appears plausible to millions of investors that Pets.com should have sported a market cap in excess of the entire U.S. annual market for pet products, and hold on to it. Consumers probably won't scramble to click their mice on line and receive bulk dog food via Federal Express because this is such an extraordinarily cool thing to do, we've begun to realize.

It was quite a ride, but the Mother Goose Economy is behind us now, except for a few tenacious bedtime stories. We may have become too jaded for economic miracles, but hacker mythology lives on. Vendors promote it because customers frightened by hackers will spend more on security. Hackers promote it because it lands them high-paying jobs in the security racket. The combination of computer security and hacker mythology is something I call *hacker-centric security*, one of the last unchallenged con games of the New Economy.

There's a foolish notion still in circulation that to foil hackers you should hire hackers. This is because hackers sometimes find and leverage flaws that security professionals don't notice. But there's little logic behind the practice: the fact that someone can break a system is hardly a guarantee that they'll know how to fix it. There's also no guarantee that a hacker will know anything about a complex, multifaceted system beyond the parts susceptible to his own tricks. It's plausible to imagine a quite successful hacker with a narrow field of expertise and little appreciation of the larger security picture. One hacker might excel at breaking database servers, another at breaking Web servers. They may be completely ignorant of each other's tricks. Even if a hacker knows enough to secure a component that he can break, there's no reason to believe he'll be capable of securing any other elements of a complex system. Hacker-centric security is a marketing tactic, *not* a strategy.

The mythology persists because the media are in love with hackers and innocently credit them with far more expertise than they actually possess. Some readers will recall the late-nineties media circus surrounding the L0pht, a Boston-based crew of self-proclaimed "ethical hackers." They did some programming and a fair amount of original research and often posted advisories and exploits to BugTraq, as most researchers do. But they also donned the wizard's robes for the press, with aliases like Mudge and Space Rogue, Dildog and Brian Oblivion. "Eight brilliant geniuses," TruSecure Surgeon General Russ Cooper once called them. They took in Bruce Gottlieb, a former columnist for *Slate*, who wrote a puff piece called "HacK, CouNterHaCk" for the *New York Times Magazine* in October of 1999.

The public expects geniuses to be weird, and Gottlieb is careful to establish the L0pht crew's satisfying eccentricity: "Their six-room suite is an adolescent geek's fantasy clubhouse. One wall is papered with antiquated circuit boards while another has a signed picture from Julie, Penthouse Pet. Junk food in the cupboard is taken seriously. There are three different kinds of Cheez-Its: hot and spicy, plain and white cheddar," he explains.

One of the L0pht's more successful tactics in achieving media stardom was ambiguity, encouraging people to wonder which side they're really on. For example, they created a password cracker for Windows NT and 2000 called L0phtCrack (now called LC3). It's useful for admins to identify weak passes, and it's also a fabulous script-kiddie tool. But the L0pht crew liked to play coy when their motives were questioned, knowing that ambiguity and intrigue will always attract journalists.

"Mudge frankly admits that he'll answer anyone's technical questions about hacking," Gottlieb says. And Mudge plays coy: "If a blackhat approaches us and says, 'hey, this is the project or problem I'm looking at...' we'll talk to them, no problem. And if a government agency approaches us and says, 'how do you do this,' or, 'how does this work,' we'll talk to them." (Note the subtle implication that blackhats are dealing with problems, while government agencies are trying to figure out how things work. A gentle reminder that hackers are geniuses.)

Next, Gottlieb establishes the crew's qualifications as Very Mysterious People: "Perhaps because of their ties to the blackhat community, L0pht members refuse to be identified, although they will let themselves be photographed. As Space Rogue explains (and any hacker knows), pictures are next to useless if you're trying to dig up private data on someone."

And now for the kicker: "When L0pht testified before the Senate [Committee on Governmental Affairs in May of 1998], members would not accept checks for hotel and travel expenses. As with members of the Witness Protection Program who have come before the Senate, they were reimbursed with cash."

To enhance the mystique, Gottlieb catalogs their kit as if it belonged to the set of a Tom Clancy technothriller: "Black cables, yellow cables and jumbles of thin rainbow-colored wires drip from the ceiling, all jacked in to steel racks of oscilloscopes, radio transmitters, DSL modems, ISDN modems, half-opened CPUs and a 50-foot roof antenna."

Only one problem there: you can't half-open a CPU. You could break one in half, I suppose, if your fingers are callused enough not to be pierced by the pins, but "half-opened" is not a valid state of affairs. Gottlieb doesn't quite know what he's talking about, so it's no wonder that, without a hint of skepticism, he lets Mudge get away with saying, "Any of us could leave L0pht right now and take six-figure jobs.... The fact that we don't and we're on the ramen-noodle, mac-and-cheese diet, that speaks for our ethics right there. It's not a job for us; this is what drives us through life."

Mudge said that to Gottlieb three months before taking a (presumably) six-figure job with a security startup called @Stake in January of 2000.

A group of investors and salespeople from Forrester Research, Cambridge Technology Partners, and Compaq suffering from dot-com fever decided to burn some venture capital and get into the security racket. They hired a respected security researcher named Daniel Geer, and bought some instant street cred by hiring a hacker crew, the L0pht, which had been dangling itself as a tempting target for acquisition via the media for some time. Perhaps Gottlieb's puff piece, so well placed in the *New York Times Magazine*, helped seal the covenant.

The marriage would not be harmonious. One by one, the L0pht crew would resign or be forced out of the organization, although the company would persist in using them as mascots even in their absence. But lately, the transformation from hacker-centric marketing to a more vanilla corporate image is nearing completion. At this writing, it appears that Chris Wysopal (aka Weld Pond) is the sole surviving L0pht member. It's tempting to imagine that the hacker-centric marketing gimmick never quite worked for @Stake, and that the company slowly dissociated itself from the L0pht crew as they became old news and their brand value deteriorated. In time, the liabilities of being identified with hackers began to outweigh the publicity benefits. Once the L0pht crew went mainstream, they ceased to be the mystifying media darlings once fawned over by Bruce Gottlieb and many others. In time, they were left to trade on their technical expertise, which, apparently, didn't quite suit the company's ambitions.

@Stake has struggled for credibility since conception. It has steadily shed its hacker airs in favor of a more mainline track, courting major corporate clients, including Microsoft. Here again, poor judgment has been an inescapable curse. The company sacked Chief Technology Officer Dan Geer only days after he and several other security researchers released a whitepaper called "CyberInsecurity: The Cost of Monopoly" in September of 2003. The paper argued that the computing monoculture created by Microsoft Corporation is itself a major threat to cyber security.

According to the authors, "Because Microsoft's near-monopoly status itself magnifies security risk, it is essential that society become less dependent on a single operating system from a single vendor if our critical infrastructure is not to be disrupted in a single blow. The goal must be to break the monoculture. Efforts by Microsoft to improve security will fail if the side effect is to increase user-level lock in. Microsoft must not be allowed to impose new restrictions on its customers and then claim that such exercise of monopoly power is somehow a solution to the security problems inherent in its products. The prevalence of security flaws in Microsoft's products is an *effect* of monopoly power; it must not be allowed to become a *reinforcer*."

Within days of posting that bit of self-evident wisdom, Geer found himself unemployed. Rumors circulated that Microsoft had intimidated @Stake with threats of contract cancellations, but a far more plausible explanation is that @Stake sacked Geer out of its own irrational fear of reprisal and its obsequious deference to the Redmond behemoth. The security outfit made its loyalties evident. Clearly, Microsoft can trust @Stake. The question remaining is, can you?

Throughout its journey from hacker-centric media phenomenon to Redmond suck-up, @Stake has found credibility an elusive goal. But it would be unwise to single out this one company. @Stake illustrates the pitfalls and regrets involved in hacker-centric security nicely, but it's not alone. Many security companies hire hackers. Some advertise it; others struggle to conceal it; but the practice is widespread.

A couple of years ago, while covering a security industry conference, I noticed a large banner in the conference hall hung by one of the vendors. "Are Hackers Threatening Your Network?" the banner asked rhetorically in foot-tall lettering.

"And are you paying them a hefty retainer?" I wondered quietly.

The Cyber-Terror Hoax

When it comes to such topics as computer security, cybercrime, hacking, and cyberterror, the guesswork and mythology routinely passed off as expert analysis can get positively comical. I began this book with a chapter describing the many superstitions surrounding the hacking underground. I presented that material early for a reason: hacking embodies the greatest misconception most people harbor about computer security. As you can see from the emphasis throughout the remaining chapters, users concerned about security need to worry far more about their software and far less about hackers. You need to control your operating system so it isn't offering scores of insecure services to millions of strangers on the Internet; you need to worry about spyware hidden in applications, about viruses and worms and Trojans, about controlling data traces on the Net and on your machine, and about using encryption to keep your private business private. Software is the paramount security concern. Hackers, while not irrelevant, are the least of our worries. Skilled hackers *are* a threat to high-value targets, but for most of us they figure only marginally.

And yet most people mistakenly imagine that hackers represent the greatest threat to their online security. And there's a reason for this: the security establishment and the news media have been selling hackers as the number-one cybersecurity concern for years. This has happened in part because most reporters can't understand the things hackers say, so they imagine them to be smarter than the rest of us, therefore frightening. It's happened in part because hackers like to talk in riddles and wear outrageous clothes and dye their hair blue and pierce themselves as if they'd had a near-death experience with a malfunctioning nail gun. This makes them telegenic and sexy (in the news sense of *sexy*), hence compelling targets of media attention. They look scary and they're largely unintelligible; therefore they must be dangerous, the reporter supposes.

Ever since the evil-genius hacker became a permanent fixture of IT culture, the stage has been set for another popular tech fiction: cyberterror. With the click of a mouse, we're told, the floodgates of dams will be opened and villages swept away; aircraft will be crashed into mountains; food supplies will be poisoned; and national economies will be wiped out. Behind this hoax are some well-heeled and powerful players: technology and security vendors hoping to feed heavily on Homeland Security pork, and government bureaus seeking additional funding, power, and importance.

And once again, propping it up is a vast pool of naïve journalists who print whatever FUD their sources supply because they don't understand the basic technology involved. Some readers will recall the media frenzy surrounding the so-called Millennium bug, or Y2K bug, that was supposed to visit digital scourges of every description upon mankind. Then–U.S. President Bill Clinton set up a Y2K working group to prepare an electronic catastrophe recovery plan, and the U.S. Senate even set up a Y2K Committee, chaired by Robert Bennett (Republican, Utah) and Christopher Dodd (Democrat, Connecticut), to entertain self-interested witnesses in the technology and security sectors, both public and private, who testified with predictions of mayhem and doom.

During one such Senate hearing, a witness, one Nick Gogerty of British Y2K consulting outfit International Monitoring lashed out at a soothing report by the Clinton Administration's Y2K working group and denounced it as "potentially reckless."

"We believe Y2K will be the second costliest accident in history," Gogerty exclaimed, oddly neglecting to mention his pick for the all-time worst. But, he added, "barring nuclear or major chemical failures, loss of life should be minimal in the United States." He had perhaps meant to reassure the Committee with that little qualification, but one could have heard a pin drop when he finished his speech.

At another Y2K Committee hearing, U.S. Critical Infrastructure Assurance Office (CIAO) director John Tritac (coiner of the inane phrase "electronic Pearl Harbor") remarked, with an eccentric scientist's anticipation of some fascinating calamity, that the Y2K rollover would at least provide "essential lessons" and a golden opportunity for the security establishment to "observe the impact of cyber failure."

Michael Vatis, then director of the FBI's National Infrastructure Protection Center (NIPC); John Koskinen, chairman of the President's Information Coordination Center (ICC); and Richard Schaeffer, director of infrastructure and information assurance for the Department of Defense, also testified. Their theme, endlessly repeated, was that Y2K stuff-ups were going to provide cover for terrorists and hostile military organizations to attack the U.S. and its allies.

No one mentioned the ultimate horror, an attack or a critical breakdown involving nuclear power or weapons facilities, but the terrible implication lurked throughout the discussion. Indeed, much of John Koskinen's testimony focused on potential "energy" problems, obvious code for "nuclear" problems, though neither he nor anyone else dared utter the dreaded *n*-word. It was the elephant in the room that no one would acknowledge.

NIPC's Vatis claimed it would be extremely difficult to distinguish between a malicious cyberattack and an innocent Y2K breakdown when the rollover arrived. He predicted that foreign militaries might try to "equalize their disadvantage in conventional warfare with the United States by going after our soft underbelly—our dependence on information technology" and try to "take out" essential infrastructure services such as energy, transportation, and banking.

Committee Ranking Member Christopher Dodd asked Vatis if there existed any "hard evidence" that hostile military organizations were involved in cyberattacks or related planning against the U.S. and its allies.

"I wouldn't want to answer in this forum," Vatis sniffed.

Dodd pressed him again: "I'm not going to ask for specifics; I'm just asking if there's hard evidence of that occurring."

Again Vatis brushed him off, appealing to the public nature of the hearing and the need to maintain secrecy.

"Well, *you* raised the issue," Dodd observed with sarcasm. He concluded that Vatis's "reluctance to answer" was itself an indication that such evidence must exist. Vatis did not contradict him.

It was a superb performance. Vatis didn't answer and therefore could not later be accused of lying to Congress, a serious felony. And yet he successfully planted in the minds of the Senators, and the journalists in the audience, that cyberterror is a real and present danger rather than the hoax it actually is.

In the end, the Y2K rollover occurred and human life inexplicably went on in spite of it.

Security vendors are as eager to capitalize on the cyberterror myth as government agencies, and also regularly participate in Congressional festivals of fear. Such hearings are a handy forum of free advertising because there are always reporters in attendance copying down the most sensationalist quotes. Private companies also testify regularly, while positioning themselves as government contractors, and in this way reach out for rich, juicy gobbets of security pork. Frightening Congress is one way of getting programs funded, especially those that generate lucrative government contracts. Since the atrocities of 11 September 2001, American security pork has become exceptionally rich and juicy and plentiful. Tech companies have been descending on Washington like a modern-day swarm of '49ers. Everyone has a new gimmick to defeat the forces of evil; everyone has discovered some new, diabolical threat to life and limb and economic stability. We're all just a mouse-click away from some digital apocalypse, Congress is repeatedly told.

Some Truth

In July of 2002, IT consulting outfit Gartner and the U.S. Naval War College enacted a mock cyberwar named Digital Pearl Harbor, apparently in tribute to government alarmist John Tritak. The exercise brought together a team of specialists in several areas related to critical infrastructure for a three-day hackfest, but failed to validate the Clancyesque predictions of mass devastation envisioned by the leading security paranoiacs of the Clinton and Bush administrations.[5]

Now, it's important to bear in mind that this was an *exercise*, not a *simulation*. In a simulation, there are red teams that attack and blue teams that defend, just as there are in the real world. But in this exercise there were no blue teams.

---

5. For details, see www.gartner.com/2_events/audioconferences/dph/dph.html.

Therefore, the findings were necessarily skewed in favor of the attackers. If the participants had tried any of this in the real world, they would have had to contend with competent admins and supervisors struggling against them.

The red teams were divided into telecom, Internet, electric power, and finance subgroups. To make the exercise as realistic as possible, the popular cliché of brilliant geek-misfits wreaking mass mayhem from some deluxe hobbyist dungeon was abandoned. Instead, the presumed attackers came from the upper levels of the tech world: engineers, programmers, and mathematicians, many with Ph.D. degrees and decades of practical experience to their credit.

It was assumed that the attackers would be bankrolled with at least $200 million, would have access to state-level intelligence, and would take five years to plan their assaults. The goal would be to create not mass destruction, but rather a crisis in public confidence sufficient to shift the balance of power, presumably as a supplement to a real war.

Technically speaking, a dream team like the one described with the money and time assumed can do some damage. But it would be very difficult to keep an operation that size secret for five years, because the attackers would have to recruit inside help. Obviously, in the real world someone would inevitably do something stupid, say something stupid, or approach the wrong person for assistance. And indeed, one of the team leaders, David Fraley in the telecom group, made a similar observation. It's unlikely that all the teams would be able to maintain secrecy long enough to carry out a real attack. It's difficult enough for five people to keep a secret for a matter of weeks; here we're talking about hundreds keeping one for five years. The burden of secrecy alone is enough to make the following scenarios implausible. And keep in mind that the attacks would have to be integrated in order to do much damage; yet the discovery of one or two plots would likely lead to the discovery of the others.

One basic assumption that strikes me as particularly fraudulent is the belief that disruptions, even coordinated disruptions, in these areas would result in a crisis of public confidence. We've seen cities immobilized for days by natural events like blizzards, the severest of which are often accompanied by power and communications breakdowns, financial inconveniences, and failures of emergency response teams to function, and yet life mysteriously goes on. We humans aren't as fragile or as dependent on state intervention as government desires us to be and generally imagines us to be. We shift for ourselves rather well when the infrastructure of state guidance lets us down and the life-giving commercial heartbeat flatlines. People are remarkably adept at solving problems, both individually and in small, *ad hoc* groups. Thus we routinely survive earthquakes, floods, blizzards, economic depressions, disease epidemics, hurricanes, foreign occupations, famines, plagues, slavery, tsunamis, volcanic eruptions, sustained V-1 and V-2 bombing campaigns, and the like. If we couldn't, we wouldn't be here now.

That said, it's clear that a fair amount of mischief can be brought about by a large, well-funded technical dream team. Telecom group member David Fraley reported that it's possible to cause telephone network capacity to collapse for a brief period. However, it would take a very large investment in both personnel and money (bribes, presumably) to accomplish even that much. Perhaps 200 people would be needed, he reckoned. A satchel bomb thrown down a manhole in Manhattan would be far easier, far cheaper, and still fairly destructive, he remarked.

As for the power grid, it's national and controlled by complex SCADA (supervisory control and data acquisition) systems. SCADA devices are automated computer systems that monitor complex mechanical systems. Still, it's only feasible to target a large metropolitan area, team member John Dubiel noted. Attacking the entire grid would be quite impractical. The best approach would be to launch physical attacks on major transmission corridors, all of which are well known, followed by the malicious use of compromised control systems to create a pattern of cascading failures throughout the target region. "At this point the system [would be] attacking itself," he observed. Finally, the team would attack and damage the SCADA systems themselves to hamper recovery efforts.

It's possible to launch remote attacks against some SCADA systems connected to public infrastructure, but insiders would have to be recruited to attack others, he added. Furthermore, this would have to be coordinated brilliantly and carried out in hours, not days, to thwart ongoing recovery efforts. We can assume that with a $200 million war chest, the attackers will have little trouble buying cooperative insiders, assuming they don't blow their cover. Still, the more people involved, the greater the chance that someone will slip up and expose the operation.

It's also important to know that few critical SCADA systems are controlled via an Internet connection or the public telephone system. Some may be, but it's not a common setup. Most such systems are networked on private intranets and leased phone lines that don't communicate with the outside world. Destroying them would require *insiders* to corrupt the software that controls them. So this means that one would need saboteurs who not only know how to operate the control systems, but also how to damage the software that runs them. And since most systems are on relatively local loops, one would need a lot of people who are both qualified and willing to do the deed. Furthermore, those SCADA systems foolishly left accessible via the Net or the public phone system still require a good deal of specialized training to operate. A hacker might gain remote access to one, but it's unlikely that he'll have any knowledge of the complex system it's connected to. It's a lot more likely that he would cause accidental damage by poking about and tinkering with it. Finding a competent hacker who also happens to be an expert in the operation of power grid or petroleum refinery SCADA systems is a long shot. And finally, and most importantly, 200 people are unlikely to be able to keep their mouths shut for five years. I think the odds of pulling this off are very slim to none.

In the finance area, group member Annie Earley recommended disrupting cash flow and credit availability in the consumer, corporate, and institutional realms simultaneously to undermine public confidence. To get the most long-term damage from the smallest investment, she advised attacking the ACH (automated clearing house) payments system.

According to the Federal Reserve, in 2000 the ACH system handled 4.8 billion items valued at $12 trillion, including salary deposits, consumer and corporate bill payments, stock dividends, Social Security and other U.S. Treasury entitlements, insurance premiums, and stock purchases.

Earley said it's painfully easy to replicate the ACH format and simulate a valid transmission while substituting bogus transactions. She suggested initiating the attack at the start of the Thanksgiving holiday weekend. Social Security benefits would be paid during the weekend, creating a flood of activity within which to conceal numerous malicious efforts involving salary deposits and scores of other transactions handled via ACH. All of the bogus payments would be formatted legitimately and be small enough not to attract attention (i.e., under $10,000 each). Short-staffing on the holiday weekend reduces the chance that oddities will be noticed. Earley expects 30 to 45 days' lag in the public's discovery of the monkey business, but once people begin to reconcile their monthly statements, call centers will start going berserk, bank branches will be flooded with confused, demanding patrons, and it will be impossible to answer everyone's questions. Staff capacity will simply be exceeded, and all hell will break loose.

Earley seems to have forgotten the media, which will disseminate whatever cheerful message the government and Wall Street see fit to feed it. You may not be able to reach your bank's call center, but the major newspapers and networks will remain ahead of the curve. We will be told that the authorities are aware of the difficulty, that they understand it, that they're working around the clock to fix it, and that in the end, no one is going to lose any money. Unless this attack can be coordinated with an effective communications infrastructure attack that would knock out national TV, I don't see it sowing panic. Anger and irascibility, yes; fist-fights, yes; but widespread panic, no.

Next we come to the Internet, the very nexus of cyberterror superstition. In this case, the team assumed $50 million to spend, four cells of operators, and six months in which to plan.

Team member John Mazur recommended establishing a covert network to undermine confidence in the Internet. This network would make use of P2P applications, compromised VPNs, and hijacked machines in the enterprise space. High-value targets might include media outlets through which malicious hackers could spread disinformation. Other handy targets would include network service providers; financial, power, and enterprise networks; and corporate and government networks entrusted with sensitive information.

Member Paul Schmitz imagined four cells: a recon and intelligence cell (probing, mapping, scanning), an architecture cell (compromising remote machines), a disruption cell (corrupting data and launching denial-of-service attacks), and a destruction cell (finally switching off the Internet).

Note that "destruction" is a relative term in the context of the Net. There are no commands that will cause physical damage to equipment. Servers and routers have not been fitted with remote self-destruct buttons; and systems over-loaded by computational tasks do not blow up as they do on *Star Trek*. Destruction, in this context, would mean corrupting operating systems, applications, and data caches badly enough to render the machinery temporarily dysfunctional. If all went well for the hacker dream team, it might be possible to create local, cascading failures extending for a few days' time. This would involve widespread software corruption and finally disabling DNS servers and DNS data caches so that what remains of the Internet would be difficult for ordinary users to navigate. To some extent, this process could be sustained by rapidly changing attack methods; but the more local infrastructure one disables, the more difficult it is to reach out to other portions of the Net that haven't been affected. And once again, there are always blue teams in the real world. Such attacks will be continually countered in real time, and most might not succeed at all.

The Naval War College's Craig Koerner pointed to the need for "synergies" in making the attacks interoperable, hence marginally feasible. For example, the group would likely attack the Internet last to preserve it for other attacks. However, if the Internet is used to attack other critical systems, the activity will be detected and countermeasures will be used. Furthermore, "saving" the Internet and using it as an attack platform would become difficult when the power and telecom infrastructures, on which it depends, are also under attack. Finally, the *value* of the Internet as an attack platform is quite limited. Most of the important target systems simply aren't connected to it. Koerner pointed out that while local attacks are possible, it's virtually impossible to bring off any lasting, nationwide horror. The stereotypical scenario of a hacker crew bringing down the national communications and power infrastructure is quite preposterous.

And yet the security establishment, Congress, and the press remain infatuated with this sexy myth. Fear sells, and its chief booster for the past several years has been Richard Clarke, an advisor to two U.S. presidents and America's former "cybersecurity czar." Clarke has pushed the cyberterror myth harder than anyone. His motivation seems to be a sincere personal conviction that terrorists will one day strike hard via the Internet and do serious harm to people. Whether this is because he doesn't understand the technology and therefore overestimates its power, or because he's spent too many years hunkered down in dark NSC bunkers I can't say, but after covering him for several years, I sense he's convinced that he's a true Cassandra who sees what ordinary mortals can't. The NIPC's former director, Michael Vatis, was also an incontinent doomsayer, though his motivation seemed to be the endless pursuit of Congressional funding for his outfit. Since his withdrawal from NIPC, the organization's subsequent director, Ron Dick, has struggled to restore its credibility by studiously avoiding sensationalist predictions. He's fond of saying that the scenario he worries most about is a conventional terror attack accompanied by an attack on local communications that would interfere

with rescue efforts. The Internet won't have much to do with it: attacking communications infrastructure is best accomplished with explosives, backhoes, and bolt
cutters; but the combination of attacking a population center and local communications simultaneously *is* something to worry about. Dick deserves recognition
for trying to bring common sense back to the cyberterror conversation. It's an
uphill battle, of course, and one he'll lose, but he is struggling for some truth.

Airplanes will not be crashed by hackers, nor will they be so long as human
pilots continue to fly them instead of Web bots. The floodgates of dams will not
be opened and no villages will be swept away, because people will step in when
problems emerge. Chemical additives will not be incorporated into foodstuffs in
toxic quantities, because there are human beings working on the production lines
who will notice the anomalies in additive supplies and investigate them. Only a fully
automated system controlled via public networks is truly vulnerable to cyberattack.
And if someone should design a complex system with serious public safety implications that has no human supervision and can be controlled via the Internet or
the public phone system, he deserves to be hanged.

Finally, the presumed threat of cyberterror, that the populace will lose confidence in public institutions and rise up in rebellion after an infrastructure attack,
is tied more to institutional and bureaucratic condescension than any real danger.
Personally, I find it extremely offensive to see people portrayed in this way. But
Messiah complexes are widespread in the elite quarters that draw those who feel
uniquely qualified to wield state authority and regulate the lives and activities of
others. The fragile civilian is an enduring bureaucratic and law-enforcement fetish,
but history tells a different story. People are a lot smarter and a lot tougher than
public officials like to imagine. Populations simply are not going to curl up in
a fetal position and demand emergency services because they can't download
their e-mail for a day or two or because their ATM has gone haywire. We're just
not that delicate. The human race exists today *because* we're not that delicate.

Your Children Are in Terrible Danger

It's natural for us to be alarmed by anything that threatens children. It's an
inescapable feature of human nature. Children are defenseless, both physi-
cally and mentally, and they are therefore entitled to greater protection than
adults. Ideally, a child should be entitled to trust any adult, though obviously
they can't. The real world can be hard on children sometimes.

Unfortunately, danger to children has become a tremendously fashionable
class of FUD. Manipulators in business and government use it against us every
day, appealing to the protection of children when they can't make a better argument for what they propose, or wish to sell.

A good example comes from the Recording Industry Association of America
(RIAA), which, in addition to pursuing its lawsuit vendetta, has lately sought to

warn consumers away from P2P file sharing by using the taint of child exploitation as a repellent. The Senate Judiciary Committee held hearings in September of 2003 to expose the problem on the RIAA's behalf.

Youngsters are encountering the most appalling images of child sexual abuse when they search for music files, a number of witnesses claimed. But only U.S. General Accounting Office (GAO) Information Management Issues Director Linda Koontz had done any hands-on research. "In one search, using 12 keywords known to be associated with child pornography on the Internet, GAO identified 1,286 titles and file names, determining that 543 (about 42 percent) were associated with child pornography images. Of the remaining, 34 percent were classified as adult pornography and 24 percent as nonpornographic," she said.

Of course, it's unlikely that children would search for music using keywords associated with child pornography, but Koontz was prepared for that objection and brought along some research based on more innocent keyword searches. Here the torrent of child porn by which our youngsters are being swept away slowed to a trickle. "Searches on innocuous keywords likely to be used by juveniles, such as names of cartoon characters or celebrities, produced a high proportion of pornographic images: in our searches, the retrieved images included adult pornography (34 percent), cartoon pornography (14 percent), child erotica (seven percent), and child pornography (one percent)," Koontz admitted. Obviously, it would be quite unusual for a youngster to stumble upon child porn while looking for music.

Suffolk County, New York District Attorney Thomas Spota has had some experience prosecuting online pedophiles who've used P2P services. Appealing to his expertise, but to no verifiable facts, he implied that the kiddie porn available on KaZaA and other services is actually *worse* than the filth found elsewhere on the Internet.

"The images of child pornography available on peer-to-peer networks are some of the worst seen by law enforcement to date. Included in the images seized by police in the cases being prosecuted by my office are still photographs of very young children engaged in sexual acts with other children and adults and video clips lasting several minutes of children being subjected to unspeakable acts of sexual violence," Spota claimed. How this might be worse than the same vile material found elsewhere in vastly greater quantities was not explained.

Later, National Center for Missing and Exploited Children Chairman Robbie Calloway asserted that there is a direct connection between the availability of child pornography images and the likelihood that children will be assaulted in the real world. A pedophile "can convince himself that his behavior is normal, and eventually he will need more and increasingly explicit child pornography to satisfy his cravings. When mere visual stimulation no longer satisfies him, he will often progress to sexually molesting live children," he claimed, though he offered no evidence in support of what he said.

When RIAA President Cary Sherman's turn to testify came around, he spent the bulk of his time whining about a "drastic decline in record sales" brought about by "the astronomical rate of music piracy on the Internet," for which P2P file sharing is believed responsible. After mentioning child pornography in passing, he then launched an elaborate attack against telecom behemoth Verizon, which has not been as cooperative with the RIAA as Sherman would wish, having moved in court to protect the privacy of its subscribers from the music lobby's do-it-yourself subpoenas.

He then recapitulated the RIAA's legal arguments against Verizon at considerable length and detailed exhaustively the various provisions of the DMCA that Verizon is supposedly violating, as if invited to give court testimony in the dispute. The exploited children quickly faded into memory. Sherman concluded that "the DMCA information subpoena represents a fair and balanced process that includes important and meaningful safeguards to protect the privacy of individuals" and protect the music cartel's revenues, as if this had been the hearing's topic all along.

And of course it always was the topic. It was clear from Sherman's tirade that the day's exercise was an attack against P2P technology for its presumed negative effects on the music cartel's profits, not on children. The specter of child abuse may have hung over the proceedings, but it was nothing more than an atmospheric effect. If Sherman had the slightest concern for the welfare of children, he hid it well.

The sheer hypocrisy of decrying child porn on behalf of an industry that sexualizes children wholesale represents the very apotheosis of *chutzpah*. A music video by band Blink 182 called "Feeling This" could be the closest thing to kiddie porn ever shown on television. And most mass-produced rap and hip-hop videos are nothing more than a booty revue set to monotonous music and illiterate doggerel. Music industry creations VH1, MTV and BET have become almost uninterrupted soft-core porn channels. But this isn't adult pay-per-view; it's 24/7 entertainment for teenagers.

And the labels are concerned about the effects of P2P porn on the young. Sure they are.

Certainly there are plenty of threats for parents to worry about, but an appeal to child welfare is often the sign of an impending swindle. Any claims of special danger must be evaluated rigorously because exaggeration is the rule, not the exception. It's simply too easy to get attention and inspire action with a reference to endangered children. Abuse of this universal hot button is as old as the trial of Socrates, who, we may recall, was sentenced to death for "corrupting the young." One of the more shameless abusers of the child-danger button in recent memory is former U.S. Attorney General Janet Reno, who, during her tenure, repeatedly pressed Congress for crypto controls, key escrow, expanded Internet surveillance, and greater wiretap authority on behalf of endangered sprouts. It was a rare occasion when Reno didn't justify the need for total electronic transparency because exploited and kidnapped children somehow depend on it. Nothing that she or FBI Director Louis Freeh proposed would have been much use to exploited children, however. Their requests were for the fulfillment of a long-sought FBI wish list that the atrocities of 11 September 2001 vouchsafed to federal law enforcement a few years later.

The Soft Pedal

So far, we've considered security and safety issues, threats, and risks that are deliberately exaggerated to create public anxiety that can be exploited by commerce and government. But there is a disinformation flip side: the soft pedal. In Chapter 3, I wrote about mad cow disease (BSE) for two reasons: first, to illustrate the often very personal nature of risk and threat assessment; and second, to make the point that social engineering clouds our view of risks and threats and makes it difficult for us to perceive them accurately. In the realm of public safety and security, assessments are often made by parties who may be hopelessly incompetent, who may profit from our fears, or who may overdo security and safety measures driven by their own professional survival instincts. Threats can be exaggerated, and often are, but it's important to bear in mind that they can also be obscured for equally self-serving reasons.

When the American BSE infection was first disclosed around Christmas of 2003, the U.S. Department of Agriculture (USDA) hastened to reassure the public that the meat supply was safe. The official line was a masterpiece of soft-pedaling. The public was told that meat cut from the infected animal, which had already been sold, would have been safe to eat. It's probable, but not certain, that meat cut from skeletal muscles is not a vector of variant Creutzfeldt-Jakob disease (vCJD) in humans when the source animal is infected with BSE. Yet the public was told that *only* central nervous system (CNS) tissue can spread the disease. Actually, although it's true that vCJD transmission through skeletal muscle has not been documented, it's not known with certainty to be impossible. The fact that over a hundred unfortunate Britons contracted vCJD from BSE-infected meat tends to contradict this claim, unless they were all tucking in to plates full of brains, spinal cords, and eyeballs—in other words, unless they were all big fans of hotdogs, sausages, and cheap ground beef. A more accurate statement would be that skeletal muscle from infected animals is *believed* safe to eat, while tasty internal bits like kidneys, livers, and sweetbreads might be a tad risky. So that's lie number one.

Another dodgy claim was that CNS tissue *never* enters the human food supply. This is untrue. Beef neck bones are usually on sale in my local supermarket, spinal cords and all. Bovine CNS tissue certainly is sold in the consumer market. Second, slaughtered cattle are struck in the head with a powerful mechanical device called a bolt, which kills them instantly. Unfortunately, bits of brain and eye matter, which are a confirmed vCJD vector, can become airborne and land on parts of the carcass meant for direct human consumption. Third, a recent technology called advanced meat recovery (AMR) takes chopped-up skeletons and crushes the chunks to force the last scraps of meat off the bone, creating a paste that's used in cheap ground beef, hotdogs, and sausages. Nervous system tissue and bone grit always end up in it. It may be true that brains and spinal cords aren't deliberately commingled with food except by unscrupulous processors, but such matter is routinely commingled inadvertently as a consequence of modern processing techniques. So that's lie number two.

Yet another bit of fancy rhetorical footwork by the USDA was a claim that the sick animal's infectious bits could not enter the human food supply because they went to a rendering plant. That's not quite true: rendered cattle remains can be fed to other animals, such as chickens, pigs, farmed fish, and household pets, which in turn may be rendered and fed back to cattle or to us, though this is not believed to be dangerous. BSE spreads primarily through animal feed contaminated with BSE-infected cattle remains and scrapie-infected sheep remains. In the U.S. and Canada, the practice of feeding cattle remains, or the remains of other ruminants (the family to which cattle belong: cud-chewers including sheep, goats, deer, etc.), to any ruminant is against the law, but that hardly prevents it from happening. It's illegal, not impossible. And ruminant CNS tissue can be fed to nonruminants that are later rendered and fed back to ruminants. Downers and dead livestock; euthanized pets; road kill; restaurant and supermarket waste; carcasses from veterinary practices, animal shelters, circuses, and zoos; and similar tidbits all become animal feed, fish feed, meat and bone meal, gelatin, dog and cat food, protein additives, soap, soil treatments, and other quality products. Rendering does *not* destroy the proteins, called prions, that are responsible for BSE and vCJD. To say that BSE-infected tissue can't enter the human food supply because it ought to be reserved for rendering, and because the rendered matter ought not to be fed to ruminants or people, is false. Ideally it *shouldn't*, but we don't live in an ideal world. So that's lie number three.

> **NOTE** *Readers who want the lowdown on BSE and CJD in excruciating detail should check out the British government's report at* www.bseinquiry.gov.uk.

When the diseased dairy cow in the U.S. was first discovered, long after her meat had been sold, U.S. Agriculture Secretary Ann Veneman hastened to hold a press conference, during which she glossed over the details with cheerful platitudes to reassure the public, and announced plans to serve beef at her own Christmas dinner. As usual, no one in the mainstream press dared ask an inconvenient question. Veneman's script was a verbatim rundown of a press release issued by the National Cattlemen's Beef Association, a powerful industry lobby. According to the Association:

"The BSE agent is not found in meat like steaks and roasts. It is found in central nervous system tissue such as the brain and spinal cord." (*And in cheap hamburger and sausages thanks to AMR, and perhaps in organ meats to a lesser degree. And don't forget that neck bones are a popular consumer product.*)

"All U.S. cattle are inspected by a USDA inspector or veterinarian before going to slaughter. Animals with any signs of neurological disorder are tested for BSE." (*But their meat, edible organs, trimmings, and waste are sold before the test results are known.*)

"BSE affects older cattle, typically over 30 months of age. The vast majority of the cattle going to market in the U.S. are less than 24 months old." (*The fact that younger animals rarely exhibit symptoms is no guarantee that they can't spread the disease.*)

"The only way BSE spreads is through contaminated feed." (*Not even close. It can spread through meat accidentally contaminated with bovine CNS tissue during processing, and possibly through nonruminants like pigs and chickens fed on bovine CNS tissue, though this is believed to be unlikely.*)

"The U.S. Food and Drug Administration (FDA) in 1997 instituted a ban on feeding ruminant-derived meat and bone meal supplements to cattle. This is a firewall that prevents the spread of BSE to other animals." (*This is hardly a firewall; feed might be mislabeled, accidentally contaminated with other feed, or deliberately contaminated by unscrupulous processors and suppliers.*)

The National Cattlemen's Beef Association has an agenda: to sustain the demand for beef and to defend production and processing techniques that are profitable. The USDA also has an agenda: to support the industry and pacify the public. The Department is concerned with protecting the cattle industry, an important economic asset responsible for over $175 billion in trade for the U.S. alone. This is why the Agriculture Secretary never once deviated from the lobbying organization's PR script. The official line was designed to prevent a loss of confidence in the food supply and thus to preserve profits for the industry. The Association is very afraid that consumers in North America might demand that animal-derived feeds and related ingredients be banned from all livestock fed to humans. A cattle diet containing waste animal protein is economical and helps U.S. and Canadian beef compete on price within a vast, and lucrative, international market. It also plays a role in public health: if the millions of tons of waste animals and unusable remains couldn't be processed and sold at a profit as feed, we would all be exposed to a health threat considerably worse than BSE from mountains of rotting carcasses. The existing system, unappetizing though it may be, is not as bad as it sounds. Something has got to be done with the millions of tons of waste animals that die or are killed each year. If they can't be turned into a commodity, we will all have to pay for their proper disposal or suffer the consequences.

One reason the public never got the whole story is institutional condescension: the belief among many bureaucrats and industry illuminati that we, the great unwashed, are incapable of drawing rational conclusions from complete, accurate data without mounds of sugar coating and an energetic sweeping under the carpet of the unpleasant facts of life. And yet, the unvarnished truth was never that bad to begin with. There is little reason for Americans and Canadians to fret about vCJD. Personally, I've long assumed that the North American meat supply is infected with BSE and I've taken measures to reduce my exposure by preferring meat from animals reared on grass and grain, and fish and seafood caught in the wild, though not rigidly excluding more risky commercial meats and processed foods. As I said in Chapter 3, everyone's perception of risk, and everyone's tolerance of it, will vary. But we can't respond individually unless the information we receive is as accurate and as complete as possible. When we've got good information, we can make choices that suit us personally. When we haven't got good information, our choices are more likely to suit someone else. Like the National Cattlemen's Beef Association, say.

Soft-pedaling causes two problems: first, consumers who innocently trust bad information may assume more risk than they would if they were better informed; second, those who detect that crucial information is being withheld may suspect a cover-up, presume the worst, and respond with excessive worry and caution.

Yet even without the government and lobbyist gilding, the North American BSE risk is a minor concern. Personally, I'd like to see more animals tested and more frequent and more rigorous inspections of feed supplies, and I'd like to see advanced meat recovery (AMR) products relegated to renderers, not food processors, but I'm not anxious about it. I was pleased to see that within a week of the BSE scare, the USDA finally outlawed the widespread practice of selling meat from downers as groceries. But BSE is rather low on my list of daily terrors; I worry a lot more while crossing a busy avenue than I do while shopping for food. And there are more important diseases to be concerned about. For example, HIV kills millions of people each year, and the flu can kill hundreds of thousands in a *moderate* year. Some flu pandemics have claimed the lives of *tens of millions* in a single year. On the other hand, vCJD kills a few tens: as of December 2003, a total of 153 cases have been reported worldwide. There's more risk of deadly illness lurking in most nightclubs than in all the slaughterhouses of North America.

Although the BSE risk is negligible, the USDA still couldn't bring itself to be honest with the public, and neither could the Cattlemen's Association. Too much money is at stake. So always keep in mind that while some people and organizations will profit from frightening you unnecessarily, others will profit from lulling you into complacency. Remember that the tobacco lobby for decades insisted that the connection between smoking and lung cancer was mere speculation and that nicotine is not addictive. There was no need to be afraid of their very profitable product, Big Tobacco repeatedly insisted. The auto industry fought seat belts, air bags, pollution controls, and antilock brakes because these handy items cut into their bottom line. The energy industry rarely misses an opportunity to scoff at the danger of greenhouse gasses. And the food production and service industries have long maintained that campylobacter, *E. coli*, hepatitis A, and salmonella are natural ingredients for which they are in no way responsible.

While the odds of encountering threats like cyberterror are comically exaggerated, others, like food poisoning, are soft-pedaled. In both cases, we end up with distorted views that make it impossible to choose a sensible course of action that suits our own priorities and sense of risk tolerance. We worry about exotic threats that may never harm anyone while ignoring important ones that loom large every day. As author Bruce Schneier noted in the 2003 book *Beyond Fear*, "people underestimate risks they willingly take and overestimate risks in situations they can't control."

This is a very important observation. When our safety and security are in the hands of others, we often demand unrealistic standards of performance. We expect the USDA to make BSE go away because we can't control the situation: most of the major risk factors are in the hands of strangers whose motives and level of competence we can't know. We expect others in positions of responsibility to operate with the utmost caution, skill, and wisdom, though we ourselves would not. For example, many people drink and drive occasionally, but even though they do, they would be outraged by a drunk airline pilot flying them about. Instead of some fallible workaday schmoe just like themselves,, they expect instead to find a cross between Aristotle and Chuck Yeager at the controls. In other words, when our safety and security are in the hands of others, we expect the impossible. That's another reason why we're lied to constantly by commerce and government: we expect more than the truth will bear.

Propaganda, both commercial and governmental, frequently invites us to expect the best this and the finest that. Our local restaurant uses only the best ingredients. Our furniture is made by old-world artisans using the finest exotic hardwoods. Our soldiers are equipped with the best weapons and the most reliable defensive gear, while the latest space-age technology watches over them. And when they're shot to bits, the world's most skilled surgeons stitch them back together. The plain truth doesn't sound very impressive in the blizzard of patronizing superlatives to which we're subject every day.

Unrealistic expectations also help explain why the bureaucratic response to any public threat often comes down to a choice between overprotection, an elaborate rain dance suggesting that everything that can be done is being done whether it helps or not, and soft-pedaling, a performance underplaying concerns about, say, living downstream of a chemical processing plant. FUD is plentiful where public anxiety is profitable; soft-pedaling blossoms where public overconfidence is lucrative. We live in an ocean of disinformation in which the habit of relentless skepticism is our only defense.

Unintended Consequences

On 17 October 2003, six people lost their lives and eight others sustained critical injuries in a Chicago office building, thanks to a foolish security measure. Since the violent destruction of the Alfred Murrah Building in Oklahoma City and the World Trade Center in New York, the idea of terrorists attacking office buildings has become a security obsession. These attacks are shocking and terribly destructive, but they're also extremely rare. Nevertheless, many public buildings now require identification of visitors and limit access from side entrances, garages, and similar routes. The ID requirement is nothing more than a security rain dance: knowing a visitor's name makes no one any safer unless the name can be compared against a list of known terrorists and pyromaniacs. ID cards can be faked easily, and the people checking them are unlikely to be competent at spotting counterfeits. A metal detector, on the other hand, actually *is* useful. Knowing a visitor's name or his phony alias may be worthless, but learning whether or not he's armed is news you can use. Unfortunately, metal detectors are expensive: the ID requirement is a cheap dodge that gives people the false impression that security is being taken seriously.

In the Chicago case, all of the stair doors were locked from inside the stairwell, no doubt to inhibit the movements of terrorists should they ever decide to operate in the building. Unfortunately, the locked stairwells became a death trap when a familiar, everyday threat emerged: a fire. Building residents and visitors were made safe from an exotic, virtually nonexistent threat, yet made vulnerable to one that kills people every day. The person responsible for this blunder probably thought he knew something about security, but he was wrong. No doubt he confused the volume and intensity of media attention with the actual risk of terrorism. And no doubt he meant well. Unfortunately, he had the authority to translate his lopsided risk assessment into a security protocol, killing six people and injuring eight others who had no choice but to trust him. This is important to keep in mind: the minute you leave your house, your safety and security are in the hands of people who, more often than not, are well-meaning dolts. To make matters worse, the security establishment loathes public scrutiny and replies with hostility whenever its wisdom is questioned. "Professionals" appeal to their advanced tactical training and knowledge of secret information to dismiss cynics as uninformed trouble makers. A common-sense critic who persists in questioning security rules and procedures publicly will eventually be maligned as the dupe of criminals and terrorists.

The Chicago tragedy illustrates the tension between two similar concepts: security and safety. They're closely related, but they're *not* the same. Security is concerned with preventing or defeating deliberate attacks. Safety is concerned with preventing or defeating accidents and natural threats. For example, as we travel from warmer to colder regions, we may notice that buildings change subtly in form. In colder climates, roof pitch is steeper. This roof angle allows snow to slide off, preventing a dangerous buildup that can weaken the structure. In warm regions, this is not a concern. But in cold climates, snow load on a roof can cause structural damage and hence create danger. Sharpening the roof pitch on houses in colder regions is a simple example of safety engineering. We're surrounded by other examples: safety glass and airbags in cars, guard rails on highways, circuit breakers in houses, child-proof lighters. Sometimes we hardly notice it: bridges, for example, are often designed with an open structure that lets the air pass through to reduce wind load. All of these measures, and thousands of others like them, are designed to reduce the risk or mediate the threat from accidents and natural forces.

Locks on doors and burglar alarms are different. Locking your door doesn't improve matters much during a blizzard; closing it firmly will suffice. But locking it does help when someone is deliberately trying to break in to your house. Door locks are a simple example of security engineering. But notice that security and safety are related. For extra security, you might install entrance door locks that require a key on both sides, called automatic deadlocks. These are very difficult for burglars to defeat, and so offer good security. But suppose there's a fire in the middle of the night. People are woken suddenly in a dark, smoke-filled house. They can't see well; they're not thinking clearly so soon after waking; alarms are ringing; and each is worried about the other. And now they've got to run about in the dark and find the key so they can get out of a burning house. They're in a lot more danger they would be if the entrance doors opened easily from within.

Security often comes at the expense of safety. In general, people enjoy greater safety when they have more freedom and suffer greater danger when they have less freedom. Of course there are exceptions: sometimes people are safer and more secure when their movements are restricted, which is why there's a moat or a fence preventing you from offering tidbits to the polar bear at the zoo, but this is the exception, not the rule. Unfortunately, proscriptions tend to be the default when it comes to public security and safety. It's always cheaper and easier to restrict freedoms and regulate behavior. The locking stairwell doors in Chicago are a classic example of restricting people's freedom in the name of security, and killing them in the bargain. This is why risk assessment is crucial. Fires kill and injure tens of thousands of people throughout the world every year. Terrorists rarely kill and injure more than a few hundred, though 2001 was a rare and tragic exception. The risk of fire is thousands of times higher, and the threat is the same: death and crippling injury. Fire safety is *enormously* more important than counterterrorism. Of course, you wouldn't know that from the media circus surrounding terrorism and the pronouncements of politicians, bureaucrats, and public officials. Terrorism is weighted disproportionately because it's extremely sexy news, and because of its symbolic and political dimensions. But if you hope to die a natural death, you should think *fire* a thousand times more often than you think *terrorist*.

You and I make numerous assessments every day and willingly accept some risk that we believe is worth living with. Bureaucrats and public officials think differently. If they tolerate risk and the worst happens, they will be excoriated for doing too little. If they overreact to threats, people may complain, but the bureaucrat or official can always reply with the familiar slogan that they're protecting people, or better yet, protecting children. The bureaucratic urge to overprotect is universal and everlasting. If overprotection were merely an inconvenience, it could be justified. Unfortunately, excessive security and neurotic risk-aversion can create extremely dangerous conditions, such as those responsible for the unnecessary loss of six innocent souls in Chicago.

Sadly, if a building resident had objected to the stairwell door policy on common-sense grounds, he would no doubt have got an earful of platitudes from management invoking solemn responsibilities for public safety and warnings that such matters are best left in the hands of professionals. "For your safety" is a hollow incantation, yet a common preamble to some of the worst possible security procedures. When a public official worries about risk, he inevitably worries about losing his job if things should go badly. Risk to the public is risk to his career. His risk aversion is fundamentally personal, yet it will be refracted in public policy affecting thousands, perhaps millions. With his job always on the line, he ceases to think rationally and instead thinks politically. Unfortunately, you and I have little choice but abide by his rules, even if it kills us.

While it may be futile for individuals to dig in their heels and object to foolish policies connected with public safety and security, this is no reason for us to follow a bad example in our daily lives. It's important to bear in mind that there *is* such a thing as too much security. All of the security measures you implement have consequences. They can cost more than they're worth and hence represent a waste of time or money; they can lead to a false sense of security, hence complacency; they can create needless inconvenience; they can even increase threats and risks associated with other, more relevant dangers. Whenever you're thinking about computer and Internet security, or even household safety for that matter, it's important always to consider the consequences of your actions. Automatic deadlocks might thwart a burglar, but they might also kill you and your family during a fire.

Let's look at an example related to personal computing. Throughout this book I've been pushy about the importance of encryption and data hygiene. That's because, in some situations, privacy *is* security. You may not be able to prevent some novel attack against your system, but if the attacker comes away empty-handed, you've still defeated him. Many of us share computers with others at work and at home, and occasionally we may share one with someone we don't trust. Let's suppose that you've gone on holiday and left your flatmate at home with access to your computer. Let's also suppose that you've done a good job of setting up separate accounts for him and yourself, and have protected your user account and administrator or root account with strong passwords as I've recommended. Is your personal data safe from your flatmate's snooping while you're away?

Not at all. He may never be able to guess your passwords, but he doesn't have to. He could simply boot the machine with a DOS floppy disk, then run Norton DiskEdit or a similar program and browse the hard disk at will.

But now let's suppose that you've anticipated this possibility and taken steps to prevent it. Personal computers are fitted with battery-powered memory chips that hold the date, time, and system setup. This is done so that you won't have to re-enter all these values and reset the BIOS (basic input–output system) options after unplugging your machine. On a PC, the BIOS controls the keyboard, disk drives, serial ports, and similar items. You control the BIOS options from a setup interface that's often accessed with a hotkey during booting. BIOS is what operates your computer before the operating system has a chance to load. Indeed, it's what loads the operating system in the first place. It tells your computer which disk to boot from.

Now, since booting the machine from a floppy or CD can allow someone else to examine your hard disk, you might wish to configure your BIOS options to prevent booting from these drives. And indeed you can. You can even password-protect the BIOS setup interface so that your flatmate won't be able to change your options, and therefore won't be able to boot the machine from external media. You might think that this is a good security measure, and it may give you confidence when you leave your computer in your flatmate's hands for a couple of weeks, but you'd be wrong to trust it. An attacker with unsupervised physical access to your machine can get around this with ease. He might discharge the battery-powered CMOS (complementary metal oxide semiconductor) chip where the BIOS options are saved, thereby restoring the factory defaults and eliminating your password. He could then reconfigure the BIOS options to allow booting from external media. Or he might simply remove your hard disk drive and connect it to another machine. The disk can then be read with a utility like DiskEdit or mirrored with the Linux utilities DD or DDrescue and read with an ordinary text editor. Limiting your boot options and password-protecting your BIOS setup will prevent naïve users from mucking about with system settings they're better off not adjusting, which is a good thing, but it won't provide much security.

The scheme fails in two ways. First, it's inconvenient; every time you want to start your machine from external media you'll have to change the system's boot options with the BIOS setup interface. You'll have to boot twice to change it and twice again to restore it, and it doesn't offer enough protection to be worth the bother. Second, it creates a false sense of security; it seems rather clever, but it's actually quite easy to defeat. To protect your data from others with unsupervised physical access to your machine, you have to encrypt the files you wish to keep private and practice data hygiene to keep your duplicate data traces under control. It's impossible to lock someone out of a PC unless you resort to heavy-duty physical barriers, which are, obviously, far too expensive and inconvenient for personal computing. Trying to achieve physical security with a PC is an example of effort and inconvenience greatly disproportional to the potential benefit. It's a handy model for a lot of other security blunders based on the natural urge to overdo things.

Better Is Better than More

Most of us are familiar with the story of Moses's big mistake in the desert, when God spared the Israelites from slow death by providing water from a rock. Earlier, near Mount Sinai, God had instructed Moses to strike a rock with his staff to provide water, and at that time everything went well. But on this occasion, God said, "Take the staff and assemble the congregation, you and your brother Aaron, and command the rock before their eyes to yield its water." There was no mention of hitting anything, but Moses struck the rock anyway, twice for good measure. God was displeased to see his instructions ignored, and the Israelites spent 40 years suffering in the desert as a result. The problem was *more*. If one smack had yielded results, two smacks ought to yield better results, Moses apparently reckoned. Poor Moses died in the desert and never saw the promised land, but things would have gone differently if he'd kept in mind the crucial difference between *better* and *more*. Indeed, what God had in mind *was* better. The Israelites were by this time frightened and thirsty and rebellious. God knew that providing water merely by issuing a verbal command would impress the people more than using the staff, the power which had become routine to them. The miracle God was planning to perform was a good deal more impressive. Too bad Moses went for more when he could have gone for better. He, and more to the point, his many followers, paid a terrible price for that blunder.

Excessive security, and excessive concern with it, are based on the universal human impulse persuading us that if a is good, then $(a)^2$ or $(a+b)$ must be better. Sometimes more *is* better, and that's why there's an engineering concept called *redundancy* that provides secondary and even tertiary backups to crucial systems. An airplane flying over the open ocean simply cannot afford to have a fuel pump malfunction. Thus it's equipped with backups. A better fuel pump is little comfort; what we're looking for is three quite decent ones. We routinely make backup copies of our data for a similar reason; if our computer fails radically, we need that redundancy. And I've written several times that security needs to be layered because computers are complicated devices capable of hundreds of functions. Securing one function is not necessarily going to provide security for another. So it's true that more can be a good thing, but better is still better.

No doubt this seems contradictory. It's not. Three decent fuel pumps on an airplane is better than one improved model that's three times as reliable. Why? Because a pump with only one-third the risk of failure will fail enormously more often than three pumps with three times the risk of failure. It's simple: let's say a standard fuel pump has a one in one-thousand chance of failing during a flight.

For the sake of argument, let's say it will fail during every thousandth use. The secondary pump also has a one in one-thousand chance of failing. Thus it, too, will fail during every thousandth use. But remember, a thousand flights have to be completed before it will have been used *once*. After two thousand flights, it will have been used twice, and so on. It won't fail until one million flights have been completed, at which point the third pump will take over for the first time. If that pump fails on every thousandth use like the others, the plane will be disabled only after it's made *one billion* flights, which of course is an impossible number. But a single pump three times as reliable will fail after only three thousand flights, an entirely possible number.

So in that situation, more *is* better, and better is what we're after. The problem is that in many situations, more can make things worse. Demanding ID of visitors to a building is "more" security. But because it's a mere rain dance, it makes matters worse by promoting a false sense of security. Locking a stairwell is "more" security, and it may protect us from an exotic threat like al-Qaeda commandos trying to take over an office building, but it will kill innocent people trying to escape a fire, hundreds of which happen every day. Armed air marshals on commercial flights are "more" security, but guns and planes do not mix well. So far, the marshals have proved themselves adept at subduing obstreperous drunks, but five or six beefy guys with some commando training are another matter. Terrorists no longer need to worry about sneaking guns onto planes. They can simply overpower the air marshal and use his gun instead. And they will. It's only a matter of time. One of the hijackers can pretend to be drunk and behave in an increasingly threatening manner until the air marshal steps in, thereby revealing himself. The other hijackers can pounce on the air marshal. So then we'll have five or six beefy guys with commando training *and* a gun. Suppose there's an armed pilot in the cockpit. The way I figure it, within a few minutes the hijackers are going to have two guns. It's a classic: more security, less safety. If there were *no* deadly weapons on the plane, the passengers would be able to deal with the hijackers themselves. That's a classic too: less security, more safety.

It's very important, whenever you think about security, to think about unintended consequences, and safety consequences in particular. Often there is a balance to be struck between security and safety. Just as often there will be another kind of compromise involved that may be unacceptable. Few people would walk around their neighborhood in body armor, but if you live in a battle zone you would. Ordinary folks do get shot from time to time, but going about in a hot, cumbersome outfit that your friends will ridicule isn't worth the bother. Of course, if you were a soldier in battle, it would be. Something that works well in one situation is often not appropriate in another. Resist the temptation to learn security by analogy. Think instead of the immediate situation and ask yourself these questions:

- What asset am I trying to protect?

- Who is likely to attack and how might they attack?

- Is the primary threat more likely to be the result of an accident or someone's deliberate efforts?

- How much is the asset worth?

- How fragile is it (e.g., if a computer file is merely read or copied by someone else, will its value suffer)?

- How likely is it to be attacked or accidentally damaged?

- What are the most effective, yet the least expensive, least time-consuming, and least cumbersome methods of securing it?

- Finally, and most importantly, are there any hidden safety compromises involved? Often there will be, so it's always important to look for them.

Our Friend the Hidden Transponder

One of my favorite security ironies is connected with RFID (radio frequency identification) chips that can be implanted in everyday objects. An RFID chip is a small radio transponder. Some are passive and can only be read with a powered reader. Others are active and contain their own power source for broadcasting. The popular Speedpass toll system, which automatically bills one's credit card or debits one's bank account, uses an active RFID chip, or transponder.

Manufacturers, transportation outfits, and retailers are very much taken with RFID technology because it can be used to simplify inventory and shipping control. Scores of products, or even scores of full pallets and containers, can be read electronically in a fraction of the time it would take an individual to read and record the information. RFID is a very useful technology, at least for some people. Unfortunately, the people it's good for are a small minority and the people it's bad for are just about everyone else: there are serious privacy implications in hidden transponders that turn up in virtually every consumer product. Thus, the chip makers and their potential clients have done what every well-heeled group does when their agenda is in direct conflict with public interests: they've formed a lobbying outfit called the Auto-ID Center at MIT, and retained the services of a public relations firm.

A watchdog outfit, called CASPIAN (Consumers Against Supermarket Privacy Invasion and Numbering) recently discovered a trove of marketing materials on the MIT Auto-ID Center Web site. According to the documents, the RFID lobby sees public resistance as nothing more than an obstacle to be overcome with shallow slogans. Many of the documents are related to focus-group surveys in which consumers wisely note that RFID offers them very few benefits while posing a considerable threat to privacy. In response, PR firm Fleischman-Hillard recommended that the industry communicate several inaccuracies, the most egregious being that the RFID transponder is "nothing more than an improved bar-code," as if broadcasting data were an inconsequential difference.

In another document, it's anticipated that the public will resign itself to the inevitability of this innovation, though they may not much care for it. In yet another, it's recommended that RFID tags be renamed Green Tags to slap on an overlay of environmental rectitude. But it seems likely that they will be renamed eTags to give them a jolt of Silicon Valley cachet instead. Note the condescension at the heart of these calculations: the public is too stupid to grasp the difference between a bar code and a transponder, and too spineless to object to measures it doesn't like.

Now, RFID can also be used in a security context. Some governments are already giving thought to chipping bank notes to deter counterfeiters. RFID chips can also make inventory control of large shipments of cash, say from a national treasury to a bank, more convenient. If each note emits a unique radio signal, it would be easy for a supervisor at the treasury to use an electronic reader and take a final count of the shipment. When the shipment arrives at the bank, a supervisor there can make a quick count and detect any discrepancies immediately. If theft is suspected, the armored truck can be impounded and its occupants detained until the police arrive to investigate. So this is a fine security system indeed—for some people, anyway.

Imagine that the bank notes in your country have been chipped and all your cash is broadcasting its presence for several feet in every direction. RFID chip readers are easy to come by and quite cheap. Even if the bank-note chips are protected in some way, a clever hobbyist will inevitably find a way to modify the readers so they can be used to scan crowds of people and determine at a distance whose pockets are especially full. Suppose you've got a substantial amount of money on you one night while you're walking alone. A man holding an electronic box in one hand suddenly appears and menaces you with a weapon he's holding in the other. Congratulations, citizen; you've just been pre-qualified for a mugging.

Chipping bank notes is a fine security system indeed. Unfortunately, it's also a major threat to personal safety. It's good for a few people in a limited set of circumstances and bad for everyone else, like a lot of security measures. The political influence and financial power of those for whom it's good will always determine whether or not you and I get stuck with it. Common sense is rarely a factor in these decisions.

Security and safety are *not* the same; at times, they're mutually exclusive. There is such a thing as too much security and too much emphasis on it. You must always ask yourself, is this *better*, or just *more*? Both cost money, but "more" is a waste of it and a needless inconvenience, and perhaps even dangerous, unless it *is* better. There are security practitioners acting on your behalf whose agendas are in direct conflict with yours, yet whose decisions you can't escape. It is, quite simply, important not to trust. Cooperate if you must, but don't put your faith in the mysterious. Security is chiefly a matter of common sense; if a scheme is too complicated or too opaque for you to understand, chances are there's a rain dance going on.

Database Hell

The amount of information stored in databases connected to the Internet is staggering: a person's entire financial, medical, travel, and commercial history can be reconstructed from vast electronic repositories. Worse, businesses and government agencies are now using the Internet to make accessing data convenient from remote locations. A database that ten years ago could be accessed only by local users on an internal network can now be accessed from any computer equipped with a modem. This represents a tremendous multiplication of data access points and a multiplication of people who have access to data, and this development in itself poses a tremendous security risk. The more convenient it is for authorized users to access a database, the easier it is for intruders to access it as well.

The growth of data storage and retrieval mechanisms and their complexity ensures that abuse is inevitable. It also ensures that mistakes are both more plentiful and increasingly difficult to identify and correct. You may one day find that a business or government bureau that you deal with has inaccurate information about you, and you may find it fairly easy to correct that particular problem. But because data is shared promiscuously nowadays, you may find that a dozen other databases have obtained the same inaccurate information. Getting all of that sorted out is a real trial. For one thing, you may not be able to identify all of the databases in which inaccurate information is being stored: some may never come to your attention. Another problem is that when you attempt to correct the record, the people in charge of it may trust the source more than they trust you, and make correcting it next to impossible.

For example, let's imagine that you've discovered an error in your records maintained by the Social Security Administration, and let's suppose that you've been able to get it corrected. But let's imagine further that the motor vehicle administration has that same inaccurate information in its own database. If so, they may well tell you that the information can't be wrong because it comes from a trusted source: the Social Security Administration. Anyone who's ever attempted to hold a rational conversation with a clerk at the motor vehicle administration knows that getting a problem like that sorted out can be a monumental endeavor fraught with frustration and frequent temptations to violence. Now imagine that six other government bureaus and two credit bureaus have received the same inaccurate data. You could spend years trying to correct a simple error caused by one bureau, but propagated to numerous others thanks to the ease with which information can now be shared and databases merged. Anyone who's been a victim of identity theft already knows how maddeningly resistant to challenge erroneous data can be in today's information economy. Errors successfully cleared from one database may later be reintroduced from another "trusted" source containing the same erroneous data.

Welcome to database hell.

CAPPS II

The Computer Assisted Passenger Prescreening System (CAPPS II) is a database disaster in waiting. It is supposed to prevent terrorists and violent criminals from flying in commercial airplanes. It works by searching commercial and government databases to create a risk profile of each ticket holder before they board a plane. The system is a product of Lockheed Martin Corporation, an aviation defense contractor no doubt anointed by Bush administration Transportation Secretary Norman Mineta, a former Lockheed Martin vice president. CAPPS II is complicated, and expensive, and prone to monumental failure. It's a prime example of an elaborate security rain dance.

There is a lot wrong with this system. For one thing, it represents a tremendous invasion of privacy for the traveling public. For another, it amounts to a virtual interrogation in anticipation of suspicion, rather than interrogation in reply to suspicion, for centuries a general principle of good criminal justice and civil liberty.

CAPPS II creates profiles of each passenger based on the their credit history, financial stability, travel history, and criminal history, with a liberal sprinkling of secret intelligence data. Some of the criteria will be kept secret by the Department of Transportation and the Department of Homeland Security. Each traveler will be assigned a code indicating that they are fit for a standard, minimal security check, require a more elaborate and intrusive security check, or should not be permitted to fly at all. Bringing all this data together from both government and commercial sources and making it accessible to every airline clerk in the United States makes data security and data integrity impossible to ensure, and invites abuse by administrators, bureaucrats, incompetent clerks, contractors and their staff, and overzealous law-enforcement officials.

In testimony before the U.S. Senate Committee on Commerce, Science, and Transportation in November of 2003, Transportation Security Administration (TSA) Deputy Administrator Stephen McHale explained that, "CAPPS II will conduct a risk assessment of each passenger using national security information and information provided by passengers during the reservation process, including name, date of birth, home address, and home phone number, and provide a 'risk score' to TSA. The 'risk score' includes an 'authentication score' provided by running passenger name record (PNR) data against commercial databases to indicate a confidence level in each passenger's identity. CAPPS II will be a threat-based system under the direct control of the federal government and will represent a major improvement over the decentralized, airline-controlled system currently in place.

"CAPPS II would not retain data on U.S. passengers who are permitted to fly. Information would be stored only for a sufficient time to assess that a U.S. traveler is who he or she claims to be and to evaluate government information related to terrorist threats and practices. Information would not be kept after completion of the traveler's reserved itinerary, apart from a necessary audit trail that would not be searchable by passenger name or other personal identifier," McHale explained.

The system won't maintain records of its search results, which means that each traveler will be assessed each time he flies. This is a necessary precaution allowing the system to respond to new data and shifting threat conditions. But it also means that an innocent person cleared repeatedly for years might be flagged later, as erroneous data inevitably leaks into the system. Worse, a victim of bad data who goes to the trouble of clearing his record will be susceptible to a new error as soon as he's finished sorting things out. Because the system will be used repeatedly and will remain open to new information, a person can fall victim to errors at any time, initiating a fresh game of database whack-a-mole.

CAPPS II won't prevent most terrorists from flying; instead, it will increase the probability of a successful terrorist attack using commercial aircraft. The reason should be obvious: a group can very conveniently use this system to prescreen its members and find out which of them have profiles that result in extra scrutiny. CAPPS II is a good tool for terrorists to use in assessing airport defenses. A group of unarmed terrorists can simply board two or three flights in succession and observe how the system reacts to them. If, after a few trial runs, they discover that they're allowed to board unchallenged, they can assume that their profiles do not trigger a warning. Armed with that information, they'll stand a good chance of mounting a real attack.

The CAPPS II system is a product that a big defense contractor wishes to sell at a tidy profit. It is a security solution in search of a problem to solve. Lockheed Martin's agenda is to sell the system and serve its shareholders, not make flying safer.

The scheme fails in two ways: first, it creates a false sense of security among airline staff and passengers who would otherwise be more watchful; second, it gives terrorists an excellent training device that they can use as often as necessary to assemble a group of people who can get onto airplanes without arousing suspicion. CAPPS II is an effective terrorist tool and a preposterous security system. It makes it far more likely that another spectacular terrorist atrocity involving aircraft will be carried out in the future. Here again: *more* security, *less* safety. If the system were not used, then it would fall to airport and airline staff and passengers to remain observant, an immensely saner and more effective approach.

A false sense of security is always more dangerous than no security. However, corporations have been eager to capitalize on terrorism fears with expensive technological Band-Aids like face recognition gear and CAPPS II, and bureaucrats and politicians are always eager to pacify the public with frequent reference to mystifying high-tech gizmos, even when reassurance creates a more dangerous situation. A vigilant public is the best possible deterrent to terrorist attacks; unfortunately, bureaucrats, law-enforcement officials, and security vendors would sooner hang themselves than confess this essential truth.

Any experienced database administrator (DBA) will tell you that data integrity is a constant challenge, one where success rates above 95 percent are considered excellent. Even at a good rate like this, with hundreds of millions of people cataloged in thousands of different databases, the chance of some Kafkaesque misunderstanding becomes significant for quite a lot of people. This is one reason why it's important to control the data traces that you leave in real life and on the Internet, as we discussed in Chapter 5. The less data you leak, the fewer chances there are that you will become the victim of damaging but false information with your name on it.

The American Civil Liberties Union (ACLU) has called CAPPS II "the logical outgrowth of a bureaucratic fixation on technological quick-fixes to highly complicated international and domestic security problems."[6] I mention it here because it is undoubtedly going to involve Internet databases and the myriad points of failure, error, and insecurity that this implies. It will be abused very often and it will fail very often—far more often than it will succeed. It's an example of database hell taken to an extreme. It's also an example of IT dollars being thrown blindly at a security problem with superstitious faith that things will get better simply *because* very expensive and very complicated technology is involved.

Mindless enthusiasm for technology is hardly new. I'm reminded of Robert Graves's 1929 memoir *Good-Bye to All That,* where the British military command's superstitious faith in poison gas, then the latest thing in weapons technology, is illustrated. The gas device is called, with typical bureaucratic euphemism, "the accessory." It was scheduled for use on a still morning with no wind to carry it to the enemy, with tragicomic results. According to Graves, "A captain commanding the gas company in the front line phoned through to divisional headquarters: 'Dead calm. Impossible discharge accessory.' The answer he got was: 'Accessory to be discharged at all costs.' The spanners for unscrewing the cocks on the cylinders proved, with two or three exceptions, to be misfits. The gas men rushed about shouting for the loan of an adjustable spanner. They managed to discharge one or two cylinders. The gas went whistling out, formed a thick cloud a few yards off in No Man's Land, then gradually spread back into our trenches."

Total Poindexter Awareness

In November of 2002, the Pentagon's Defense Advanced Research Projects Agency (DARPA) unveiled plans to develop a massive database system, called the Total Information Awareness (TIA) network, under the direction of Iran–Contra scandal alumnus Admiral John Poindexter. The system would link commercial

---

6. See www.aclu.org/SafeandFree/SafeandFree.cfm?ID=13355&c=206.

databases with intelligence and law-enforcement systems to make it possible for the authorities to investigate and track virtually every citizen quickly and conveniently. A public outcry followed, and the program's name was hastily changed from *Total* Information Awareness to *Terrorism* Information Awareness, but this dodge didn't fool many people. After considerable public debate, during which time Poindexter resigned, the U.S. Congress restricted some of the TIA program but allowed other parts to proceed, though it neglected to mention which bits are being pursued.

Meanwhile, the dream of establishing law-enforcement and military intelligence databases of virtually everything done by every citizen is coming to fruition, only it's being sneaked in under state, not federal, auspices. The TIA program may have been partly de-clawed by Congress, but it lives on at the state level in an incarnation called, ominously, the MATRIX (Multistate Anti-Terrorism Information Exchange). This state scheme is a deliberate end-run around Congressional oversight. Yet there are federal dollars behind it—four million from the Department of Justice to date—which makes it clear that the Feds will be expecting to benefit from it. It's hard to resist seeing the MATRIX as an underhanded way for three-letter agencies to keep tabs on ordinary folk and their foibles, sidestepping restrictions on domestic spying instituted since the Church Committee convened in the 1970s. The conspicuous use of the phrase *anti-terrorism* in the project's name is a bright warning signal, being the standard incantation with which assaults on the liberties and privacy of ordinary citizens are justified these days.

"The MATRIX pilot project is an effort to increase and enhance the exchange of sensitive terrorism and other criminal activity information between local, state, and federal agencies," the project's Web site (www.iir.com/matrix) explains. The system will use "data analysis and data integration technology to improve the usefulness of information contained in multiple types of document storage systems."

The system is designed to give the Feds what they're not allowed to have, simply by repackaging it and delivering it through a side channel. It's also designed to track and prosecute garden-variety criminals while surrounding itself with a smokescreen composed of counterterrorist vapors. Bureaucrats and vendors alike have learned that people will tolerate greater assaults on their freedom, privacy, and dignity whenever terrorism is mentioned. There's always money to be made and power to be gained by frightening people.

The company profiting from this security pork bonanza, Florida outfit Seisint, Inc., is run by a gentleman implicated two decades ago in a drug-smuggling ring, according to the Associated Press. At this writing, the states of Alabama, Connecticut, Florida, Georgia, Kentucky, Louisiana, Michigan, New York, Oregon, Pennsylvania, South Carolina, Ohio, and Utah have signed on to the scheme. Residents of other states are safe—for the moment.

In January of 2004, the *Washington Post* reported that Northwest Airlines turned over personal data related to millions of its passengers to the U.S. National

Aeronautics and Space Administration (NASA) for experiments in counterterrorist data mining. This occurred only months after the company stated that it "did not provide that type of information to anyone." The data handed over to NASA included names, credit card details, addresses, and phone numbers. When confronted with evidence of its quite obvious and bald-faced lie, Northwest confessed the deed, but, incredibly, insisted that it hadn't violated its privacy policy.

"Our privacy policy commits Northwest not to sell passenger information to third parties for marketing purposes," the *Post* quotes the company as saying. However, "this situation was entirely different, as we were providing the data to a government agency to conduct scientific research related to aviation security and we were confident that the privacy of passenger information would be maintained," it hastened to add.[7]

This is why I said earlier that a company's privacy policy is a legal instrument enabling it to violate customer privacy without being called to answer for it. It doesn't safeguard your privacy at all; rather, it indemnifies the company against complaints brought by irate customers. Whenever you agree to a policy of this sort, you are almost always signing away rights.

In September of 2003, it was revealed that airline JetBlue had secretly turned over the personal details of five million of its passengers to a contractor developing a data-mining project for the U.S. military. The contractor, Torch Concepts of Huntsville, Alabama, merged JetBlue's passenger data with extremely sensitive personal information purchased from data-mining outfit Acxiom, one of the heavyweights of the privacy-invasion industry. Torch Concepts then attempted to estimate each JetBlue passenger's security risk with some manner of analytical hocus pocus. Needless to say, JetBlue's customers had never volunteered to be guinea pigs in this experiment.

The politically ambitious General Wesley Clark served on Acxiom's board of directors, and has gone foraging in search of Homeland Security pork on the company's behalf, according to the *Washington Post*.[8]

"A senior executive at Acxiom said Clark began knocking on doors for the company, without pay, out of patriotic impulses shortly after the September 11 attacks. Jerry Jones, Acxiom's general counsel and business development leader, said the company also wanted to do its part in the war on terrorism," the *Post* reports.

Patriots all, these well-paid consultants and wealthy corporations sacrificing our privacy and liberty on the altar of counterterrorism. But if you think terrorism is a good enough pretext to allow governments to catalog the public *en masse*, consider that Acxiom was made sport of by a malicious hacker who maintained

---

7. See www.washingtonpost.com/ac2/wp-dyn/A26037-2004Jan17?language=printer.

8. See www.washingtonpost.com/ac2/wp-dyn?pagename=article&node=&contentId=A7380-2003Sep26&notFound=true.

access to one of its databases for two years without being detected. Acxiom maintains such details as our Social Security number, sex, date of birth, occupation, income, number of offspring, address and years in residence, and vehicle ownership. The attacker, one Daniel Baas, obtained 300 passwords to Acxiom's systems and downloaded millions of sensitive records that the company maintains and sells to outsiders. Bass, who worked for one of Acxiom's contractors, even had sufficient access to *tamper* with the data. The company's clients include banks, credit associations, manufacturers, telecom companies, and now, apparently, the Transportation Security Administration and the Department of Homeland Security. Not only are these colossal commercial databases susceptible to constant error, data corruption, and misuse by employees, contractors, partners, and their employees, they are also vulnerable to malicious attack from without. Opening them to law-enforcement and national security officials is a recipe for future authoritarian nightmares.

If that weren't enough, the Markle Foundation Task Force on National Security in the Information Age, a think tank under the direction of NIPC alumnus Michael Vatis, is busy developing a plan for mass data mining through the Department of Homeland Security. Members of the outfit include former U.S. Senators, former security establishment operators, General Wesley Clark of JetBlue/Acxiom fame, and current representatives of major software vendors like Microsoft and Sun. There are also two privacy advocates, who one hopes are not mere token appointments but suspects will be used chiefly as window dressing.

The Markle Foundation will be applying PR spin and slick marketing tactics to create a monster federal database with a friendly face. They're proposing what they call "a trusted network for Homeland Security"[9] with the palpably nonthreatening acronym SHARE, standing for *Systemwide Homeland Analysis and Response Exchange Network*. This is the warm and cuddly version of Total Poindexter Awareness: a new system "which would empower all participants to be full and active partners in protecting our security, and which would be governed by guidelines designed to protect our liberties," we're assured.

"As the recent controversies surrounding DARPA's Terrorist Information Awareness program and an Army contractor's use of JetBlue passenger data demonstrate, government access to, and use of, privately held data remains a vexing problem ... the Task Force notes that the government should effectively utilize the valuable information that is held in private hands, but only within a system of rules and guidelines designed to protect civil liberties," the organization says.

There's that phrase again: "protect liberties," a perennial favorite of U.S. Attorney General and Lord Protector John Ashcroft. Clearly, the public-relations emphasis will be on privacy assurance. But the unholy union of vast commercial databases maintained by the American privacy-invasion industry and those maintained by government authorities should not inspire confidence in anyone.

---

9. See www.markle.org.

Such a system will be riddled with erroneous data that citizens may never succeed in correcting, assuming they ever come to know of it. And it will be hacked: there will be too many points of access for it ever to be made secure. It will be abused daily by overzealous police officials in thousands of jurisdictions; it will incriminate the innocent; it could be used as leverage in extorting confessions ("Look, we *have* your records; we *know* you're guilty; sign the confession and spare your family any more grief"); it might even be used to target minority populations both political and ethnic; and it will almost certainly fail to prevent any terrorist attacks. But it will be used. It's inevitable: sooner or later the U.S. government *will* have its point-and-click digital dragnet. It amounts to investigation and interrogation *prior* to suspicion according to criteria that the subject is ignorant of and defenseless against, a practice reminiscent of the Salem witch trials and the Spanish Inquisition, only now festooned in modern, high-tech costume. It will do far more harm than good. It will injure innocent people, but it won't prevent terrorist atrocities. Still, tech companies and bureaucrats alike will tout its "advanced technology" and speak of it with a warm, patriotic glow. This may sound like the arrival of Big Brother, but it's not so much Orwell's *1984* as Kafka's *The Trial* we should be reminded of here.

Palladium

Microsoft and other software giants, along with hardware giants Intel and AMD, are involved in a security scheme called Next-Generation Secure Computing Base (NGSCB), previously known as Palladium. As *Total* Information Awareness became *Terrorism* Information Awareness in response to public criticism, so *Palladium*, when it was denounced in the technology press, quickly became the yawn-inducing *NGSCB*, an eminently forgettable name. Whatever it's called, it's essentially is a low-level authentication scheme that will enable your hardware to recognize certified software. It makes it possible for a user to prevent untrusted software from running on his machine. That is, a user might choose only certain vendors whose products he trusts. The Palladium system would work at the hardware level and automatically verify that any software attempting to run conforms to the user's preferences. It would make it more difficult for attackers to forge software certificates and feed malware or bogus updates and patches to unsuspecting victims. It could also be used to verify the origin of documents, even e-mail.

There are other uses. Devices could be certified for access to a network. Even software such as network clients could be certified. In the corporate realm, this sort of authentication might be used to lock unwanted devices, unwelcome users, and even unwanted systems and clients, out of a network. It would make it easier for companies to prevent local users from inadvertently installing insecure clients or malware behind the firewall.

It sounds like a security panacea, and that fact alone should be setting off alarm bells. While Palladium has the potential to make securing large, private networks easier and offers clear benefits to network admins, there are several nasty implications for Internet users and retail consumers of PCs and software.

First off, Palladium is, at its core, a mechanism for denying access and privileges on a computer system. This is fine when the system is entirely under the administrator's control, but it's a dangerous mechanism that could allow software makers, OEMs, and even ISPs to dictate to users what software they can and cannot use on their own PCs. For example, if AOL doesn't want you to use an open-source chat client on its AIM network, it could, if it wished, force you to use an adware-infected proprietary client from which it derives revenue. The Palladium system would simply reject connections from unauthorized clients. If Microsoft doesn't want you to use OpenOffice or Mozilla on a Windows computer, the company could prevent them from running or break their functionality in the name of "security" and "trusted computing." If a media content provider doesn't want you to use an open-source media player on your computer, it could prevent its content from running on any but approved ones. This could get as bad as, say, a Sony DVD playing only on a Sony device. Game consoles already work this way.

If an OEM wanted only software from Microsoft and its approved partners to run on the PCs it sells, it would be able to enforce this discipline easily with Palladium. The machine would simply fail to boot with any other operating system or refuse to launch any unapproved software. It would even be possible for an ISP to prevent you from using an open-source operating system. It would be quite easy to prevent all PCs except those running a Palladium-enabled version of Windows from connecting to the Internet. It would also be trivial to lock out e-mail from clients not similarly approved. An ISP could force customers to use a Palladium-enabled version of Microsoft Outlook, say, in the name of spam reduction.

Palladium or NGSCB could also be used to enforce *digital rights management* (DRM) access controls that go far beyond the stated goal of piracy prevention. Indeed, it would give content providers unlimited control over what consumers can do with movies and music they've purchased. If you wish to rip a CD to your hard disk in order use your computer to play music that you've paid for, Palladium could make it impossible. If the content distributor doesn't *authorize* you to make a copy, your computer can be designed so that it simply will not perform the task.

The entertainment industry has put tremendous effort into spreading disinformation that associates unauthorized copying with piracy. It is important to know that *unauthorized* use is not the same as *illegal* use, and that copying is not the same as piracy. Copying content for personal use is a right affirmed by the U.S. Supreme Court's 1984 Sony decision. Piracy, on the other hand, is a federal crime.

DRM allows content providers to enforce their own use restrictions independent of the legal system. It may be legal for you to copy a piece of music, but it's also legal for the entertainment cartel to prevent you from doing so with a technological access control. The industry uses DRM to thwart piracy, but it also uses it to prevent legal copying. This is because the cheapest way to thwart pirates is to stamp out the copying of digital media in every situation. By declining to authorize copying, the entertainment industry is curbing legal behavior in order to curb illegal behavior. Unfortunately, through the DMCA, Congress granted the industry the right to do this. According to the Act, even when what you wish to do is perfectly legal, circumventing a DRM scheme is a federal crime. The law allows content providers to interfere with the legal activities of consumers, yet makes it a crime for consumers to circumvent these measures. DRM schemes and Palladium can be used together to prevent consumers from taking legal action that the music and movie cartels simply decline to authorize.

This is not to say that these things will happen, but Palladium/NGSCB makes them all possible. And the technology itself establishes a rationale for moving in these directions: it offers security; it promises fewer viruses, less malware, and less spam. The public has become so exasperated with Microsoft bugware that Palladium, bad as it might be for consumers, could be well received if it were marketed properly. The Redmond behemoth has enough partners such as content providers, ISPs, OEMs, and independent software vendors (ISVs) eager to please it that Palladium could be pushed on consumers from several directions.

There are good profits to be made from product lock-ins, and Palladium could become the foundation for a network of IT industry partners seeking to limit consumer choice for their collective benefit. Businessmen and PR bunnies like to use the fatuous word *synergy* to describe mutually beneficial forces in commerce where *a* promotes the growth of *b* and *b*'s growth promotes either *a* or another facet of the company that sells *a*. A simple example of this would be if your ISP were to offer a discount to users of Palladium-enabled Windows computers on the rationale that such users represent a lower risk for spam, virus propagation, and bandwidth abuse. Microsoft would kick money back to the ISP through a partnership back channel in exchange for promoting the use of Windows and Microsoft clients. The kickback would exceed the cost of the discount, and both companies would profit. That's synergy: two or more companies collectively pressuring you to lock in with a particular product line, arranged so that they all benefit. It boils down to this: "To use our service, you must buy our partner's product." This is good for trade and bad for consumers because it limits choice, a factor that exerts downward pressure on retail prices. When choice is limited, prices rise. Unfortunately, Palladium could easily be used to enforce profitable product and vendor lock-ins.

In time, Microsoft could begin to regulate the applications you'll be permitted to run on your own computer. This would bring the PC in line with the Xbox, a device that simply will not run any software that MS hasn't approved. Eventually, the PC might evolve into nothing more than a slave appliance controlled by Microsoft, or perhaps by one's ISP or OEM in partnership with Microsoft, and merely *operated* by its owner, like a game console or a cable TV set-top box. Redmond is already marketing Palladium as a security enhancement to protect your system from malware and spam. However, it can as easily become a tool to protect your system from *you*.

The only question is whether the big tech firms would try to use it as a means of limiting consumer choice and increasing their revenues with excessive lock-ins, forced upgrades, or worse, continual payment plans (pay-per-use). Imagine that in the future, consumer software licenses will be granted for a fixed period. Palladium would make it trivial for a vendor to disable your software automatically unless you either pay to extend the license or purchase an upgrade. It would allow content providers to enforce a pay-per-use scheme as well. That's not far from extortion, but it is a real possibility. Large corporations will not have to put up with this abuse because they have market clout. No ISP is going to reject a large corporate customer because they prefer Linux or BSD over Windows. But retail consumers are easy to push around; they're poorly organized and have few lobbyists. They'll have serious difficulty voting with their wallets when there are no practical alternatives for them to turn to.

It would be wise for consumers to reject Palladium, or Next-Generation Secure Computing Base (NGSCB) as it's now called, because its potential for abuse by content providers, software vendors, ISPs, and OEMs is virtually limitless. It makes no sense to place this much power in their hands and simply hope that they'll never abuse it.

Aside from its obvious potential to enslave consumers, Palladium has other problems. Conceptually, it's a rather fragile security system, a measly elaboration of the company's failed "trust zones" scheme. If users are granted control over it, then it's merely something else to click Yes to. In other words, when the user is about to install a piece of malware, a warning dialog will pop up asking something like, "Windows cannot certify wicked_trojan.exe. Install anyway? Y/N." This is why I would expect Palladium to evolve toward regulating user control over the system. It won't afford much security so long as it allows such decisions. On the other hand, as the personal computer becomes even more of a black box, a different set of security problems emerges. A loss of user control makes it difficult, perhaps impossible, to apply temporary workarounds, to simplify a system so that there are fewer openings for attack, and to control data traces and verify their destruction. Remember, to enhance security, your system has got to be transparent and you have got to be in complete control of it. Palladium will never offer good security, but it will make it impossible for us to achieve better. It will become a mediocre security baseline that we cannot move past. Furthermore, there is always the danger with any one-size-fits-all security scheme that when one system is compromised, all systems may be compromised. A single exploit could affect every user. Palladium will be yet another Microsoft system requiring regular patching and firmware updates, as if there weren't enough already.

As we discussed in Chapter 6, two of the most objectionable properties of Microsoft software are its lack of transparency to the user and the company's control over its functions. Palladium will eventually make both of these conditions worse than they already are. Redmond's own history in software development tells us that the Windows PC will steadily become more of a black box and that MS will assert ever greater control over it. Neither of these developments is good for computer security or for consumers, but they offer a lot of potential to industry heavyweights. And not just Microsoft: Palladium is a general mechanism for delivering mediocre security on the condition that vendor lock-ins be tolerated. Palladium, like so many security schemes, will serve the interests of a few at the expense of many.

Trust Nothing, Fear Nothing

I hope by now I've made you quite paranoid. Paranoia is a healthy perspective from which to approach computer security, but it is grossly unhealthy and quite unnecessary to be riddled with anxiety. By using common sense and layers of protection, you can make your system an unattractive target. By being paranoid in a healthy way, I mean quite simply that you must never trust anything that you don't grasp fully. And you must never accept as truth what another person tells you unless you understand what they're saying. But I definitely *don't* mean "be afraid." There's a whole antivirus and computer-security industry and a plethora of government agencies devoted to frightening you with constant reference to imminent threats. It's very much in their interest that you be frightened at all times and that new threats surface regularly to revive public anxiety as older ones fade into story.

There's far more myth than truth in circulation and a lot more bad security than good. It's hardly a record that inspires confidence. And that's my point. We become victims for one reason: because we trust. We assume that the computer guys at Kinko's know how to protect their systems from malware, but in truth, most of them probably know less than you do right now. We trust journalists to give us the straight dope, but most of them wouldn't know it if they stumbled over it. We trust that professional programmers and Webmasters know enough about security to design software and systems that we can rely on. And that's where we go wrong. There is no minimum level of experience or education required of programmers or computer technicians, or even tech journalists. There is no regulatory agency ensuring that sensitive applications are designed, built, and installed by qualified people. We are all free to hire anyone who seems to know more than we do about computers to advise us, and even design and install our systems, applications, and networks. The fellow who installed the shopping cart software on an e-commerce Web site that you do business with may not have had the faintest idea how to secure it. If he did a default installation, it will almost certainly be riddled with holes. He can know a good deal more than the site owner or Webmaster, and to him appear to be an expert, and still not know a fraction of what's needed to perform a reasonably secure installation.

Trust is where we go wrong. So stop doing it. Don't trust your firewall; don't trust your anonymizing proxy; don't trust crypto; don't trust SSL or SSH; don't trust your software vendor; don't trust files you get from anywhere, including your friends and "official" download sites; don't trust patches; don't trust your file-wipe utility. Indeed, don't trust *me*. Trust only what you understand. Trust only what you can verify.

In the past few years, we've seen Microsoft patches that break applications; we've seen more security holes in Internet Explorer, Outlook, and Outlook Express than just about any applications ever designed; we've seen Microsoft neglect to fix a major flaw in Passport and Wallet because it wanted to conceal the problem; we've seen a backdoored version of OpenSSH; we've seen that SSL is vulnerable on a LAN; we've seen an anonymizing service backdoored by the Feds; we've seen a PGP plugin for Outlook that coughs up your passphrase, not due to a flaw in the algorithm or cryptosystem, but because the application itself is susceptible to a buffer overflow. We've also seen man-in-the-middle attacks against SSL, PGP, and GnuPG. You've got three layers there—algorithm, cryptosystem, and application—any one of which might be broken in any number of ways. If you wouldn't know how to spot a subtle security flaw in a complex piece of software like that, then why would you trust it?

Your crypto application's own text editor is supposed to prevent clear-text versions of encrypted files from being held in RAM or swapped to disk, both while they're being composed and again when they're decrypted. But are you *certain* that it does?

By all means *use* security utilities and services, but never trust any of them fully. No single product, no one procedure or scheme, will make your system secure. You must use layers of defense, apply common sense, and always assume that no matter what you do, there will be ways to compromise your privacy and security. You can make it difficult, but you can't make it impossible. So don't expect it to be impossible, and don't *need* it to be impossible. Think about how to get by with its being difficult instead.

Again, the three essential layers of computer security are

- *Prevention:* Keeping a low profile on line, using more trustworthy open-source clients and applications, and avoiding risky behavior like opening e-mail attachments

- *Resistance:* Making your machine difficult to attack by firewalling, disabling services, and tightening user permissions

- *Tolerance:* Using encryption and practicing data hygiene so that the fruits of a compromise are worthless to an attacker

Security professionals call this strategy *defense in depth*, and it is the core concept behind all effective computer security tactics. It is absolutely the way to go, so long as it doesn't become *defense in excess*.

Don't overdo things. Use layers of protection, and keep them simple. Leave the smallest footprint possible on the Web by taking advantage of an anonymizing service; use aliases and alias e-mail accounts liberally on line; be extremely stingy with personal information; never trust other people's equipment; and make your machine difficult to crack so that 95 percent of remote attackers will simply move on to one of the millions of easier targets hooked up to the Net. But be assured that nothing will make a compromise impossible except keeping your computer locked in a vault with no Internet access, which of course is no fun at all.

To use your computer and surf the Web without anxiety, simply refuse to trust your own machine, any network whether local or remote, any single security tool or service, any crypto scheme, any slogan like Trustworthy Computing, any digital certificate, any trust authority, any local client, or any remote host. Practice defense in depth, but never assume that it's foolproof.

Now you're paranoid in a healthy way, yet free from anxiety. Your computer, his network, their shopping cart—these things aren't the digital equivalent of bank vaults. So don't treat them as if they were, and move on and enjoy your life.

If you're cautious and skeptical, and apply common sense to security, the odds against a system compromise or major invasion of privacy will be very much in your favor. But always remember that, regardless of the odds, it's foolish to wager something you can't afford to lose. Your credit card number is not a big deal: your total liability is $50 if you report its misuse promptly and you can get a new one in a week or so. The combination of your credit card number, Social Security number, name, date of birth, and address packaged together is a far greater worry because it makes identity theft easy, so never give out more information than absolutely necessary to complete a transaction, and never let the merchant store your data.

Be aware that sending your computer to a repair shop can result in legal complications. Authorities in most jurisdictions actively pressure computer repairmen to search for evidence of bad behavior, such as P2P software, large caches of MP3s or movies, cracking tools, unlicensed software, and the like. Searching for kiddie porn and catching pedophiles is the blanket justification for this activity, but a good deal of unrelated snooping goes on. People whose files and electronic correspondence may be confidential, such as doctors, lawyers, journalists, and the like, can inadvertently violate confidentiality agreements simply by turning a machine over to a repairman. When a computer breakdown is not related to a hard disk drive (i.e., the problem persists when you boot from other media), you should remove all of your hard drives before having the machine repaired. The technician can boot it from removable media to confirm that his repairs were effective.

Use as many online aliases and Web-mail accounts as you please. If you create, and always access, a Web-mail account through a good anonymizing service and decline to give out any identifying information while registering, mail sent from that account can't be traced to you or your computer. Identify yourself only to people and businesses you know and trust in real life. Never open e-mail attachments, or files proffered via IRC, IM, P2P, or Web sites without scanning them; but always bear in mind that virus scans won't catch all malware. Use a firewall or packet filter and an anonymizing proxy. Encrypt your sensitive files and electronic correspondence. Practice good data hygiene. Disable unnecessary services. Take advantage of a multiuser system. Keep an eye on your children whenever they go on line. And always use open-source products whenever you can.

Now breathe. And enjoy your computer.

Glossary

*nix	Abbreviation of UNIX, often meant to indicate a family of operating systems including BSD and Linux.
0-day	See *zero-day*.
ActiveX	A set of Microsoft programming technologies related to OLE (object linking and embedding) and COM (Component Object Model). Not a programming language, but a set of approaches for enabling programs to interact with other programs and computer systems, often without user supervision or control.
ActiveX controls	ActiveX-based programs that can be downloaded from a Web page and executed automatically. Microsoft unwisely gives these programs more authority and privilege on a Windows system than the user running them. When malicious or poorly designed, ActiveX controls are among the most dangerous forms of malware in circulation. They should be avoided.
Admin	See *sysadmin*.
Administrator	The most powerful user account on a Windows system.
Adware	Putatively "free" software programs that fetch advertisements and display them on the user's desktop to pay for development. It is trivial to design adware that violates a user's privacy without their knowledge. Vendor assertions of privacy protection and other platitudes cannot be trusted, and adware should always be avoided. Open-source substitutes should be sought.

NOTE *Some material derived from Webopedia (www.webopedia.com) and used by permission. Copyright 2004 Jupitermedia Corporation. All Rights Reserved.*

Algorithm	A mathematical routine or series of mathematical steps for solving a problem or accomplishing a task.
Anonymity	1. A condition in which one might be observed but cannot be recognized or identified. 2. A condition in which a group's behavior might be observed but cannot be associated with a particular member.
Anonymous proxy server	See *proxy server*.
API	Acronym for application program interface, a set of protocols and tools for developing software applications. APIs can be thought of as modular building blocks. The use of common APIs in different programs helps promote consistency in the user experience, or "look and feel," of different applications.
Applet	A program designed to be executed by an application rather than the operating system. For example, Java applets embedded in Web pages are executed by the browser's Java Virtual Machine.
Application	A software program that enables users to perform tasks, such as word processing, as opposed to software that provides system functionality, such as an operating system, daemon, driver, or utility.
Application-layer firewall	A specialized firewall designed to protect particular applications, capable of detecting malicious network traffic.
Authentication	The business of verifying a user's claimed identity without necessarily identifying him personally. A username and password combination is a common form of authentication.
Authorization	The business of regulating access to a system or a resource.
Backdoor (also *trapdoor*)	An undocumented means of access to a program, service, or system. Programmers often code backdoors into software, sometimes to aid in system recovery, sometimes for malicious purposes.
Bash	Bourne Again Shell. A popular open-source UNIX-compatible command shell.
Batch file	A text file containing a series of commands to be executed automatically, also called a shell script. On Windows, it usually has the extension .bat, .btm, or .cmd. On Linux, it usually has the extension .sh or .run.
Binary	An executable file.

BIOS	Acronym for basic input–output system. Software that boots a computer independent of the operating system. The BIOS program usually resides on a ROM (read-only memory) chip or a flash memory chip.
Blackhat	A malicious hacker or cracker. A computer criminal.
Buffer	A temporary data storage area in RAM. Many programs hold data in a buffer while computational tasks are being performed.
Buffer overflow	Buffers are created in fixed sizes. When a buffer is sent more data than it can hold, the data overflows. Attackers can cause a buffer to overflow in order to fill it with malicious code and force a computer to execute malicious instructions.
Cache	Any one of several data storage methods designed to improve performance. For example, when system resources are in demand, a disk cache will hold data in memory and write it later, when the system is idling. Data recently read from the disk is stored in memory so that programs can access it quickly, without searching the disk. A Web site might cache its pages or images on several proxy servers, thereby accommodating more users at a time.
Carding	The practice of stealing or counterfeiting credit cards and credit card account information.
Checksum	See *message digest*.
Circuit proxy	A type of firewall that sits between a computer and a network and acts as a gateway, shielding the computers behind it. A NAT router is a common example of a circuit proxy.
Client	A software program used to access a server. For example, a browser is a client that fetches Web pages and allows a user to interact with a Web server. An e-mail program is a client that sends mail to an SMTP server or fetches it from a POP server.
CMOS	Acronym for complementary metal oxide semiconductor. A type of chip often used in battery-powered devices. For example, a computer's BIOS setup data is often stored on a battery-powered CMOS chip.

Command	An instruction entered by a user that is then translated into an instruction that a computer can execute. Text entered at the command shell, mouse clicks, and hotkey combinations can all serve as commands.
Command interpreter	A software component that translates commands into instructions a computer can execute. Sometimes used interchangeably with command processor.
Command processor	A software component that executes commands. Sometimes used interchangeably with command interpreter.
Command shell	The user interface to a command processor, for example, the DOS prompt in Windows.
Cookie	A small file downloaded from a Web server onto a computer, often without user interaction or consent. Originally, cookies were a means of maintaining connection state information during an HTTP session. They are now used for authentication and for commercial tracking and profiling.
CPU	Acronym for central processing unit. The hardware component of a computer that executes instructions and performs calculations. On large machines, the CPU is often integrated with a circuit board and other components such as memory chips, and removed or inserted as a module. On most PCs, the CPU is contained in a single chip called a microprocessor, which can be removed from the motherboard and replaced independent of other components.
Cracker	A person adept at defeating technological access controls. Cracking emphasizes analysis over creativity, though both elements are involved. Often used by the media as a synonym for computer criminal. See also *hacker*.
Cross-site scripting (XSS)	Malicious scripts in Web pages or sent via HTML e-mail that enable a remote attacker to interfere with a browser session. Any Web page that accepts user input can be susceptible to XSS. Microsoft's Internet Explorer browser has proved exceptionally easy to attack in this manner. See also *man in the middle*.
Cryptosystem	The basic architectural model with which encryption is put to use. A one-way hash function is one type of cryptosystem. An asymmetrical paired-key system is another.

CVS	Acronym for concurrent versions system. An open-source system used by developers to organize and merge various versions of source code. CVS maintains the code and records the changes made by each developer involved. When a developer requests a particular version, CVS automatically creates it from the records of changes that it maintains. When a bug is discovered, CVS makes it easy to identify the change that caused it. The combination of CVS and the modular design of open-source software helps developers fix bugs quickly.
Daemon	A background process invoked by software programs as needed to provide special functions. Daemons are usually not invoked directly by users, but rather by software in response to user demands. On Windows, a daemon is called a *system agent*, and a daemon process is called a *service*.
Database	Essentially, an electronic filing system. A large collection of data structured to simplify the retrieval of particular items according to a wide range of criteria. A telephone directory is a database organized alphabetically. The same information stored in a modern electronic database can be searched according to virtually limitless criteria: e.g., the names of every person living on a certain street with an odd-numbered address containing the numeral 5. Everyone whose given name is seven letters long and ends in the letter *o*. Everyone whose surname contains the letter combination *dz* and lives on a street containing the letter combination *ka*.
Datagram	A data packet. A piece of a message transported via a network.
Data hygiene	The practice of controlling access to data, eliminating duplicate data traces on a local machine and across a network, and destroying data securely.
Data trace	A secondary or tertiary copy of data created by an operating system or a software application, or stored on a remote server, often without the user's knowledge.
DBA	Acronym for database administrator. A sysadmin in a lab coat.

DDoS	Acronym for distributed denial of service: a nuisance attack that overwhelms bandwidth, server capacity, or other system resources. It is called *distributed* when numerous compromised hosts are used.
Dead drop	An abandoned or unattended location where goods or data can be delivered. Credit card fraudsters often arrange delivery of pilfered goods to an abandoned house or office where they can collect the merchandise without calling attention to themselves. On line, spammers and malicious hackers can use an unattended server or an anonymous Web-mail account as a destination to collect harvested data such as passwords and credit information.
Defense in depth	The practice of layering several different defensive strategies. The central concept of good computer security.
DHCP	Acronym for Dynamic Host Configuration Protocol. A system that automatically assigns IP addresses to hosts on a network. Many ISPs use DHCP to assign IP addresses to users each time they connect. It can also be used on a LAN to simplify network administration.
Digital signature	Code using one of several encryption techniques that identifies the creator or sender of a file or message.
Distro	Abbreviation of distribution.
DMCA	Acronym for the Digital Millennium Copyright Act. U.S. legislation, written by entertainment industry lobbyists and coaxed through Congress, intended to legitimize the cartel's monopolistic control over content production, distribution, and use.
DNS	Acronym for domain name service (also DN *system*). A network of machines dedicated to converting domain names to IP addresses. A domain name must be converted to an IP address for a connection to be made. DNS enables users to surf the Web according to domain names, which are easier to recall than their corresponding IP addresses.
Domain	A collection of hosts on a network that share address space and can be administered collectively. For example, machines at the addresses 123.1.1.1 and 123.1.1.2 would belong to the same domain.
DoS	Acronym for denial of service: a nuisance attack that overwhelms bandwidth, server capacity, or other system resources.

DOS	Acronym for disk operating system. Microsoft's early contribution to the PC revolution, comparable to Ford's early contribution to the automobile age and McDonald's early contribution to American cuisine.
DRM	Acronym for digital rights management. An electronic control scheme that regulates consumers' access to digital content, increasingly to their disadvantage.
Dynamic account	An online credit-card scheme in which a unique card number is created for each purchase. This helps ensure that a customer's credit data will be safe from fraud when a merchant's database is hacked.
Egress filtering	A feature of some personal firewalls, or *packet filters,* that will alert users when a program attempts to access the Internet. An excellent warning system for discovering malware that antivirus software neglects.
Encryption	The practice of scrambling or encoding data so that it cannot be decoded except under strict, controlled conditions.
Entropy	A state of disorganization or randomness. On Linux, system noise created by devices that is used to generate random numbers.
Ethernet	A very popular LAN architecture.
Filesystem	The basic scheme that an operating system uses to organize data on a disk. There are many different filesystems, each with its advantages and disadvantages. The Windows filesystem FAT-32 and the Linux filesystem ext2 are recommended for users concerned with data hygiene.
FSF	Acronym for Free Software Foundation. An organization dedicated to the creation and distribution of open-source software.
FTP	Acronym for File Transfer Protocol. A protocol for exchanging files via the Internet.
FUD	Fear, uncertainty, and doubt. A public appeal to danger in pursuit of money or political gain. FUD is an important product of security vendors, bureaucrats, law-enforcement officials, politicians, and gullible news reporters.
Gay	In the hacker world, a term of abuse: exhibiting poor hacking skills.

GNU	Acronym for GNU's not UNIX. A project started in 1983 by Richard Stallman, in connection with the Free Software Foundation (FSF), dedicated to the development of open-source software.
GPL	Acronym for the GNU General Public License.
GUI	Acronym for graphical user interface. A computing environment that uses graphical elements such as menus, icons, and pointing devices to accept and enter commands. A GUI is essentially a graphical command shell.
Hacker	Originally, a talented programmer. Now used chiefly to indicate talented computer enthusiasts interested in system security. Those motivated to improve security are called whitehats; those motivated to misuse what they learn are called blackhats. Hacker is often mistakenly used by the media as a synonym for computer criminal. See also *cracker*.
Handshake	An initial data exchange between two devices in anticipation of a network connection. A malicious attack based on the handshake, called a SYN flood, can tie up system resources and lead to a denial of service. See also *SYN flood*.
Hash	A one-way cryptographic function creating scrambled data that is resistant to decryption. Hashed data is not meant to be recovered.
Honeypot	1. A decoy computer system designed to attract hackers and allow others to observe their behavior. 2. A remote service, such as a free anonymizing proxy, designed to spy on users.
Host	A computer offering data or services to another computer. For example, a server is a kind of host. The term is confusing because all personal computers act as hosts, though they act as clients more often. Any machine with an IP address is called a host. Usually, one speaks of a PC as a client system because it normally requests data and services, but it's called a host by virtue of being connected to the Net or a LAN.
HTML	Acronym for Hypertext Markup Language. An easy-to-learn language used to create Web pages.

HTTP	Acronym for Hypertext Transfer Protocol. The protocol that browsers use to interact with Web servers. HTTP is stateless, meaning that connections do not maintain a history of previous activity. Cookies are used to maintain connection state information.
HTTPS	An indication that SSL (Secure Sockets Layer) is in use. Web servers that accept HTTP connections encrypted with SSL are addressed with HTTPS in the URL (uniform resource locator). See also *SSL*.
Hyperlink	A big word for a small thing: HTML code in a Web page or an HTML e-mail that acts as a pointer to other Web pages. Clicking on a hyperlink directs a Web browser to the page indicated. Note the word *hype* within.
Identity theft	A growing criminal industry in which fraudsters impersonate others and make purchases in their name. The recent, explosive growth of commercial databases has been a great boon to identity thieves.
IDS	Acronym for intrusion detection system. Software that inspects network traffic and local system behavior for patterns indicating malicious activity.
IM	Acronym for instant messaging, e.g., AOL Instant Messenger (AIM), MSN Messenger, ICQ, etc. A network of servers designed to broadcast chats among groups of users in real time. The system also accommodates individual chats. The user interface is more graphics based than IRC. All traffic is logged by the provider.
Infosec	Abbreviation of information security.
Inline script	Code delivered in the message body of an e-mail memo that can be executed without user interaction. Often dangerous.
Integrity check	The business of using a message digest or checksum to determine whether data has been altered. See also *message digest*, *MD5*.
IP	Acronym for Internet Protocol, a component of the TCP/IP protocol that makes the Internet work. IP is concerned with the format of packets, or datagrams.

IP address	A number that identifies a device uniquely on a network or the Internet. On the Net, each device must have a unique IP address. On a LAN, one can assign any IP address to any machine within it, even if it duplicates an Internet address, but its gateway must have a valid, unique Internet address. The format is four numbers separated by periods where each number can be zero to 255. Thus 123.132.231.213 is a valid IP address, while 123.321.132.312 is not.
IRC	Acronym for internet relay chat. A network of servers designed to broadcast chats among groups of users in real time. The system also accommodates individual chats. The user interface is more text based than IM. All traffic is logged by the provider.
ISP	Acronym for Internet service provider.
ISV	Acronym for independent software vendor.
Java	A popular programming language developed by Sun Microsystems that creates executable files that run on numerous computing platforms.
JavaScript	A scripting language based on Java but developed independently by Netscape to add pulsating distractions to Web sites and HTML e-mail, and consume bandwidth. Easy to learn and easy to misuse, it has become a major source of script-kiddie mischief.
Java Virtual Machine	A runtime environment enabling Java to execute on different platforms and within applications.
Kernel	The core, memory-resident component of an operating system. The kernel typically manages low-level services such as essential processes, memory, and disks. The kernel resides just above the BIOS. Higher-level components, such as drivers, libraries, and daemons, deal with peripherals, clients, applications, and the like.
Key	The component of a crypto application responsible for scrambling and unscrambling data.
Keystroke logger	Perhaps the greatest single threat to computer security. A keystroke logger captures all keyboard input in plain text. Passwords can be intercepted, leaving a well-defended system naked to an attacker. Keystroke loggers are available in both software and hardware forms. Many commercial spyware programs and rootkits contain them.

LAN	Acronym for local area network.
Legacy code	Programming code in current software left over from previous versions, sometimes to provide compatibility with older hardware and applications, sometimes left for no reason by hurried programmers.
LinTel	Linux systems running on Intel-based hardware.
Localhost	An internal, or loopback, network interface with the IP address 127.0.0.1. It enables client programs on a computer to exchange data with each other without crossing the network interface, which is useful for Internet privacy. It also enables users and developers to test network applications without crossing the network interface.
Loopback interface	See *localhost*.
Macro	A scripted routine or series of commands that can be initiated conveniently, usually with a hotkey combination.
Malware	Any software or firmware code that causes unintended system behavior or impedes intended system behavior.
Man in the middle (MIM or MITM) attack	Any of several attacks in which a malicious third party interposes himself between two points where data is being exchanged.
MD5	A popular hashing algorithm used for integrity checking, password hashing, and generating a message digest. See also *message digest*.
Message digest	Also called a *fingerprint* or a *checksum*. A brief hash created when a file is used as input. If a file is altered, its message digest will change. If the message digest of the original file is known, tampering can be detected quickly and easily by comparing the message digests.
Motherboard	The main circuit board of a PC, connecting the CPU, memory modules, and peripherals. Designed so that components can be swapped easily.
Nastygram	A threatening e-mail memo sent by lawyers in thrall to Big Business to Web site operators and their ISPs. Often used to intimidate and silence small-fry curmudgeons, satirists, and naysayers.

NAT	Acronym for network address translation. A device that enables a LAN to distribute its own internal IP addresses while using another address as an Internet gateway. It serves as a firewall by concealing the IP addresses of computers from the Internet.
NetBIOS	Acronym for network basic input–output system. A group of protocols for designing local area network (LAN) technology.
Newbie	Synonym for novice. A person ignorant of technology but willing to learn. By no means an unflattering word.
Next-Generation Secure Computing Base (NGSCB)	A new name for Palladium, Microsoft's elaboration of a failed trust scheme. When Palladium received bad reviews in the technology press, Microsoft chose this brutally dull moniker so that the public would have difficulty associating the two.
NGSCB	See *Next-Generation Secure Computing Base*.
NIC	Acronym for network interface card. An expansion card permitting computers to connect directly to a local network.
OEM	Acronym for original equipment manufacturer. Companies such as Dell, Gateway, HP, and the like, that build computer systems according to terms and specifications dictated by Microsoft and Intel.
Open source	Software distributed along with its original source code so that users can build it themselves if they wish. Providing source code ensures that the software can be examined freely and understood thoroughly, so that undesirable functions cannot be concealed.
P2P	Acronym for peer-to-peer. A networking scheme in which each machine operates in the same manner, as opposed to a client/server arrangement, where functions are specific.
Packet	A datagram. A part of a message transported via a network.
Packet filter	A software firewall that regulates access to ports.
Packet sniffer	A software program that intercepts all traffic crossing a network interface.
Palladium	See *Next-Generation Secure Computing Base*.

PC	Acronym for personal computer.
Personal firewall	See *packet filter*.
Phreak (also *phreaker*)	A person adept at manipulating the telephone system.
Ping	A packet sent to an Internet address to determine whether there is a machine at that address. Some firewalls will drop ping packets to conceal the machine they're defending.
POP	Acronym for Post Office Protocol. The protocol used to fetch messages from an e-mail server.
Port	A simple network connection interface. A logical opening through which packets flow between client and server.
Port forwarding	The practice of forwarding a client's port to a remote location from which it can be accessed via another client or a different protocol. For example, HTTP port 80 can be forwarded to an SSH server, and Web pages fetched with an SSH client, thereby concealing the HTTP traffic from prying eyes.
Power user	A person who has learned to configure and control a computer system or a software application expertly. One who can tweak a system for superior utility, performance, and security.
Privacy	The state of freedom from observation. A rare and fleeting experience in the modern world.
Privacy policy	A legal instrument enabling businesses to violate promises of confidentiality without fear of legal retaliation.
Process	Any running program executable or binary.
Protocol	Any widely accepted format for exchanging data, creating software, or designing systems.

Proxy server	A server that lies between a client and another server. Useful for distributing load on a network. For example, if a request is sent by a client, the proxy will attempt to satisfy the request before forwarding it to the server upstream. Proxies are often left open by careless admins and can be used by others without the owner's knowledge. A proxy can also be designed to provide anonymity by forwarding requests from users who connect to it. If designed properly, the traffic forwarded by the proxy cannot be associated with any particular user.
Queue	A group of pending tasks lined up sequentially and completed in turn.
Rain dance	A theatrical performance indicating that problems are being dealt with, but accomplishing little or nothing and often making the problems worse. Confiscating tweezers and corkscrews at airport security checkpoints is an example of a rain dance.
RAM	Acronym for random access memory.
Read only	An attribute of a disk volume, directory, or file that prevents data from being written, or regulates the conditions under which data can be written. See also *write protect*.
Registry	A large database used by Windows to store configuration information and numerous data traces.
RFID	Acronym for radio frequency identification. A retailing gimmick using transponders in place of bar codes.
Risk	The relative likelihood that an undesirable event will occur. Compare with *threat*.
Root	The administrator account on UNIX-compatible systems. Unlike a Windows administrator, root is omniscient and omnipotent.
Rootkit	Malware that yields complete system control to an attacker.
Router	1. A device that forwards packets along a network. 2. A gateway between two networks.
RPM	Acronym for Red Hat Package Manager, a popular, open-source software manager capable of installing, maintaining, and uninstalling pre-built software packages or source packages. Developed by Red Hat Linux, RPM can be used on any Linux system to simplify software installation and maintenance.

SCADA	Acronym for supervisory control and data acquisition. Automated computer systems that monitor and sometimes control complex mechanical systems.
Scene whore	Term of abuse: a female script kiddie.
Script	Commands or other code that can be executed without user interaction.
Script kiddie	Term of abuse: a pseudohacker or pseudocracker who uses tools and exploits developed by others. See also *wannabe*.
SE	See *social engineering*.
Sequence number	A numerical tag in TCP packets that indicates the correct order for message reassembly and helps a client and server verify that a connection has been established. There are man-in-the-middle attacks based on sequence-number guessing.
Server	A computer system that offers services to other computers over a network.
Service	See *daemon*.
Session	A two-way connection across a network.
Shell	The user interface to a program or operating system. A shell accepts commands or other user input, such as mouse actions, and translates them into instructions that a computer or a program will execute.
Shell script	See *batch file*.
SMB	1. Acronym for server message block, a Windows scheme for sharing files, directories, and devices over a network. UNIX-compatible network applications such as Samba use SMB to provide share compatibility with Windows systems. See also *NetBIOS*. 2. Acronym for small-to-medium business.
SMTP	Acronym for Simple Mail Transfer Protocol: The protocol used to send e-mail from a client to a mail server, or from one server to another.
Social engineering (SE)	The practice of manipulating people. High-tech word inflation for *con game*.
SOHO	Acronym for small office/home office.

Source code	The original product written by a programmer. A human-readable file that must be compiled to create code that a computer can execute. Executable code cannot be read by people; however, when source code is distributed along with compiled executables, or binaries, a programmer can see precisely how the executable code will function.
Spam	Unsolicited commercial e-mail. The great bounty of the New Economy.
SPI	See *stateful packet inspection*.
Spool	Acronym for simultaneous peripheral operations on line. A means of holding peripheral operations, such as print jobs, in a queue so that they can be performed as system resources permit.
Spyware	Powerful rootkits sold commercially and deliberately overlooked by antivirus products.
SSH	Acronym for secure shell. A TCP protocol providing an encrypted link between two computers. SSH can also encrypt and transport other protocols, such as HTTP, POP, FTP, etc.
SSH tunneling	The practice of using SSH to transport other network and Internet protocols through an encrypted link.
SSL	Acronym for Secure Sockets Layer. A TCP protocol that enables other network protocols to be encrypted. Often used for establishing an encrypted link between a browser and a Web server, indicated with a URL containing HTTPS. SSL is also used for authentication and certification.
State	The status and history of a network connection.
Stateful	Having the ability to use or maintain state information.
Stateful packet inspection	A feature enabling a firewall or packet filter to remember the state of existing and recent connections, automatically accepting connections from hosts the user has contacted voluntarily and rejecting others.
Stateless	A protocol, such as UDP or HTTP, that does not maintain or make use of connection state information.
Swap file/swap partition	An area of a disk reserved for memory reads and writes. See also *virtual memory*.

SYN flood	A DoS attack against a server in which the initial hand-shake is faked. When a client seeks to connect, it sends a SYN (synchronize) packet. The server sends a SYN/ACK (synchronize/acknowledge) packet in reply and allocates system resources in anticipation of a connection, or session. Finally, the client replies with an ACK (acknowledge) packet and the session begins. However, if the ACK packet fails to arrive, the server will wait for a period of time with system resources allocated. Obviously, if thousands of bad SYN packets are sent, a server can be overwhelmed. Defenses include specialized firewalls and a packet verification scheme for Linux called SYNcookies.
Sysadmin (also *admin*)	Abbreviation of systems administrator. An underpaid drudge who maintains computer systems and is blamed for all that goes wrong.
System agent	See *daemon*.
TCP	Acronym for Transmission Control Protocol, part of the TCP/IP communications protocol that makes the Internet possible. TCP is the component concerned with establishing connections, data transport, and keeping packets in order for correct reassembly.
TCP/IP	Acronym for Transmission Control Protocol/Internet Protocol. The chief communications protocol used by the Internet.
Threat	An undesirable event that is possible. Compare with *risk*.
TLS	Acronym for Transport Layer Security. A network protocol similar to SSL that encrypts traffic between a client and a server.
Transponder	A wireless communication device that both transmits and receives radio signals.
Trapdoor	See *backdoor*.
Trojan	A seemingly desirable program with a hidden malicious payload, like the legendary horse for which it's named.
UDP	Acronym for User Datagram Protocol, a stateless, or connectionless, protocol used for broadcasting messages but not for establishing a session.
URL	Acronym for uniform resource locator, the universal Internet address format consisting of the protocol followed by the domain name or the IP address.

Utility	A program that manages system resources or performs tasks related to system maintenance.
Vector	Anything that spreads or enables the spread of malware.
Virtual memory	A scheme enabling disk space to be used as memory address space. See also *swap file*.
Virus	Malware capable of replicating itself unnoticed, though with user interaction.
VPN	Acronym for virtual private network. A network using public infrastructure and relying on encryption to establish privacy.
WAN	Acronym for wide area network, e.g., the Internet.
Wannabe	Term of abuse: a script kiddie eager to be mistaken for a capable hacker or cracker.
Web bug	A small, often invisible, remote image linked in a Web page or an HTML e-mail memo. The browser or e-mail client will fetch the image automatically. When it does so, the remote server from which it's fetched can log the user's IP address and other personal information. The Mozilla browser and Mozilla e-mail client can be configured to ignore remote images.
Webmaster	A person who maintains a Web site.
WEP	Acronym for wired equivalent privacy. A mediocre encryption scheme for wireless networks.
Whitehat	A nonmalicious hacker or cracker. A security researcher.
WinTel	A Windows-based computer system running on Intel-based processors.
Wipe	To destroy a computer file by writing data over it repeatedly.
Worm	Malware that propagates without any user interaction.
Write-protect	1. To set the attributes of a disk volume, directory, or file so that no data can be written to it. 2. To confine write privileges to particular users and system components.
XSS	See *cross-site scripting*.
Zero day (also *0-day*)	The day when a previously unknown exploit is detected and reported, after which its value depreciates. The phrase is sometimes used to indicate unknown exploits.

Procedures, Processes, and Ports

Procedures

> **NOTE** *The tilde (~) can indicate two things: a shortened directory path, or a directory whose name would vary on different computers. Thus C:\Windows\Temp and C:\Program Files\Temp might be shortened to ~\Temp, and /home/*username*/Documents might appear as /home/~/Documents.*

Configuring the Mozilla Browser and Mail Client

Figure B-1 shows the History option, where I prefer to use a value of zero days. This makes the browsing history available so long as Mozilla is open. When it's closed, the history will be deleted, except for the typed-URL history. Notice that there is a button enabling you to clear the URLs that you've typed into the address bar, or location bar.

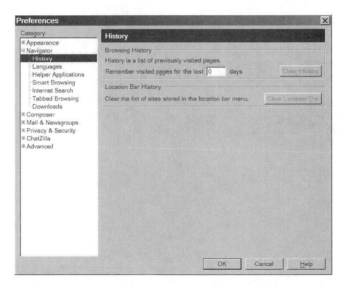

Figure B-1. Controlling data traces with the History options dialog

Next is the Downloads menu (Figure B-2), where I recommend choosing the progress dialog option over the download manager, which makes it too easy for other users to see what you've been up to. Mozilla will still record your downloads, but in Chapter 5 and later in this Appendix there are instructions to prevent Mozilla from recording your download history. The download history is the only item where Mozilla records your comings and goings without enabling you to control your data traces easily from the Preferences menu.

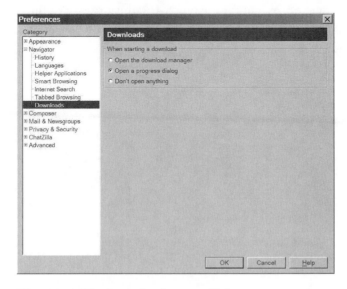

Figure B-2. The Downloads setup dialog

The option for sending automatic replies that confirm your receipt of an e-mail memo appears in Figure B-3. Obviously, it's best left off because spammers, marketers, and other Internet parasites can abuse this feature.

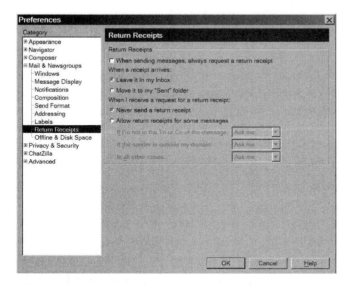

Figure B-3. Blocking return receipts

Figure B-4 shows a good, yet simple setup for handling cookies. Accepting cookies only from the originating server prevents third-party marketers from tracking you, though some Web sites, such as banking and e-commerce outfits, will sometimes use third-party cookies for authentication. In that case, you can accept cookies from those sites by using the Manage Stored Cookies feature. However, I prefer to leave third-party cookies blocked and simply toggle the setting occasionally, because the sites I visit that have legitimate uses for third-party cookies are few. It is also important to block *all* cookies in the Mozilla mail client using the second option, *Disable cookies in Mail & Newsgroups*, to help defeat spammers, and finally to limit the lifetime of cookies to your current browser session as indicated. This way, cookies will stay alive for as long as you have Mozilla open, then be deleted automatically when you close the browser. This prevents cookies from accumulating data about your comings and goings over time.

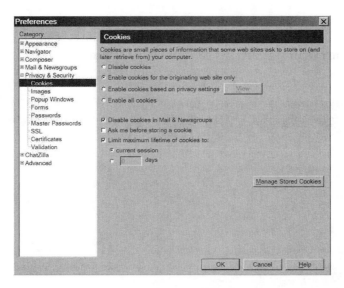

Figure B-4. Blocking third-party cookies in the browser and e-mail client

Next we have the Images setup (Figure B-5), and I strongly recommend limiting images to the originating server. This will cut down on third-party Web bugs and on third-party advertisements that only cause Web pages to load slower. You will miss a bit of content, but most of it will be junk anyway. It's very important to check *Do not load remote images in Mail & Newsgroup messages*, as indicated. This will help defeat spammers' tracer images and porn. Images attached to a memo will still display normally.

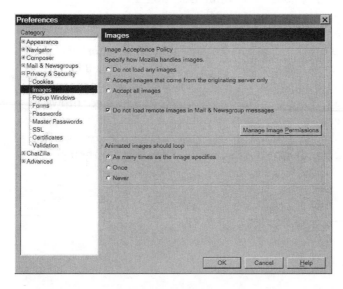

Figure B-5. Blocking third-party images in the browser and e-mail client

The option for preventing popup windows from launching is shown in Figure B-6. It's a good feature, but it doesn't work all the time. To defeat popups with certainty, you need to disable Java and JavaScript, but this will make Web surfing rather inconvenient because the majority of sites stubbornly insist on using both. On the plus side, disabling Java and JavaScript will positively eliminate popups and cause Web pages to load faster, which is an issue for 56K-ers. Choose your poison.

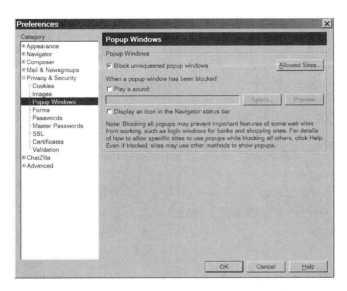

Figure B-6. Blocking popup ads

Now we come to a tricky set of options. Mozilla can collect a good deal of user information related to Web shopping, including credit card data, so that it can be entered quickly and conveniently during an online purchase. If this is configured right, it can be made adequately secure. If it's done carelessly, remote attackers and local snoops can easily obtain this data from you. The Forms, Passwords, and Master Passwords options need to be set as shown in the four examples that follow. It is reasonable to let Mozilla save form data (Figure B-7).

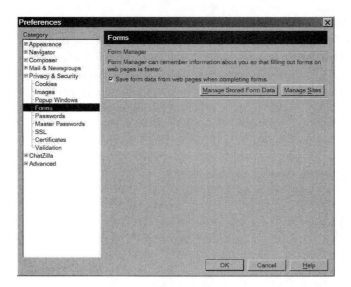

Figure B-7. Saving form data, step one

When the options are set correctly, you will receive a password prompt whenever you attempt to access the data using the Manage Stored Form Data button (Figure B-8).

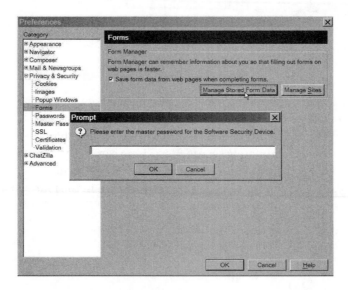

Figure B-8. The password prompt

The Passwords menu should be set so that Mozilla will remember and enter Web site passwords for you, but only if the option *Use encryption when storing sensitive data* is also selected, as shown in Figure B-9.

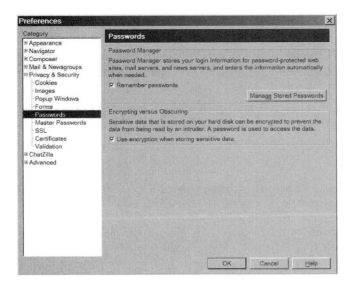

Figure B-9. Saving passwords and encrypting them

Finally, it is necessary to set a good password using the Master Passwords menu, and also to require the password each time the information is accessed (Figure B-10).

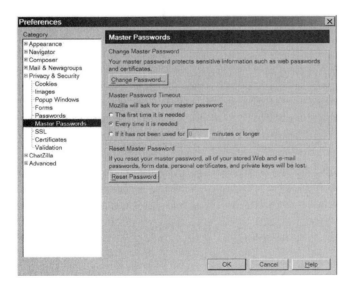

Figure B-10. Proper settings for the Master Password

Once this is done, your Web site passwords and form data will not be accessible without the master password. To verify this, go to the Form Data and Passwords menus and select the Manage buttons. You should be prompted for the master password each time. It's important that the master password be very difficult to guess, but you mustn't forget it. You can write it down and keep it in a secure place until you're confident you've memorized it, then destroy the record.

The Advanced menu enables you to toggle Java on and off (Figure B-11). Java is not much of a security hassle with Mozilla on Windows, and even less of one on Linux. There are annoyances, and there have been exploits, but the inconvenience of trying to surf the Web with it shut off is fairly daunting. If your computer is otherwise well configured for security, Java should not be a problem.

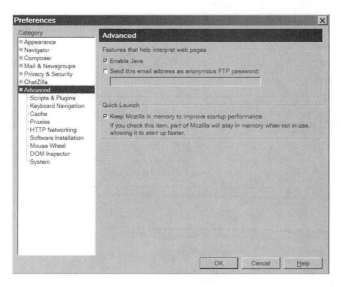

Figure B-11. Enabling Java and letting Mozilla load at boot time

The toggle for JavaScript (Figure B-12) is an item with a bit more potential for mischief, including exploit code, popups, cookie manipulation, and the like. On a Windows computer, even with Mozilla, I would be somewhat more inclined to disable JavaScript, though on a well-configured Linux machine I wouldn't worry about it, so long as the popups are under control. Allowing JavaScript, but denying its most offensive "features," as pictured in Figure B-12, is a reasonable compromise between security and convenience. Note in particular that both JavaScript and plugins are disabled for Mozilla Mail, which is quite important. Like remote images and cookies, these are things you do *not* want in your e-mail.

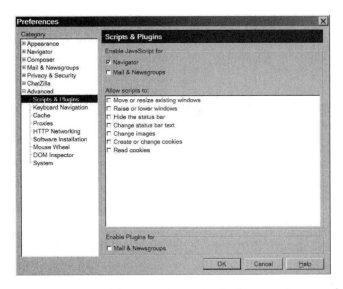

Figure B-12. Enabling JavaScript in the browser but restricting its functions, and disabling it in e-mail

The browser cache stores local copies of all the Web pages you've visited. Obviously, this is a security issue on shared computers. You can control it by limiting the available disk space and clearing it periodically (though not securely) with the Clear Cache button. I would recommend a value of 0 MB for disk space if you have a fast Internet connection (Figure B-13). Dialup users should limit its size to a few tens of MB and remember to clear it regularly.

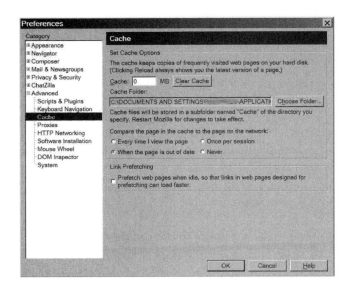

Figure B-13. Controlling the page cache

Finally, to make Mozilla Mail display incoming memos in plain text, open the mail client, go to the menu bar, and choose View ➤ Message Body As ➤ Plain Text (Figure B-14).

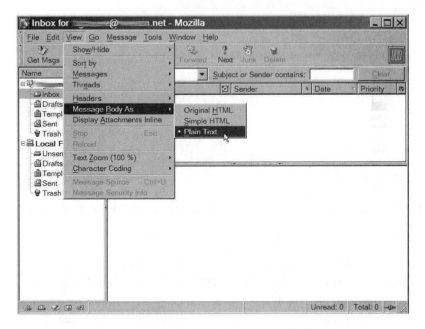

Figure B-14. Choosing plain-text display in Mozilla Mail

Finding and Disabling Windows Services

To see which services are running on Windows

1. Go to the Start menu, choose Run, and type in *services.msc*. Click OK.

2. You will now be confronted with an enormous list of running services with obscure names like Application Layer Gateway Service, Background Intelligent Transfer Service, and COM+ Event System (Figure B-15). Highlight any service and right-click. You will get a menu allowing you to start it, stop it, or view its properties.

3. Use the right-click menu to display the properties of the service you chose above. The Properties dialog will launch (Figure B-16).

4. You will find four tabs at the top of the dialog: General, Log On, Recovery, and Dependencies. The General tab will show you the service's name, a brief description, the path to the relevant executable file, a drop-down menu allowing you to choose how it should start (i.e., Automatic, Manual, or Disabled), and finally, four buttons allowing you to start, stop, pause, and resume the service.

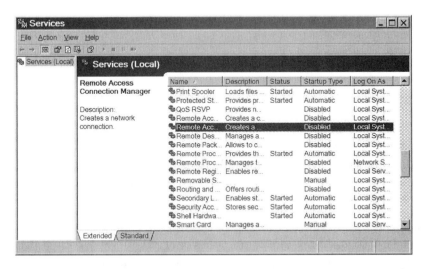

Figure B-15. The Windows Services menu with the Remote Access Connection Manager service highlighted

Figure B-16. The Properties dialog associated with the Remote Access Connection Manager service

You will notice right away that the descriptions tell you little of value, such as how much memory the service uses, how many remote exploits have been found against it, or whether or not you can safely disable it. It's best to stop a service using the Properties dialog as we just described, then use the system normally for a while and observe its behavior. You can usually re-enable a service if shutting it off causes problems. If nothing untoward happens after a bit of daily use, you can disable it permanently.

Windows Services Worth Disabling

Automatic Updates: This service will automatically connect to the Internet, check for available patches, and install them. I recommend running Windows Update manually and choosing the upgrades and patches to be downloaded, unless you like the idea of letting Microsoft decide what code belongs on your system and when it should be installed. Set it to Disabled. (But don't forget to run the update manually on a regular basis. Just click on Start ➤ Windows Update.)

ClipBook: This service stores cut and paste information and allows you to share it with other computers. It multiplies data traces, which complicates the practice of good data hygiene, and also wastes memory. Set it to Disabled.

Error Reporting Service: This service phones home to Microsoft when application errors occur. Set it to Disabled.

Indexing Service: This service essentially maintains data *about* your data (i.e., *metadata*) to speed up searching the local drive and the contents of files. It multiplies data traces, completely undermines the practice of good data hygiene, and wastes a good deal of memory. Set it to Disabled.

Internet Information Service (IIS): This is Microsoft's notoriously insecure Web server. It is usually not installed on XP systems, but if it has been installed it should be uninstalled *with prejudice* unless you're actually using it. If you need a Web server, Apache for Windows is a safer alternative that I recommend. However, you should never install *any* sort of server on a home system unless you need one and know how to run it securely.

Messenger: Often called *Windows Messenger*, this service broadcasts messages on a network. It is *not* the MSN Messenger chat client. It is often exploited to broadcast spam across the Internet but has no other useful function on a home or small business network, though it can be useful on large networks when the administrator needs to broadcast a message to all users. Set it to Disabled.

Net Logon: This service allows logging on to a *domain controller*. This is not required for home and small office networks. Set it to Disabled unless your machine is a member of a domain.

NetMeeting Remote Desktop Sharing: This service permits others to access your computer using NetMeeting. This is a major security hole. Set it to Disabled unless you need it.

Network DDE: This service enables applications on different computers to share data. It's of no use to most home and SOHO users. Set it to Disabled.

Network DDE DSDM: This service manages network shares. It's of no use to most home and SOHO users. Set it to Disabled.

Network Location Awareness: This service collects location and configuration information about networked computers. It's of no use to most home and SOHO users. Set it to Disabled.

Protected Storage: This service saves your login passwords for e-mail, your ISP, and the like. This is not dangerous on a properly configured PC, but I do recommend disabling it on laptop computers, which have a tendency to grow legs. If your laptop is stolen, stored passwords will enable the thief to access your ISP account, VPN, e-mail, etc. Set it to Disabled on laptop computers, and get into the habit of logging in manually.

QoS RSVP: This service provides network traffic information to certain applications. It's of no use to most home and SOHO users. Set it to Disabled.

Remote Access Auto Connection Manager: This service creates a connection to a remote network whenever a program references a remote DNS or NetBIOS name or address. In other words, it's a shortcut for embedded links. Set it to Disabled unless you need it.

Remote Access Connection Manager: This service establishes a network connection when Windows Internet Connection Sharing is in use. Using a router for connection sharing makes this service unnecessary. Set it to Disabled unless you need it.

Remote Desktop Help Session Manager: This service controls the Windows Remote Assistance feature, which allows remote users, such as malicious script kiddies, to connect to your machine and tweak all its settings. I *strongly* recommend against using this service; it is far too susceptible to abuse. Set it to Disabled.

Remote Packet Capture Protocol: This service allows remote users to intercept packet traffic on your machine. This is useful for remote administration, but it is suicidal otherwise. A great boon to malicious hackers and script kiddies; set it to Disabled, with prejudice.

Remote Registry Service: This service allows remote users, such as malicious script kiddies, to tweak your Registry settings to their liking. Set it to Disabled.

Routing and Remote Access: This service allows other computers to dial in to yours through a modem to access the local network. You may need it for some VPN software. Unless you need it, set it to Disabled.

Server: This service permits file and print sharing from your computer, which is a very foolish thing to allow if the computer also connects to the Internet. Unless you are using these features (and preferably on a LAN only), set it to Disabled.

SNMP Service: This is a network monitoring service. It is not necessary on most home or small office computers. Set it to Disabled.

SNMP Trap Service: This service handles messages exchanged between SNMP agents on networked computers. It's of no use to most home and SOHO users. Set it to Disabled.

SSDP Discovery Service: This service enables discovery of UPnP (Universal Plug and Play) devices on your network. UPnP is *very* insecure, easily exploited, and should never be used on a machine with Internet access (see *UPnP* later on this list). Set it to Disabled.

TCP/IP NetBIOS Helper Service: This service provides support for NetBIOS over TCP/IP. However, you should not be using NetBIOS over TCP/IP because it is *very* insecure. Uninstall NetBIOS if you have it (see the instructions that follow), then set this "helper service" to Disabled.

Telnet: This is a *very* insecure mechanism allowing remote users to log on to your computer. Never make Telnet available for any reason. If it is installed, set it to Disabled.

Terminal Services: This is an insecure service allowing remote users to log on to your computer. However, a very useful feature called *Fast User Switching* depends on it. Fast User Switching allows users to move between accounts without ending their sessions. Tasks in one account will remain active while another user is logged in. Unfortunately, Microsoft has made this handy feature dependent on an insecure service. If you disable Terminal Services, your computer will be more secure, but whenever you log out of an account you will have to save all your work because your applications and tasks will be shut down. Choose your poison.

Universal Plug and Play (UPnP): Don't confuse this with *Plug and Play*, which is useful and safe. The UPnP service detects and configures UPnP-compatible devices over a network. It is *very* susceptible to remote exploitation, so set it to Disabled. It works with the SSDP Discovery Service, which should also be set to Disabled (see *SSDP Discovery Service* earlier on this list).

Upload Manager: This service manages file transfers between clients and servers on a network. Very few home users will have any use for it. It also phones home to Microsoft seeking driver information when devices are installed. Set it to Disabled.

WebClient: This service allows Windows and MS applications to modify Web-based content. Some Microsoft applications may need it. If you have difficulty with MSN Messenger or Media Player, you may need to enable WebClient later. However, if you follow my recommendations and substitute more secure Internet clients for the ones Microsoft supplies, there is little chance you will ever need this service. Set it to Disabled.

Uninstalling TCP/IP NetBIOS on Windows

It is important to uninstall TCP/IP NetBIOS. This is not a good service to have on any machine connected to the Internet. To remove it, follow these steps:

1. Go to the Start menu and choose Settings ➤ Network Connections, or ➤ Control Panel ➤ Network Connections. Click on your network connection device, then on the Properties button.

2. A dialog will launch. Under the General tab you will find your installed network protocols, services, and clients. If your PC is used for Internet access and does not require additional networking capability, you should uninstall *everything* except Internet Protocol (TCP/IP). Get rid of File and Print Sharing, NetBIOS, Client for Microsoft Networks (unless you use PGP), and the rest of these superfluous whistles and bells. TCP/IP is the *only* component you need for an Internet connection to work.

3. After uninstalling all the unnecessary networking components, left-click on Internet Protocol (TCP/IP) to launch its Properties dialog.

4. Click the Advanced button and another dialog will launch, labeled Advanced TCP/IP Settings. Choose the WINS tab at the top (Figure B-17).

5. Choose the option labeled Disable NetBIOS over TCP/IP at the bottom. You will need to reboot for all of these settings to take effect.

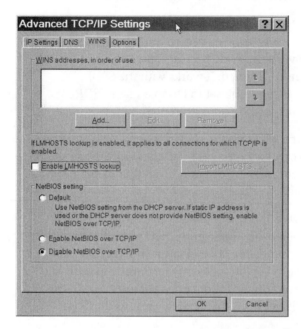

Figure B-17. The Advanced TCP/IP Settings dialog with proper WINS settings

Disabling DCOM on Windows

There is one more notoriously insecure service that we need to disable on Windows, called DCOM (Distributed Component Object Model), which enables software components to communicate directly over a network. It is quite unnecessary for home users, terribly obscure, and the particular service that enabled the MSBlaster worm to attack the Windows RPC service. Power users can open the Registry and alter the key HKEY_LOCAL_MACHINE\Software\Microsoft\OLE\EnableDCOM with a value of *N* and reboot. Novices should disable DCOM thus:

1. Go to the Start menu, choose Run, and type in *dcomcnfg*. Click OK, and the Component Services dialog will launch.

2. In the left pane, choose the menu item Component Services and expand the tree below it. Next choose Computers, expand the tree again, and choose My Computer.

3. In the left pane, right-click on My Computer and choose Properties from the drop-down menu (Figure B-18). The My Computer Properties dialog will launch.

4. Choose the Default Properties tab on the My Computer Properties dialog and *clear* the checkbox in front of the option Enable Distributed COM on this computer (Figure B-19). You will need to reboot for the change to take effect. If the option is not available, you'll need to use the Registry hack above.

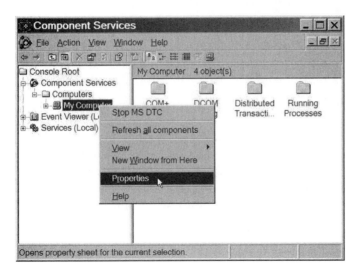

Figure B-18. The Component Services dialog with tree expanded, right-click menu activated

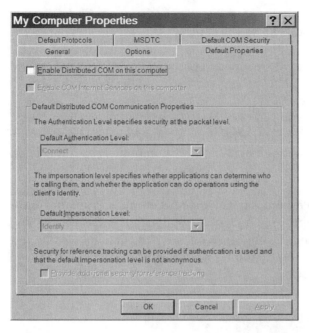

Figure B-19. The My Computer Properties dialog with proper DCOM settings

Linux Services Worth Disabling

Apache: This is a fine Web server. Most Linux distributions are filled with more packages than any person could possibly use, and sometimes, due to this embarrassment of riches, servers like Apache can be installed without the user's realizing it. If you don't need a Web server or don't know how to run one securely, you should uninstall it promptly.

Berkeley Internet Name Domain (BIND): This service translates domain names to IP addresses. Unless you are operating a server, you have no use for it. Disabling it will not affect your Internet clients: your ISP will provide BIND or DNS services for you. The daemon is called *named* and should be disabled.

File Transfer Protocol (FTP): This is a file server. Few home users will have any use for it. The daemons are called *wuftpd* and *proftpd;* get rid of them unless you need to make FTP available and know how to secure it.

Line Printer Daemon (LPD): This service allows users to connect to a printer across a network. It is *exceptionally* insecure and should be disabled with prejudice.

Nessus: This is a vulnerability scanner that runs a daemon process. It's not terribly dangerous, but there is no point leaving it running when it's not in use, lest others connect to it. I recommend enabling and disabling the nessusd daemon from the command line and leaving it out of your runlevels.

Network Information Service (NIS): This service allows networked machines to share a common interface. It is not so much vulnerable in itself but it requires RPC, which is. Home users should not have any use for it.

Network File System (NFS): This service provides remote access to shared file systems across a network. As with NIS, it is not so much vulnerable in itself but it requires RPC, which is. Home users should not have any use for it.

Postfix: This is a fairly reliable mail server. Few home users need a mail server or know how to run one securely, so this should be disabled, but not uninstalled. Some mail clients may require it to be present, though not running.

Remote Procedure Call (RPC): Sometimes called *sunrpc* or *portmap*, this should be disabled except when NIS or NFS is in use. Any daemon with *rpc* or *portmap* in the name is a good candidate for disabling.

Rlogin: This service accepts remote logins. It is only slightly more secure than Telnet and should be disabled. Use SSH or Webmin if you need to log in to your machine remotely.

Samba: This is a file and print sharing service that offers Windows compatibility. It's unnecessary on most home machines. Computers used primarily to contact the Internet should not be offering such services unless they have to, though Samba can be quite useful in an office if you know how to run it securely.

Secure Shell (SSH): This service accepts remote logins. You should disable the SSH daemon (sshd) unless you need to connect remotely to your computer. If you do connect remotely, SSH is the most secure method and should always be preferred to Telnet and rlogin. Disabling the SSH daemon will not cause any problems when using an SSH client.

Sendmail: This is a mail server. You probably don't need a mail server, so uninstall it. If you do need a mail server, you should *still* uninstall Sendmail and replace it with Postfix, which is more secure. Some e-mail clients may require Postfix to be installed, though not running, so disabling it is better than uninstalling it.

Simple Network Management Protocol (SNMP): This service allows for configuring devices over a network. Home users should have no use for it. There are plenty of exploits against it, so disable the snmpd daemon unless you really need it.

Squid: This is a proxy server, and a fine one, but it's a security issue if you don't need it and don't know how to secure it. If you don't know what a proxy server is, then you absolutely don't need one. Uninstall it if you find it's been installed.

Telnet: This is a *hopelessly* insecure service that permits remote logins. Disable it; remove it from /etc/init.d; exorcise it.

Webmin: This is a fairly trustworthy server for remote administration. However, if you don't need it, uninstall it. If you're not going to use it, there's no point making it available to others on the Internet, like malicious script kiddies.

Ypbind: This daemon supports Network Information Services (NIS). There have been exploits against it. Again, as with any service, if you don't need it, disable it.

Setting File Display Properties in Windows

1. Go to the desktop Start menu and choose Settings ➤ Control Panel ➤ Folder Options. The Folder Options dialog will launch.

2. Choose the tab labeled View from the top of the Folder Options dialog.

3. Check the boxes or radio buttons next to the items labeled *Display the contents of system folders* and *Show hidden files and folders* (Figures B-20 and B-21).

4. Next, *clear* the checkbox next to the item labeled *Hide protected operating system files (Recommended)*. You will be warned against clearing this box, but you need to know what's on your system if you want to make it more secure. Ignore the warning (Figures B-20 and B-21).

5. Finally, *clear* the checkbox next to the item labeled *Use simple file sharing (Recommended)*. Click Apply and finally OK (Figures B-20 and B-21).

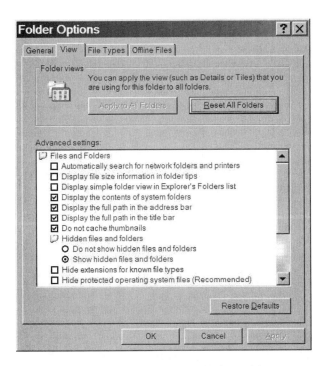

Figure B-20. The Folder Options dialog with recommended settings

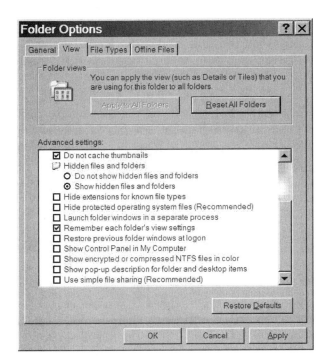

Figure B-21. The Folder Options dialog with recommended settings, continued

Setting Up User Accounts in Windows

1. Go to the desktop Start menu and choose Run and type in *compmgmt.msc*. Click OK, and the Computer Management dialog will launch.

2. In the left pane, select Local Users and Groups, expand the tree, and choose Users.

3. You will see several users listed in the right pane, such as the Administrator, Guest, and the name you chose for yourself when you installed Windows, which is also an administrator (Figure B-22). Windows XP sets the person who installs the system as *an* administrator, but not *the* Administrator. What's the difference between *the* Admin and *an* admin? Basically, *the* Admin is an inbuilt account coded into Windows, whereas *an* admin is whoever installed the system, plus any other users he decides to nominate for the honor. Let's concern ourselves first with *the* Admin, or the built-in account.

4. Highlight the Administrator account and right-click. The drop-down menu allows you to set or reset the password. If you've already set a password but think it might be weak, then you should reset it with a better one, using the instructions that follow.

Make your password a difficult one, combining uppercase and lowercase letters, numerals, and special characters like the dollar and pound signs. It should be at least eight characters in length, though when it comes to passwords, longer is always better. I recommend using a short phrase that makes no sense, like *sleazy bricks*. Use some uppercase and some lowercase letters, and substitute characters that resemble a few of the other letters so it looks something like this: sl34ZybR1@k$. Note that we've substituted numbers and special characters that, at least vaguely, resemble the letters they're standing in for to make the password easier to memorize. You can write it down and keep it in a secure place until you're sure you've memorized it. A password like this will be practically impossible to brute force or crack with a dictionary attack.

When you set the Admin password, you will receive a warning that numerous problems might arise. Ignore it.

5. Once you've password-protected the built-in Administrator account, set a strong password for yourself as *an* administrator, associated with the username you chose when you installed Windows XP. You can use the same password for both accounts with little risk, so long as it's a tough one according to our guidelines. It is usually safe for home users to disable the remaining built-in accounts provided by Microsoft, except the Guest account, which may prove useful. Personally, I would disable every account except *the* Admin, *your* admin account, and the Guest account at this point (unless you've already added users, obviously).

6. To enable or disable an account, select it in the Computer Management dialog, use the right-click menu, and choose Properties. In the Properties dialog, under the General tab, find the checkbox next to the option *Account is disabled* (Figure B-23).

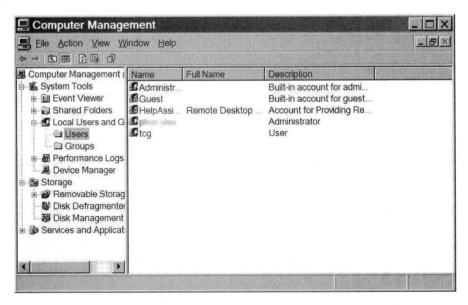

Figure B-22. The Computer Management dialog with Users selected

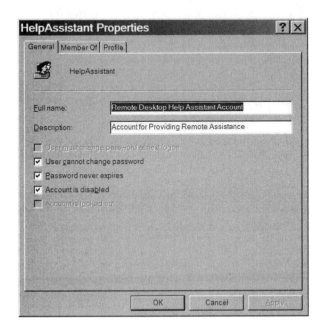

Figure B-23. The Computer Management Properties dialog with the default MS account disabled

If you haven't established a user account for yourself or added any other users, you should do so now. But you can close the Computer Management dialog at this point; things will get easier from here.

Now it's time to add users, and this means *you too*. You'll remain an administrator, of course, but you're going to set up and start working from an unprivileged account except when admin access is needed for altering system settings or installing software, just like any security-savvy person. This is not difficult:

1. Open the Start menu and go to Settings ➤ Control Panel ➤ User Accounts. A window will open, most likely reminding you that you are the system administrator.

2. Create a user account for yourself. Choose Create a new account, and then choose a login name. Choose limited for the account type and click the Create Account button.

3. Now create a password for the account. This is the account you should use at all times, except when you need to perform administrative tasks.

4. Simply repeat the process, choosing limited accounts for each user. You can also activate the Guest account so that occasional visitors and house guests can use your computer without accessing any of the established user accounts. However, the Guest account is not password protected, so *anyone* can use the machine with it. Privileges are low, but this is not a good option if you are unable to supervise use of the computer for extended periods. If you don't set up the Guest account, it will not appear on the boot screen.

Adjusting User and File Permissions in Windows

1. Log in to your administrator account and left-click on the My Computer desktop icon.

2. Under Hard Disk Drives, click on Local Disk (C:). You will see a list of top-level directories such as Program Files, WINDOWS, etc. (Alternatively, you can launch the Windows Explorer file browser; the procedure is the same.)

3. Let's assume that you have a user called tcg with an account on your machine and you want to disable access to the system directory for him alone. Navigate to the WINDOWS\system directory.

4. Highlight the directory, right-click, and select Properties from the right-click menu (Figure B-24).

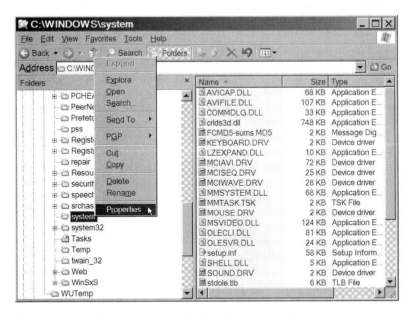

Figure B-24. Selecting properties for the system directory

5. When the Properties dialog pops up, choose the Security tab. There will be two fields: at the top, a list of user groups, and below, a list of possible permissions. However, if you apply restrictions to a group such as Users, then every user will be denied use of the program. To specify an individual user, click on the Advanced button (Figure B-25).

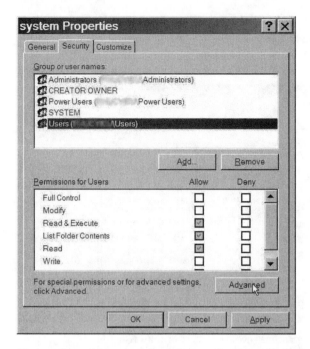

Figure B-25. Choosing the Advanced user permissions dialog

6.   This will bring up the advanced security settings dialog. Again, you will see Users listed as a group. Click the Add button and enter the desired username, tcg, manually in the lower field under Enter the object name to select (Figure B-26). Click OK.

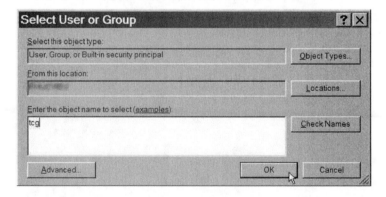

Figure B-26. Choosing a user instead of a group

7. You will then get another dialog showing the user you chose associated with the system directory. You can now choose the user's permissions for that directory. Unfortunately, there is a plethora of options. To make it simple, choose Deny in the top line labeled Full Control to remove the user's permission to view or launch files in the system directory. This will change all of the options at once (Figure B-27).

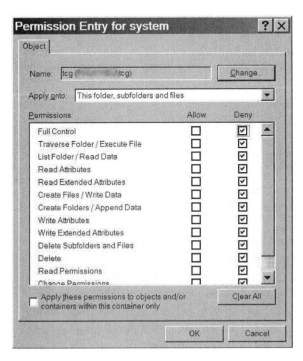

Figure B-27. Denying a user access to the system folder

8. Click the OK button; you will return to the advanced security settings dialog. Click Apply.

9. You will see a new line with the word *Deny* followed by the username. Click OK and close the system directory Properties box. The user you chose will not be able to view or activate any files in the system directory.

You can use this basic procedure to fine-tune file and directory permissions for each user. You could, for example, deny a small child permission to use a chat client like ICQ or an e-mail client on his own. But remember, if you apply limits to the Users group, *all* users will be kept from the directory or program file chosen. To specify users for particular file and directory restrictions, you must bring up the advanced security settings dialog and apply the restrictions individually as just described.

Adjusting User and File Permissions in Linux

When you wish to restrict users on a Linux system from directories or program files, a simple approach is to raise the level of privilege needed, then increase the privileges of users to whom you wish to grant access by adding them to a group with greater privileges. (You can do this on Windows too, but with so many options it can become confusing.) For example, on Linux you might restrict the ICQ (licq) program file to access by the group *trusted*, and then add yourself, your spouse, and your older children to that group. Young children would remain in the group *users* only, and not be able to access the ICQ binary from their accounts. The other users would belong to two groups, users and trusted, and so be permitted access by virtue of their membership in the trusted group.

The easiest way to change file and directory permissions is by using a GUI file browser like Krusader or Nautilus, because if you have a lot of files to deal with, making these changes at the command line will be tedious. You can certainly make these changes from a user account with a root shell if you understand the commands *chmod*, *chuser*, and *chgroup* (well worth leaning, by the way), but if you want to use a GUI method, you'll have to log in as root. Simply navigate to the files you wish to restrict, right-click, and pull up their properties. You will find a simple dialog for setting permissions. The options are *read*, *write*, and *execute*. If you want only one user to have access, then clear the checkboxes on the lines labeled Group and Others. If you wish to allow a group to access it, simply check off the permissions you intend to grant on the line labeled Group and then specify the group in the field below. If you wish to allow every user to have some access, check off the permissions you intend to grant to members of additional groups on the line labeled Others.

In Figure B-28, the user tcg is the only one permitted to view, enter, or write to his /home/tcg/Documents directory. Root has free access to the entire system by default, but fellow members of the group to which tcg belongs (users), and all others, are denied access.

Figure B-28. Setting directory permissions with Krusader

Because permissions are simpler on Linux than on Windows, it's easier to work with groups than with individual users. If you wish to grant file or directory access to some but not all users, you can assign a directory's or a file's access rights to a more privileged group, such as trusted, then add only the users you choose to that group. And that's all there is to it. Linux makes this procedure quite painless.

You can do permission tweaking with directories, but the cautions in Chapter 2 about *recursive* changes still apply. If you overprotect a directory, you may block user access to program files or configuration files that you wish to make available. It's also very easy to edit group permissions in terms of the system services available. Small children can have Internet access disabled, for example, by raising the permission level needed to access the service and then denying them membership in the group authorized to do so.

Viewing and Killing System Processes in Windows

To see what's running on Windows

1. Go to the Start menu and choose Run.

2. Type in *taskmgr* and click OK. The Windows Task Manager dialog will launch.

3. The first two tabs at the top, labeled Applications and Processes, are the ones we're concerned with.

Figure B-29. The Windows Task Manager Applications dialog

Under the Applications tab (Figure B-29), you should find only those applications that you've launched yourself or added to your startup directory. If there's an application listed that you don't recognize, don't be alarmed, but investigate it with a Web search. Chances are that once you learn what it is, you'll recognize it. But if not, or if you gather that it might be malicious, you will need to kill it and remove it.

First, you will have to stop it so that it can be removed. To find its related executable file, right-click on the application name and choose the option Go To Process (Figure B-30). In this example, we are going to kill Mozilla.

Figure B-30. The Windows Task Manager: Go To Process

This will bring up the processes list with the executable file highlighted. Kill the process by right-clicking and choosing the option End Process Tree from the drop-down menu, which will kill the primary process and each child process it invokes in one go (Figure B-31).

Figure B-31. The Windows Task Manager: End Process Tree

The best way to rid yourself of unnecessary or suspicious applications is to use the Windows Add or Remove Programs utility. So long as you've killed the process tree as just described, you can go to the Start menu and choose Settings ➤ Control Panel ➤ Add or Remove Programs. Your applications should all be listed, and you can uninstall a questionable one easily with the Change/Remove button. If this is impractical, or if it fails, you can manually delete or wipe the executable file, and even the directory in which it's located, so long as you've killed its related process tree. To remove it manually, note the process name, search your hard disk for the executable file or the program directory, and wipe it—so long as you've confirmed that you don't need it.

Under the Task Manager Processes tab, you'll find a complete list of executable routines running on your computer. There will likely be a large number of them, and they can have very arcane names that give little indication of what they actually do. If you followed my advice about eliminating unnecessary Windows services in Chapter 2 and previously in this Appendix, the processes list will be a good deal more manageable.

Viewing and Killing System Processes in Linux

1. Open a few instances of the Mozilla browser.

2. You will need root access to see all of the system processes and kill them. Open a shell, type in the command *su,* and supply the root password. Now type the command *ps ax.*

3. You will see a list of running processes with their corresponding Process IDs, or *PIDs,* and the paths to the relevant binaries.

4. To kill a single process only, enter the command *kill* followed by the PID. To kill the process and all of its child processes, enter the command *killall* followed by the process name. The *killall* command is similar to the End Process Tree option in Windows.

5. Enter the command *killall mozilla-bin.* All of the Mozilla instances you started and all of the child processes they invoked will be killed in one go.

The *kill* and *killall* commands are handy and easy to use, but the same cautions for Windows users apply. If you're logged in as root, you can kill a crucial system process by mistake and you might have to reboot your machine to recover. If you're only concerned with processes you started as a user, then you should use the *ps ax* and the *kill* and *killall* commands as a user. This way, the worst you can do is kill your own applications or your X session. You won't be able to interfere with system processes or other users' processes. Attempts to kill important system processes from a user account will fail, and the shell will report "operation not permitted."

Installing and Using PGP on Windows

If you followed my earlier advice about uninstalling Client for Microsoft Networks, you will have to reinstall it to use any version of PGP. To do this, follow these steps:

1. Go to the Start menu and choose Settings ➤ Network Connections.

2. Click on the icon corresponding to your network connection, and a status dialog will appear. (The name will depend on what sort of connection you make.)

3. Choose Properties, and a connection Properties dialog will appear.

4. Click on Install.

5. The Select Network Component Type dialog will appear asking you what to install; choose Client and click the Add button.

6. Finally, the Select Network Client dialog will appear, in which you should specify Client for Microsoft Networks. Click OK and clear the dialogs.

You will have to reboot Windows after installing PGP, so it's wise to save any work you have open before you begin.

Now you can unzip the PGP file and activate the installer, a typical GUI wizard. After clicking through the welcome and license screens, etc., you will be asked if you have an existing keyring or if you're a new user. Next you will be asked to choose a directory for the program or accept the default. Either is fine. The next screen offers you several plugins. (The plugins won't work if you're using the free version.) Next the wizard will install several files and prompt you to reboot, which you must do before using the program.

When Windows restarts, you'll have to launch PGP and create your key pair. There should be a new tray applet with a little padlock icon that launches PGP. Bring it up and select the PGPkeys feature. (Or go to the Start menu and choose Programs ➤ PGP ➤ PGPkeys.) A dialog will pop up, called PGPkeys, allowing you to create your own keys and to add or import other people's public keys to your keyring.

Now it's time to create your first key pair:

1. Using the menu bar at the top of the PGPkeys dialog, go to Keys ➤ New Keys. Another wizard will start, to simplify creating them.

2. On the first screen, type in your name and e-mail address, or your alias and a corresponding e-mail address. (You can repeat this for as many e-mail accounts and aliases as you own.)

3. On the next screen, you will choose your passphrase. Make it a good one. There is a little progress bar that indicates the passphrase quality. Shoot for somewhere past the halfway mark. Write it down if you need to and keep the record secure; destroy it only when you're confident that you've memorized it. It is crucial that you not forget this passphrase, or anything you encrypt will be impossible to decrypt later.

4. Once that's done, the program will generate your new keys. When it's finished, clear the wizard and you should find the keys listed in the original dialog. If there are no error messages or warning symbols, you're done (Figure B-32). But leave the original PGPkeys dialog open until we've finished.

Figure B-32. The PGPkeys dialog with a new key pair illustrated

You're now ready to encrypt and decrypt files on your computer. Let's give it a quick try:

1. Open Notepad, type in a brief message, then save the file as test-pgp.txt.

2. Open the Windows Explorer file browser and find the file. You'll see, as you right-click on the file, that PGP is now integrated with Windows Explorer. Use the right-click menu and scroll down to PGP (Figure B-33). You'll be able to encrypt, sign, decrypt, or wipe the file.

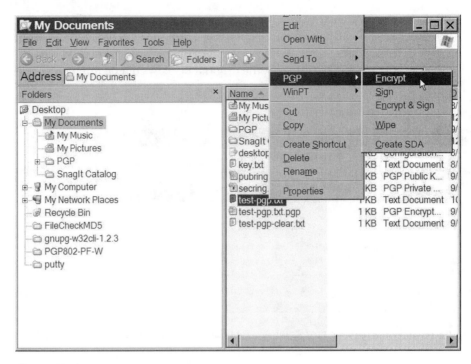

Figure B-33. The PGP right-click menu

3. Choose Encrypt. A second dialog will appear, listing the Recipients in the top field and yourself in the bottom field. Since we haven't added any other people's public keys, the upper field will be blank (Figure B-34). Once you've added other public keys, your contacts will be listed in the upper field, and you can drag them to the lower field if you wish. The lower field lists the public key or keys to be used for encryption. If you should add others later, PGP can encrypt the file so that these people will be able to decrypt it as well.

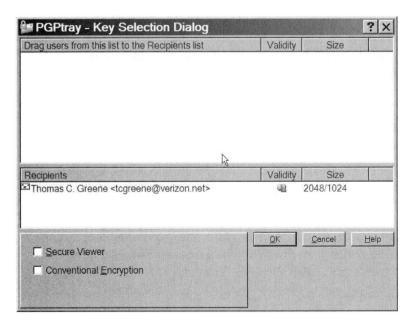

Figure B-34. The PGP Key Selection dialog with one recipient selected

4. For now, only you should appear in the lower field. Since this is a test, make sure that the option Wipe Original is *not* selected in the bottom left field of the PGP Options dialog (Figure B-35). Just click on OK, and in a moment you'll find that you have two files with the same name, your original and one encrypted (indicated with a little padlock icon), named test-pgp.txt.pgp.

5. To decrypt the file you just created, simply left-click as if to launch it. You will be prompted for your passphrase. Enter the passphrase, and a dialog will appear. A decrypted version of the encrypted file will be created. Call the decrypted version test-pgp-clear.txt and save it.

6. Now you can verify that your original file, test-pgp.txt, and the decrypted file, test-pgp-clear.txt, are identical. To see the contents of the encrypted file, right-click on it in Windows Explorer and choose Open With ➤ Notepad. The encrypted version will be a lot of meaningless characters. Now that you've verified that PGP is working properly, you can decrypt this file again whenever you please. It's safe to wipe both the original file and the decrypted file so that only the encrypted one remains.

7. To wipe your original file and the decrypted file, select them in Windows Explorer, right-click, and choose PGP ➤ Wipe. This will not merely delete the files but will actually obliterate them. And now only the encrypted file remains.

Next, let's create, sign, and send an encrypted e-mail memo. Since you haven't yet added anyone else's public key to your keyring, you can only send it to yourself, encrypted for yourself. But that's fine; this is merely a test.

1. Open Mozilla Mail and choose Compose. Enter your own e-mail address in the To field. Now type in a brief message.

2. Go to the PGP tray applet and select Current Window ➤ Encrypt & Sign. The Key Selection dialog will pop up so that you can choose the key or keys to use. Your key will already be chosen, so just click OK. You'll get a password prompt, and after a moment the text in the e-mail memo will change to a lot of gibberish.

3. Now send the memo and wait for it to return. When it comes back, it will still be a lot of gibberish. Return to the PGP applet, choose Current Window from the menu, and select Decrypt & Verify.

4. In a moment, a password prompt will appear. Enter your passphrase. A text editor will pop up, showing the memo contents in clear text and informing you that the signature is valid. Digitally signing e-mail is useful when you want a recipient to be confident that a memo appearing to be from you actually *is* from you. E-mail is ludicrously easy to forge.

What you've just done is encrypt a memo using your public key, decrypt it using your private key, sign it with your private key, then verify the signature with your public key, though it all happened automatically.

If you wish to send an encrypted memo to someone else, you will first have to add their public key to your keyring. If you want another person to be able to verify your digital signature, you will have to send them your public key. You cannot verify the signature of, or encrypt a memo for, someone whose public key is not in your keyring. Similarly, a person who hasn't got your public key in their keyring can't verify your signature or encrypt a memo for you. So if you want to use PGP for e-mail, you've got to exchange public keys with your correspondents.

If these two tests have been successful, everything is working as it should and it's time to back up your keyring and adjust a few options.

1. First, choose a backup medium such as a blank, formatted floppy disk or CD and put it into its related drive.

2. Return to the PGPkeys dialog, which should still be open. From the menu bar, choose Keys ➤ Export. You'll get a Windows dialog allowing you to save the keys wherever you wish. Choose the appropriate disk drive and make sure that the checkbox labeled Include Private Key(s) is checked. Save your key pair, and store the disk in a secure place.

If your computer ever crashes hopelessly, you can restore your keys from the disk later using the PGPkeys Import feature. Again, you needn't save your keyring on external media each time you add someone's public key, but you *do* need to do it each time you generate a fresh key pair for yourself.

The PGP default options and settings are all sensible, but let's go over a few that are important to understand. Using the PGPkeys dialog, go to Edit ➤ Options. Another dialog will launch with a row of tabs at the top (Figure B-35). We're not going to deal with each tab or all the available options, but only those that need reviewing.

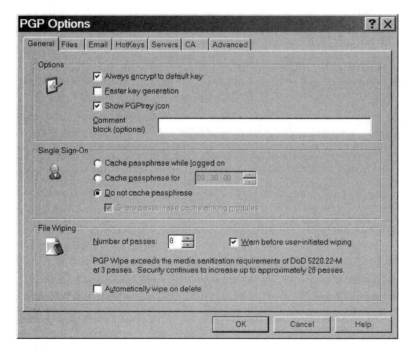

Figure B-35. The PGP Options dialog

Under the General tab, I recommend the option Always encrypt to default key for most users. This way, whenever you encrypt a file or a memo with someone else's public key, you'll retain a copy of it encrypted with your own key so you can access it later. If you don't choose this option and you also choose to wipe the original file automatically after encrypting it, you could end up encrypting one of your own files so that only someone else can read it. Your recourse then would be to ask the recipient to decrypt it, reencrypt it with *your* public key, and send it back—assuming that person hasn't wiped it in the meantime.

The next set of options under General concerns the Single Sign-On feature, which allows your passphrase to be cached in memory. Home users who don't share their account with others can select the first option, which keeps the passphrase in memory for as long as they're logged in. You will enter your passphrase once and not need to again until you log out of your account or reboot Windows. People in a non-hostile but busy computing environment can choose the second option, which caches the passphrase for a set period of time. The default is two minutes, and this is reasonable for those who work with encrypted files but are frequently called away from their workstation. A home user or a business person with a private office might safely choose one or two hours. People in a hostile environment, where others might attempt to spy on them, or who work with extremely sensitive files, should choose the third option, no memory caching, which requires a passphrase every time an encrypted file or memo is accessed.

Finally, there is the File Wiping option for data destruction. This deletes a file and overwrites it with random characters several times so that the original can't be recovered. The default is three passes, which is good enough for most purposes.

Under the Advanced tab, there is a checkbox at the bottom enabling you to back up your keyring each time PGPkeys closes. The default is to save it to your keyring folder. This is a good feature that will keep your keyring current as you add other people's public keys to it. But it's important to know that this is *not* the same as saving your key pair on removable media for safekeeping. Backing it up on your hard drive is not adequate; if there's a major computer breakdown, your backup will be lost along with the original.

Using GnuPG on Linux with KDE

We have to assume that you already have GPG and KGpg installed. Novices should try to obtain RPM (Red Hat Package Manager) packages built by their Linux vendor. These may not always be the latest binaries, but they will be configured to work on your system without bother.

KGpg will install a tray applet with a key manager and an editor. Go to the applet and select Open Key Manager from the menu (Figure B-36). If you already have keys, it will search in /home/ ~/.gnupg for them. If they're not located there, go to the menu bar, select Keys ➤ Import Key, and browse to the directory where your keys are located. Be sure to check the option *Allow import of secret keys* when you're importing your own keys. You can also use this same procedure to add other people's public keys to your keyring.

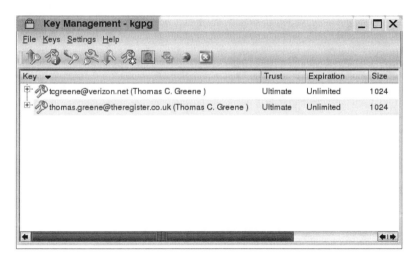

Figure B-36. The KGpg Key Management dialog

If you have no keys, it's time to create them. From the Key Manager menu bar choose Keys ➤ Generate Key Pair. Another dialog will pop up, prompting you for your name and e-mail address. The defaults for Key Size and Algorithm are perfectly adequate, but you can change them if you wish. The Advanced button will open a shell so that you can use the standard, interactive GPG setup, but novices can use the Key Generation dialog in GUI mode without worry (Figure B-37). You will then be prompted to supply a passphrase, and the keys will be generated. While this is going on, you will be asked to do things with your computer such as launching programs to create *entropy*. Linux generates random numbers from system "noise" caused by device drivers and the like. This noise is gathered and stored in an *entropy pool*, which helps improve the randomness of numbers generated.

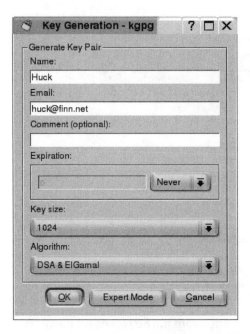

Figure B-37. The KGpg Key Generation dialog

Importing GnuPG Keys to KMail

Once your keys are generated, you should test them. Let's start by importing them to KMail:

1. Open KMail and go to Settings ➤ Configure KMail. The KMail Configure dialog will launch (Figure B-38).

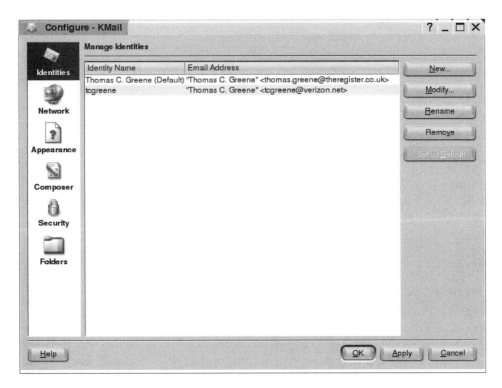

Figure B-38. The KMail Configure dialog

2. Choose Identities from the left menu and highlight the e-mail account corresponding to the key pair you just created.

3. Click the Modify button and the Edit Identity dialog will launch. From the tabs at the top, choose Advanced.

4. In the middle of the Advanced dialog, there will be a line labeled Open PGP key (Figure B-39). If your new key appears along that line, skip to step 7.

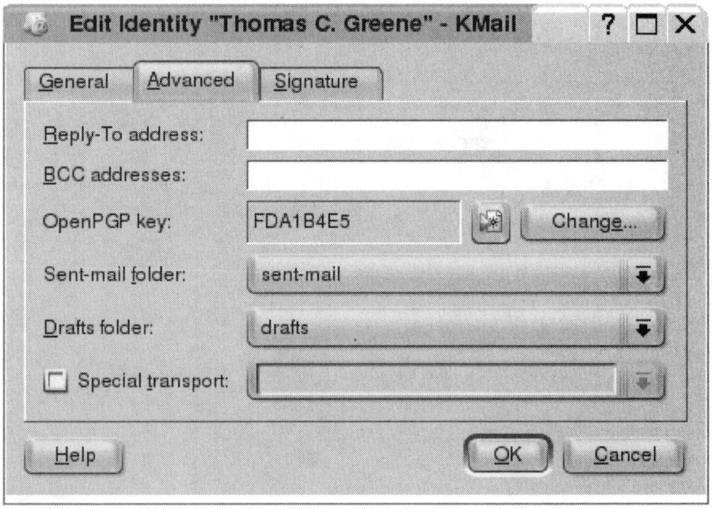

Figure B-39. The KMail Edit Identity Advanced dialog

5. If your new key doesn't appear, verify that the Security dialog (Figure B-41) option *Select encryption tool to use* is set to *GnuPG—Gnu Privacy Guard,* as illustrated. Then return to the Edit Identity Advanced dialog and click the button labeled Change. Another dialog, labeled Your Open PGP Key, will pop up, showing your key pair (Figure B-40). If the pair *still* is not listed, click the button at the bottom labeled Reread Keys. Your new key pair will now appear in the window.

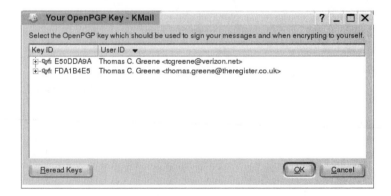

Figure B-40. The KMail Open PGP Key dialog—notice the button labeled Reread Keys.

6. Select your new key pair in the Open PGP Key dialog and return to the KMail Edit Identity Advanced dialog. Your key will be listed in the line labeled Open PGP key. Click OK.

7. Next, choose Security from the left-hand menu in the KMail Settings dialog, and click on the OpenPGP tab (Figure B-41). Here are your basic options for using GPG. I recommend *not* choosing *Keep passphrase in memory*, unless you trust all of the people who might have unsupervised access to your machine while you're logged in to your account. I do recommend choosing the option *Always encrypt to self*, so that you will be able to read the messages you've sent to others. The remaining options are chiefly a matter of personal preference. Now you can close the KMail Settings dialog.

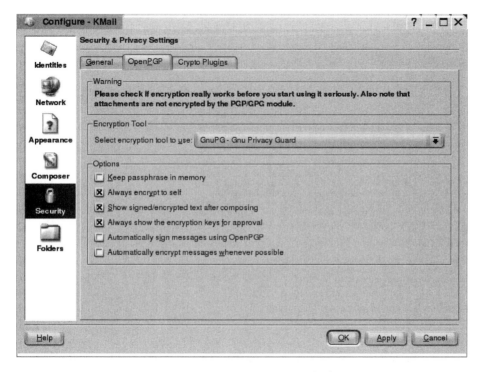

Figure B-41. The KMail Security & Privacy Settings dialog

You can create a key pair for each of your e-mail accounts and aliases, and import public keys from all of your correspondents. KMail will automatically select the correct key for the identity you choose whenever you compose a memo. It will also automatically choose the public key for each recipient, so long as you've added their public keys to your keyring and indicated that you trust the keys using the Key Manager ➤ Edit Key feature. This way, you can easily send an encrypted memo to several people in a single operation.

Now it's time to create an e-mail memo addressed to yourself. Open a new message and type in a few sentences, then go to the menu bar and choose Options ➤ Encrypt Message, and Options ➤ Sign Message. Send the message, and you will be prompted for your crypto passphrase. Enter it, and the memo will be sent immediately or the encrypted text will be displayed, depending on the options you've chosen. When the memo returns, you'll be prompted for your passphrase. Enter it, and the memo should be decrypted and indicate that you've signed it. If you don't enter your passphrase, only the encrypted text will be displayed.

Now let's try the KGpg editor. Open the KGpg tray applet and select Open Editor from the menu. Type in a brief message, then click on the Encrypt button. A dialog will pop up, asking which key to use. Select your key and the text will change to something like the example in Figure B-42.

Figure B-42. A short phrase encrypted

With most versions of KGpg, you can use the editor to encrypt the text, sign it using the Sign/Verify button, and paste it into an e-mail memo or IM client. If you do copy and paste the encrypted text, be sure to include the opening and closing lines -----BEGIN PGP MESSAGE----- and -----END PGP MESSAGE-----.

You can also save the message to your hard disk and send it as a file attachment later. From the KGpg Editor menu bar, choose File ➤ Save, or File ➤ Save As. The standard KDE dialog will launch with your /home/~/Documents directory as the default location. Name the file and save it, and then attach it to an e-mail memo if you like. The editor is also quite handy if you wish to type out a brief note and save it locally or on removable media as an encrypted file.

Encrypting files on your local hard disk is easy. There are two ways to go about it. First, you can use the KGpg Editor, and from the menu bar choose File ➤ Encrypt File, or File ➤ Decrypt File. You will be able to browse to the file you wish to work with. Second, on later versions of KDE, KGpg integrates itself with the Konqueror file and Web browser and the Krusader file browser, allowing you to select a file, right-click, and encrypt or decrypt it from the right-click menu. This ability to select and encrypt or decrypt files easily is important because KMail doesn't automatically encrypt file attachments. You'll need to encrypt them separately, which you can do conveniently with the KGpg Editor or the right-click menus in Konqueror or Krusader.

Here's how to test this feature:

1. Open Konqueror or Krusader and navigate to a file you'd like to encrypt. Right-click on it and find the options Encrypt and Decrypt in the menu. (If the options are unavailable, you may have to update your version of KDE or KGpg.) Now choose Encrypt.

2. You will be prompted for the key you wish to use. When the key selection dialog pops up, you can choose more than one encryption key by using the Shift key with the mouse to select them. If you're encrypting the file with someone else's public key, be sure to select your own key as well.

3. The encrypted file will have the extension .asc and receive a little pad-lock icon, indicating that it's a GPG file.

4. Now you can decrypt it, again using the right-click menu. The decrypted file will have the same name as the original, so you will be warned that decryption will overwrite it. To keep the original, simply change the proposed name of the decrypted file and click the Rename button.

5. Next, enter your passphrase. The file will be decrypted and the renamed output file can be compared with the original input file. If everything is working, you can right-click on the two clear-text versions and choose Shred or Wipe from the right-click menu. This will obliterate the files by wiping them several times with random data so that only the encrypted file remains.

The KGpg editor also allows for convenient comparison of MD5 checksums:

1. First, copy the checksum supplied by the vendor to the clipboard. Then open the KGpg Editor, and from the menu bar choose Signature ➤ Check MD5 Sum. A file browser will launch.

2. Navigate to the file you wish to check and click on it.

3. The file's MD5 sum will be displayed in a dialog box. There is a button labeled Compare MD5 With Clipboard that you can click to compare the file's sum against the sum you copied to the clipboard to see if they match. A green radio button will appear to let you know that the sums are the same.

Once you've verified that GPG is working as it should, it's time to back up your key pair to removable media for safekeeping. The easiest way is simply to copy your /home/~/.gnupg directory to a CD or floppy. You should do this whenever you create a new key pair for yourself. Backing up your correspondents' public keys is a good idea as well, but it's not crucial because you can always ask them to send the keys again if your computer should suffer a major malfunction. Your own private keys, however, can never be recovered if they're lost.

Configuring the Windows Swap File

1. Go to the Start menu and choose Settings ➤ Control Panel ➤ System.

2. The System Properties dialog will pop up. Click the tab labeled Advanced. On the Advanced dialog, in the field labeled Performance, click the Settings button (Figure B-43).

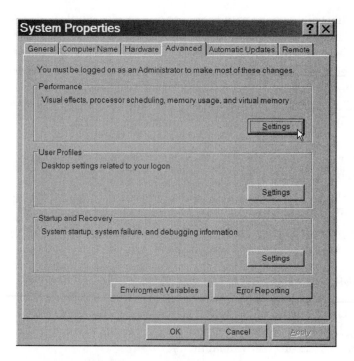

Figure B-43. The System Properties dialog

3. The Performance Options dialog will pop up. Again, choose the Advanced tab and click the Change button in the field labeled Virtual memory (Figure B-44).

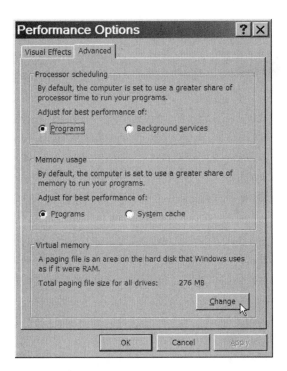

Figure B-44. The Performance Options dialog

4. The Virtual Memory dialog will pop up. Choose Custom size and ensure that the fields labeled Initial size and Maximum size have the same value (Figure B-45). A popular rule of thumb for Windows is to choose a swap-file size equaling twice the amount of RAM you have installed. For example, if you have 128 MB of RAM, you might choose 256 MB for both the Initial and Maximum sizes of your swap file. (Opinions differ on the optimal size for a swap file; my example is simply a common one. It's most important that the Initial and Maximum sizes be the same.)

Once you've changed your swap file to a single, fixed size, you will need to reboot. You can then use a wipe utility to clear unused disk space, eliminating the old data traces created by the swap file.

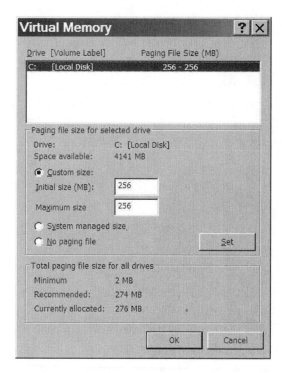

Figure B-45. The Virtual Memory dialog

Disabling the Windows Indexing Service

1. Go to the Start menu and choose Run.

2. Type in *services.msc* and click OK. The Services dialog will launch.

3. Right-click on the Indexing Service to bring up the Properties dialog, and click Stop if the service is running. Then select Disabled. Click Apply and close the dialog.

To prevent the service from being re-enabled

1. Activate the My Computer desktop icon. Next, select (Local Disk C:) under Hard Disk Drives.

2. Right-click on the (Local Disk C:) icon and choose Properties from the right-click menu. The Local Disk Properties dialog will pop up. Near the bottom you will see the option Allow Indexing Service to index this disk for fast file searching. (The option will not be available on all systems, so don't worry if you don't see it.)

3. *Clear* the checkbox, click Apply, and select the option Apply changes to C:\, subfolders and files. Click OK.

Disabling Windows System Restore

1. Go to the Start menu and choose Settings ➤ Control Panel ➤ System to launch the System Properties dialog (or right-click on the My Computer icon and choose Properties).

2. Choose the System Restore tab at the top of the System Properties dialog and check the box on the line reading Turn off System Restore. Click OK.

3. Next, go to the Start menu, choose Run, and type in *services.msc* to launch the Services dialog. Find the System Restore service, stop it if it's running, and set it to Disabled.

Write-Protecting the Mozilla Downloads History in Windows

1. First, open the Windows Explorer file browser, navigate to C:\Documents and Settings\, and choose the subdirectory associated with your username.

2. Now go to ~\Application Data\Mozilla\Profiles. Drop down to your Mozilla profile, which could be named "default" or your username.

3. Drop down again to the directory just below (the directory name will end in .slt) and find a file named downloads.rdf. (Or simply search for downloads.rdf.) This is your download history.

4. Open downloads.rdf with Notepad, delete all the text, save the blank file, and then write-protect it (i.e., right-click and choose Properties ➤ Attributes ➤ Read-only).

Write-Protecting the Mozilla Downloads History in Linux

On Linux, navigate to /home/~/.mozilla and find your profile name, which could be "default" or your username. Drop down to the directory below (the directory name will end in .slt) and find the file named downloads.rdf. (Or search for downloads.rdf.) Open it with a text editor, delete all the text, save the blank file, then write-protect it (right-click in Krusader or Konqueror, choose Properties, and deny *Write* to all users).

Notes on NAT

Network address translation (NAT) is an inexpensive and fairly secure means of hooking several computers to a single broadband Internet connection. Most NAT routers for home use cost in the $100 range, and ones with a bit more capability for the small office cost in the $250 range. Many offer both wired and wireless access from a single device.

Broadband Internet gear consists of three basic items: a modem that will connect you to your ISP, a router that will connect a number of computers to the modem, and a network interface card (NIC) for each computer.

A NAT router acts as a gateway between your home network, or LAN, and the Internet. It will acquire an external IP address from your ISP, and then distribute private, internal IP addresses to itself and to each of your computers. Thus the router will have two IP addresses: one assigned by your ISP, which is its external IP address that outsiders will see, and an internal IP address that you can see from the LAN, so that you can access it conveniently with a Web browser and tweak its settings. For example, a router might acquire virtually any external IP address—let's say 123.132.213.120, for example—but it will usually have an internal IP address of 192.168.1.1 or 192.168.0.1. You will need to consult your router's documentation to find out its default internal IP address, but it will be in the format 192.168.*x.x*. The computers on the LAN—i.e., on *your* side of the router—will also be given IP addresses in the format 192.168.*x.x*.

Let's say the router's default internal IP address is 192.168.1.1, which is not unusual. You can point your browser to that IP address (http://192.168.1.1) and log on to the router's admin interface. Be sure to change the default password right away: *admin* is a common one. You will then be able to set up the router to work with your ISP's equipment, according to their documentation. If your ISP requires PPPoE (Point-to-Point Protocol over Ethernet) for an ADSL connection, the router can provide it so you won't need a PPPoE client on your computers. The computers can be set up for a LAN connection, using the router's internal IP address as the default gateway. The router will log in to your ISP for you and keep the connection alive.

I recommend buying a NAT router with both wired and wireless capability. It won't cost more than a strictly wired or strictly wireless router, and its flexibility can save you money. Sometimes it's cheaper to go wired; sometimes it's cheaper to go wireless. And sometimes, a combination of wired and wireless will save you money, depending on where each piece of equipment is located.

When setting up a private network, you first need to decide where each piece of equipment will be kept. Bear in mind that the modem will need to be plugged into a phone jack or cable point, and that it, the router, and your computers will need power points nearby. So try to visualize the entire setup before you go shopping; this way, you won't buy longer cables than you need, which will save money and prevent your home office from becoming an agility training course. The router can go close to the modem or close to the computers, but remember, one long cable between the modem and the router is cheaper than four long cables between the router and the computers. So think carefully about how best to minimize the tangle, and the costs. Ethernet cables are expensive; so are wireless NICs. Consider the distance between each piece of equipment and the costs involved. Sometimes a wireless NIC will be cheaper than a cable.

If you intend to use the wireless capability, set it up with WEP enabled. This will prevent outsiders from intercepting your signals or freeloading on your connection. But if you don't need the wireless capability, disable it. Never make *any* service available unless you intend to use it.

A NAT router can be set up to act as a DHCP (Dynamic Host Configuration Protocol) server for your private network if you wish. That is, it can assign internal IP addresses to each of your computers automatically. You can enable the router's DHCP server feature and configure each computer to use DHCP. If this feature doesn't work for you, you can assign IP addresses to each computer manually. In that case, assuming the router has an internal IP address of 192.168.1.1, the first computer should be set to 192.168.1.2. The next one should be 192.168.1.3, and so on. In every case, your subnet mask should be 255.255.255.0.

When NAT is set up properly, Netstat will report each computer's local address in the format 192.168.*x.x*. If, for some reason, the local IP address shown is the one assigned by your ISP, you'll know that the computer is accessing the Internet directly due to some misconfiguration. You will have to consult your router's documentation and your ISP's documentation to sort it out.

Linux broadband users who are not running any servers and who have disabled unnecessary daemons, as explained in Chapter 2, need nothing more than a NAT router capable of stateful packet inspection (SPI). Because undesirable Internet functions can't be hidden in open-source software, a packet filter is superfluous.

However, Windows users with a NAT router *do* need a packet filter capable of *egress filtering* because so many native Windows processes, and so much third-party software, will connect to the Internet without alerting the user.

Notes on Packet Filters

Linux home users with a dialup connection obviously won't be using NAT and will need a simple packet filter. Bastille is an easy-to-use front end to the

IPchains and IPtables packet filters, available from `www.bastille-linux.org`. It will also tighten permissions to help harden a Linux system, though this can be over-done. I would not recommend the paranoid option for a home computer. Indeed, even the moderate option is a bit more than required unless the system is running servers.

All Windows users, regardless of how they connect to the Internet, need a packet filter capable of egress filtering. There is too much malware and spyware written for Windows, and too much phone-home capability built into Windows itself and into the applications it runs, for a user to depend on a router alone. NAT is a perfectly adequate defense against external attacks, but Windows and the software written for it are filled with hidden functions that open the door to system exploitation and privacy invasion from within. Indeed, this inherent promiscuity with Internet access is a greater risk than that of remote attackers trying to break in. On a Windows system, egress filtering is actually more important than firewalling.

Most Windows packet filters, with the glaring exception of Microsoft's own Internet Connection Firewall, will alert users whenever a system process or application is attempting to access the Internet. Usually there will be a setup option enabling users to choose access rights for each application or system process. My advice is to deny Internet access to everything that requests it except for known clients, such as the browser, e-mail, IM, IRC, etc., and perhaps one or two select processes that have value to you. If you've just installed a packet filter for the first time, you will be alerted whenever a program attempts to access the Internet and asked if the service or process should be allowed to connect. It's important to know what each one is before deciding. Virtually all Windows processes should be denied Internet access, though a few, such as automatic updates, may be useful to you. Perform a Web search and find out what you can about any system component or executable file that tries to connect. Readers who have been using a packet filter for a while should review the items that they've already permitted access and shut down those they don't need or that seem suspicious.

Adware programs may not work unless the corresponding ad functions are allowed to connect. I recommend replacing adware with open-source equivalents whenever possible and uninstalling the original. But keep in mind that some adware outfits are unscrupulous, and sometimes, when the uninstall routine is activated, the adware portion of the program will remain and continue to operate. Egress filtering will help you locate any adware leftovers.

Many packet filters will let you control whether or not a client or other service should be allowed to act as a server. Some P2P and IM clients may need this level of permission to function properly, but it is generally a bad idea to allow any piece of software to act as a server unless it has to. Be *very* stingy with the "allow server" option.

Windows Processes

A *process* is a running program executable. Following are three lists of Windows processes that one might discover by using the Task Manager, although the lists are not exhaustive. The first group contains common malicious processes. The second group contains common Windows processes, though the fact that they're listed here by no means indicates that you should *want* them running. The third group lists common application processes, though, there again, the fact that they're known by no means indicates that you should welcome them on your machine. When you find a running process that piques your interest, you should perform a Web search on it, learn what it does and how it works, and decide if it ought to be allowed to run on your machine. Indeed, many of the "normal" processes listed here are ones that I've advised users to disable for security reasons. Others can be disabled to improve system performance.

Bear in mind that allowing a process to run is one thing; allowing it to access the Internet is quite another. The only programs that should be granted Internet access are clients such as browsers, IM and e-mail clients, and the like, as noted previously.

The Windows Task Manager and the procedures for killing and disabling processes are covered in Chapter 4. The lists of process names that follow are provided courtesy of LIUtilities (www.liutilities.com) and include a few of my own additions. Interesting items should be researched. The LIUtilities online process library at www.liutilities.com/products/wintaskspro/processlibrary[1] is a good place to start, and Google will provide additional leads if a process that concerns you isn't listed or explained in enough detail. Pay close attention to spelling, because malicious processes are deliberately spelled to resemble normal ones.

Malicious Processes

adaware.exe	alevir.exe	aom.exe	arr.exe	backweb.exe
bargains.exe	blss.exe	bootconf.exe	bpc.exe	brasil.exe
bundle.exe	bvt.exe	cfd.exe	cmd32.exe	cmesys.exe
datemanager.exe	dcomx.exe	divx.exe	dllreg.exe	dpps2.exe
dssagent.exe	emsw.exe	explore.exe	fsg_4104.exe	gator.exe
gmt.exe	hbinst.exe	hbsrv.exe	hxdl.exe	hxiul.exe
iedll.exe	iedriver.exe	iexplorer.exe	infus.exe	infwin.exe

---

1. Process library descriptions copyright LIUtilities.

intdel.exe	isass.exe	istsvc.exe	jdbgmrg.exe	kazza.exe
keenvalue.exe	kernel32.exe	launcher.exe	loader.exe	mapisvc32.exe
md.exe	mfin32.exe	mmod.exe	mostat.exe	msapp.exe
msbb.exe	msblast.exe	mscache.exe	msccn32.exe	mscman.exe
msdm.exe	msiexec16.exe	mslaugh.exe	msmgt.exe	msmsgri32.exe
msrexe.exe	mssys.exe	msvxd.exe	netd32.exe	nssys32.exe
nstask32.exe	nsupdate.exe	onsrvr.exe	optimize.exe	patch.exe
pgmonitr.exe	powerscan.exe	prizesurfer.exe	prmt.exe	prmvr.exe
ray.exe	rb32.exe	rcsync.exe	run32dll.exe	rundll.exe
rundll16.exe	ruxdll32.exe	sahagent.exe	save.exe	savenow.exe
sc.exe	scam32.exe	scrsvr.exe	scvhost.exe	svc.exe
svchosts.exe	svshost.exe	service.exe	showbehind.exe	soap.exe
spoler.exe	srng.exe	start.exe	stcloader.exe	support.exe
svc.exe	svchosts.exe	svshost.exe	system.exe	system32.exe
teekids.exe	trickler.exe	tsadbot.exe	tvmd.exe	tvtmd.exe
webdav.exe	win32.exe	win32us.exe	winactive.exe	win-bugsfix.exe
windows.exe	wininetd.exe	wininit.exe	winlogin.exe	winmain.exe
winnet.exe	winppr32.exe	winservn.exe	winssk32.exe	winstart.exe
winstart001.exe	wintsk32.exe	winupdate.exe	wnad.exe	wupdt.exe

Windows Processes

agentsvr.exe	alg.exe	autorun.exe	cconnect.exe	cidaemon.exe
cisvc.exe	clisvcl.exe	cmd.exe	csrss.exe	ctfmon.exe
ddhelp.exe	dfssvc.exe	dllhost.exe	dns.exe	dumprep.exe
explorer.exe	grpconv.exe	helpctr.exe	hidserv.exe	iexplore.exe
inetinfo.exe	internat.exe	ireike.exe	ismserv.exe	kernel32.dll
launch32.exe	lights.exe	llssrv.exe	locator.exe	lsass.exe
mad.exe	mapisp32.exe	mdm.exe	mmc.exe	mmtask.tsk
monitor.exe	mprexe.exe	msconfig.exe	msdtc.exe	msgsrv32.exe
msiexec.exe	msoobe.exe	mssearch.exe	mstask.exe	mtx.exe

nddeagnt.exe	netdde.exe	ntfrs.exe	ntvdm.exe	pstores.exe
regsvc.exe	regsvr32.exe	rnaapp.exe	rpcss.exe	rundll32.exe
runonce.exe	sage.exe	scanregw.exe	scardsvr.exe	scm.exe
services.exe	smss.exe	snmp.exe	smss.exe	snmptrap.exe
spool32.exe	spoolss.exe	spoolsv.exe	srvany.exe	svchost.exe
system	system idle process	systray.exe	tapisrv.exe	taskmgr.exe
taskmon.exe	taskswitch.exe	winlogon.exe	winmgmt.exe	winoa386.mod
wins.exe	wkdetect.exe	wmiexe.exe	wowexec.exe	wuauclt.exe

Application Processes

acrobat.exe	acrord32.exe	acrotray.exe	acsd.exe	actalert.exe
agrsmmsg.exe	aim.exe	apoint.exe	ati2evxx.exe	atiptaxx.exe
atrack.exe	avsynmgr.exe	backweb-8876480.exe	bcmsmmsg.exe	carpserv.exe
ccapp.exe	ccevtmgr.exe	ccpxysvc.exe	ccregvfy.exe	cdac11ba.exe
cdplayer.exe	cmmpu.exe	cpd.exe	cthelper.exe	ctsvccda.exe
cvpnd.exe	dadapp.exe	damon.exe	ddcman.exe	defwatch.exe
devldr32.exe	directcd.exe	dit.exe	dlg.exe	dsentry.exe
dw.exe	dxdllreg.exe	em_exec.exe	evntsvc.exe	ezsp_px.exe
findfast.exe	firedaemon.exe	gamechannel.exe	hh.exe	hkcmd.exe
htpatch.exe	iamapp.exe	igfxtray.exe	javaw.exe	jusched.exe
kazaa.exe	kbd.exe	lexbces.exe	lexpps.exe	livenote.exe
loadqm.exe	loadwc.exe	lucomserver.exe	lvcoms.exe	mcshield.exe
mgabg.exe	mmtask.exe	mobsync.exe	mozilla.exe	mplayer2.exe
msgsys.exe	mshta.exe	msimn.exe	msmsgs.exe	msnmsgr.exe
mspaint.exe	mspmspsv.exe	mssvc.exe	navapsvc.exe	navapw32.exe
nerocheck.exe	netscape.exe	netscp6.exe	nisum.exe	nopdb.exe
notepad.exe	nwiz.exe	nvsvc32.exe	osa.exe	osd.exe

pctspk.exe	pds.exe	pinger.exe	point32.exe	promon.exe
prpcui.exe	ps2.exe	psfree.exe	ptsnoop.exe	qserver.exe
qttask.exe	ramsys.exe	realplay.exe	realsched.exe	reboot.exe
regedit.exe	rnathchk.exe	rndal.exe	rtvscan.exe	rulaunch.exe
sagent2.exe	sbhc.exe	schwizex.exe	sentry.exe	setup.exe
sgtray.exe	smc.exe	sndvol32.exe	soundman.exe	ssdpsrv.exe
starteak.exe	steam.exe	stimon.exe	stisvc.exe	studio.exe
tcpsvcs.exe	tfswctrl.exe	tgcmd.exe	tkbell.exe	unwise.exe
updatestats.exe	updreg.exe	uptodate.exe	urlmap.exe	userinit.exe
vsmon.exe	wanmpsvc.exe	wcescomm.exe	wcmdmgr.exe	webscanx.exe
winamp.exe	winword.exe	winzip32.exe	wjview.exe	wkcalrem.exe
wkufind.exe	wmplayer.exe	wordpad.exe	vptray.exe	wscript.exe
vshwin32.exe	vsmon.exe	wuser32.exe	wzqkpick.exe	xfr.exe
xl.exe	ypager.exe	zlclient.exe		

Ports

Two lists of ports follow, the first indicating standard ports for typical services on Windows and Linux, and the second, immensely longer one, listing common Trojan rootkit ports on Windows and Linux. The fact that a port is associated with a common service does *not* mean that it should be open, or that the service behind it should be running on your machine. As we discussed in Chapter 2, the vast majority of services are unnecessary and only represent an invitation to exploitation. These lists are meant as a quick reference when Netstat reports unusual connections, but they are not comprehensive. Unexpected port activity should always be investigated with a Web search.

Bear in mind that malware often uses ports associated with normal services. The fact that a malicious program *might* be using a particular port does not necessarily mean that one is. More often than not, the culprit will be a service that you've neglected to disable, or a Windows "feature" or a third-party application that's accessing the Internet without your knowledge. Always eliminate the common causes of unexpected port activity before fretting about the more exotic ones.

Common Ports

15: Netstat

20: FTP (File Transfer Protocol)

21: FTP (File Transfer Protocol)

22: SSH (secure shell), pcAnywhere

23: Telnet

25: SMTP (Simple Mail Transfer Protocol)

33: DSP (Display Support Protocol)

37: Time

42: WINS (Windows Internet Naming Server)

43: Whois

53: DNS (domain name service)

63: Whois

68: DHCP (Dynamic Host Configuration Protocol)

69: TFTP (Trivial File Transfer Protocol)

70: Gopher

79: Finger

80: HTTP (Hypertext Transfer Protocol)

88: Kerberos

98: Linuxconf

101: Hostname

109: POP2 (Post Office Protocol version 2)

110: POP3 (Post Office Protocol version 3)

111: SunRPC (Sun RPC Portmapper)

113: Ident

115: SFTP (Secure File Transfer Protocol)

117: UUCP (UNIX to UNIX copy)

119: NNTP (Network News Transfer Protocol)

123: NTP (Network Time Protocol)

135: RPC (remote procedure call), DCE (distributed computing environment)

137: NetBIOS Name Service

138: NetBIOS UDP

139: NetBIOS

143: IMAP (Internet Message Access Protocol)

161: SNMP (Simple Network Management Protocol)

194: IRC (Internet relay chat)

220: IMAP3 (Internet Message Access Protocol version 3)

389: LDAP (Lightweight Directory Access Protocol), MS Exchange, NetMeeting

443: SSL (Secure Sockets Layer)

445: SMB (NetBIOS over TCP)

465: SMTP/TLS (Simple Mail Transfer Protocol via Transport Layer Security)

512: Rlogin

515: Line printer daemon (LPD)

563: NNTP via SSL, MS Exchange

593: RPC

636: Secure LDAP (LDAP via SSL or TLS)

666: Doom

993: SIMAP (Secure Internet Message Access Protocol—IMAP via TLS)

995: SPOP (Secure Post Office Protocol—POP via TLS)

1080: Socks

1352: Lotus Notes

1433: Microsoft SQL Server

1434: Microsoft SQL Monitor

1521: Oracle SQL

1604: Citrix ICA/Microsoft Terminal Server

1755: Windows Media

1758: TFTP (Trivial File Transfer Protocol)

1863: MSN Messenger

1900: UPnP SSDP (Universal Plug and Play Simple Service Discovery Protocol)

2049: NFS (network file system)

3306: MySQL

3128: Squid

3306: MySQL

3389: Terminal Server

4000: ICQ

5000: UPnP (universal plug and play)

5010: Yahoo! Messenger

5190: AIM (AOL Instant Messenger)

5631: pcAnywhere

5632: pcAnywhere

5800: VNC (virtual network computing)

5900: VNC

6000: X Window System

6660–6670: IRC

6970: RTP (Real-Time Protocol)

6699: Napster

7007: Windows Media

7070: RealServer/QuickTime

7778: Unreal

8080: HTTP

14237: Palm

14238: Palm

17001: Quake World

26000: Quake

27010: Half-Life

27960: Quake III

Trojan Ports[2]

0: REx

1: Sockets des Troie

2: Death

5: Yoyo

11: Skun

16: Skun

17: Skun

18: Skun

19: Skun

20: Amanda

21: ADM worm, Alpha Force, Back Construction, Blade Runner, BlueFire, Bmail, Cattivik FTP Server, CC Invader, Dark FTP, Doly Trojan, FreddyK, Invisible FTP, KWM, MscanWorm, NerTe, NokNok, Pinochet, Ramen, Reverse Trojan, RTB 666, The Flu, Voyager, WinCrash

22: InCommand, Shaft, Skun

23: ADM worm, Aphex Remote Packet Sniffer, AutoSpY, ButtMan, Fire HacKer, My Very Own Trojan, Pest, RTB 666, Tiny Telnet Server, Truva

---

2. Courtesy of, and copyright by, Braun Consultants and Simovits Consulting (www.simovits.com).

25: Antigen, Barok, BSE, Email Password Sender, Gip, Laocoon, Magic Horse, MBT, Moscow Email Trojan, Nimda, Shtirlitz, Stukach, Tapiras, WinPC

27: Assassin

28: Amanda

30: Agent 40421

31: Agent 40421, Masters Paradise, Skun

37: ADM worm

39: SubSARI

41: Deep Throat, Foreplay

44: Arctic

51: Fuck Lamers Backdoor

52: MuSka52, Skun

53: ADM worm, li0n, MscanWorm, MuSka52

54: MuSka52

66: AL-Bareki

69: BackGate Kit, Nimda, Pasana, Storm, Theef

69: Pasana

70: ADM worm

79: ADM worm, Firehotcker

80: 711-Trojan (Seven Eleven), AckCmd, BlueFire, Cafeini, Duddie, Executor, God Message, Intruzzo, Latinus, Lithium, MscanWorm, NerTe, Nimda, Noob, Optix Lite, Optix Pro, Power, Ramen, Remote Shell, Reverse WWW Tunnel Backdoor, RingZero, RTB666, Scalper, Screen Cutter, Seeker, Slapper, WebDownloader, Web Server CT

80: Penrox

81: Asylum

101: Skun

102: Delf, Skun

103: Skun

105: NerTe

107: Skun

109: ADM worm

110: ADM worm

111: ADM worm, MscanWorm

113: ADM worm, Alicia, Cyn, DataSpy Network X, Dosh, Gibbon, Taskman

120: Skun

121: Attack Bot, God Message, JammerKillah

123: Net Controller

137: Chode, Nimda

137: Bugbear, Msinit, Opaserv, QAZ

138: Chode, Nimda

139: Chode, Fire HacKer, Msinit, Nimda, Opaserv, QAZ

143: ADM worm

146: Infector

146: Infector

166: NokNok

170: A-Trojan

171: A-Trojan

200: CyberSpy

201: One Windows Trojan

202: One Windows Trojan, Skun

211: One Windows Trojan

212: One Windows Trojan

221: Snape

222: NeuroticKat, Snape

230: Skun

231: Skun

232: Skun

285: Delf

299: One Windows Trojan

334: Backage

335: Nautical

370: NeuroticKat

400: Argentino

401: One Windows Trojan

402: One Windows Trojan

411: Backage

420: Breach

443: Slapper

445: Nimda

455: Fatal Connections

511: T0rn

513: ADM

514: ADM

515: MscanWorm, Ramen

520: Backdoor

555: 711-Trojan (Seven Eleven), Phase Zero

564: Oracle

589: Assassin

600: SweetHeart

623: RTB 666

635: ADM worm

650: Assassin

661: NokNok

666: Attack FTP, Back Construction, BLA Trojan, NokNok, Reverse Trojan, Shadow Phyre, Unicorn, Yoyo

667: NokNok, SniperNet

668: Unicorn

669: DP Trojan, SniperNet

680: RTB 666

692: GayOL

700: REx

777: Undetected

798: Oracle

808: WinHole

831: NeuroticKat

901: Net-Devil, Pest

902: Net-Devil, Pest

903: Net-Devil

911: Dark Shadow

956: Crat Pro

991: Snape

992: Snape

999: Deep Throat, Foreplay

1000: Der Späher/Der Spaeher, Direct Connection, GOTHIC Intruder, Theef

1001: Der Späher/Der Spaeher, GOTHIC Intruder, Lula, One Windows Trojan, Theef

1005: Pest, Theef

1008: AutoSpY, li0n

1010: Doly Trojan

1011: Doly Trojan

1012: Doly Trojan

1015: Doly Trojan

1016: Doly Trojan

1020: Vampire

1024: Latinus, Lithium, NetSpy, Ptakks

1025: AcidkoR, BDDT, DataSpy Network X, Fraggle Rock, KiLo, MuSka52, NetSpy, Optix Pro, Paltalk, Ptakks, Real 2000, Remote Anything, Remote Explorer Y2K, Remote Storm, RemoteNC, Yajing

1026: BDDT, Dark IRC, DataSpy Network X, Delta Remote Access, Dosh, Duddie, IRC Contact, Remote Explorer 2000, RUX The TIc.K

1026: Remote Explorer 2000

1027: Clandestine, DataSpy Network X, KiLo, UandMe

1028: DataSpy Network X, Dosh, Gibbon, KiLo, KWM, Litmus, Paltalk, SubSARI

1029: Clandestine, KWM, Litmus, SubSARI

1030: Gibbon, KWM

1031: KWM, Little Witch, Xanadu, Xot

1032: Akosch4, Dosh, KWM

1033: Dosh, KWM, Little Witch, Net Advance

1034: KWM

1035: Dosh, KWM, RemoteNC, Truva Atl

1036: KWM

1037: Arctic, Dosh, KWM, MoSucker

1039: Dosh

1041: Dosh, RemoteNC

1042: BLA Trojan

1043: Dosh

1044: Ptakks

1047: RemoteNC

1049: Delf, The Hobbit Daemon

1052: Fire HacKer, Slapper, **The Hobbit Daemon**

1053: The Thief

1054: AckCmd, RemoteNC

1080: SubSeven 2.2, WinHole

1081: WinHole

1082: WinHole

1083: WinHole

1092: Hvl RAT

1095: Blood Fest Evolution

1097: Blood Fest Evolution

1098: Blood Fest Evolution

1099: Blood Fest Evolution

1104: RexxRave

1111: Daodan, Ultors Trojan

1115: Lurker, Protoss

1116: Lurker

1122: Last 2000, Singularity

1133: SweetHeart

1150: Orion

1151: Orion

1160: BlackRat

1166: CrazzyNet

1167: CrazzyNet

1170: Psyber Stream Server, Voice

1180: Unin 68

1183: Cyn, SweetHeart

1200: NoBackO

1201: NoBackO

1207: SoftWAR

1208: Infector

1212: Kaos

1215: Force

1218: Force

1219: Force

1221: Fuck Lamers Backdoor

1222: Fuck Lamers Backdoor

1234: KiLo, Ultors Trojan

1243: BackDoor-G, SubSeven, Tiles

1245: Voodoo Doll

1255: Scarab

1256: Project nEXT, RexxRave

1272: The Matrix

1313: NETrojan

1314: Daodan

1349: BO dll

1369: SubSeven 2.2

1386: Dagger

1415: Last 2000, Singularity

1433: Voyager Alpha Force

1441: Remote Storm

1492: FTP 99CMP

1524: Trinoo

1560: Big Gluck, Duddie

1561: MuSka 52

1600: Direct Connection

1601: Direct Connection

1602: Direct Connection

1703: Exploiter

1711: Yoyo

1772: NetControle

1777: Scarab

1826: Glacier

1833: TCC

1834: TCC

1835: TCC

1836: TCC

1837: TCC

1905: Delta Remote Access

1911: Arctic

1966: Fake FTP

1967: For Your Eyes Only, WM FTP Server

1978: Slapper

1981: Bowl, Shockrave

1983: Q-taz

1984: Intruzzo, Q-taz

1985: Black Diver, Q-taz

1986: Akosch 4

1991: PitFall

1999: Back Door, SubSeven, TransScout

2000: A-Trojan, Der Späher/Der Spaeher, Fear, Force, GOTHIC Intruder, Last 2000, Real 2000, Remote Explorer 2000, Remote Explorer Y2K, Senna Spy Trojan Generator, Singularity

2001: Der Späher/Der Spaeher, Duddie, Glacier, Protoss, Senna Spy Trojan Generator, Singularity, Trojan Cow, Scalper

2002: Duddie, Senna Spy Trojan Generator, Sensive, Slapper

2004: Duddie

2005: Duddie

2023: Ripper Pro

2060: Protoss

2080: WinHole

2101: SweetHeart

2115: Bugs

2130: Mini BackLash

2140: The Invasor, Deep Throat, Foreplay, The Invasor

2149: Deep Throat

2150: R0xr4t

2156: Oracle

2222: SweetHeart, Way

2281: Nautical

2283: Hvl RAT

2300: Storm

2311: Studio 54

2330: IRC Contact

2331: IRC Contact

2332: IRC Contact, Silent Spy

2333: IRC Contact

2334: IRC Contact, Power

2335: IRC Contact

2336: IRC Contact

2337: IRC Contact, The Hobbit Daemon

2338: IRC Contact

2339: IRC Contact, Voice Spy

2343: Asylum

2345: Doly Trojan

2407: Yoyo

2418: Intruzzo

2555: li0n, T0rn Rootkit

2565: Striker Trojan

2583: WinCrash

2589: Dagger

2600: Digital RootBeer

2702: Black Diver

2772: SubSeven

2773: SubSeven, SubSeven 2.1 Gold

2774: SubSeven, SubSeven 2.1 Gold

2800: Theef

2929: Konik

2983: Breach

2989: Remote Administration Tool—RAT

3000: InetSpy, Remote Shut, Theef

3006: Clandestine

3024: WinCrash

3031: MicroSpy

3119: Delta Remote Access

3128: Reverse WWW Tunnel Backdoor, RingZero

3129: Masters Paradise

3131: SubSARI

3150: Deep Throat, The Invasor, Foreplay, Mini BackLash

3215: XHX

3292: Xposure

3295: Xposure

3333: Daodan

3410: Optix Pro

3417: Xposure

3418: Xposure

3456: Fear, Force, Terror Trojan

3459: Eclipse 2000, Sanctuary

3505: AutoSpY

3700: Portal of Doom

3721: Whirlpool

3723: Mantis

3777: PsychWard

3791: Total Solar Eclypse

3800: Total Solar Eclypse

3801: Total Solar Eclypse

3945: Delta Remote Access

3996: Remote Anything

3997: Remote Anything

3999: Remote Anything

4000: Remote Anything, SkyDance

4092: WinCrash

4128: RedShad

4156: Slapper

4201: War Trojan

4210: Netkey

4211: Netkey

4225: Silent Spy

4242: Virtual Hacking Machine

4315: Power

4321: BoBo

4414: AL-Bareki

4442: Oracle

4444: CrackDown, Oracle, Prosiak, **Swift Remote, MSBlaster**

4445: Oracle

4447: Oracle

4449: Oracle

4451: Oracle

4488: Event Horizon

4567: File Nail

4653: Cero

4666: Mneah

4700: Theef

4836: Power

5000: Back Door Setup, Bubbel, **Ra1d, Sockets des Troie**

5001: Back Door Setup, Sockets des **Troie**

5002: Shaft

5005: Aladino

5011: Peanut Brittle

5025: WM Remote KeyLogger

5031: Net Metropolitan

5032: Net Metropolitan

5050: R0xr4t

5135: Bmail

5150: Pizza

5151: Optix Lite

5152: Laphex

5155: Oracle

5221: NOSecure

5250: Pizza

5321: Firehotcker

5333: Backage

5350: Pizza

5377: Iani

5400: Back Construction, Blade Runner, Digital Spy

5401: Back Construction, Blade Runner, Digital Spy, Mneah

5402: Back Construction, Blade Runner, Digital Spy, Mneah

5418: DarkSky

5419: DarkSky

5430: Net Advance

5450: Pizza

5503: Remote Shell

5534: The Flu

5550: Pizza

5555: Daodan, NoXcape

5556: BO Facil

5557: BO Facil

5569: Robo-Hack

5650: Pizza

5669: SpArTa

5679: Nautical

5695: Assassin

5696: Assassin

5697: Assassin

5742: WinCrash

5802: Y3K RAT

5873: SubSeven 2.2

5880: Y3K RAT

5882: Y3K RAT

5888: Y3K RAT

5889: Y3K RAT

5933: NOSecure

6000: Aladino, NetBus, The Thing

6006: Bad Blood

6267: DarkSky

6400: The Thing

6521: Oracle

6526: Glacier

6556: AutoSpY

6661: Weia-Meia

6666: AL-Bareki, KiLo, SpArTa

6667: Acropolis, BlackRat, Dark FTP, Dark IRC, DataSpy, Network X, Gunsan, InCommand, Kaitex, KiLo, Laocoon, Net-Devil, Reverse Trojan, ScheduleAgent, SlackBot, SubSeven, SubSeven 2.1.4, Trinity, Y3K RAT, Yoyo

6669: Host Control, Vampire, Voyager, Alpha Force

6670: BackWeb Server, Deep Throat, Foreplay, WinNuke eXtreame

6697: Force

6711: BackDoor-G, Duddie, KiLo, Little Witch, Netkey, Spadeace, SubSARI, SubSeven, SweetHeart, UandMe, VP Killer, Way

6712: Funny Trojan, KiLo, Spadeace, SubSeven

6713: KiLo, SubSeven

6714: KiLo

6715: KiLo

6718: KiLo

6723: Mstream

6766: KiLo

6767: KiLo, Pasana, UandMe

6771: Deep Throat, Foreplay

6776: 2000 Cracks, BackDoor-G, SubSeven, VP Killer

6838: Mstream

6891: Force

6912: Shit Heep

6969: 2000 Cracks, BlitzNet, Dark IRC, GateCrasher, Kid Terror, Laphex, Net Controller, SpArTa, Vagr Nocker

6970: GateCrasher

7000: Aladino, Gunsan, Remote Grab, SubSeven, SubSeven 2.1 Gold, Theef

7001: Freak 88, Freak 2k

7007: Silent Spy

7020: Basic Hell

7030: Basic Hell

7119: Massaker

7215: SubSeven, SubSeven 2.1 Gold

7274: AutoSpY

7290: NOSecure

7291: NOSecure

7300: NetSpy

7301: NetSpy

7306: NetSpy

7307: NetSpy, Remote Process Monitor

7308: NetSpy, X Spy

7312: Yajing

7410: Phoenix II

7424: Host Control

7597: QAZ

7626: Glacier

7648: XHX

7673: Neoturk

7676: Neoturk

7677: Neoturk

7718: Glacier

7722: KiLo

7777: God Message

7788: Last 2000, Singularity

7789: Back Door Setup

7800: Paltalk

7826: Oblivion

7850: Paltalk

7878: Paltalk

7879: Paltalk

7979: Vagr Nocker

7983: Mstream

8011: Way

8012: Ptakks

8080: Reverse WWW Tunnel Backdoor, RingZero, Screen Cutter

8090: Aphex Remote Packet Sniffer

8097: Kryptonic Ghost Command Pro

8100: Back streets

8110: DLP

8111: DLP

8127: 9_119, Chonker

8130: 9_119, Chonker, DLP

8131: DLP

8301: DLP

8302: DLP

8311: SweetHeart

8322: DLP

8329: DLP

8488: KiLo

8489: KiLo

8685: Unin 68

8732: Kryptonic Ghost Command Pro

8734: AutoSpY

8787: Back Orifice 2000

8811: Fear

8812: FraggleRock Lite

8821: Alicia

8848: Whirlpool

8864: Whirlpool

8888: Dark IRC

9000: Netministrator

9090: Aphex Remote Packet Sniffer

9117: Massaker

9148: Nautical

9301: DLP

9325: Mstream

9329: DLP

9400: InCommand

9401: InCommand

9536: Lula

9561: Crat Pro

9563: Crat Pro

9870: Remote Computer Control **Center**

9872: Portal of Doom

9873: Portal of Doom

9874: Portal of Doom

9875: Portal of Doom

9876: Rux

9877: Small Big Brother

9878: Small Big Brother, TransScout

9879: Small Big Brother

9919: Kryptonic Ghost **Command Pro**

9999: BlitzNet, Oracle, Spadeace

10000: Oracle, TCP Door, XHX

10001: DTr, Lula

10002: Lula

10003: Lula

10008: li0n

10012: Amanda

10013: Amanda

10067: Portal of Doom

10084: Syphilis

10085: Syphilis

10086: Syphilis

10100: Control Total, GiFt Trojan, **Scalper, Slapper**

10167: Portal of Doom

10498: Mstream

10520: Acid Shivers

10528: Host Control

10607: Coma

10666: Ambush

10887: BDDT

10889: BDDT

11000: DataRape, Senna Spy Trojan Generator

11011: Amanda

11050: Host Control

11051: Host Control

11111: Breach

11223: Progenic Trojan, Secret Agent

11225: Cyn

11660: Back streets

11718: Kryptonic Ghost Command Pro

11831: DarkFace, DataRape, Latinus, Pest, Vagr Nocker

11977: Cool Remote Control

11978: Cool Remote Control

11980: Cool Remote Control

12000: Reverse Trojan

12310: PreCursor

12321: Protoss

12345: Ashley, BlueIce 2000, Mypic, NetBus, Pie Bill Gates, Q-taz, Sensive, Snape, Vagr Nocker, ValvNet, Whack Job

12346: NetBus

12348: BioNet

12349: BioNet, The Saint

12361: Whack-a-mole

12362: Whack-a-mole

12363: Whack-a-mole

12623: ButtMan, DUN Control

12624: ButtMan, Power

12631: Whack Job

12684: Power

12754: Mstream

12904: Rocks

13000: Senna Spy Trojan Generator

13013: PsychWard

13014: PsychWard

13028: Back streets

13079: Kryptonic Ghost Command Pro

13370: SpArTa

13371: Optix Pro

13500: Theef

13753: Anal FTP

14194: CyberSpy

14285: Laocoon

14286: Laocoon

14287: Laocoon

14500: PC Invader

14501: PC Invader

14502: PC Invader

14503: PC Invader

15000: In Route to the Hell, R0xr4t

15092: Host Control

15104: Mstream

15206: KiLo

15207: KiLo

15210: UDP remote shell backdoor server

15382: SubZero

15432: Cyn

15485: KiLo

15486: KiLo

15500: In Route to Hell

15512: Iani

15551: In Route to Hell

15695: Kryptonic Ghost Command Pro

15845: KiLo

15852: Kryptonic Ghost Command Pro

16057: MoonPie

16484: MoSucker

16514: KiLo

16515: KiLo

16523: Back streets

16660: Stacheldraht

16712: KiLo

16761: Kryptonic Ghost Command Pro

16959: SubSeven, SubSeven 2.1.4

17166: Mosaic

17449: Kid Terror

17499: CrazzyNet

17500: CrazzyNet

17569: Infector

17593: AudioDoor

17777: Nephron

18753: Shaft

19191: BlueFire

19216: BackGate Kit

20000: Millennium, PSYcho Files, XHX

20001: Insect, Millennium, PSYcho Files

20002: AcidkoR, PSYcho Files

20005: MoSucker

20023: VP Killer

20034: NetBus 2.0 Pro, NetBus 2.0 Pro Hidden, Whack Job

20331: BLA Trojan

20432: Shaft

20433: Shaft

21212: Sensive

21544: GirlFriend, Kid Terror

21554: Exploiter, FreddyK, Kid Terror, Schwindler, Sensive, Winsp00fer

21579: Breach

21957: Latinus

22115: Cyn

22222: Donald Dick, G.R.O.B., Prosiak, Ruler, RUX The TIc.K

22223: RUX The TIc.K

22456: Clandestine

22554: Schwindler

22783: Intruzzo

22784: Intruzzo

22785: Intruzzo

23000: Storm worm

23001: Storm worm

23005: NetTrash, Oxon

23006: NetTrash, Oxon

23023: Logged

23032: Amanda

23321: Konik

23432: Asylum

23456: Clandestine, Evil FTP, Vagr Nocker, Whack Job

23476: Donald Dick

23477: Donald Dick

23777: InetSpy

24000: Infector

24289: Latinus

25002: MOTD

25123: Goy'Z TroJan

25555: FreddyK

25685: MoonPie

25686: DarkFace, MoonPie

25799: FreddyK

25885: MOTD

25982: DarkFace, MoonPie

26274: Delta Source

26681: Voice Spy

27160: MoonPie

27184: Alvgus Trojan 2000

27373: Charge

27374: Bad Blood, Fake SubSeven, **li0n, Ramen, Seeker,** SubSeven, SubSeven 2.1 Gold, SubSeven 2.1.4, SubSeven 2.2, SubSeven Muie, The Saint

27379: Optix Lite

27444: Trinoo

27573: SubSeven

27665: Trinoo

28218: Oracle

28431: Hack´a´Tack

28678: Exploiter

29104: NetTrojan

29292: BackGate Kit

29559: AntiLamer BackDoor, DarkFace, **DataRape,** Ducktoy, **Latinus,** Pest, Vagr Nocker

29589: KiLo

29891: The Unexplained

29999: AntiLamer BackDoor

30000: DataRape, Infector

30001: Err0r32

30005: Litmus

30100: NetSphere

30101: NetSphere

30102: NetSphere

30103: NetSphere

30133: NetSphere

30303: Sockets des Troie

30331: MuSka52

30464: Slapper

30700: Mantis

30947: Intruse

31320: Little Witch

31335: Trinoo

31336: Butt Funnel

31337: ADM worm, Back Fire, Back Orifice, BlitzNet, BO client, BO Facil, BO2, Freak88, Freak2k, NoBackO, Deep BO

31338: Back Orifice, Butt Funnel, NetSpy

31338: Deep BO, NetSpy

31339: Little Witch, NetSpy

31340: Little Witch

31382: Lithium

31415: Lithium

31416: Lithium

31557: Xanadu

31745: BuschTrommel

31785: Hack´a´Tack

31787: Hack´a´Tack

31788: Hack´a´Tack

31789: Hack´a´Tack

31790: Hack´a´Tack

31791: Hack´a´Tack

31792: Hack´a´Tack

31887: BDDT

32000: BDDT

32001: Donald Dick

32100: Peanut Brittle, Project nEXT

32418: Acid Battery

32791: Acropolis, Rocks

33270: Trinity

33333: Prosiak

33545: G.R.O.B.

33567: li0n, T0rn Rootkit

33568: li0n, T0rn Rootkit

33577: Son of PsychWard

33777: Son of PsychWard

33911: Spirit 2000, Spirit 2001

34312: Delf

34313: Delf

34324: Big Gluck

34343: Osiris

34444: Donald Dick

34555: Trinoo (Windows)

35000: Infector

35555: Trinoo (Windows)

35600: SubSARI

36794: Bugbear

37237: Mantis

37651: Charge

38741: CyberSpy

38742: CyberSpy

40071: Ducktoy

40308: SubSARI

40412: The Spy

40421: Agent 40421, Masters Paradise

40422: Masters Paradise

40423: Masters Paradise

40425: Masters Paradise

40426: Masters Paradise

41337: Storm

41666: Remote Boot Tool

43720: KiLo

44014: Iani

44444: Prosiak

44575: Exploiter

44767: School Bus

45092: BackGate Kit

45454: Osiris

45632: Little Witch

45673: Acropolis, Rocks

46666: Taskman

47017: T0rn Rootkit

47262: Delta Source

47698: KiLo

47785: KiLo

47891: AntiLamer BackDoor

48004: Fraggle Rock

48006: Fraggle Rock

48512: Arctic

49000: Fraggle Rock

49683: Fenster

49698: KiLo

50000: SubSARI

50021: Optix Pro

50130: Enterprise

50505: Sockets des Troie

50551: R0xr4t

50552: R0xr4t

50766: Schwindler

50829: KiLo

51234: Cyn

51966: Cafeini

52365: Way

52901: Omega

53001: Remote Windows Shutdown—RWS

54283: SubSeven, SubSeven 2.1 Gold

54320: Back Orifice 2000

54321: Back Orifice 2000, School Bus, Yoyo

55165: File Manager Trojan

55555: Shadow Phyre

55665: Latinus, Pinochet

55666: Latinus, Pinochet

56565: Osiris

57163: BlackRat

57341: NetRaider

57785: G.R.O.B.

58134: Charge

58339: Butt Funnel

59211: Ducktoy

60000: Deep Throat, Foreplay, Sockets des Troie

60001: Trinity

60008: li0n, T0rn Rootkit

60068: The Thing

60411: Connection

60551: R0xr4t

60552: R0xr4t

60666: Basic Hell

61115: Protoss

61337: Nota

61348: Bunker-Hill

61440: Orion

61603: Bunker-Hill

61746: KiLo

61747: KiLo

61748: KiLo

61979: Cool Remote Control

62011: Ducktoy

63485: Bunker-Hill

64101: Taskman

65000: Devil, Sockets des Troie, Stacheldraht

65289: Yoyo

65421: Alicia

65422: Alicia

65432: The Traitor (th3tr41t0r)

65530: Windows Mite

65535: RC1 Trojan

Online Resources

Security News

The Register,
www.theregister.co.uk

The most skeptical and perhaps the last fully independent tech news publication. Covers all aspects of the IT industry, including security. Shares content with SecurityFocus.

SecurityFocus,
www.securityfocus.com

Computer and network security are the only topics. Offers news articles, opinion columns, advisories, and technical how-tos, ranging from newbie-friendly to advanced. Shares content with *The Register*.

Wired News, wired.com

Owned by Lycos, but apparently enjoys considerable editorial independence. Covers all aspects of the IT industry, including security articles.

LinuxSecurity,
www.linuxsecurity.com

A daily roundup of Linux security stories.

Linux Today,
linuxtoday.com

A daily roundup of Linux stories from the press, including security articles.

FreeOS, www.freeos.com

News and resources for systems such as BSD and Linux.

Security News Portal,
www.securitynewsportal.com

A daily roundup of security news. Ironically, the site appears to be optimized for Internet Explorer, which is the least secure browser available, and displays poorly in Mozilla.

Whitehats,
www.whitehats.com

A daily security news roundup.

SecuriTeam,
www.securiteam.com

A portal with security news, tools, and separate focus areas for Windows and *nix.

Resources

Anonymizer, www.anonymizer.com	A site offering both free and premium Internet anonymity services. Highly recommended.
SourceForge, sourceforge.net	A vast repository of open-source software for Windows and Linux. The site can be overwhelming, but it has a search engine to help users locate packages.
Free Software Foundation (FSF) and GNU Project, www.gnu.org	The home base of the open-source movement. A repository of open-source products, chiefly for UNIX-compatible systems.
SANS Institute, www.sans.org	An educational and research organization with a vast archive of security research documents, news, and advisories.
CERT/CC, www.cert.org	Computer Emergency Response Team Coordination Center at Carnegie Mellon University. An archive of advisories, statistics, and administrative worst and best practices.
NIST CSRC, csrc.nist.gov/publications/nistpubs	An archive of security research maintained by NIST (National Institute of Standards and Technology) CSRC (Computer Security Resource Center). Recommended for advanced users and security professionals.
Federation of American Scientists (FAS), www.fas.org	A site concerned with the social and political implications of technology and security. Not limited to computing.
Attrition, attrition.org	A pleasantly quirky site offering a good deal of security information with a skeptical point of view.
Sam Spade, samspade.org	A site with CGI gateways to many useful Web resources, such as whois, traceroute, etc.
GeekTools, www.geektools.com	A site similar to Sam Spade with lots of online tools.
F-Secure virus library, www.f-secure.com/v-descs	A searchable database of viruses.
Sophos virus library, www.sophos.com/virusinfo/analyses	A searchable database of viruses.
Simovits Consulting Trojan ports, www.simovits.com/nyheter9902.html	A list of ports used by Trojan rootkits with brief descriptions.

WinGuides Registry library, `www.winguides.com/registry`	A large collection of Windows Registry tips, tweaks, and explanations.
LIUtilities process library, `www.liutilities.com/products/wintaskspro/processlibrary`	A large, searchable collection of Windows processes.
Computer Bytes Man, `www.computerbytesman.com`	A site detailing online privacy threats and political issues connected with technology.
Center for Democracy and Technology (CDT), `www.cdt.org`	A site detailing online privacy threats and political issues connected with technology.
Electronic Frontier Foundation (EFF), `www.eff.org`	A site detailing online privacy threats and political issues connected with technology.
Vmyths, `vmyths.com`	Scathing criticism of the antivirus industry and media-hyped virus scares.
Cryptome, `cryptome.org`	An online repository of government documents and anonymous submissions. Information is not checked for accuracy, by design.
Webopedia, `www.webopedia.com`	A searchable online dictionary of computer terminology.
Wikipedia, `www.wikipedia.org`	A searchable online encyclopedia of technology terms. More detailed than Webopedia.
Victoria TelecommunityNet, `sun.soci.niu.edu/~rslade/secgloss.htm`	A glossary of technical terms chiefly related to security, maintained by Rob Slade.
Risks Digest, `catless.ncl.ac.uk/Risks`	An archive of general privacy, security, and safety articles. Not limited to computing.
Victoria TelecommunityNet, `sun.soci.niu.edu/~rslade/mnbksccd.htm`	A list of security books for professionals and power users, maintained by Rob Slade. Definitely not light reading.

E-mail Lists

Counterpane Crypto-Gram	A monthly newsletter by Bruce Schneier, one of the better class of security expert. Sign up at `www.counterpane.com/crypto-gram.html`.
Politech	A mailing list of news stories and topics concerning Internet privacy, free speech on line, and legislation related to technology. Sign up at `politechbot.com/mailman/listinfo/politech`.
ISN	InfoSec News from Attrition. A daily roundup of security news items. Sign up at `www.c4i.org/isn.html`.
The Register	An e-mail roundup of the day's tech stories, including security. Sign up at *The Register*'s home page, lower left.
Sans Institute NewsBites	A weekly roundup of important security news items. Sign up at `www.sans.org/newsletters`.
SecurityFocus News	Sign up at `www.securityfocus.com/subscribe`.
SecurityFocus Microsoft Security News	Sign up at `www.securityfocus.com/subscribe`.
SecurityFocus Linux Security News	Sign up at `www.securityfocus.com/subscribe`.
BugTraq	A high-volume mailing list of bugs and exploits geared toward security researchers. Sign up at `www.securityfocus.com/subscribe`.
Focus on Microsoft	A high-volume mailing list of bugs and exploits geared toward Windows researchers. Sign up at `www.securityfocus.com/subscribe`.
Focus on Linux	A high-volume mailing list of bugs and exploits geared toward Linux researchers. Sign up at `www.securityfocus.com/subscribe`.

Index

Symbols

*nix, 196, 279
@Stake, 239, 240
0-day, 12, 227, 279, 296
~ (tilde), 68, 297

Numbers

802.11 standard, 154

A

abduction of children, 194
ACH (automated clearing house) payments
    system, 246
ACLU (American Civil Liberties Union), 267
ACPI (advanced configuration and power
    interface), 201
Acrobat Reader, 203
ActiveX, 34–35, 279
Acxiom, 269–70
Ad-aware utility, 13, 112
Administrator password, 60–63, 318
Adobe Acrobat Reader, 203
Adobe Photoshop, 203
advanced configuration and power interface
    (ACPI), 201
advanced power management (APM), 201
Advanced TCP/IP Settings dialog, 312
Advanced user permissions dialog, 66, 322
adware, 12–13
    defined, 279
    detecting, 112–13
aggregate data, 188
Airsnort, 154
Akamai, 183
algorithms
    defined, 121, 279
    and hashed passwords, 22
AMaViS, 114
American Civil Liberties Union (ACLU),
    267
AN.ON Project, 221, 222
anonymity
    defined, 181–82, 280
    importance of, 186–88
anonymity services, 185
    Anonymizer, 147–48, 153, 184, 390
    Java Anonymous Proxy (JAP), 220–22
anonymous proxy servers, 19, 280
antivirus software, 28, 113–14
Apache Web server, 56, 203, 314
API (application program interface), 280
APM (advanced power management), 201
applets, 280

application processes, 353–54
application program interface (API), 280
application vulnerabilities, 40–41
application-layer firewall, 280
applications
    defined, 280
    third-party, 40
Apress Web site, 98, 145, 162
Ares, 23
The Art of Deception, 75
Ashcroft, John, 270
asymmetrical paired-key cryptosystems,
    122
ATMs (automatic teller machines), 26
attachments, e-mail, 34
attack tools, 5
Attritition.org Web site, 229, 390
Austen, Ian, 42–43
authentication, defined, 280
authorization, defined, 280
automated clearing house (ACH) payments
    system, 246
automatic teller machines (ATMs), 26
automatic updates, 40, 49
Automatic Updates service, 308
AVG tool, 10, 113

B

Baas, Daniel, 270
Back Orifice, 6
backdoor, defined, 280
Ballmer, Steve, 205, 206, 209, 212
Barrett, Joe, 25
bash (bourne again shell), 177–78, 280
basic input–output system (BIOS), 259, 281
Bastille, 349–50
batch files, 35, 280
BCWipe, 161
Bennett, Robert, 242
Berkeley Internet Name Domain (BIND)
    service, 41, 56, 203, 314
Bill and Melinda Gates Foundation, 212
binary, defined, 280
BIND (Berkeley Internet Name Domain)
    service, 41, 56, 203, 314
BIOS (basic input–output system), 259, 281
blackhats, 5, 281
bookmarks, 176
Borland Kylix, 203
bourne again shell (bash), 177–78, 280
Brooks, David, 208
browsers, 34–35, 175–77
brute force attacks, 7
BSD operating system, 196
BSE (mad cow disease), 88–90, 251–55

buffers, 172
    defined, 281
    overflows, 34, 38, 281
bugs, defined, 32
BugTraq mailing list, 392
bulletin boards/forums, and IP address, 15
Bzip utility, 203

C

caches, 132, 176, 177, 281, 305
Calloway, Robbie, 249
CAPPS II (Computer Assisted Passenger
    Prescreening System), 265–67
carding. *See* credit card accounts
CDA (Communications Decency Act), 192
CDT (Center for Democracy and Technology)
    Web site, 391
censorship, 186–87
Center for Democracy and Technology (CDT)
    Web site, 391
central processing unit (CPU), defined, 282
Central Intelligence Agency (CIA), 92–93
CERT/CC Web site, 390
CGI (common gateway interface) exploiters,
    7
CGI Proxy, 185
chat. *See* IRC (Internet relay chat)
checksums, 143, 144, 281
children
    exaggeration of threats to, 248–51
    as marketing target, 191–94
    protecting from Internet threats, 191–94
Children's Online Privacy Protection Act
    (COPPA), 191–92
CIA (Central Intelligence Agency), 92–93
circuit proxies, 281
Claria Corporation, 12
Clark, Wesley, 269, 270
The Cleaner utility, 86
ClearChannel Communications, 186
Client for Microsoft Networks, 125, 126, 133,
    329–30
clients, defined, 281
Clinton, Bill, 242
clipboard, 172–73
ClipBook service, 49, 308
Clipper Chip, 120
CMOS (complementary metal oxide
    semiconductor), 281
Code Red worm, 10–11, 231–35
code-execution environments, 33
CodeWeavers, 200
Collins, Susan, 75
command, defined, 282
command interpreters, 36, 282
command processor, defined, 282
command shell, defined, 282
common gateway interface (CGI) exploiters, 7
Communications Decency Act (CDA), 192
complementary metal oxide semiconductor
    (CMOS), 281
Component Services dialog, 54, 313

compression utilities, 20
Computer Assisted Passenger Prescreening
    System (CAPPS II), 265–67
Computer Bytes Man Web site, 391
Computer Management dialog, 62, 319
concurrent versions system (CVS), defined,
    283
consumer profiles, 190–91
cookies
    dangers of, 34
    and data traces, 175–77
    defined, 282
    setting options with Mozilla, 299
Cooper, Russ, 232, 238
COPPA (Children's Online Privacy Protection
    Act), 191–92
Coremetrics, 35
Corley, Eric, 80–81
cost of ownership
    of Linux, 202–3, 216
    of Windows, 216
Cottrell, Lance, 184
Counterpane Crypto-Gram newsletter, 392
CPU (central processing unit), defined,
    282
crackers, 282. *See also* hackers
credit card accounts, 24–26, 80
Creutzfeldt-Jakob disease (vCJD), 88–90,
    251–52
Cringely, Robert X., 233
CrossOver Office, 200
cross-site scripting (XSS), 36, 282, 296
crowds, 183–85, 220–22
cryptosystems, 121, 122, 282
CVS (concurrent versions system), defined,
    283
CyberPatrol, 192
CyberSitter, 192
cyber-terror hoax, 241–43

D

daemons, 41, 283
DARPA (Defense Advanced Research Projects
    Agency), 267
data destruction, 132, 143, 164
data hygiene, 155–94
    defined, 283
    local data, 156–78
        bash history, 177–78
        browser traces, 175–77
        clipboard, 172–73
        e-mail traces, 171–72
        file slack and unallocated space,
            162–64
        print spool, 172
        recently accessed files, 173–75
        shadow data, 164–65
        system restore, 169
        temporary files, 170–71
        virtual memory, 156–62
        Windows Indexing Service, 167–69
        Windows registry, 165–67

online data, 181–94
    children as marketing target, 191–94
    importance of anonymity, 186–88
    lack of security on Internet, 178–81
    privacy invasion, 188–91
    proxy servers, 183–85
    overview, 155–56
data packets, 180–81
database security, 264–75
    CAPPS II, 265–67
    Palladium, 271–75
    Total Poindexter Awareness, 267–71
databases, defined, 283
datagram, defined, 283
date of birth, 28
DCOM (distributed component object
    model), removing, 53–55, 312–14
DDoS (distributed denial of service), defined, 284
DDrescue, 259
Debian Project, 227
Deep Throat rootkit, 20
Defense Advanced Research Projects Agency
    (DARPA), 267
defense in depth, 276–77, 284
Defensive Thinking, 75
destruction of data, 132, 143, 164
Deutch, John, 92–93
DH Brown report, 211
DHCP (dynamic host configuration
    protocol), 15, 284, 349
Dick, Ron, 246–47
dictionary attacks, 7, 22–23
Diebold Election Systems, 187
digital certificates, 44, 226
Digital Millennium Copyright Act (DMCA),
    38–39, 284
Digital Pearl Harbor, 243–44
digital rights management (DRM), 272–73, 285
digital signatures, 123, 124, 130, 284
DirectAdvertiser, 98–99
disk space, unallocated, 158–59, 162–64
disk tracks, 164–65
DiskEdit, 259
distributed component object model
    (DCOM), removing, 53–55, 312–14
distributed denial of service (DDoS), defined,
    284
distros, 197, 199, 284
Dixie Chicks, 186
DMCA (Digital Millennium Copyright Act),
    38–39, 284
DNS (domain name service), defined, 284
Dodd, Christopher, 242, 242–43
domain, defined, 284
domain name service (DNS), defined, 284
DOS operating system, 196–97, 284
DoubleClick, 176
DrakX, 64
drivers, open-source, 201, 214
DRM (digital rights management), 272–73, 285
Dubiel, John, 245
dynamic accounts, 28, 285
dynamic host configuration protocol
    (DHCP), 15, 284, 349

E

Earley, Annie, 245–46
eBay, 84, 188–89
Ebert, Roger, 3
eBlaster, 193
eEye Digital Security, 226, 231–35
EFF (Electronic Frontier Foundation) Web
    site, 391
egedit32.exe tool, 166
egress filtering, 285
Electronic Frontier Foundation (EFF) Web
    site, 391
"elite" hackers, 4
e-mail, 33–34. *See also* encryption
    attachments to, 20
    data traces from, 171–72
    hoaxes, 82–86
    "out-of-the-office" replies, 77–78
    SirCam e-mail worm, 82–83
    and social engineering, 77–78
        hoaxes, 83–84
        sending viruses, 82–83
        spam, 84–85
e-mail addresses
    finding, 14–15
    precautions against detection, 18–19
e-mail lists, security-related, 39, 392
encryption, 96, 119–54. *See also* PGP (Pretty
    Good Privacy)
    creating encrypted e-mail, 334
    defined, 285
    GPG, 133–41
    MD5, 143–46
    overview, 121–23
    PGP, 125–33
    SSH, 146–52
    SSL, 152–54
    and virtual-memory swapping, 157
    WEP, 154
End User License Agreement (EULA), 100
EnGarde, 215–16
Enigmail, 134
entropy, 135, 285, 337
Error Reporting Service, 49, 308
Ethereal, 96, 99, 100, 102, 110–12, 203
Ethernet, 108, 285
EULA (End User License Agreement), 100
Evolution, 200
execute privileges. *See* read, write, execute
    permissions
experts, security, 228–31
exploits, 11–12, 32
ext2 filesystem, 216
ext3 filesystem, 164

F

face recognition technology, 235–36
family-friendly ISPs, 193
FAS (Federation of American Scientists) Web
    site, 390
Fast User Switching, 51, 311
FAT-32 filesystem, 164

fear, uncertainty, and doubt (FUD), 231, 285
Federal Trade Commission (FTC), 26, 27, 192
Federation of American Scientists (FAS) Web site, 390
file slack, 162–64
File Transfer Protocol (FTP), 56, 203, 285, 314
FileCheckMD5 utility, 145
files
  recently accessed, 173–75
  setting display properties, 316–17
  temporary, 170–71
file-sharing
  P2P, 203
    and adware/spyware, 12
    and children, 248–49
    defined, 290
    KaZaA, 37, 87, 249
    security dangers of, 37–39
    and social engineering, 86–87
  SMB (server message block), 16, 41, 293
filesystems, 216, 285
file-wipe utility, 203
FileWiping option, 132
filtering programs, 192–93
fingerprints, 143, 145
firewalls, 28, 203, 291
floppy disks, 165
Focus on Linux mailing list, 392
Focus on Microsoft mailing list, 392
Folder Options dialog, 59–60, 317
forms, setting options with Mozilla, 301–4
forums/bulletin boards, and IP address, 15
fragmentation, 163
Fraley, David, 244–45
free Internet services, 222
Free Software Foundation (FSF), 144, 198, 285
Free Software Foundation Web site, 390
free speech, 186–87
FreeBSD operating system, 204, 208–9
Freedom WebSecure, 184
Freeh, Louis, 120, 250–51
FreeOS Web site, 389
Frljuckic, Iljmija, 26
fsck utility, 216
F-Secure, 10, 113, 150, 390
FSF (Free Software Foundation), 144, 198, 285
FTC (Federal Trade Commission), 26, 27, 192
FTP (File Transfer Protocol), 56, 203, 285, 314
FUD (fear, uncertainty, and doubt), 231, 285

G

Gaa Moa Exploiter (GME), 23–24
Gaim instant messenger, 37
Gartner, 27, 209, 243
Gates, Bill, 212. *See also* Microsoft
  Corporation; Windows operating system
Gator, 12
"gay" hackers, 4–5, 285
GCC (GNU C Compiler), 203
GeekTools Web site, 390
Geer, Daniel, 239, 240

Gentoo, 215
Gibson Research Corporation, 232
Gibson, Steve, 232–33
Giga Research, 209
GIMP (GNU Image Manipulation Program), 203
GME (Gaa Moa Exploiter), 23–24
Gnome desktop, 216
GnomePGP, 133
GNU C Compiler (GCC), 203
GNU General Public License (GPL), 197, 198, 286
GNU Image Manipulation Program (GIMP), 203
GNU Privacy Assistant (GPA), 133
gnu.org site, 144
GnuPG (GPG) utility. *See* GPG (GnuPG) utility
Gogerty, Nick, 242
Goldstein, Emmanuel, 80
Gottlieb, Bruce, 238, 239
governments, views on encryption, 119–21
GPA (GNU Privacy Assistant), 133
GPG (GnuPG) utility, 133–42, 203
  asymmetrical paired-key cryptosystem used by, 122
  creating e-mail memo addressed to yourself, 139–40
  creating keys, 135–36
  encrypting files with KGpg Editor, 140–41
  importing GnuPG keys to KMail, 338–44
  testing keys, 136–39
  use with e-mail, 96
  using with KDE, 336–38
GPL (GNU General Public License), 197, 198, 286
GPS (global positioning system) transponders, 189
graphical user interface (GUI), 5, 209, 286
Graves, Robert, 267
Grokster, 37
groups, 69–70
Guess, Inc., 26
Guest account, 61, 63, 319
GUI (graphical user interface), 5, 209, 286
Gzip utility, 203

H

Hacker Generations, 3
hacker-centric security, 237–41
hackers
  blackhats, 5, 281
  defined, 286
  jargon of, 4–5
  portrayal by Hollywood, 2
  portrayal in journalism, 2–3
  whitehats, 4, 296
hacking, defined, 4
handshake, defined, 286
hardware, Linux support for, 201, 214
hashing, 22–23, 286
HighSpeed Junki, 231
hoaxes, e-mail, 82–86
Hollywood, portrayal of hackers in, 2

honeypots, 185, 286
host, defined, 286
Hotmail, 37, 208, 222–23
HTML
    defined, 286
    in e-mail, 33–34
HTTP, defined, 286
HTTP exploiters, 7
HTTPS, defined, 287
hyperlink, defined, 287

I

IBM, 213
identity checks, 256
identity theft. *See also* credit card accounts
    defined, 287
    insurance for, 27–28
IDS (intrusion detection systems), 76, 287
IIS (Internet Information Service), 49, 308
IM (instant messaging), 36–37, 84, 287
images, setting options with Mozilla, 300
Independent Media Center, 187
independent software vendors (ISV), 40, 288
Indexing Service, 167–69, 308, 346–47
India, and Microsoft, 212
infosec, 287
inline script, defined, 287
installing Linux, 200–201
instant messaging (IM), 36–37, 84, 287
integrity checks, 143, 287
Intel platform, 210–11
Internal Revenue Service, 74
International Monitoring, 242
Internet Explorer browser, 34–35, 43
Internet forums and bulletin boards, and IP
    address, 15
Internet Fraud Prevention Advisory Council
    (IFPAC), 25
Internet Information Service (IIS), 49, 308
Internet, lack of security on, 178–81
Internet monitoring. *See* network and
    Internet monitoring
Internet relay chat. *See* IRC (Internet relay
    chat)
Internet services, free, 222
intrusion detection systems (IDS), 76, 287
Invisible KeyLogger Stealth, 224–25
IP address
    assigning manually, 349
    defined, 288
    finding, 14–15, 19–20
    precautions against detection, 18–19, 108
IPchains and IPtables packet filters, 350
IRC (Internet relay chat)
    clients and server, 203
    defined, 287
    social engineering via, 84
ISN mailing list, 392
ISPs
    defined, 288
    family-friendly, 193
ISV (independent software vendors), 40, 288

J

Jacks, Jeremiah, 25, 26
Java, 203
Java Anonymizing Proxy, 184
Java Anonymous Proxy (JAP), 220–22
Java, defined, 288
Java Virtual Machine, defined, 288
JavaScript, 33, 288, 304–5
JetBlue airline, 269
JFS file system, 164, 216
John the Ripper (JtR) passfile cracker, 7, 22
Jones, Jerry, 269
journalism
    coverage of security issues, 229–31
    portrayal of hackers in, 2–3
JtR (John the Ripper) passfile cracker, 7, 22
JuJu Jiang, 224–25

K

Kaczynski, Theodore, 182
KaZaA, 37, 87, 249
KDE desktop, 216
    font installer, 201
    and GPG, 133–34, 136
    history files on, 177
    Klipper clipboard, 172–73
    recently accessed files, 174–75
    using GnuPG with, 336–38
Kerberos service, 41
kernel, defined, 288
kernel-level patches, 40
key loggers, 225
keyrings, 125, 126, 130, 334
keys, encryption. *See* encryption
keyservers, 132
keystroke logging, 225, 288
KGpg editor, 140–42, 343, 343–44
KGpg utility
    creating keys, 135–36, 337–38
    obtaining, 134
    purpose of, 134
kill and killall commands, 118–19, 329
Kinko's computers, infecting of, 224–25
Klipper, 172–73
KMail, 134
    and e-mail traces, 171–72
    importing keys to, 136–39, 338–44
KMPlayer, 201
Koerner, Craig, 246
KOffice, 203
Kolla, Patrick, 112
Konqueror browser, 215
    integration with KGpg, 140–41
    and recently accessed files, 174
Koontz, Linda, 249
Koskinen, John, 242
Krusader browser, 69–71, 215
    changing file/directory permissions,
        324–25
    integration with KGpg, 140–41
    and recently accessed files, 174
Kssh, 150

L

L0pht hacker group, 238–40
L0phtCrack, 238
LAN (local area network), 288, 348
laptops
    and Linux, 201, 214
    Protected Storage service on, 50
Lavasoft's Ad-aware utility, 13, 112
law-enforcement community, 178–79
"leet" hackers, 4
legacy code, 39, 289
Legion tool, 16–17, 18
Lettice, John, 210
Lieberman, Joseph, 75
lifetime individual visitor experience (LIVE)
    profile technology, 35
Lindows, 215, 216
Line Printer Daemon (LPD) service, 56, 314
Linmodems.org Web site, 201
LinTel systems, 210, 289
Linux on Laptops Web site, 201, 214
Linux operating system
    2.6 kernel attacks, 226–27
    bash history, 177–78
    caveats, 199–201
    cost of ownership, 202–3, 216
    data destruction for, 164
    developers for, 205–6
    and GPG, 133–42
    GPL (GNU General Public License) of, 198
    history of, 196–97
    in India, 212
    installing, 200–201
    kernel of, 198
    and laptops, 201, 214
    LUGs (Linux user groups), 201–2
    Microsoft propaganda against, 210–13
    migrating from UNIX to, 210–11
    overall superiority in security, 195–96, 199
    patches for, 40–41
    preventing X server from listening on Net,
        58
    and print spools, 172
    procedures
        adjusting user and file permissions,
            324–25
        importing GnuPG Keys to KMail,
            338–44
        services worth disabling, 314–16
        using GnuPG with KDE, 336–38
        viewing and killing system processes,
            329
        write-protecting Mozilla downloads
            history, 347–48
    SCO Group's attacks against, 213–14
    services, 55–58
    single vs. multi-user editions of, 41–42
    vs. Solaris and Oracle, 210
    swap partition on, 162
    and system privileges, 44–45, 63–64,
        69–71
    temporary files, 170–71
    why infected by less viruses, 114

Linux Today Web site, 389
LinuxSecurity Web site, 389
LIUtilities process library, 350, 391
LIVE (lifetime individual visitor experience)
    profile technology, 35
local area network (LAN), 288, 348
local data, 156–78
    bash history, 177–78
    browser traces, 175–77
    clipboard, 172–73
    e-mail traces, 171–72
    file slack and unallocated space, 162–64
    print spool, 172
    recently accessed files, 173–75
    shadow data, 164–65
    system restore, 169
    temporary files, 170–71
    virtual memory, 156–62
    Windows Indexing Service, 167–69
    Windows Registry, 165–67
localhost, 104–5, 109, 148–52, 289
Lock Screen option, 64
Lockheed Martin Corporation, 265–66
lolita, 85
loopback interface, 109, 289
LPD (Line Printer Daemon) service, 56, 314
LUGs (Linux user groups), 201–2
Luhn number test, 24–25

M

Mac OSX, 204
MacNeill, Mike, 98
macros, 36, 289
mad cow disease (BSE), 88–90, 251–55
Maiffret, Marc, 232
MainActor, 201
malicious processes, 114–19
malware, 32, 289
Manage Stored Cookies feature, 299
Mandrake Linux, 40, 64, 197, 215
man-in-the-middle (MIM) attacks, 36–37,
    289
manual updates, 40
marketing surveys, 190–91
Markle Foundation Task Force on National
    Security in the Information Age, 270
Markoff, John, 2–3
Marshall, James, 185
MATRIX (Multistate Anti-Terrorism
    Information Exchange), 268–71
Matrix Reloaded, 3
Mazur, John, 246
McAfee Firewall, 202
McAfee Virus Scan Home Edition, 202
McHale, Stephen, 265
MD5 algorithm, 143–46, 289, 343–44
Media Player, 52
Meinel, Carolyn, 233–34
Melbourne, Jody, 99
memory, virtual, 156–62, 296
message digets, 143, 289
Messenger service, 49, 309

Microsoft Corporation. *See also* Windows operating system
 and @Stake, 240
 admission of Linux being a threat, 210
 Bill and Melinda Gates Foundation, 212
 comment about FreeBSD, 208–9
 comment about UNIX, 208–9
 connecting users without their knowledge, 99–100
 October 2000 attack on, 19–21
 Passport service problem, 222–24
 propaganda against Linux, 210–13
 use of social engineering, 97–99
Microsoft DOS operating system, 196–97
Microsoft Outlook e-mail client. *See* Outlook e-mail client
Microsoft Passport service, 222–24
Microsoft SQL, 203
Microsoft Word, 200
Microsoft Works, 202
Millennium bug, 241–43
MIM (man-in-the-middle) attacks, 36–37, 289
Mineta, Norman, 265
MINIX operating system, 197
Mitnick, Kevin, 2, 73–75, 80, 93
modem drivers, 201
monitoring. *See* network and Internet monitoring; system monitoring
monocultures, 32–33
Moosoft's The Cleaner utility, 86
Morpheus, 37
motherboard, defined, 289
Motion Picture Association of America (MPAA), 39
Motorola, 74–75
Mozilla browser, 205–6
 caches, 305
 controlling data traces, 176–77
 cookies, 35, 299
 forms, 301–4
 images, 35, 300
 and index.dat files, 169
 JavaScript, 304–5
 passwords, 301–4
 popup windows, 301
 user data/Web activity storage, 166
 write protecting downloads history, 347–48
Mozilla Form Manager, 224
Mozilla Mail, 33, 171
 creating encrypted e-mail, 334
 plain text display, 306
MPAA (Motion Picture Association of America), 39
MS Office Clipboard, 172–73
MSBlaster worm, 10, 41, 53, 207, 312
MSN Messenger, 37, 52
multi vs. single-user systems, 41–43
Multistate Anti-Terrorism Information Exchange (MATRIX), 268–71
multi-user editions of Windows, 41–42
MySQL database server, 203

N

NASA (National Aeronautics and Space Administration), 268–69
nastygram, defined, 289
NAT (network address translation), 108, 290, 348–49
National Cattlemen's Beef Association, 252–53
National Infrastructure Protection Center (NIPC), 83
Nautilus browser, 69, 324–25
NeoLite, 20
Nessus service, 16, 56, 203, 315
Net Logon service, 49, 309
NetBIOS, 51, 290
NetMeeting Remote Desktop Sharing service, 49, 309
NetNanny, 192
Netstat, 96
 and popup spam, 99
 revealing active ports with, 101–9
Netstumbler, 154
NetVizor, 193
network address translation (NAT), 108, 290, 348–49
network and Internet monitoring, 99–112
 Ethereal, 110–12
 Netstat, 101–9
Network Associates, 226
Network DDE DSDM service, 50, 309
Network DDE service, 309
Network File System (NFS) service, 57, 315
Network Information Service (NIS) service, 57, 315
network interface cards (NICs), 154, 290
Network Location Awareness service, 50, 309
New York Times, 212
New York Times Magazine, 238, 239
newbies, 13, 22, 24, 290
news organizations, 231, 389
Next-Generation Secure Computing Base (NGSCB)
 defined, 290
 possible future use of, 271–74
 problems with, 44–45, 274–75
 use to thwart piracy, 272–73
NFS (Network File System) service, 57, 315
NGSCB. *See* Next-Generation Secure Computing Base (NGSCB)
NICs (network interface cards), 154, 290
NIPC (National Infrastructure Protection Center), 83
NIS (Network Information Service) service, 57, 315
NIST CSRC Web site, 390
Nmap, 203
Northwest Airlines, 268–69
Norton SystemWorks, 202
NortonWipeinfo, 161
notebook computers. *See* laptops
Notepad utility, 19
NSA's SE-Linux, 216
NTFS filesystem, 164

O

OEMs (original equipment manufacturers), 202, 205, 272, 273, 274, 290
Office XP, 202, 203
online data, 181–94
    children as marketing target, 191–94
    importance of anonymity, 186–88
    lack of security on Internet, 178–81
    privacy invasion, 188–91
    proxy servers, 183–85
online databases. *See* database security
online resources, 389–92
online shopping. *See* credit card accounts
OpenOffice, 200, 203
open-source software, 198. *See also* Linux
        operating system
    and adware/spyware, 13
    and bugs/attacks, 227
    defined, 290
    overview, 195–96
OpenSSH, 150, 203
operating systems, 39–40. *See also names of*
        specific operating systems
Oracle, 210
original equipment manufacturers (OEMs), 202, 205, 272, 273, 274, 290
Orlowski, Andrew, 214
Outlook e-mail client, 33
    Linux clone for, 200
    security zones, 43
    and Sircam worm, 82–83, 234
    Windows Messenger integration with, 97–99
"out-of-the-office" e-mail replies, 77–78

P

P2P file-sharing, 203
    and adware/spyware, 12
    and children, 248–49
    defined, 290
    KaZaA, 37, 87, 249
    security dangers of, 37–39
    and social engineering, 86–87
packaging software, 198
packet filters, 290, 349–50
packet sniffers, 11, 96, 110, 290
packet switching, 179–80
packets, defined, 290
paging files. *See* swap files
paired-key encryption. *See* encryption
Palladium. *See* Next-Generation Secure
        Computing Base (NGSCB)
passfile crackers, 7
passfiles, hashed, 22–23
passphrases, encryption, 142
Passport accounts, 37
Passport service, 222–24
passwords
    Administrator password, 60–63
    and dictionary crackers, 7
    and encryption, 122
    hashed, 22–23
    setting options with Mozilla, 301–4

patches
    Linux vs. Windows, 206
    and operating system vulnerabilities, 39–40
    and scripted exploits, 11–12
PayPal, 84, 189
PC, defined, 291
pedophiles, sting against, 85–86
Performance dialog, 118
Performance Options dialog, 160, 345
periodic service packs, 206–7
Perl, 203
permissions. *See* read, write, execute
        permissions
personal firewalls, 28, 203, 291
PGP (Pretty Good Privacy), 96, 125–33
    asymmetrical paired-key cryptosystem
        used by, 122
    available options, 131–32
    backing up keyring, 130–31
    cost of, 125
    creating key pairs, 126–27
    creator of, 119
    encrypting/decrypting files, 127–30
    installing and using, 329–36
    obtaining, 125–26
    obtaining other's keys/publishing own, 132–33
    reinstalling Client for Microsoft Networks
        before using, 126
PGP Wipe, 143
PGPkeys, 126, 127, 330–31
PGPWipe, 161
phone, and social engineering, 78–81
Photoshop, 203
phreaks, defined, 291
ping, defined, 291
Poindexter, John, 267–68
point-and-click attack tools, 5
police community, 178–79
Politech mailing list, 392
POP (post office protocol), 184, 291
pop-up ads. *See* adware; spyware
popup windows, preventing with Mozilla, 301
pornography, 21–24, 85
port forwarding
    defined, 291
    examples of, 148, 150–51
    use with all IP clients, 149
port scanners, 8–9
portmap. *See* Remote Procedure Call (RPC)
ports, 354–88
    active, revealing, 101–9
    common ports, 355–58
    defined, 291
    Trojan ports, 358–88
Postfix mail server, 203
Postfix service, 57, 315
power user, defined, 291
power-management features, on laptops, 214
prevention, 276
print spool, 172
privacy, defined, 181, 291
privacy policy, defined, 291

private keys. *See* encryption
privilege escalations, 227
privileges. *See* system privileges
procedures, 297–348
    configuring Mozilla browser/mail,
        297–306
    Linux
        adjusting user and file permissions,
            324–25
        importing GnuPG Keys to KMail,
            338–44
        services worth disabling, 314–16
        using GnuPG with KDE, 336–38
        viewing and killing system processes,
            329
        write-protecting Mozilla downloads
            history, 347–48
    Windows
        adjusting user and file permissions,
            320–23
        configuring swap file, 334–46
        disabling DCOM, 312–14
        disabling indexing service, 346–47
        disabling system restore, 347
        finding and disabling services, 306–11
        installing and using PGP, 329–36
        setting file display properties, 316–17
        setting up user accounts, 318–20
        uninstalling TCP/IP NetBIOS, 311–12
        viewing and killing system processes,
            325–28
        write protecting Mozilla downloads
            history, 347
processes
    application processes, 353–54
    defined, 291
    malicious processes, 114–19, 351–52
    viewing and killing, 325–29
    Windows processes, 352–53
proftpd daemon, 56
Protected Storage service, 50, 309
protocol, defined, 291
proxy servers
    anonymous, 19, 220–22
        Anonymizer, 147–48, 153, 184
        Java Anonymous Proxy (JAP), 220–22
    defined, 292
    setting up online crowds, 183–85
public computers, 224–25
public keys. *See* encryption
PuTTY, 150–51

Q

QAZ rootkit, 19–20
QoS RSVP service, 50, 309
queues, 172, 292

R

radio frequency identification (RFID), 189,
    262–63, 292
rain dance, defined, 292

RAM (random access memory), 156, 292
RATs (remote access trapdoors), 6–7
read, write, execute permissions, 64–71
    definition of "read only," 292
    Linux operating system, 69–71
    setting with Krusader browser, 324–25
    Windows operating system, 64–69
    write-protect, defined, 296
    write-protecting Mozilla downloads
        history, 347–48
RealNetworks RealPlayer, 203
recently accessed files, 173–75
Recording Industry Association of America
    (RIAA), 38–39, 248–50
Red Hat Linux, 197, 215
Red Hat Package Manager (RPM), 198,
    214–15, 292, 336
redundancy, 260
regedit.exe tool, 166
The Register, 389, 392
Registry. *See* Windows Registry
Regulation of Investigatory Powers (RIP) Act
    of 2000, 120
ReiserFS file system, 164
Remote Access Auto Connection Manager
    service, 50, 309
Remote Access Connection Manager service,
    47–48, 50, 307, 309
remote access, dangers of, 6–7
remote access trapdoors (RATs), 6–7
Remote Desktop Help Session Manager
    service, 50, 310
Remote Packet Capture Protocol service, 50,
    310
Remote Procedure Call (RPC), 41, 52, 55, 57,
    315
Remote Registry Service, 50
Remote Registry Service service, 310
remote systems
    tool for finding active ports, 8–9
    tool for scanning for vulnerabilities, 8
Reno, Janet, 120, 250–51
resistance, 276
resources, online, 389–92
restore points, 169
RFID (radio frequency identification), 189,
    262–63, 292
RIAA (Recording Industry Association of
    America), 38–39, 248–50
RIP (Regulation of Investigatory Powers) Act
    of 2000, 120
risk, 88–90, 292
Risks Digest Web site, 391
Rlogin service, 57, 315
root, defined, 292
rootkits
    Deep Throat rootkit, 20
    defined, 292
    example of use, 17
    explanation of, 6–7
    QAZ rootkit, 19–20
    SubSeven rootkit, 6, 17, 18, 86
Rosenberger, Rob, 234
router, defined, 292

Routing and Remote Access service, 50, 310
RPC (Remote Procedure Call), 41, 52, 55, 57, 315
RPM (Red Hat Package Manager), 198, 214–15, 292, 336

S

safety, vs. security, 256–57
Sahin, Tamer, 208
SAINT, 203
Sam Spade Web site, 390
Samba service, 41, 57, 203, 315
SamSpade.org, 110
Sans Institute NewsBites mailing list, 392
SANS Institute Web site, 390
SCADA (supervisory control and data acquisition), 245, 293
scene whores, 5, 293
Schaeffer, Richard, 242
Schmitz, Paul, 246
Schneier, Bruce, 255
Scientific American, 233–34
SCO Group, 213–14
script kiddies
    defined, 293
    devices used by, 4–13
        dictionary crackers, 7
        HTTP exploiters, 7
        packet sniffers, 11
        port scanners, 8–9
        rootkits and RATs, 6–7
        scripted exploits, 11–13
        Trojans, 6
        viruses, 9–11
        vulnerability scanners, 8
        worms, 10–11
    examples of attacks by, 13–30
        to access pornography, 21–24
        attack on lawyer's computer, 14–19
        attack on Microsoft, 19–21
        to steal credit card numbers, 24–29
scripted exploits, 11–13
scripts, 35–36, 293
SE. *See* social engineering
Seahorse, 133
Secure Shell. *See* SSH (Secure Shell)
secure socket layer (SSL), 119, 152–54, 294
SecureCRT, 150
SecureIIS, 231
SecuriTeam Web site, 389
security experts, 228–31
security industry, 220
Security News Portal Web site, 389
security news resources, 389
security specialists, 228
security, vs. safety, 256–57
security zones, 43, 45
SecurityFocus News mailing list, 392
SecurityFocus Web site, 389
Seisint, Inc., 268
SE-Linux, 216
Sendmail server, 315
Sendmail service, 57

sequence number, 179, 293
server, defined, 293
server message block (SMB) file sharing, 16, 41, 293
Server service, 310
service, defined, 293
service packs, for Windows, 206–7
services
    defined, 41, 293
    finding and disabling, 306–11
    worth disabling, 314–16
shadow data, 164–65
SHARE (Systemwide Homeland Analysis and Response), 270
shared browsing, 37
Sharman Networks, 37, 87
shell, defined, 293
shell scripts, 35, 293
Sherman, Cary, 249–50
shopping online. *See* credit card accounts
Shred utility, 143, 164
Simovits Consulting Trojan Web site, 390
Simple Network Management Protocol (SNMP), 51, 57, 293, 310, 316
Simple Nomad, 2
Single Sign-On feature, 132, 336
single vs. multi-user systems, 41–43
Sircam worm, 82–83, 234
skimming, 25–26, 27
slack space, 163
Slackware, 215
Slapper.A worm, 10
Slemko, Marc, 222, 223
SMB (server message block) file sharing, 16, 41, 293
SNMP (Simple Network Management Protocol), 51, 57, 293, 310, 316
SNMP Trap Service, 310
Snort, 203
Sobig worm, 207
social engineering, 73–94
    countermeasures, 90–93
    defined, 293
    e-mail use, 77–78
        hoaxes, 83–84
        for sending viruses, 82–83
        spam, 84–85
    instant messaging use, 84
    overview, 73–75
    P2P file-sharing use, 86–87
    reasons for success of, 80–81
    sting against pedophiles, 85–86
    Sydney International Airport example, 76–77
    telephone use, 78–81
Social Security Administration, 74
Social Security number, 28
software
    open-source, 198. *See also* Linux operating system
        and adware/spyware, 13
        and bugs/attacks, 227
        defined, 290
        overview, 195–96

packaging, 198
upgrades, 226–27
SOHO, defined, 293
Solaris operating system, 196, 204, 208
    Gnome desktop, 216
    vs. Linux, 210
Sophos, 10, 113, 390
source code, defined, 294
SourceForge Web site, 390
spam, 82–86, 294
specialists, security, 228
SPI (stateful packet inspection), 148, 294
sploits, 4
spool, defined, 294
Spota, Thomas, 249
Spybot Search & Destroy, 112
spyware
    defined, 294
    detecting, 102
    for monitoring children's Internet use,
        193
Squid service, 58, 316
Squid Web proxy/caching software, 203
SSDP Discovery Service service, 51, 310
SSH (Secure Shell), 315
    defined, 294
    on Linux, 57
    overview, 146–47
SSH tunneling, 109, 146, 148–50, 153, 294
SSL (secure socket layer), 119, 152–54, 294
Stallman, Richard, 197
Starbucks employee con, 80–81
StarOffice, 200
Startup directories, 69
state, defined, 294
stateful, defined, 294
stateful packet inspection (SPI), 148, 294
stateless, defined, 294
Strauss, Howard, 211–12
SubSeven rootkit, 6, 17, 18, 86
Sullivan, Joseph, 188–89
Sun Solaris operating system, 196, 204, 208
    Gnome desktop, 216
    vs. Linux, 210
sunrpc. *See* Remote Procedure Call (RPC)
Sun's StarOffice, 200
super nodes, 38
supervisory control and data acquisition
    (SCADA), 245, 293
surveys, marketing, 190–91
SuSE Linux, 40, 197, 203, 206, 215
SuSE MainActor, 201
SuSE YaST, 64
swap files
    configuring, 334–46
    data traces on, 157–62
    defined, 294
swap partition, 157, 162
Sydney International Airport, 76–77
Syllabus Magazine, 211–12
syn flood, defined, 295
system administrator, 225, 295
system agents, 41, 295
system folders, denying users access to, 323

system monitoring, 112–19
    Adware/Spyware detection, 112–13
    antivirus software, 113–14
    malicious processes, 114–19
system privileges, 58–64
    Linux operating system, 44–45, 63–64,
        69–71
    and NGSCB, 44–45
    read, write, execute, 64–72
        on Linux, 69–72
        on Windows, 64–69
    single vs. multi-user systems, 41–43
    Windows operating system, 41–44
        read, write, execute permissions,
            64–69
        setting up individual user account,
            58–63
System Properties dialog, 159, 344
system restore, 169, 347
Systemwide Homeland Analysis and
    Response (SHARE), 270

T

Tanenbaum, Andrew, 197
TCP/IP, defined, 295
TCP/IP NetBIOS service, 51, 52–53, 310,
    311–12
telephone, and social engineering, 78–81
Telnet service, 51, 58, 310, 316
temporary files, 170–71
Terminal Services, 51, 311
Thieme, Richard, 3
third-party applications/utilities, 40
Thompson, Fred, 75
threats
    assessment of, 88–90
    defined, 295
TIA (Total Information Awareness) network,
    267–71
tilde (~), 68, 297
Tinfoil Hat Linux, 216
TLS (transport layer security), 181, 295
tolerance, 276
tools for hacking, 5
    adware/spyware, 12–13
    dictionary crackers, 7
    HTTP exploiters, 7
    packet sniffers, 11
    port scanners, 8–9
    rootkits
        Deep Throat rootkit, 20
        defined, 292
        example of use, 17
        explanation of, 6–7
        QAZ rootkit, 19–20
        SubSeven rootkit, 6, 17, 18, 86
    scripted exploits, 11–12
    Trojans, 6
    viruses, 9–10
    vulnerability scanners, 8
    worms, 10–11
Torch Concepts, 269

Torvalds, Linus, 197
Total Information Awareness (TIA) network, 267–71
transponders, 262–63, 295
transport layer security (TLS), 181, 295
trapdoors, 6–7, 295
Trillian, 37
Tripwire utility, 145, 203
Tritac, John, 242
Tritak, John, 243
Trojan ports, 358–88
Trojans, 6, 295
TrueType fonts, 201
TruSecure, 232, 238
trusted content, 43, 45
Trustworthy Computing initiative, 206
tunneling, SSH, 109, 146, 153, 294

U

UDP (user datagram protocol) ports, 52, 101, 103, 106–7, 208, 295
unallocated disk space, 158–59, 162–64
unices, 196
Universal Plug and Play (UPnP), 51, 311
UNIX operating system, 196
    Microsoft comment about, 208
    migrating to Linux from, 210–11
updates, 40
upgrades, 226–27
Upload Manager service, 52, 311
UPnP (Universal Plug and Play), 51, 311
URL, defined, 296
U.S. Department of Agriculture (USDA), 252–55
U.S. National Aeronautics and Space Administration (NASA), 268–69
user accounts. *See* system privileges
user datagram protocol (UDP) ports, 52, 101, 103, 106–7, 208, 295
UserLinux distro, 215
utilities
    defined, 295
    third-party, 40

V

Valentine, Brian, 210–11
Vatis, Michael, 242, 243, 246, 270
vCJD (Creutzfeldt-Jakob disease), 88–90, 251–52
vectors, 31–72, 33–39. *See also* system privileges
    application vulnerabilities, 40–41
    browsers, 34–35
    defined, 32, 296
    e-mail, 33–34
    instant messaging, 36–37
    Linux services, 55–58
    operating system vulnerabilities, 39–40
    overview, 31–33
    P2P software, 37–39
    scripts, 35–36

    vulnerable services, 41
    Windows services, 46–55
Veneman, Ann, 252
Verizon, 38–39, 250
Victoria TelecommunityNet Web site, 391
Viisage, 236
virtual buffer zone, 183
virtual memory, 156–62, 296
Virtual Memory dialog, 346
virtual private networks (VPNs), 37, 296
viruses, 9–11
    defined, 296
    scanners for, 10
    sent via e-mail, 82–83
Visionics/Identix, 236
Vmyths, 234, 391
VPNs (virtual private networks), 37, 296
VShell, 150
vulnerabilities, 32, 41
vulnerability scanners, 8, 16

W

Wallet service, 222–24
WAN, defined, 296
wannabe, defined, 296
Web bugs, 35, 296
WebClient service, 52, 311
webmaster, defined, 296
Webmin, 58, 203, 316
Webopedia Web site, 391
WEP (wired equivalent privacy), 154, 296
WhenU, 12
whitehats, 4, 296
Whitehats Web site, 389
Whitten, Alma, 120, 123
whois database, 110
Why Johnny Can't Encrypt, 120
Wikipedia Web site, 391
Windows Indexing Service, 167–69, 308, 346–47
Windows Internet Connection Sharing, 50
Windows Messenger service, 49, 97–99, 309
Windows operating system, 204–18
    comparison with UNIX, 208–9
    cost of ownership, 202
    image size, 209
    marketing technique for, 204–7
    and Microsoft's fear of Linux, 210–13
    overall inferiority in security, 195–96, 199
    patches for, 40–41
    poor quality of, 208–10
    popularity of, reasons for, 204–6
    procedures
        adjusting user and file permissions, 320–23
        configuring swap file, 334–46
        disabling DCOM, 312–14
        disabling indexing service, 346–47
        disabling system restore, 347
        finding and disabling services, 306–11
        installing and using PGP, 329–36
        setting file display properties, 316–17
        setting up user accounts, 318–20

uninstalling TCP/IP NetBIOS, 311–12
viewing and killing system processes, 325–28
write protecting Mozilla downloads history, 347
and SCO's attack on Linux users, 213–14
seeing what's running on, 114–18
services, 46–55
    DCOM, disabling, 53–55
    insecure services enabled by default, 48–52, 48–52
    overview, 46
    seeing which services are running, 46–48
    TCP/IP NetBIOS, removing(uninstalling), 52–53
single vs. multi-user editions of, 41–42
and system privileges, 41–44
    read, write, execute permissions, 64–69
    setting up individual user account, 58–63
whether to use different OS, 214–18
why OEM's promote, 204–5
XP
    benefits of, 42–43
    Professional Edition, cost of, 202
    Search Companion, 99–100
    swap file on, 158–59
Windows Privacy Tools (WinPT), 133
Windows Registry, 35, 165–67
    and data hygiene, 165–67
    defined, 292
    editing to delete swap file, 158
    and recently accessed files, 173–74
Windows Task Manager, 114–18, 326–28
WinGuides Registry library, 391
Winkler, Ira, 5
Winmodem drivers, 201
WinPcap, 111
WinPT (Windows Privacy Tools), 133
WinTel systems, 210, 296
WinZip, 20
Wipe utility, 143, 164
Wipeinfo, 161
wipeswap.sh script, 162, 164

wired equivalent privacy (WEP), 154, 296
Wired News Web site, 389
Word application, 200
wordlists, 22–23
Word-of-Mouth.org, 84–85
workplace surveillance, 225–26
worms
    Code Red worm, 10–11, 231–35
    defined, 296
    MSBlaster worm, 10, 41, 53, 207
    Sircam worm, 82–83, 234
    Slapper.A worm, 10
    Sobig worm, 207
write privileges. *See* read, write, execute permissions
wuftpd daemon, 56
WWWGet clones, 203
Wysopal, Chris, 240

X

Xandros Desktop OS, 215, 216
XFS file system, 164
Ximian Evolution, 200, 203
XP, Windows
    benefits of, 42–43
    Professional Edition, cost of, 202
    Search Companion, 99–100
    swap file on, 158–59
XSS (cross-site scripting), 36, 282, 296

Y

Y2K bug, 241–43
YaST, 64
Ypbind service, 58, 316

Z

zero-day, 12, 227, 279, 296
ZeroKnowledge Systems' Freedom WebSecure, 184
Zimmermann, Phil, 119, 120, 182
Zip disks, 165
Zip utility, 203

forums.apress.com

FOR PROFESSIONALS BY PROFESSIONALS™

JOIN THE APRESS FORUMS AND BE PART OF OUR COMMUNITY. You'll find discussions that cover topics of interest to IT professionals, programmers, and enthusiasts just like you. If you post a query to one of our forums, you can expect that some of the best minds in the business—especially Apress authors, who all write with *The Expert's Voice*™—will chime in to help you. Why not aim to become one of our most valuable participants (MVPs) and win cool stuff? Here's a sampling of what you'll find:

DATABASES

Data drives everything.

Share information, exchange ideas, and discuss any database programming or administration issues.

INTERNET TECHNOLOGIES AND NETWORKING

Try living without plumbing (and eventually IPv6).

Talk about networking topics including protocols, design, administration, wireless, wired, storage, backup, certifications, trends, and new technologies.

JAVA

We've come a long way from the old Oak tree.

Hang out and discuss Java in whatever flavor you choose: J2SE, J2EE, J2ME, Jakarta, and so on.

MAC OS X

All about the Zen of OS X.

OS X is both the present and the future for Mac apps. Make suggestions, offer up ideas, or boast about your new hardware.

OPEN SOURCE

Source code is good; understanding (open) source is better.

Discuss open source technologies and related topics such as PHP, MySQL, Linux, Perl, Apache, Python, and more.

PROGRAMMING/BUSINESS

Unfortunately, it is.

Talk about the Apress line of books that cover software methodology, best practices, and how programmers interact with the "suits."

WEB DEVELOPMENT/DESIGN

Ugly doesn't cut it anymore, and CGI is absurd.

Help is in sight for your site. Find design solutions for your projects and get ideas for building an interactive Web site.

SECURITY

Lots of bad guys out there—the good guys need help.

Discuss computer and network security issues here. Just don't let anyone else know the answers!

TECHNOLOGY IN ACTION

Cool things. Fun things.

It's after hours. It's time to play. Whether you're into LEGO® MINDSTORMS™ or turning an old PC into a DVR, this is where technology turns into fun.

WINDOWS

No defenestration here.

Ask questions about all aspects of Windows programming, get help on Microsoft technologies covered in Apress books, or provide feedback on any Apress Windows book.

HOW TO PARTICIPATE:

Go to the Apress Forums site at **http://forums.apress.com/**.
Click the New User link.